iOS Game Programming
with Xcode and Cocos2d

iOS Game Programming with Xcode and Cocos2d

Justin Dike

Focal Press
Taylor & Francis Group

NEW YORK AND LONDON

First published 2014
by Focal Press
70 Blanchard Road, Suite 402, Burlington, MA 01803

Published in the UK
by Focal Press
2 Park Square, Milton Park, Abingdon, Oxon OX14 4RN

Focal Press is an imprint of the Taylor & Francis Group, an informa business

Library of Congress Cataloging in Publication Data
Dike, Justin.
iOS game programming with Xcode and Cocos2d/Justin Dike.
    pages cm
    1. iPhone (Smartphone)—Programming. 2. Computer games—
Programming. 3. iOS (Electronic resource) I. Title.
QA76.8.I64D55 2013
794.8′1536—dc23   2013022253

ISBN: 978-0-415-71269-9 (pbk)
ISBN: 978-1-315-88375-5 (ebk)

Typeset in Helvetica Neue
by Florence Production Ltd, Stoodleigh, Devon, UK

Printed by Bang Printing in the United States of America.

SFI label applies to the text stock

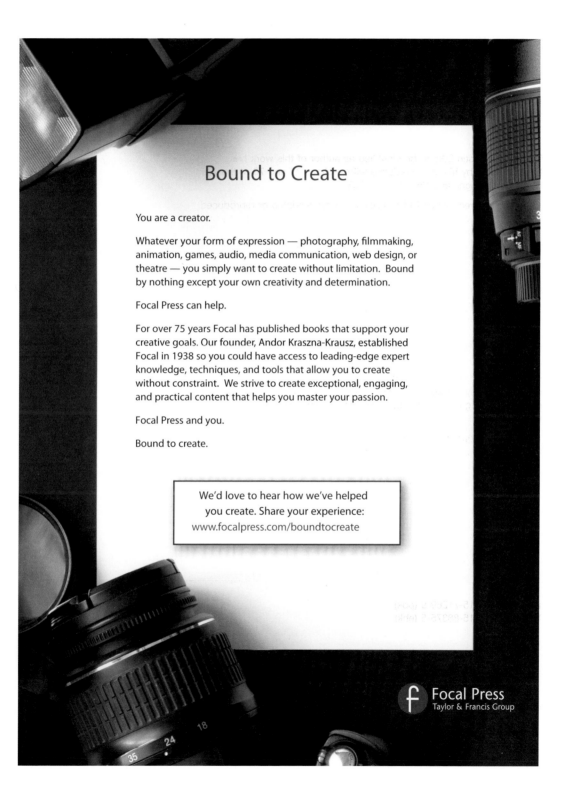

Dedicated to My Parents

Dad, I know you won't read much of this book, at least not to learn programming, but you believed in it. Even daring to ask, "So *now* when do you think it will be finished?", which I know means you were excited to see it done. You reminded me many times that a book was worth investing the time in to do right, so thanks for not rubbing it in (too much) that I seriously under-estimated how long this would take to finish.

Mom, you love telling stories about your three-year-old son that could sit quietly and draw for hours without interruption. Now that I'm a parent, I realize how odd and wonderful that must have been. Thanks for giving me the crayons, paper, and time to be myself. I still have trouble not drawing something on blank pages …

Contents

About the Author

Justin Dike is the creator and lead developer at CartoonSmart.com, an education channel and video production company specializing in high definition tutorials for Xcode, Cocos2d, HTML5, Adobe Flash, Adobe Illustrator, Toon Boom Animate, SketchBook Pro, and other software / frameworks. He received his BFA in Computer Art from the School of Visual Arts, with a focus on 2D and 3D animation. Justin worked for what eventually became a mid-sized animation studio in Manhattan, directing web shorts and longer length cartoons for broadcast. During that time, he led training sessions for new artists and animators to work with Flash in a fast-paced production environment. Teaching a roomful of people inspired him to found Cartoon Smart in 2004 to educate students worldwide. Cartoon Smart has been his professional home since then. One of his many jobs now is organizing piles of notes reminding him to learn something new or update something old. Justin enjoys spending time with his wife, sons, daughter, parents, sisters, brothers and the rest of his family of Atlantans (and wishes he had more time to visit the Texans, Coloradans, and Pennsylvanians).

The Code

The code in this book has been tested on iOS 7 and takes into account the latest devices, including the iPhone 5, iPad with Retina display, even the iPad mini. Even though I wrote it, this book is my own personal reference manual. When I forget something, I'll be relying on it to be accurate too.

Chapter 1

The Hardest Part: Starting

Right now there is a suitcase next to my bed that hasn't been unpacked from a vacation weeks ago. I am a procrastinator. Fortunately, I'm also a perfectionist. Once a job has started, it must be done right. It's just that starting part that trips me up. Whether it's cleaning mountains of clothes off the floor, reading unread emails, or writing an entire book.

Here's my challenge to you: overcome what is keeping you from not building that clever app festering in the back of your mind. Embrace whatever will tip the scales from doing nothing to doing something. It might be as simple as convincing yourself, "The time is right".

Swear this oath ... by turning to the next page, I promise to actually begin the project I've been dreaming of. It may bring fortune, fame, or even failure, but I will undertake a new adventure.

Why Program with Cocos2d?

Hopefully many of you reading this book are
"on the fence" about whether or not to use
Cocos2d for your next app. I say hopefully, because I want to convert you. I'd love to hear
back from readers that tell me this book was the reason they got started using Cocos2d, or
programming in general. I think Cocos2d is a very easy language to learn because it was
made specifically for building 2D games and interactive applications. Think about that for a
second, it was created with game developers in mind. If your main reason for reading this
book is to create a game for the App Store, then this is a good language for you. I say,
language but Cocos2d is better described as a framework. It uses Objective-C. So while
you are learning Cocos2d in this book, you are also learning the Objective-C language.
There will be times when it makes more sense to teach you something outside of the
Cocos2d framework and work solely with the native code Apple provides for the iOS.

Some of you might be wondering if this is an iOS 7 book? At the time I'm writing this,
iOS 7 has been released and the version of Xcode I'll be using to test my projects can
build an iOS 7 app, but what we'll be doing in this book is largely independent of Apple's
OS cycle. More important to us, is what version Cocos2d is at. Right now, Cocos2d is at
version 2.x. I'll throw a little "x" in there because there's always some updates to the
framework to account for things like iOS 7 being released. To train along with this book,
your best bet is to use the latest version of Cocos2d, although most of my examples have
been tested with Cocos2d version 1.x and run the same. Why is that?

The basics tend to stay the same for a long time. I think that's an important point to
remember for anyone new coming to programming, because it's easy to fret over how much
there is to learn when there's so much new code being introduced every year. If you worry
about the latest code for the camera, Facebook integration, Passbook, etc., while you're still
learning the basics, it's overwhelming. To encourage you, just remember that what you learn
now rarely gets undone. New code to play with new things doesn't usually affect the old
code to build the essentials. It's just new code, there when you want it. Also, because we
are using Cocos2d in this book and focusing mostly on games, we are in a "walled garden"
in a sense. The games we create don't even need to tap into the fancier features of the iOS
(but they could if you wanted). My goal for you in this book is to keep things simple and
focused on making games.

Who Am I? ... A Programmer, Maybe?

I'm probably a lot like you. Even if you've never programmed anything before, I'll bet we're still more similar than dissimilar when it comes to programming. My background is in art and for all my past years working with code, I still don't think I'm all that smart. Somehow a decade and a half of fumbling around with code has flown by. It still doesn't seem that long ago that I was living in a closet-sized apartment in Manhattan spending my mornings in life drawing classes and evenings in a computer lab learning animation. The fact is though, I've probably spent ten thousand hours more as a professional programmer than I ever did as a professional animator. Still, for some reason, I feel like a fish out of water at times. That same feeling can drag you down throughout the learning process. Like, if you don't understand something **now**, you weren't meant to **ever** understand it. Disregard those thoughts. Will it take a decade to feel like you belong in front of a page full of code? Maybe. Maybe not. It doesn't matter, because feeling unsure of yourself doesn't have to stop you from making your first app or landing your first paid freelance gig as a programmer. There is a beginning to learning how to code, but there won't be an end. Every project can require knowing a little more than before. Maybe that's why countless other professional programmers like myself will always feel like they haven't mastered anything. We are all just students. Some of us double as teachers as well.

My main profession for almost a decade has been teaching video tutorials. That's longer than YouTube has been around. Weird, right? When my company CartoonSmart.com began I mostly taught Flash developers how to draw and animate. The illustration in the header of this section dates back to those past glory days of teaching simple things like how to draw. Eventually I started recording tutorials for Flash's programming language, which at the time was Actionscript 2. I taught some simple games, similar to Battleship, Missile Command, even a crude Mario Bros clone. Then Actionscript 3 came along and the language got less simple. I had to learn some better coding habits, like object-oriented programming. Just when I felt comfortable again, I tried an entirely new programming language because I got my first iPhone. It was a difficult switch at first, but a worthwhile adventure for sure.

There is something almost magical about publishing your work to an iOS device. Yes, I'll confess I've drunk the Kool-Aid of the Apple cult, but long before they ever made phones. My dad bought the first Mac computer. It's exciting to see a project you've coded get run on your Mac, but for some reason it is completely different to see what you've made on an iPhone or iPad. Maybe it's because running an app on your computer feels confined to **only your** computer. Whereas running an app on your iPhone feels like it could also be running on **every iPhone** too. You'll see some random stranger's phone and think, "my app could be on there right now."

Let's get back to **us**. If you already have some programming experience, tell me if we share any of these qualities in common:

- You can eventually code something close to what you originally set out to do, but for better or worse, you took some serious detours.
- You rarely finish reading programming books (like this one).
- Googling is your greatest source of information.
- Your second greatest source is all those fantastic people that just happen to have asked the same exact question on a forum that you currently need answered. Praise them.
- You sidetrack yourself for hours relentlessly trying to solve an issue you've already figured out a different approach to.
- You can be obsessive, learning everything about one subject and be completely stubborn about learning nothing on another.

That about sums me up as a programmer. Lucky for you, I do know the material in this book quite well. Although in writing this book over a few month's time, I've found myself using my own examples for reference in other projects. So once again, I find myself being both a teacher and my own student. Someone once said to me, "If you really want to learn the material, teach it."

So with that in mind, let's **both** get started. As you can see, there's a lot of fun projects ahead …

What You Need to Begin

Here's what you need to start building a fantastic app for the iPhone, iPad, iPad mini or iPod touch:

- **An Intel-based Mac with Lion** (or a higher OS) I use a middle-of-the-road iMac from early 2011, so depending on when you read this, you might laugh at the specs of my machine compared to what you can buy today.

- **Xcode,** which is available free in the Mac App Store. Once this big app downloads and installs, it will live in your **Applications** folder.

- **Cocos2d**, a free coding framework which makes creating games much easier. We'll go over the installation steps on the next couple pages.

- **The last thing you need is an iPad or iPad mini**, as the example projects in this book will be setup for the iPad screen sizes. I'll show you how to switch your project settings back and forth between iPhone-only, iPad-only, or Universal app later on. You can jump back and forth whenever you want.

The Different Cocos2d Versions to Install

Cocos2d isn't an application to "install" in the traditional sense, it is a coding library that extends what you can do with Objective-C. So what we'll actually be doing is adding new templates to Xcode that will create projects with the extended coding library included. Cocos2d is not an extra piece of software to install.

Head over to Cocos2d–iphone.org and make your way to their Download section. You'll probably see a couple different links to download (or branches) labeled **Stable** or **Unstable**. I would recommend the most recent stable release of version 2, but the choice is yours. This book will be using Cocos2d v2.x, but as far as the basics go, the two versions are largely similar. I'll try to point out any differences throughout this book for anyone still using v1. The templates you'll install will let you create a project for either version. One thing to consider too, is that your project will always stay at the version you created it at (unless you were to copy and replace a newer library of Cocos2d files to the project). So just because you upgrade your Cocos2d templates to a newer version, that doesn't affect any of your previously saved projects.

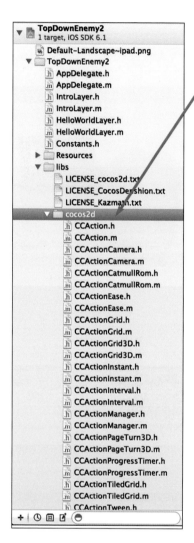

Take a look at this screenshot of an Xcode project using Cocos2d. Notice how it contains a **libs** folder, and within that a folder called **cocos2d.** Those files are the "Cocos2d engine" so to speak, and they'll be included in your project folder every time you create a new one. Usually upgrading a project just involves overwriting those older files, but when in doubt, I think your best bet is to Google something like, "migrating Cocos2d project from version (whatever) to version (whatever)" and you should find a blog article or forum posting with specific instructions to follow. A wise developer always makes a back up of their Xcode project before upgrading the Cocos2d library.

Install the Cocos2d Templates

Download the 2.x version and locate it on your computer. I pulled mine out of the usual Downloads folder and put it on my Desktop. Double click the **.tar.gz** file, and it should un-stuff itself and you'll have a regular folder full of Cocos2d files.

Right click on the terminal icon in your App Bar, and find New Window with Settings. I like Homebrew.

Next you'll need to open your Mac's **Terminal** app. Don't worry, every Mac has this pre-installed. You can do a Spotlight search or find it in **Applications > Utilities**. It is absolutely non-essential to using Cocos2d that you make your **Terminal** window feel like you're in a *Matrix* movie, which makes it all the more important I show you how. Because who else will?

The next steps I'll describe below, or you can watch the example movie at **www.focalpress.com/cw/Dike**:

- In the Terminal window, type in **cd** . This stands for "change directory". A directory is a fancy name for folder.
- Then drag the folder into the Terminal window. Doing so will automatically type in the location of that folder. Hit **Return.**
- Now type the line below and hit **Return**.

./install-templates.sh -f

You are done! You can quit **Terminal**, or leave it open to make anyone passing by your computer think you're doing freelance work for Morpheus.

Watch a bonus movie on this topic at **www.focalpress.com/cw/Dike.**

Open Xcode and Build Your First App

Now that you've got every thing installed, let's open Xcode and build an app. I know that seems premature at this point, but I'd rather get this out of the way now so you have the option to test and build your project at any stage, instead of patiently waiting until we've actually programmed something worth building (which could take a while).

We can even talk about some things now that you'll need to know when you submit a finished app for review to Apple.

First let's just create a new project using the Cocos2d v2 template under the iOS section. If this is your first time opening Xcode, you'll see the window in the screenshot on the top right. Click on **Create a new Xcode Project** from here.

Welcome to Xcode

Version 5.0 (5A1412)

Create a new Xcode project
Start building a new iPhone, iPad or Mac application.

Check out an existing project
Start working on something from an SCM repository.

↻ Open Other...

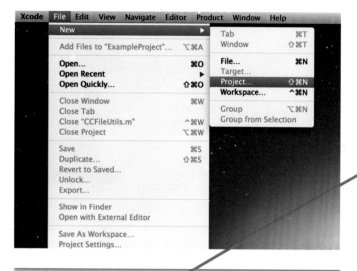

If you didn't see the previous startup image, go to **File > New > Project** as seen in the screen grab on the lower right.

Choose the **iOS > Cocos2d v2.x.** template that is selected in the top right screenshot above. Don't confuse this option with the similarly named template in the **Mac OS X** section.

You can name your project whatever you want in the **Product Name** field. The project name has no effect on the actual title of the app you submit to the Apple Store. One suggestion though, I don't ever recommend adding spaces in file names, and that goes for any resources you add to the project (such as images or audio files). I really don't think spaces belong in file names, instead use an underscore if you want your names to look pretty. A space in a name might not ever backfire on you, but programming is picky enough as it is, you shouldn't confuse yourself (or possibly the compiler) with something unnecessary.

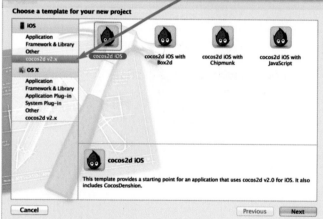

For **Company Identifier**, many people use a reverse of their domain name. So instead of "*cartoonsmart.com*", I'm using "*com.cartoonsmart*".

That's it. Your project has been created.

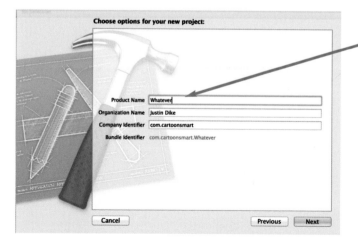

Let's save some of the reading for later and get started with a movie. You can watch it at **www.focalpress.com/cw/Dike.**

This will give you a brief overview of:

- How to build (run) your app.
- Switching between your iOS device or the Simulator to test on (without the paid Apple Developer fee the Simulator will only be available to you).
- Choosing between iPhone-only, iPad-only or Universal App.
- Setting your version number.
- Adding icons, startup images and finding out what size is required for which device.
- Adding Resources to the project folder (resources could be images, sounds, movies, etc.).
- Keeping your Resources organized.
- Entering your Bundle Identifier.
- Some frequently clicked buttons in the general user interface.
- How to find the actual app that gets built on testing or final publishing.

Notes on the Xcode interface—read the following descriptions for more details.

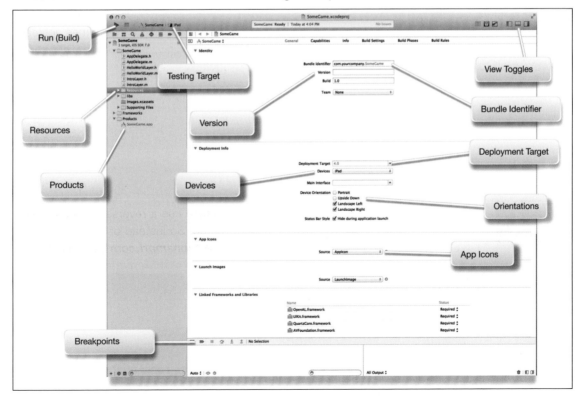

Testing Target—Choose between the iOS Simulator or your device. The Simulator lets you target devices you don't actually own. For a fast running game, the Simulator usually plays at a lower frame rate, so when in doubt, switch to testing on your iOS device for the best results.

Run (Build the App)—Press here to build your app in either the Simulator or your iOS Device. Testing on the device requires paying your Developer Fee to Apple first.

Resources—You can drag in images or files to be included in your project to here. After doing so, you'll get a prompt asking whether to copy in the resource files if needed. Typically you should leave this toggled on. Any files you import to your project should be copied into the main project folder.

Products—The App you are building gets created here. You can right click on the *.app* file and go to **Show in Finder** to locate it on your computer. Your test apps will be in the "*debug*" folder, and archived versions will be in the "*release*" folder (go up one folder from the debug version to find releases). To build a release version, you'll need to have properly signed your application.

Breakpoints—Until you are sure you want this on, leave it off. When on, the program will only execute up till your first breakpoint, then pause. This chapter discusses when to use Breakpoints later on.

Version—Most developers start with 1.0, then release new versions with 0.1 increments (1.1, 1.2 and so on). This is completely up to you, but be sure your version matches what you tell Apple in iTunes Connect.

Devices—Choose between iPhone (iPhone or iPod touches only), iPad (only), or Universal for all devices. For Universal Apps you'll need to add more icons.

Deployment Target—If you add features to your app that require a minimum OS version you can set that here. For example, if something you program can *only* run on iOS 6, than you want the Deployment Target to be 6.0. Since this is a basic Cocos2d book, you should be fine with a Deployment Target at 4.3 to 5.1. There's advantages to setting this lower than the most recent OS because not all devices have been updated or are capable of running the most recent update. For example, the iPad 1 can't go to iOS 6.

Bundle Identifier—This important ID should match the Bundle Identifier specified in the Provisioning Profiles you'll create for Development and Distribution. We'll discuss this in a later section.

Orientations—For Cocos2d projects, toggle on or off the orientations to support, but we will also set the orientation in the AppDelegate (discussed later in this chapter).

App Icons—In Xcode you can hover over these images to get the exact size required for the Icon. If your app supports Retina display, you should also include those icons as well. To add the image, just drag it into this area and the icon file will get copied into your project.

View Toggles—Collapse or reveal Xcode panels. The middle toggle opens your "All Output" panel (seen below), This is an important panel for testing your app.

Starting with the Cocos2d Templates

As you might have noticed already, the Cocos2d starting templates for either v1 or v2 will build an app that simply writes "Hello World" across the screen. The v2 template will also add a menu with two buttons to open a Game Center Leader board and Achievements board. You see this because of code written in your HelloWorldLayer class file which is divided into a header file called **HelloWorldLayer.h** and an implementation file called **HelloWorldLayer.m**. For almost all the projects in this book we will begin with the starting templates, so there will always be a HelloWorldLayer class that gets run (regardless of what you title the project). We'll talk more about using multiple scenes many chapters from now, but to keep things simple, it will be best to just use the HelloWorldLayer class for test projects.

This class is pretty stripped down as is, but we want to trim it even more because I'm sure you don't want to read "Hello World" every time your project runs. Another big reason I'm writing this section is because many of my examples show you a snippet of the

```
//
//  HelloWorldLayer.h
//  ExampleProject

|

#import <GameKit/GameKit.h>

// When you import this file, you import all the cocos2d classes
#import "cocos2d.h"

// HelloWorldLayer
@interface HelloWorldLayer : CCLayer <GKAchievementViewControllerDelegate, GKLeaderboardViewControllerDelegate>
{
}

// returns a CCScene that contains the HelloWorldLayer as the only child
+(CCScene *) scene;

@end
```

HelloWorldLayer.h and *HelloWorldLayer.m* files, but I don't want you to think that's *all* those files contain. There will be code we always leave in those files, but for the sake of saving space on these pages, I don't think you need to constantly reread the code that isn't changing from example to example.

The image on page 11 is a screen grab of a *HelloWorldLayer.h* file. We don't need to delete anything from this file, *but* since we won't be using Game Center in most of these test projects, I've highlighted the parts in orange that you COULD remove. Just note that if you do remove any of the orange code in the header file, you'll need to do the same in the implementation file.

```objc
// Import the interfaces
#import "HelloWorldLayer.h"

// Needed to obtain the Navigation Controller
#import "AppDelegate.h"

#pragma mark - HelloWorldLayer

// HelloWorldLayer implementation
@implementation HelloWorldLayer

// Helper class method that creates a Scene with the HelloWorldLayer as the only child.
+(CCScene *) scene
{
    // 'scene' is an autorelease object.
    CCScene *scene = [CCScene node];

    // 'layer' is an autorelease object.
    HelloWorldLayer *layer = [HelloWorldLayer node];

    // add layer as a child to scene
    [scene addChild: layer];

    // return the scene
    return scene;
}

// on "init" you need to initialize your instance
-(id) init
{
    // always call "super" init
    // Apple recommends to re-assign "self" with the "super's" return value
    if( (self=[super init]) ) {


    }
    return self;
}

// on "dealloc" you need to release all your retained objects
- (void) dealloc
{
    // in case you have something to dealloc, do it in this method
    // in this particular example nothing needs to be released.
    // cocos2d will automatically release all the children (Label)

    // don't forget to call "super dealloc"
    [super dealloc];
}

#pragma mark GameKit delegate

-(void) achievementViewControllerDidFinish:(GKAchievementViewController *)viewController
{
    AppController *app = (AppController*) [[UIApplication sharedApplication] delegate];
    [[app navController] dismissModalViewControllerAnimated:YES];
}

-(void) leaderboardViewControllerDidFinish:(GKLeaderboardViewController *)viewController
{
    AppController *app = (AppController*) [[UIApplication sharedApplication] delegate];
    [[app navController] dismissModalViewControllerAnimated:YES];
}
@end
```

Speaking of implementation files, Figure 1.2 shows your *HelloWorldLayer.m* file, as it should look stripped down.

This **scene** method stays unchanged. Examples of *HelloWorldLayer.m* in this book will rarely show this block, but I haven't deleted it in my project.

This **init** method got trimmed down to what you see here. Everything within the if statement got removed (where you see the red slash in the image). In Chapter 2 we'll talk more about this in detail since most of our early code to test goes in here.

This **dealloc** method stays unchanged. Examples of *HelloWorldLayer.m* in this book will rarely show this block, but I haven't deleted it in my project. We'll talk about this block more later.

> **You're done!**
>
> The only code we really HAD to delete was in one block. The rest was optional.
>
> I realize you just read some possibly unfamiliar terms like "class," "method," even "if statement," but don't worry. I'll define those properly later.

What About This Cool New IntroLayer Class?

If you build your app from the Cocos2d v2 template, the first class you'll actually see anything from is the IntroLayer class. Like the HelloWorldLayer class, it is broken into a header file and implementation file (***IntroLayer.h*** and ***IntroLayer.m***). This class is simply a convenient way to show your default launch image (or any image) before the HelloWorldLayer runs. The template is set to show this image for 1 second, then fade to white over another 1-second period. If you want to modify this transition, locate:

[self **scheduleOnce**:@selector(**makeTransition**:) **delay**:1];

Then change the number to however long you want the image to display for before running the transition. If you want to change how long the fade transition takes, skip down to this line:

[[CCDirector **sharedDirector**] **replaceScene**:[CCTransitionFade **transitionWithDuration**: 1.0 **scene**:[HelloWorldLayer **scene**] **withColor**: ccWHITE]];

Simply change the 1.0 for more or less time. Some other options for the color could be ccBLACK, ccBLUE, ccRED, and a few more easily guessed-at color names. Later on in the book, we'll look at various scene transitions you can use as well.

Skipping the IntroLayer Altogether

The IntroLayer class is a nice addition to Cocos2d because a lot of programmers were already adding their own in-between class to go from the app's default start up image to another image that credited the studio that made the app or some other branding. I would recommend using this IntroLayer class, but you could go directly from your AppDelegate to the HelloWorldLayer (or any other class). To do so, in your ***AppDelegate.m*** file, first import in the header file of the class you want to run first. For example:

#import "HelloWorldLayer.h"

Then locate this line: [director_ **pushScene**: [IntroLayer **scene**]];

and change it to: [director_ **pushScene**: [HelloWorldLayer **scene**]].

That's it! Most of the example code in this book won't mention the IntroLayer class because there really isn't much to discuss from here on out, but all the downloadable source code for the Cocos2d v2 based projects will include the IntroLayer.

Warnings Aren't Always Errors

A lot of my students freak out about Warnings.

You'll see them often when programming in Xcode, so get used to calmly dealing with a yellow triangle and exclamation point when you see it. Here's two big points to remember (accentuated with their own exclamation points):

• Something **MIGHT** be a problem!

• Something **MIGHT NOT** really be a problem!

I'm addressing this early on because you might get ahold of older project files that immediately have a Warning. This could be about deprecated code (code that one day won't be available to use) or a prompt that says something like, "This project should be upgraded". Another common, but harmless warning says, "Provisioning profile expiring". You can even get a Warning about variables you haven't used yet.

These are safe warnings.

You can also get a Warning for no good reason at all. Xcode loves to predict warnings, and occasionally it won't notice that you've corrected some code it warned you about. Those warnings can linger until you hit the almighty **CLEAN** button.

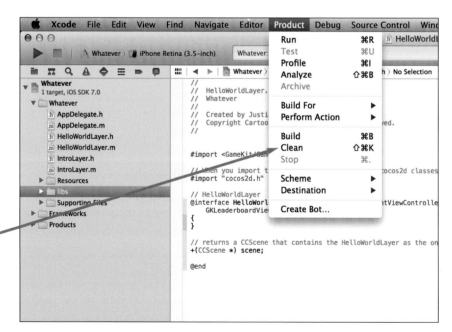

Cleaning can resolve some mysterious warnings. If the warning comes back after Xcode builds again, try this: hold down the **Option** key when the **Product** menu is open. The **Clean** button will change to **Clean Build Folder**. Give that a shot. I realize you don't really want to think about this now because you're just getting started, but if you did make a mistake, a Warning is your first sign of a problem. More often than not, you probably *did* make a mistake. Sorry, but it's true. Every programmer is capable of writing the simplest of typos. Unfortunately it's impossible for me to predict exactly what error you'll make first. Since I haven't taught you any code yet, I can't really warn you about specifics without confusing you, but I can think of three very general tips:

1. Assume the error is man-made (or woman-made). Even though I gave you some Get-Out-Of-Jail-Free Cards at the beginning of this section, it's usually safer to assume that you made the typo. So instead of pulling your hair out thinking your technology is turning against you, take a deep breath and fall on your sword. The first place to search for the problem is in what you recently wrote.

2. Undo or comment out code you just wrote. I know it's no fun to hit the Undo button on a line of code you tediously wrote, but those new lines of code are usually what introduced the problem. You can either undo OR comment out code to isolate the problem. Commenting can be done in two ways. First by writing **forward slashes** in front of a line. For example:

> *// code or text on this line will be ignored*

In general, comments aren't for code, but rather they are notes to yourself. Throughout this book, I'll often leave you notes after a line of code to explain it further. I'll make these comments easy to spot. Any text that is being commented out will be written in italics and have a yellow background.

You can also comment out larger blocks of code by writing an opening mark like this **/*** and then a closing mark like this ***/** For example:

> */* Game of Thrones was great this season*
> *I should really read the books*
> *Pick up milk later from the grocery store */*

That's not exactly the type of note you should be writing in your project, but it's been commented out, so as far as your final app is concerned, it doesn't exist.

3. Check your spelling. I'm sure I make more mistakes from misspelling variable names than I do with syntax errors, because I assume I spell things correctly. For example:

```
int myNumber = 5;
```

```
int someNumber = myNumbr + 15;
```

Do you see the error there? I left off an "e" the second time I tried to write myNumber. Fortunately Xcode would tell me about an error like this because it has no idea what the misspelled myNumbr refers to. So I should see a pop up message that says, "use of an undeclared identifier". If you're lucky, that might be the most common error you run into. Easy solution: check your spelling.

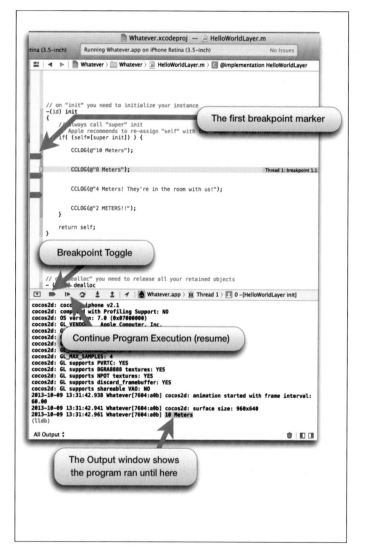

The first breakpoint marker

Breakpoint Toggle

Continue Program Execution (resume)

The Output window shows the program ran until here

Breakpoints

These aren't warnings or errors, but if you accidentally toggle on the **Breakpoints** button and build your app, you might think you've done something wrong. This debugging mode is easier to activate than you might think, because if you click in the line numbers column of Xcode, it will automatically create a breakpoint *and* toggle on the button for your next build. Meanwhile you might not have even noticed you created one. That's the danger of these tricksters. Early on, I did this a lot!

That's their only bad side, so what's the good? If you did write an error into your app, you won't always have a clue where it's occurring. The crash might occur immediately on build, or what seems immediate to you and I. The code executes much faster than we can perceive. What a breakpoint will do is pause the app and wait at the marker you created (whatever line of code that is). So you might add multiple breakpoints to isolate the problem. If your app never makes it to that first breakpoint, then you know the error is before that point. If you resume the app (by pressing the **Continue Program Execution** button), and it crashes before the second breakpoint, you know the error is somewhere between the first two breakpoints.

This can be extremely helpful in debugging your project. It's also a last resort. Most times, the Output window tells me where the error occurred with a specific line in a class file. So always check there first.

Supported Orientations

One thing you might already have planned about your first app is the rotation you want to support when your user is holding their iOS device. If you haven't thought about it, you probably should. I'm a big fan of choosing either landscape or portrait, but not both unless there's a really good reason to. Especially for games, I feel like it's perfectly fine to say, "I made this," in your best booming God-like voice, "and I'm deciding how YOU should view this game!" Apple placed a big emphasis when the iPad 1 was released on supporting every direction, but those days have passed. So if you're making a side scroller game, you probably want to support the device in landscape mode. If you're making a pinball game, it makes more sense to go with portrait. My point is, don't trouble yourself supporting both if you don't want to. Keep in mind, supporting both orientations usually means you'll be writing some extra code.

If you'll be using the Cocos2D v2 starting template, to change your app from the default landscape-only to portrait-only support, find the **AppDelegate.m** file, and scroll down to the block of code in the screenshot below (In Cocos2d version 1 this block was in the **RootViewController.m** file).

You have three options here:

return UIInterfaceOrientationIsLandscape(**interfaceOrientation**) ;
// supports both landscape directions, but not portrait

return UIInterfaceOrientationIsPortrait(**interfaceOrientation**) ;
// supports both portrait directions, but not landscape

return YES ;
// auto rotates for all directions

Then you'll need to visit your project settings and toggle on the **Supported Interface Orientation** icons for the directions you wish to include. If you ever forget how to get to these options, follow the arrow in the screenshot below. Also be sure you've selected the **Summary** tab which I've circled below.

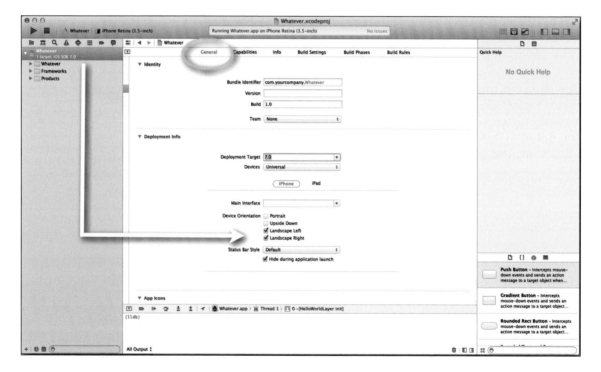

In Cocos2d version 1, toggling these icons didn't seem to make a difference, so for anyone on that version, you might be able to skip this.

Adding Retina Display Images

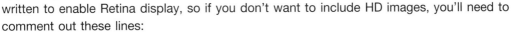

Cocos2d makes it easy to support high resolution (HD) images for the Retina display devices. Again, head over to your **AppDelegate.m** file. The code is already written to enable Retina display, so if you don't want to include HD images, you'll need to comment out these lines:

if (**!** [director_ **enableRetinaDisplay**: YES])
CCLOG(@"Retina display not supported");

You don't have to understand a lick of that code now, but in plain-speak, it basically tries to enable Retina display and if it can't it tells you so with a CCLOG message. More on logs later.

Now Cocos2d will automatically display alternate high resolution versions of your images **IF** you include them in the project with the appropriate name extension. If you don't, it will resort to showing the image with the default name. Below are the naming conventions for the various devices:

Example image name	Device
player.png (default name)	Would show on non-Retina display iPhone, iPod touch, or by default on any device if an alternately named image wasn't included
player-hd.png	Would replace **player.png** on Retina display iPhones or iPods
player-ipad.png	Would replace **player.png** on non-Retina display iPads or mini
player-ipadhd.png	Would replace **player.png** on Retina display iPads
player-iphone5hd.png	Would replace **player.png** on the iPhone 5

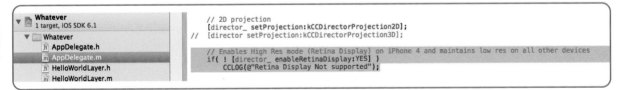

To learn about using the new Image Asset Catalogs with iOS 7, visit ...
www.focalpress.com/cw/Dike

After including an alternately named image in your Resources folder, **you don't have to make any code changes in your project to show the HD version**. Obviously though, you should actually change the size of your HD images. So if you had a 64 pixel wide by 64 pixel tall image, your HD version would be 128 by 128. Except, don't think that doubling the image size of all your current graphics makes them high resolution. They will look pixelated or blurry like this:

enemy-hd.png
128 by 128 HD image
(will be displayed at 64 by 64

enemy-hd.png
64 by 64 SD image

enemy-hd.png
128 by 128 image

A high resolution graphic needs to start big for you to see any difference. For example, the left image above is an exported PNG file from a vector illustration. PNG files are usually your image format of choice because they support transparency with an alpha channel. When I exported my image the size was 128 by 128 on export, and the resolution was the standard 72 dpi. I did this export first, because I

I'll do my best not to shamelessly plug other CartoonSmart tutorials throughout this entire book, but I'm a huge fan of working with vector graphics for games, especially now that we live in a Retina display world and exporting higher resolution graphics is key. If you need some help getting started drawing with a vector program, I use Adobe Flash. Some of my instructors use Adobe Illustrator. CartoonSmart has free tutorials on both excellent programs for game art creation.

knew later I would make a copy and shrink it down by 50 percent for my non-HD version (or SD version). That image is in the middle below. For comparison, on the far right is what you don't want to do. That image is 128 by 128 but it was created by scaling up the 64 by 64 copy. That's pointless.

Finally, Cocos2d will know at runtime to scale down your HD images by half. So a 128 by 128 image, will be displayed as a 64 by 64 sized graphic, but it maintains that extra resolution. Or simply, the extra pixel data is still in the image, so it will look much crisper.

If you're planning on making a Universal app (one that supports both the iPhone/iPod touch and iPad devices) your **-ipad.png** and **-ipadhd.png** could be bigger sizes than your

default and **-hd.png** iPhone images. Since the screen size of the iPad is obviously much bigger, it makes sense to increase the size of your graphics. In many games, you can keep the same code for a Universal app, because your game logic is using the size of the image to determine things like collision. So it's not always as painful as you might imagine to size those images differently. Worst case, it's easy to detect which device the user is playing on, and you can tweak the code where needed.

If you are building an iPad-only app, you don't need to name your standard (non-HD) files with the **-ipad.png** extension. You only need to do that for Universal apps. If you want to enable an iPad app for Retina display, you'll need to include the **-ipadhd.png** files when you use Cocos2d.

If you are on the fence about whether you should enable Retina display in your project and go to the trouble of maintaining multiple images for multiple devices, that's understandable. Honestly, it **is** more work, but if you own a Retina device, you already know the difference it makes. As a test, export a few of your images as HD and include them in your Resources folder. Once you get used to seeing *some* of your graphics look amazing, you'll probably find it unbearable to not go the extra distance and make the entire app look that good.

So what's the screen width of a Retina display iPhone in Portrait mode?
Is it 320 or 640?
Well even though the screen contains 640 pixels across, from a programming perspective you're still placing objects with a 320 surface size in mind. So instead of thinking in terms of pixels for the screen, consider them to be points. Throughout this book I'll try not to slip up and write "pixels."

My personal history as an iPhone owner went from the 3GS model to the 4S, so I skipped Apple's first high resolution phone, and really had no idea how amazing it looked until relatively recently. A personal vendetta against low resolution gameplay quickly set in and forced me to go back and upgrade a few of my games (like Pinball Showdown, seen above). So I can tell you from experience, it would have been much easier to start with the Retina display in mind, then go back and up-convert files that I didn't anticipate ever using again.

Flexible Code for Old and New iOS Devices

My dad likes to forward me tech articles where the writer will interview someone at a small gaming company and ask them how much work is required to support the latest changes to the iOS or a new device. The answer is usually from one of the cooler heads at the company that has already made their peace with whatever workload has crowbarred it's way into their weekend plans. Whereas, I'm always reminded who my developer friends are when a flurry of Tweets or Facebook postings over-exaggerate a few extra hours of work on a past app. Someone always dusts off the picture of a baby crying in front of a computer and adds a new caption about the latest release (I love that).

Unfortunately, I don't have a crystal ball to ensure everything I teach you in this book stays perfectly valid forever, but I can offer some pointers and words of encouragement. Anyone starting a project now already knows they should make high resolution images for **both** the iPhone and iPad. Unless Apple has plans for some kind of triple resolution screen, we should be safe for a while there.

The next "gotcha" would be something similar to the recent release of the iPhone 5 where the screen is slightly bigger than the previous phones. Fortunately, this can be planned for in your code. The projects in this book will try to use the width and height of the device as much as possible. So instead of hardcoding in the location of say, a health meter, with a specific value like 460, we can make that position based on a variable called screenHeight. If the health meter was always located at the height of the screen minus 20, then it shouldn't matter if the app is running on the iPhone 4, 4S, 5 or even on an iPad.

The example projects in this book will primarily be setup for the iPad, but at any time you can switch your project settings to iPhone-only or Universal and test how a drastic screen change affects your game. Hopefully if we build things right, the core engine of our games will still run fine.

Health meter located at the screen height minus 20

This is a nice lead in to some code you might need one day. You can check what kind of device family your app is running on using the exact same code that is already included in the IntroLayer class of the Cocos2d v2 template (you could paste this block into any other class):

```
if( UI_USER_INTERFACE_IDIOM( )==UIUserInterfaceIdiomPhone){
        // your device is an iPhone or iPod touch   ◄─────────────────────

} else {
        // your device is an iPad

}
```

The code in the first set of squiggly brackets would run if your device was an iPhone or iPod touch. Otherwise the code in the next set of brackets would run, meaning the device was an iPad. This would be helpful if you were building a Universal app and needed to set some position variables that were *not* based on the device's screen width or height. So inside the 'if' or 'else' statement above you could set a CGPoint value (the x and y location) for an object to be created. We'll talk more about CGPoint variables later, so ignore that term if you aren't familiar with it yet.

If you want to check a specific device model, like if your app is running on an iPhone 3GS, I'm going to let you walk down that dark alley alone. There is plenty of example code in forums to do exactly that, but as many wise people have pointed out in response to those posts, this can lead to problems where developers forget that a new model is always around the corner, and they only perform code for devices in existence. Writing from experience, it's rare you'll need to check a specific model, especially for game creation. Plus if you really must know more about the device your app is running on, you can check the screen size or whether or not it supports a Retina display.

Suppose you included this code within the first 'if' statement in our previous example:

Now you could do some further positioning based on that code (which assumes the app is set to portrait mode by the way). Hold on though, what if the next generation iPhone isn't 568 tall? Now your app is basically assuming anything that isn't 568 is probably a lower model than the iPhone 5. That 'else' statement would catch

```
CGSize size = [ [ CCDirector sharedDirector] winSize ];
if (size.height == 568 ) {
        //iPhone 5
} else {
        //not an iPhone 5
}
```

everything 'else'. So you can see how things can get a bit dodgy coding by device. Then again, that's the world we live in as developers. You can't always plan perfectly for the future.

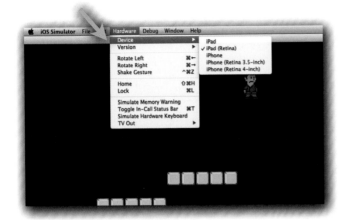

The past is a different story. You've got a window into ages long gone with the iPhone Simulator. While it isn't the smoothest way of testing your application (the actual device is almost always faster) you can test on iOS models you don't actually own. When you publish to the **iOS Simulator**, from the **Hardware** menu, scroll to **Device**, and you'll see other models to test on.

It is always smart to double check that past models run your app correctly because a simple missing image can lead to a crash. Remember, if you're including standard **and** high definition images you might forget to import one of them for the device model you don't regularly test on.

Finally, if your app ever needs to check if the device is enabled for Retina display, one easy way to do this is using code similar to what we already saw last section.

Assume we are testing an **iPad-only** project, and want to see if the device is an iPad 1, 2, mini, or iPad Retina display:

```
if ([[CCDirector sharedDirector] enableRetinaDisplay:YES] ) {
    // true if enabling Retina display worked
    CCLOG(@"Must be the iPad Retina display");
} else {
    // if enabling Retina display failed, it's an older model
    CCLOG(@"must be iPad 1 or 2, or mini");
}
```

The CCLOG statements above would send a message to the **Output** window with either of those messages above. More on log statements later. Keep in mind, that code actually enables Retina display (if it wasn't before), but it also could be used to tell us if enabling worked or not, letting us make assumptions about the model.

Now why check for this? Remember Cocos2d does all the work for you in terms of swapping in HD graphics, so that's not something we need to handle with our own code (we just have to name the files correctly). Here's one simple reason. We know the more recent iOS models are generally faster. So you could include a Cocos2d particle effect in the background of the game on a faster model device, but exclude it on the older models (keep in mind, the iPad 2 and iPad mini don't have a Retina display but are obviously much faster than an iPad 1).

Provisioning Profiles and Code Signing

I want to talk about signing your application early on because this can trip up a lot of beginners and lead to some serious frustration at the end of a project. I'd rather you tackle this hurdle soon instead of having an epic meltdown later because you got into trouble prepping your app for review. So what is a **Provisioning Profile**? Here's the official definition: "A Provisioning Profile is a collection of digital entities that uniquely ties developers and devices to an authorized iOS Development Team and enables a device to be used for testing." Translation: the app you build is tied to you. You'll need two profiles, one for testing on your device and another for your final product. These are your Development Profile and Distribution Profile. If you want to get your profiles setup now you'll need to join the **iOS Developer Program**. Sooner or later you'll want to join anyway and I don't see much point in waiting, especially if you're using Xcode frequently. The cost is still only $99, and in my opinion, well worth it—for the peace of mind alone, because while developing, you should be testing on your device. The iOS Simulator runs a lot different than an iOS device (which is usually faster). More importantly, the enrollment fee doesn't just buy you the ability to test on your device, you can eventually sell or distribute your app for free in the store. The handful of paid applications I have made sell around ten to twenty copies a day. That isn't get-rich-quick-money, but that is a little extra income each month (and it rarely ever requires customer service).

If you're signed up, you can proceed to the next steps: Login to the iOS Dev Center. In the top right, you should see a link to the iOS Provisioning Portal. There is a lot we have to do here, so I'm going to let you relax and watch a movie, which you will find at **www.focalpress.com/cw/Dike.**

Those Rascally Code Signing Errors

You will encounter a code signing error in your lifetime as a developer. Everyone does. Usually these are resolved by simply choosing the correct signing identity, so I want to give you an easy-to-find reminder in this book of where to go to fix this.

Select your project name, then select **Targets** (like the white arrow is indicating in the first image on the next page), then select the **Build Settings** tab (seen in the green circle of the same image). Aside from the **Code Signing Identity** section, this tab is full of options you will probably never adjust. So if you want to focus on only this one section, in the search bar (seen in the yellow circle of the same image) type in "code signing" and you should be left with only what you see in the screenshot below.

Notice I've selected the **Debug** row in the image. You're debugging your app when you test it on your own device, and since you're still just developing the app, you want the **Development Profile** selected that you created in the Provisioning Portal. If you click where the blue area is circled below, you'll see a secondary window pop out that gives you the signing options to select from.

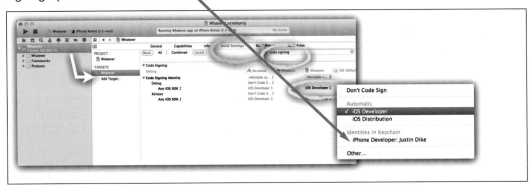

I've selected the **iPhone Developer** option under the Automatic Profile Selector field. Usually this is the best option because Xcode will try to use a profile that has a **Bundle Identifier** that matches the one specified in your **Project Settings** panel.

When you created a provisioning profile for either Development or Distribution you were asked to choose a Bundle Identifier (or App ID). Don't forget to include that same ID now in the **General** section in your Project Settings. The Automatic Profile Selector can't make a match if this isn't setup correctly.

Underneath the **Debug** row, you'll find a **Release** row, and again you'll usually be fine with the choice of the Automatic Profile Selector, just be sure it has selected the **iPhone Distribution** option. One thing to note about the **Release** version is that you'll never actually install this app on your device (that is, until it's been approved and downloaded from the App Store). This version gets built when you go to Xcode's main menu under **Product > Archive** (at least that's usually how I do it). At this point, an app should be created but not installed on your device.

Wait, Where Are These Apps Anyway?

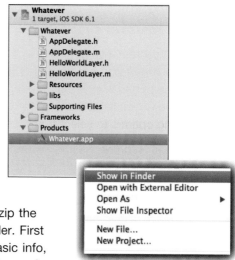

The apps you build are in the **Products** folder. Right click on the app name and select **Show In Finder** (red file names mean the app wasn't actually built). That will send you to the **Debug** folder where the development *.app* lives. If you go one folder up, you'll find a **Release** folder, which contains the distribution *.app* you will deliver to Apple or review using **Application Loader.** You already have Application Loader installed, similar to the iPhone Simulator it comes packaged with Xcode. Run a quick Spotlight search and you should find it. Typically you just need to zip the distribution *.app* file and upload it using Application Loader. First though, add a new app in iTunes Connect, fill in some basic info, and then you're ready to upload the binary (fancy name for app).

Missing Profiles

If you don't use the Automatic Profile Selector, or you still get an error after using it, then you can choose from the list of installed profiles in the pop out window. If your profile is missing, it may have expired or it wasn't actually installed.

At this point, you should check with the Organizer in Xcode. Find it from the main menu under **Window > Organizer**.

The Organizer will become your friend. Instead of visiting the Provisioning Portal online to renew or refresh your profiles, a lot of this can be done through Xcode. I've circled the **Renew** button in green on one of my many expired profiles. The **Refresh** button is circled in yellow. You'll need to sign in with your developer credentials for these buttons to work. Hopefully after renewing or refreshing these, the correct profiles are listed.

You can also use the **iOS Team Provisioning Profile** which doesn't require a Bundle Identifier. It is just a generic profile that is linked to you as a developer, but not a specific app. Using this profile is fine for testing projects, but if you want to incorporate some of the cooler iOS features like Game Center into your app, you'll need to use a profile with a bundle identifier. Otherwise Apple won't be able to recognize the app in the test environment.

Don't Code Sign
Automatic Profile Selector   (Recommended)
iPhone Developer   (currently matches 'iPh(
iPhone Distribution
BuildVehicleDev   (for bundle identifiers 'com
iPhone Developer: Justin Dike
iOS Team Provisioning Profile: *   (for bundle
iPhone Developer: Justin Dike
Testing
iPhone Developer:

The End of the Beginning

Are you ready to rock now? Are you feeling the energy of something new boiling in your blood? I hope so! I'm excited for you. Here's your Chapter 1 twist. How many programming books will tell you this?

Don't try to memorize code.

Think back to the last time you walked through a big art museum. The moment you exited the building was your best opportunity to describe to someone everything you had seen. Even then, it would be difficult to remember detailed aspects of even one painting. Your mind can only take in so much. It would take a few visits to the same museum before you could remember the location of every painting you saw, and hundreds of visits before you could memorize the exact details of a handful of favorites. So if someone asked you to describe a Van Gogh because you've been to the museum so many times, your best response isn't to pull out some oils and start painting: just take them to the museum and show them where to find it. You've *memorized the location* of that Van Gogh, not every brush stroke.

I feel the same way about code. Memorize the last place you wrote a block of code, not the block itself. I'm constantly opening old files or sneaking off to Google to refresh what I *sort of know*. Rest assured, memorizing the most common lines will happen whether you want to or not. There are lines in this book that will appear 50 or 100 times. They will cling to you like those face-huggers from Aliens.

I also use a program called 'Kousek by Fuel Collective' to jot down snippets of code. Just type in a keyword, and you'll get a copyable chunk of code that you pasted into the program at some previous time.

Of course, **this book** should serve as a fantastic reference library for finding great snippets of code. I've noticed when I copy code from sources like PDF files, or anything with hidden formatting, Xcode can get a little confused and show some mystery errors or warnings on those lines. So be aware of this when cutting and pasting code into Xcode.

Color Coding

Before we really get started, I should note that the code coloring in this book is slightly different than what you see in Xcode. I've tried to keep it close, but I think there's room for improvement in book form. The font itself is much prettier than Xcode's default font, so we might as well make things even more human-readable here in book form.

First off, when I create a variable, I'm going to color it green as opposed to plain black, which is often the case with Xcode. For example:

```
int myNumber = 5;
```

Why do this? Well, I do love the color green, but this is for your benefit. When I explain something about myNumber in a paragraph (like the one you're reading now), I want the variable to stand out. Code explanations are often just a paraphrasing of the coded statement. So which line would you rather read below:

The int type variable myNumber equals 5.

The int type variable myNumber equals 5.

That extra color coding is helpful isn't it? For the most part, though, I'll keep to the same coloring as Xcode. Basic variable types like int or bool will be pink, numbers will be blue, like 12345.

Apple's native Cocoa classes like NSString will be purple, and Cocos2d classes like CCSprite will be light blue. I'll color class names we create that same way since they are subclassed from Cocos2d classes.

Properties of Cocos2d variables, like mySprite.position will be a slightly dark blue.

Like Xcode, NSString text will be written in red, like @"hi". That @ symbol always precedes the text in quotes.

Cocoa methods will be **bold and purple**, and if it's a Cocos2d method, I'll color it **dark blue and make it bold**. Our own methods, I'll just make **bold and black**.

Did I lose anyone already? If you don't know what methods or classes are yet, that's okay! You'll learn those terms later.

My Example Projects and Resources

Throughout the book, I'll write down links to where you can find example projects I've uploaded to the companion site. I'll highlight them like the link below, but in case you ever forget where ALL these great resources are at, just bookmark the link below.

www.focalpress.com/cw/Dike

The **Resources** page has links to movies illustrating points in the book and links to zip files of *all* the chapter's projects.

If one day, the example projects aren't using the latest Cocos2d, it's still likely they will build and run fine. The important part you'll be getting from those files isn't so much the entire project itself, but the blocks of code that are worth clipping and saving. They are a safety net if you've tried making the project on your own and run into a brick wall.
So I don't want you to over-rely on those examples. It is easy to read code, download examples, re-read the code in there, hit **Run**, nod your head, and think, "Oh, I got it". Except, that isn't real practice. That's like going to karate class and watching everyone else spar with the instructor from the bench. You can say, "good workout," to everyone, but no

one will say it back. ***I can't make you get off the bench. You have to write code.*** You have to feel the frustration of a simple typo. Again, you don't have to memorize code, but you do have to practice coding and start thinking like a programmer. Part of that is dealing with mistakes you make. They happen, but they make you a better programmer.

Finally, I'm an easy instructor, I don't expect you to re-type every line of code I write in this book, but if you experiment with just half of what I teach you here, you'll have a great handle Cocos2d, Xcode and building your first app!

Chapter 2

Objective-C Basics

If you've never programmed anything before, you'll have a tougher road ahead than many readers, but that doesn't mean you can't begin right here. If terms like variables, if statements, while loops, and methods sound familiar to you, then you can probably skim or skip this chapter. Objective-C does have a unique, fun way of writing methods (or functions), so even if you have past programming experience you should pay attention to that section if you don't know the Objective-C way of doing things.

Check Yourself, Before You Wreck Yourself

Variables

So you decided not to skip this chapter, eh? I'll assume you're programming for the very first time. I've taught many students from the ground up, but mostly through video tutorials. The few times I've taught coding in a classroom or one-on-one, I've noticed some students focus more on **why** the syntax is a certain way versus **what** the syntax actually does. You might wonder, "Why are we using a semi-colon there?" or "Why is that a squiggly closing bracket instead of a straight one?" I can't answer a lot of these whimsical questions. I can't give anyone a history lesson on why the founding fathers of programming decided to use one keyboard symbol over another. I'm in my mid-thirties and I'm sure there's syntax we use today that was decided upon well before I was born.

This chapter has some basic programming syntax that is similar to almost all coding languages. For now, just give this simple code a read-through and if something doesn't click in your brain now, there's time for that later when we are actually programming a real project. For now, sit back and observe.

> Notice my usual color coding gets overridden by new index terms. These bright **orange** words are defined in the Glossary.

Variables—A variable typically represents a value that can be changed. Here are some common types of variables:

- int—**integers**, these are whole numbers both positive or negative, like 9 or –9.
- float—for **floating point** numbers, these could have a decimal value, like 9.22 or –9.22.
- NSString—a **string of characters**, like "cartoonsmart". An NSString is the Objective-C version of a string variable. The big difference is this @ symbol before the stuff in quotes. So really I should have written @ "cartoonsmart" as my example. Like Xcode, I'll color strings as red throughout this book.
- bool—a **Boolean** value, this variable type only holds two values. NO or YES. The NO essentially equals 0 and the YES equals 1. Like Xcode, I'll color bool values pink in this book.

There's plenty more variable types, but let's look at only these in this section. I should mention some variables don't vary their value. You can create a **constant variable**, or one where the value never changes. More on that later though.

Creating a variable, then assigning a value to it, can be done as a one- or two-step process. You can do this:

int myNumber = 10 ;

Or you can do this:

int myNumber ;

Take a nap, then come back later and give it a value:

myNumber = 10 ;

While you were taking a nap, that variable named myNumber existed because you created it, but it just had a default value of 0 for that variable type. A lot of times in programming, you'll set up a variable early on that you don't need right away. Think of it like actors being backstage waiting for their scene in the play. We'll talk more about why we do this in the section on **Headers and Implementation files**.

Note that when I referred to myNumber again after creating it, I didn't need to write int before it. That would cause an error because the code compiler would think I was creating the same variable twice. Once the variable type of int has been set, we don't need to write it again.

Also notice that I wrote a semi-colon after every line. This tells the compiler that particular line of code is done. In Xcode you'll usually get an error right away if you leave off a semi-colon.

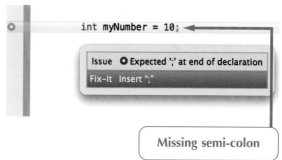

Since these are variables we are dealing with, their value can change over time. Here's some ways to change myNumber.

Take care of business with a straight-up value change:

myNumber = 11 ;

Or make myNumber equal itself plus a value:

myNumber = myNumber + 1 ;

Another way of writing that same line is:

myNumber += 1 ;

If you want to get really wild, you can make your variable equal another variable:

int yourNumber = 20 ;
myNumber = yourNumber;

Rub your goatee and meditate on that. *Ahhh-ssooooo* …

So let's look at examples of our other common variables types.

```
float someNumber = 0.1 ;
NSString *myString = @"someFile.png" ;
bool isThisBookTheBestEver = YES ;
```

No surprises with the float type. Now notice that asterisk symbol after the NSString *. That represents a pointer to the class. More often than not, you **do** need to include that pointer when creating a variable, and I'll explain that in detail below, but first notice that you can get away with putting the asterisk snuggled against the class name or the variable name. Both lines are fine below:

```
NSString *myString;
NSString* myString;
```

Since it doesn't matter, I'm sure I'll flip-flop back and forth throughout the book. You can decide where you like it best. It looks like a hair bow to me, so let's agree whoever gets to wear it, is a pretty lady for the day.

The Asterisk Pointer

The bigger mystery is **when** to include that asterisk pointer and **when not** to? You'll see it a lot in the book, and I think you'll just ignore it after a while, so don't over think any of this. I know some students get a bit crazy about this pointer because it's an odd little thing that, at first, feels like it's sometimes there and sometimes not. Here's my take on it: **when creating a variable you include it after the class name for an object**.

Now you're thinking, "Thanks Justin, so what is an object?" Well, let me tell you what's *not* an object. You don't need to include a pointer for number data, like float and int types, or data structures, like CGPoint, CGRect, and CGSize, which we will see later in the book. Now how come our bool variable didn't need it? Well remember I said that the boolean values of NO or YES are essentially just a 0 or 1 values. So a bool too is really just a basic number type.

Now you're thinking, "Stop beating around the bush, **really**, what is an object!?" Okay, okay, **classes are objects**. When I write "object", don't think it's something all that tangible. For example, later on we have some helper classes like CCJumpBy, that are used for making an object jump up. You might think, "Well, jumping isn't an object", but regardless, CCJumpBy is a class, and you can consider it an object in need of that asterisk pointer. Even classes like NSNumber require it (that's an Objective-C class dealing with numbers).

So is there an easy rule here we can remember? I might have to double check this, so don't consider it 100 percent true all the time, but if the class begins with the letters NS or CC, that should mean it is an object and will need the asterisk. Also you might do well to just remember who doesn't need the pointer, and common ones that don't are: int, float, bool, CGPoint, GRect, and CGSize. Again, we'll talk about the CG ones later.

Variable Naming Conventions ... Is there one?

On the previous page, take a look at my absurdly long and inquisitive bool variable name, isThisBookTheBestEver. It's descriptive and in the form of a question. I have a couple of reasons for naming it this way.

I like **VERY** descriptive variables. I don't feel like I need to save time typing by using a short name because Xcode will suggest a completion for the variable once I begin typing anyway. So by three or four characters in, I can just hit enter and it's all typed out. Having a descriptive variable name helps immensely when coding a large project because you stand a better chance of remembering what that variable does. Now that particular name is a bit too long for my tastes, but occassionally I code some whoopers.

I like my bool variables in the form of a question. Since the variable will always equal YES or NO, I consider those values to be the answer to the question I'm asking. By default bool variables always equal NO. So if I just wrote ... bool isThisBookTheBestEver ... that equals NO by default unless I gave it a value of YES immediately. So when my app is initially run, I typically have a lot of variables that equal NO. Or a lot of questions that I'm saying NO to, off the bat.

Take a look at some bool variable names from a recent project of mine: isTheSoundMuted, isThrowInProgress, didSomethingJustScore. Those could have been abbreviated to iTSM, iTIP, dSJS, to save me time typing, but golly, do you think I will remember what those stand for later? Later, meaning, a month later. Probably not. My brain is deleting precious childhood memories just to keep up with what I need at the grocery store.

Your naming convention is your own. Past programmers will name their variables the way they've been doing things before. For you new programmers, all I can suggest is that you make life easy on yourself. It's rare you can actually decide to do that.

Log Statements and Where to Write Your Code

It's time to write and test some code now that we have a few variables under our belt. We'll look at where to do that in the HelloWorldLayer class, although if you read the section in Chapter 1 about starting with the Cocos2d templates you already have a clue. So more importantly, we'll also look at writing a **log statement** to send a message to the **Output Window** in Xcode. By doing so, we can check the value of the variables we write at **runtime**.

I can use either a CCLOG statement or NSLog statement to output a message. Since we'll be using Cocos2d in most of our examples, I'll stick to CCLOG statements since that's the Cocos2d way of outputting messages. Here's an example:

```
CCLOG( @"I am a message" );
```

Notice my message in quotes had to include the @ symbol in front of it, just like our NSString variables. Without that you'll get a build error. Now if I wanted to see the value of a variable at runtime, I'll need to write the variable name after a comma following the string in quotes. My variable gets represented inside of the string with this syntax: **%i**. Take a look at the example:

```
int myVar = 200 ;

CCLOG( @"My variable equals %i" , myVar ) ;
```

The **%i** represents what will be replaced by an int variable. So the log message above would come back as:

My variable equals 200

Of course I would need to run a test build of the app on either the iOS Simulator or my device to see that. If you aren't seeing the Output Window while testing the app, go to the top right of the Xcode interface, find the three icons used for hiding and showing parts of the workspace and toggle the middle one to being active.

If my variable was a float type, I would use %f to log it.

If it was an object like an NSString* I would use %@.

If it was a bool variable I could also use %i , since remember bool types are just 0 or 1 integers.

There is a space between the word "equals" and the %i syntax in my example, but a space isn't necessary.

Outputting Multiple Variables

If I wanted to see multiple variables in one message I would separate them with commas. For example:

```
int myAge = 35;
NSString* myName = @"Justin" ;

CCLOG( @" %@ is almost %i ", myName , myAge );
```

So the log message above would come back as:

Justin is almost 35

Where to Start Writing Code

Whether you start your project with the Cocos2d version 1 or version 2 templates, you've got the same HelloWorldLayer class to play around in. If you don't know what the word "class" means, don't worry about it. Consider it a file for now, or more accurately, it is a couple of files: a header file named **HelloWorldLayer.h** and an implementation file named **HelloWorldLayer.m**. We'll talk more about the header file later (and why we have one), but for now we can skip over to the implementation file, and write code in the **init** statement.

Notice this small brown text below:

Go to the HelloWorldLayer.m file

Anytime I write in that format I'm doing my best to remind you of what file we are coding in. Until you get the hang of reading things like, "switch back to your header file", I think that will be helpful. Now let's find the **init** statement. It begins like this:

```
-(id) init
{
    if( (self=[ super init ]) ) {
        // we will always type below here, never above...
```

I added my own comment in there to let you know where we will begin typing. Problem is, there's a lot of other code already in the **init** statement. I want you to select that and get rid of it. So you can delete everything down to these lines below:

```
        // we won't type below here in the init statement
    }
    return self;
}
```

If you are worried we aren't on the same page, see below a screenshot of what you should be seeing:

```
// on "init" you need to initialize your instance
-(id) init
{

    if( (self=[super init]) ) {


    }
    return self;
}
```

As far as the **init** statement is concerned, we will always type between the interior two squiggly brackets that the arrows above are pointing to. If you're curious about anything else regarding the **init** statement, for now just be happy knowing it initializes the class. I'll explain more when you need to know it later. If you want a little extra help trimming down the Cocos2d starting template, watch the bonus movie at **www.focalpress.com/cw/Dike**.

Section 3

If Statements

If statements, or conditional statements, compare the value of one thing to another, and if that comparison is true we do something (perform code). Let's use an int variable of mySpeakers in this example.

```
if ( mySpeakers == 10 )

{

        // do something

}
```

> The == part is the comparison operator. Double equal signs tests equality.

> Opening and closing squiggly brackets, what's between these is the code that runs if the condition is true.

So if mySpeakers equals 10 (assume it does), we run the code between our opening and closing brackets. Right now, there's no code there, just a comment.

So let's write this again and make it an **if ... else statement**, one that does something if a condition is true (equals YES), or else it does another thing when the condition is false (equals NO).

```
if ( mySpeakers == 10 ) {

        // do something

} else {

        // do something else

}
```

Notice that this time my first, or **opening** squiggly bracket was right after my closing parenthesis symbol. Some programmers prefer to do this, but entering a line break between the two is also fine—arguably much cleaner because your opening and closing brackets can line up on top of each other like my first example.

Then obviously the big change is the inclusion of our else statement. So if mySpeakers **does not** equal 10, we perform the code inside of the brackets after the else statement.

We can also write an **if ... else if ... else statement**.

```
if ( mySpeakers == 10 ) {

        // do something if it equals 10

} else if ( mySpeakers == 11 ) {

        // do something if it equals 11

} else {

        // do something if neither statement is true

}
```

You can add as many else if statements as you want. Also, you *don't* have to include a final else statement.

Now let's take a look at more **comparison operators**. You've seen the first one in the chart already:

Operator Name	Syntax
Equal to	someNum == otherNum
Not equal to	someNum != otherNum
Greater than	someNum > otherNum
Less than	someNum < otherNum
Greater than or equal to	someNum >= otherNum
Less than or equal to	someNum <= otherNum

Our if statements can get a little trickier when we want to make two comparisons. We could write an interior if statement like so:

```
if ( mySpeakers == 10 ) {

if ( myGuitarIsLoudEnough == NO) {

    // both statements are true, do something

}

}
```

That's fine, but we can write the same thing by including a **Logical Operator** inside a single condition.

```
if ( mySpeakers == 10 && myGuitarIsLoudEnough == NO ) {

    // both statements are true, do something

}
```

The **&&** is called a **Logical AND** operator. We are testing if both statements are true. There's also a **Logical OR** operator using two pipe symbols.

```
if ( mySpeakers == 10 || myGuitarIsLoudEnough == NO ) {

        // at least one statement was true, so do something

}
```

There's one more logical operator, which I'll show you later when we talk about methods. For now though, using **&&** or || covers a lot of ground when testing conditions.

Switch Statements

Switch statements are a great way to compare a lot of values without having to write a ton of else if statements. The first line below just creates an int variable called diceRoll and uses a function called **arc4random** to give us a random number.

```
int diceRoll = arc4random( ) % 5; // will generate a value from 0 to 4

    switch ( diceRoll ) {                               Where you put the variable you are testing the value of
        case 0:
            // do something if the value is 0           In case the variable equals 0, the code below runs.
            break;
        case 1:
            // do something if the value is 1           If the following case was true, we
            break;                                      break out of the switch statement
        case 2:                                         (stop checking for other values)
            // do something if the value is 2
            break;
        case 3:
            // do something if the value is 3           Optionally, you can include a default
            break;                                      statement, so if no other condition was
        case 4:                                         met, you can run this code instead
            // do something if the value is 4
            break;

        default:
            // do something if none of the cases above were true
            break;
    }
```

Methods

Methods are the meat of your programming sandwich. Some folks call them **functions**, or **messages**, I like **methods**. In our past examples, where I had comments like

> // do something

those lines could have been replaced with calls to methods. Methods are blocks of code, which are often run many times during the life of an app. Here's an example:

–(void) **dropNinja** {

> // run code to create a ninja and add it to the game

}

This method doesn't do much, right? Again, I'm just writing a comment instead of actual code. Regardless, we've set up the method. Now let's call the method. By calling it, I mean, we will perform the code inside of the brackets above.

[self **dropNinja**] ;

I wrote self before the **method selector**, **dropNinja**, because we will usually call a method from inside of our current class. Again, just consider a class to be synonymous with the file you are typing in. In which case, self just means that the **dropNinja** method is written somewhere in that same implementation file.

This is getting a bit ahead of ourselves, but instead of self we could write a variable name if that object has it's own methods. To give you a preview of how that might look, here's an example:

[theEnemy **fireTheMostPowerfulGun**] ;

We'll come back to this when we create our own classes. For now, just realize that self isn't the only option.

You might be curious about the void part when we write the method. This means our method won't return a value when it is called. The code in the method is run, plain and simple.

> Like my variable names, I prefer descriptive method selector names. Don't be afraid to tack on a bit extra to the selector if it means you'll remember what the method does at a later date. Your current project will always be fresh in your mind, but it won't be a year later.

Methods that Return Something

Instead of void, we can include an object or data type to be returned from our method. In the example below, I'm writing bool instead of void, so I'm **committed** to return a value of that type. I'll include an if ... else statement to ensure that no matter what, either YES or NO is returned. Assume we have an int variable called numberOfNinjasInGame declared in our class:

```
-( bool ) doWeNeedToAddMoreNinjas {

        if ( numberOfNinjasInGame > 10 ) {

                return NO ;

        } else {

                return YES ;

        }

}
```

The **doWeNeedToAddMoreNinjas** method would **return** either YES or NO depending on the value of that variable. So how would this be used? Suppose every couple of seconds in a game I wanted to see if I should drop in a new ninja without going over 10. Using that method I could write:

```
if ( [ self doWeNeedToAddMoreNinjas] == YES ) {

        // if YES, then perform more code to add ninjas

}
```

Did you see what happened there? I called a method inside the conditional part of an if statement. So if numberOfNinjasInGame was equal to anything less than 10 when I ran that if statement, YES would be returned, and our game would drop another ninja into the scene.

We can actually leave off the == YES part of the if statement. The same statement could be written like this:

```
if ( [ self doWeNeedToAddMoreNinjas ] ) {

        // add code to drop a new ninja into the game

}
```

Why is that? Well, if statements are checking the truthfulness of something. So by returning YES, the comparison is considered true. Are you ready to really get your mind blown? I can add an exclamation point in front of the method, and test the opposite.

```
if ( ! [ self doWeNeedToAddMoreNinjas] ) {

    // if the method returns NO, then this code is run

}
```

That exclamation point is called a **Logical NOT operator**. Don't worry, it's rare I write logical **NOT** statements. It's also rare I leave off the == YES part in an if statement. Especially in a beginner's book, I think it's important to see the comparison value.

Methods that return something are pretty darn useful, so I want to throw one more example at you. You'll see your first bit of Cocos2d code below with the CCSprite*, which just sets up an image and adds it to the scene. We'll look at this same code later in a section dedicated to CCSprites, but for now I want you to just pay attention to the method call highlighted in green,

```
[self returnBackgroundFileName] ] ;.
```

This method returns the NSString that our CCSprite uses for the file name.

```
CCSprite* backgroundLayer ;
backgroundLayer = [CCSprite spriteWithFile: [self returnBackgroundFileName] ];
[self addChild: backgroundLayer ];
```

```
-(NSString*) returnBackgroundFileName {

  NSString* backgroundFileName;  // create a variable but with no value yet

  switch ( level ) {  // test the value of an int variable called level  (just assume we established this variable elsewhere)
    case 0:
      backgroundFileName = @"background_with_clouds.png";  // in red is the name of a .png file in our Resources folder
      break;
    case 1:
      backgroundFileName = @"background_with_sun.png";
      break;
    case 2:
      backgroundFileName = @"background_with_rain.png";
      break;
    default:
      backgroundFileName = @"background_default.png";
      break;
  }
  return backgroundFileName;  // so depending on what level equals we return a different image for the background
}
```

That previous example is very similar to a method I included in a Game Starter Kit recently. The big difference is that my method was in a different **Class** instead of self . By putting some code in different files, or classes, it keeps the project more organized. It's easy to write 2000 lines of code in one class, so to be able to take large chunks of code and put them in different files is key to keeping your sanity on a big project. You might decide to make one class deal with code related to your game's data. "Data" sounds fancy, but data could be:

- int variables for the current level or score, or float variables for how much money your character has accrued;
- NSString* variables for image file names;
- bool variables for preferences like whether the sound is muted.

These variables could all represent data that is better stored outside of the code that relates more to the actual gameplay. Or what is often described as the game's engine. The code in your **game engine** might handle things like moving your character, firing weapons, and so on. A separate **game data** class might return the number of bullets to start the level with. We'll talk plenty more about your game's **design pattern** in Chapter 9.

Methods with Parameters

Now let's look at **Methods with parameters**. Methods can be fed in parameters, or basically more data.

To do this, you'll add a colon after the method selector, then in parenthesis write the data or object type (including the * symbol if it is an object), and finally give the parameter a name. The parameter name will be used inside the opening and closing brackets of the method to refer to that value.

–(void) **checkForNewHighScore**: (int) theScore {

CCLOG (@"The number we passed in is **%i**", theScore);

// this would output the value of theScore in the CCLOG statement

}

Now to call a method with a parameter we would write:

[self **checkForNewHighScore**: 10500];

Notice I added a colon after the method selector, then I wrote the same type variable that the method is expecting, in this case an int type. It's proper to say this value was "passed into" the method.

So the amount of 10500 is passed into the method as a variable called theScore. Okay, cool, but why do this? Why complicate our methods by passing stuff into them? … *Silence, young grasshoppers.* This is easier to understand than you might think. Methods with parameters (or **messages with arguments**) can be used to do the simplest of things, like compare one variable to another. So let's add to this example and assume our project has another variable called previousHighScore:

–(void) **checkForNewHighScore**: (int) theScore {

    if (theScore > previousHighScore) {

        // make a big stink if we've set a new high score

    } else {

        // proceed to next level without any fanfare

    }

}

All we did there was check to see if we set a new high score. Of course we *could* have written that same if statement elsewhere in our file and not worried about creating a method at all, but what if we wanted to check for a new high score in multiple different places in our main file. Then it makes sense to put the code in one place, or one method, instead of writing the same thing again and again. If you ever find yourself writing the same code twice, you should consider creating a method to handle that code.

Ready for more fun? You can have multiple parameters passed into one method. We just separate them with a colon. Lets change up our example a bit. We'll write a method that creates a bonusAmount variable and sets it's value to the multiplied amount of the two parameters we pass in, which will be named theScore and livesLeft.

–(void) **calculateBonus**:(int) theScore : (int) livesLeft {

int bonusAmount;

bonusAmount = theScore * livesLeft;

}

The method call would look like this:

[self **calculateBonus**: 10000 : 3];

That method call is okay. As in, only okay. As in, it could be way better. Check out the screenshot to the right, all I've typed so far in calling the method is **"cal"** and Xcode predicts what method I'm starting to write then shows me what variable

```
[self calculateBonus:(int) :(int)
M  void calculateBonus:(int) :(int)
```

types are expected for the parameters. That's awesome of Xcode. Yet, we could make things even more awesome because just seeing **(int) : (int)** is really vague. Let's rename the method slightly and give the second parameter a name we can identify it with when we are calling the method. The changes are underlined:

–(void) **calculateBonusUsingTheScore** : (int) theScore **andLivesLeft** : (int) livesLeft {

    // no changes below ...

int bonusAmount;

bonusAmount = theScore * livesLeft;

}

Now when we start typing the call to the method in Xcode we will see the image to the right instead. Notice how much more readable that is. You

[self **calculateBonusUsingScore:**(int) **andLivesLeft:**(int)]
M void calculateBonusUsingScore:(int) andLivesLeft:(int)

would know exactly what type parameters the method is expecting, and also have an idea of which int refers to what. The previous way of writing the method wasn't wrong, it just won't be as easy for us, the ever forgetful programmer, to remember it's usage at a later date. So our more polished method call would look like this:

[self **calculateBonusUsingTheScore:**10000 **andLivesLeft:** 3];

> Throughout this book, method selectors and their parameters will be written in bold, just like this one.

Methods with Parameters that Return Something

Let's really drive these concepts home. Change that last method example to return an int value instead of just void:

– (int) **calculateBonusUsingTheScore:**(int) theScore **andLivesLeft:**(int) livesLeft {

int bonusAmount;

bonusAmount = theScore * livesLeft;

return bonusAmount;

}

Now you could make a variable equal to the returned amount from the method:

int yourBonus = [self **calculateBonusUsingTheScore:**10000 **andLivesLeft:** 3];

    // returns the multiplied amount

In practice, you probably wouldn't be using numbers above, but instead, other variables. For example:

int yourBonus = [self **calculateBonusUsingTheScore:** currentScore **andLivesLeft:** lives];

Had enough of methods yet? We will program a lot of them later so I won't fry your brains too much with them just yet. Try to remember a few key points here:

- Methods are blocks of code that help you to organize things (**functions** or **messages** are other common terms for methods).
- Methods can perform simple calculations in a couple lines of code or be hundreds of lines long, and even call other methods.
- Methods are a great way to keep from writing the same code in multiple places.
- Methods can optionally return a value to a variable or be used in a conditional statement (like an if statement).
- Methods can optionally have parameters passed in (**arguments** or **properties** are other common terms for **parameters**).

Two common errors you might get when calling methods are:

Trying to return the wrong type value

```
NSString* someVariable ;

someVariable = [self calculateBonusUsingTheScore:10000 andLivesLeft:3];
                        ⚠ Incompatible integer to pointer conversion assigning to 'NSString *' from 'int';
```

An NSString* is the wrong type variable to receive what is returned from this method (if we're using our example on the previous page, it will return an int type variable).

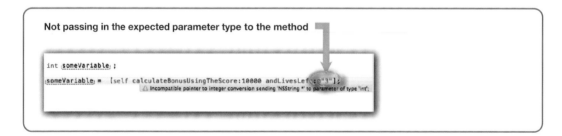

Not passing in the expected parameter type to the method

```
int someVariable ;

someVariable = [self calculateBonusUsingTheScore:10000 andLivesLeft:@"3"];
                        ⚠ Incompatible pointer to integer conversion sending 'NSString *' to parameter of type 'int';
```

The NSString* of @"3" is the wrong type parameter, an int is expected.

While and For
Statements

No proton accelerating in the living room!!

Phew. The basics are almost done. Lets take a look at two other type statements that are common to every programming language I've ever used.

The **While Loop**. Or as I sometimes think of it, the wily loop, because these can get a bit crazy if we let them. Take a peak:

```
int bullets = 0;

while ( bullets < 100 ) {

    // do code to add a bullet sprite to the scene

}
```

So in plain speak, while bullets is less than 100, the program will do whatever code is inside of the squiggly brackets. Over and over and over again. The problem is that our program can get stuck here if bullets never equals more than 100. It's like crossing the beams in Ghostbusters. It's bad. The universe can collapse in on itself, crashing the app with it.

Let's correct our example by adding 1 to bullets for every iteration of the while loop.

```
while ( bullets < 100 ) {

    // do code to add a bullet sprite to the scene

bullets += 1 ;

    // adds 1 to bullets

}
```

So now the program would iterate through the loop 100 times, then eventually bullets will equal 100 and the condition won't be true anymore (because we are using a **less than** operator not a **less than or equal to** operator).

One big thing to keep in mind with while loops is that they occur super fast. So you might think, "Neat, I could use a while loop to shoot out a bunch of bullets and they would be spaced out a few points between each bullet because the code can't run *that* fast". Wrong. A while loop would just dump out 100 sprites at once, all on top of each other and your game would appear to have fired only one bullet. Bummer. If you did want to code a gun to fire sprites spread evenly apart, you would be better off performing a method at a timed interval like every second or fraction of a second.

So what are while loops good for? Well, the previous example still holds up, just maybe not with 100 iterations. A lower number like five loops would make sense, each time adding a bullet sprite, and the code you write to position them could be randomized so visually they all don't pile in on top of one another.

While loops are also good for removing objects, often called children, from a scene. We'll look at the code to add and remove children in the next chapter.

Breaking (out of) a While Loop

You can also **break** out of a while loop before the conditional statement is false. Here's an example:

```
int bullets = 0;

int bulletsInYourVest = 52;

while ( bullets < 100 ) {

    // do code to add a bullet sprite to the scene

    bullets ++ ; // writing ++ is another way to add 1 to bullets

    if ( bullets == bulletsInYourVest ) {

        break;

    }

}
```

So plainly speaking, we tried to add 100 sprites, but our bullets variable eventually equaled the amount of bulletsInYourVest and we had to break out of the loop. Obviously it would have made more sense to just code our conditional statement:

```
while ( bullets < bulletsInYourVest )
```

Duh, but, hey, these are just examples.

It's actually rare I use a break statement in a while loop, and that's probably because they do occur so quick, I don't often find a need to break from them before the conditional statement becomes false.

For Statements

For Statements are very similar to while loops in usage, but notice how everything can be setup within the parenthesis:

```
for ( int bullets = 0 ; bullets < 100 ; bullets ++ ) {

    // do code to add a bullet to the scene

}
```

Inside the parenthesis we have three parts of code separated by semicolons. The first part sets up a variable, the second part is our conditional expression, and the last part is the increment for the loop. Note, bullets ++ is just a shorter way of writing:

```
bullets = bullets + 1; or bullets += 1 ;
```

For statements can also include break statements in the same way as while statements. They can also have **nested loops**, or other for statements within them. So you could do this:

```
for ( int bullets = 0 ; bullets < 100 ; bullets ++ ) {

    // do code to add a bullet sprite to the scene

        for ( int grenades = 0 ; grenades < 10 ; grenades ++ ) {

            // do code to add a grenade sprite to the scene

    }

}
```

In that example, how many grenade sprites are being added to the scene? Well for every iteration of the first loop, we add ten grenades sprites. So 100 iterations of the first loop would mean 1000 grenade sprites. Seem like too much? If you created a variable called allGrenades and added one to it for every iteration of our nested loop, when the initial for loop is complete allGrenades would equal 1000.

```
int allGrenades = 0;

for ( int bullets = 0 ; bullets < 100 ; bullets ++ ) {

    for ( int grenades = 0 ; grenades < 10 ; grenades ++ ) {

        allGrenades ++;

    }

}
```

Obviously those nested loops can run through a lot of code if you want them to. I should mention while loops can also have nested loops, so don't think those are only unique to for loops. If you were to break out of a nested loop, you are only breaking out of that particular loop, the outer loop of the while or for statement would continue.

Peek Into The Future!

Take a look at the for statement below, which you'll see again in Chapter 4 in a section on iterating through classes. You don't need to understand any of this code right now, but I want to give you a sneak peek at a for statement which doesn't use an int variable to decide when it's time to stop running.

```
for ( Enemy *opponent in self.children) {

        if ( [opponent isKindOfClass: [Enemy class] ] ) {

                // log each time we find an instance of this class

                CCLOG( @"found one!" );

        }

}
```

The for statement is going to run for every child in the scene because we used in self.children as the condition. As you can read above, we're checking if one of those children is of the Enemy type class. Pretty cool, right?

Another fun thing to look forward to later is using a while loop to keep a player positioned on a platform (versus falling through it). Showing you the exact code now would be a bit confusing, but I'll give you a little preview, half code, half notes:

```
while ( the player intersects with the platform ... ) {

  ... move the player up a small amount, like one point, and temporarily disable gravity

}
```

Read over that and consider what you already know about while loops: they occur lightning fast and they need to eventually be un-true or else we'll get stuck in the loop endlessly. So what this code will do later is keep testing that the player and the platform intersect each other, and move the player up until that intersection is not true. It happens so fast though, visually we won't see the player move up.

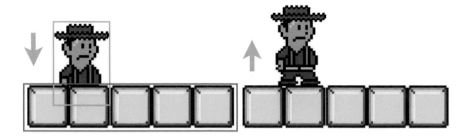

We've reached the end of what I consider the most basic concepts in programming. The code discussed in the section on methods was very specific to Objective-C, but the rest of what we looked at is common to most programming languages. There's obviously a **ton** more we could get into, but I'll introduce you to plenty more in later chapters. You might be surprised how many games could be made using the basics we've talked about here and a tiny bit more to do with positioning graphics in a scene.

Many people assume programming is all about math, but most of the time it just boils down to logical situations. It is rare we will write a program that uses mathematics beyond what a sixth grader knows. When you lie in bed thinking, "How will my game begin?", you'll probably answer yourself with a logical statement like, "Well, if the player does this thing, then this will happen or else they will have to go here". That kind of thinking isn't mathematical, it's logical. Once you start writing your game, logic is what leads you step by step through your code, not math. What you'll control with code is the flow of a sequence of logical situations.

Chapter 3

Cocos2d Basics

Some of you beginners may have gotten hit hard last chapter, while others might have yawned through those basics. Well, hopefully I can please everyone in this chapter. We are still going to keep things very light, as I introduce some of the easiest things you can do with Cocos2d, but you might be amazed at how much you can do with so little.

I'll save some higher concepts, like creating your own classes and subclasses, for later chapters. For now, I'd like you to just work with some simple images and move things around the screen. Trust me, your friends and family will be impressed.

CC Sprite

A **CCSprite** is an image. Actually it is a class used for drawing your images to the screen. The "CC" in CCSprite lets you know it's a Cocos2d class, and anytime you see a class beginning with "CC", you can keep that in mind. Uh oh, I just wrote the word **class** again didn't I? That term carries a lot of baggage,

especially for students that have been introduced to classes before and never really understood the various analogies that teachers use to try to describe them. Like Mom and Dad are a class, and they have kids that are subclasses. Or the old flow chart of classes and subclasses that new students are supposed to understand. Some of those confuse me too. So let's do this. Forget I mentioned it. If I mention it again, keep avoiding the term until you are ready to tackle it. For now, just keep these two notes in mind:

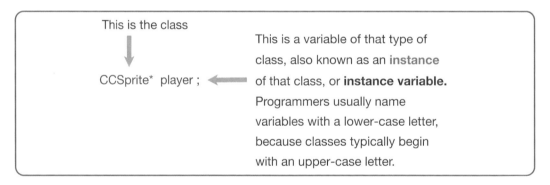

This is the class

CCSprite* player ;

This is a variable of that type of class, also known as an **instance** of that class, or **instance variable.** Programmers usually name variables with a lower-case letter, because classes typically begin with an upper-case letter.

Remember our NSString* object from last chapter? That was a class. I just didn't make a big stink about it.

Variables made from classes often have their own methods and properties. CCSprite has a method named **spriteWithFile**:

```
CCSprite*  player ;
player  = [ CCSprite spriteWithFile:@"player.png" ];
```

Now my player calls this method, **spriteWithFile**, to eventually display the file @"player.png" which would have been imported to your Xcode project (if you forgot how to to add a file to your Resources, you can just drag and drop it in). Using what you know about methods from the previous chapter, **spriteWithFile** is the method selector. Ah-ha. Then @"player.png" is the NSString* type parameter I'm expected to pass into the method. CCSprite is obviously the class. So somewhere in your Cocos2d library are two class files (**CCSprite.h** and **CCSprite.m**) that did some work for you just now. You never have to poke around in those library classes if you don't want to. Remember the dude who sold out the good guys in the first Matrix. "Ignorance is bliss," he said. Very true. Hey, what happened to that guy?

Now let's add one more crucial line:

CCSprite* player ;

player = [CCSprite **spriteWithFile**:@"player.png"];

[self **addChild**: player];

Those three lines would add an image to your scene. Come to think of it, the first two lines could be combined into one. Let's keep creating our instance variables in separate lines though. There's a reason for that which you'll see eventually.

So about our new line … [self **addChild**: player]; … it should be obvious what occurs here. We add a child, the player variable, to self. In this hypothetical example, self will just be our current scene, or really our layer.

Adding children is a great term. It implies there's a parent, and there is. When we add a CCSprite, it is a child of our **CCLayer**, which is a child of our **CCScene**. You don't have to be typing this code into an example project for now, but assuming you were, the **HelloWorldLayer.m** file already has a CCScene and CCLayer created.

CCScenes and CCLayers can be an important part of how you use Cocos2d, or they can almost be ignored entirely. You could create an entire game using the scene and layer from the HelloWorldLayer class. In fact, that's very likely for a simple game.

All your **CCSprites** can coexist on one **CCLayer** just fine. Don't feel like you need to experiment with tons of layers for each sprite because you think that's how things are supposed to be done. It's rare I work with more than one layer.

One big thing to be aware of is that the **addChild** part of … [self **addChild**: player]; … added the child to the layer. If you removed the layer, you would remove the children as well. In this case, the CCSprite would be automatically released from memory along with the layer. Which is a good thing. Cocos2d does a fantastic job of not making us worry about memory.

The only thing you really need to concern yourself with now is where exactly that CCSprite landed in the scene. If you're playing along at home, you know by now it didn't end up in the middle of the screen.

Positioning Objects

Using the example code from last section, you would see that our CCSprite ended up being displayed in the bottom left corner of the screen, like so:

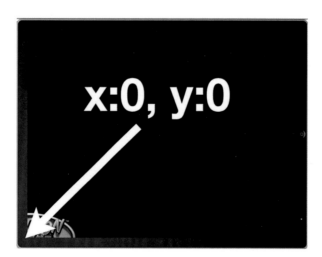

Since we didn't position the CCSprite ourselves it just got added at the default location of 0 on the x axis and 0 on the y axis. The reason we see only the top right quarter of my logo in that example is because Cocos2d puts the center point (or **anchor point**) of most objects in the middle. So if the logo in this example was 400 pixels wide, and 200 pixels tall, the center point would be where? At x: 200 and y: 100, or *half the width and half the height*.

Y on Bottom?

Are you wondering why the image was in the ***bottom*** corner of the screen if the default location it got dropped at was x: 0 and y: 0 ? Usually with design programs your 0, 0 point is in the top left. Well, the architect of Cocos2d may have hemmed and hawed about this, but for a game engine it does make sense to have 0 on the y axis be at the bottom of the screen. Think about jumping up in the air. You would say, "I jumped 3 feet up". In a game, your character might jump 30 points up starting from a lower value like 0 (or the bottom of the screen).

Let's take our previous code and modify the position.

CCSprite* player ;

player = [CCSprite **spriteWithFile:**@"player.png"];

[self **addChild:** player];

player.position = ccp(512, 384);

Should be obvious, but let's break it down anyway. Our player, or instance variable, has a property named position. To modify (some) properties we can write the variable name, then a period, and then the property (this is called **dot notation**):

player.position

Let's pause right here. Actually rewind even further and just write in Xcode— player.p—and hit **Escape**. You would see the image on the right.

Notice the code hinting has already found the position property but, more importantly, **it is also telling us what**

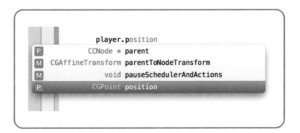

kind of value the property expects us to provide. In this case a **CGPoint**, which is a kind of data called a struct, or structure that simply defines an x and y value.

So if the position property expects a CGPoint, we had better give it one. Both lines below get the job done, and both comma-separate the x and y values in opening and closing parenthesis.

player.position = ccp(512, 384);

player.position = CGPointMake(512, 384);

Using ccp( ) is the more Cocos2d way of doing things since it is part of the Cocos2d library, and it is a heck of a lot shorter to type than CGPointMake( ). So throughout this book, I'll be using ccp whenever I can. If you want to define the abbreviation in your head, it's probably short for "Cocos2d position" or "Cocos2d point". To be honest, I've never thought about that till now.

We could also make the player.position value equal a CGPoint variable instead. To do this, let's create the CGPoint variable first:

CGPoint playerPosition = ccp(512, 384);

player.position = playerPosition;

One advantage to doing this is that we could use the playerPosition variable later possibly with other objects.

Getting the Screen Width and Height

I want to spend longer than necessary on CGPoint variables because probably everything in your game (that's visible) will get positioned with a CGPoint. I **hard-coded** in the value of my x and y locations on the previous page, meaning my values are a specific number. I didn't have to do this though. I could have put two variables in there instead. For example:

int screenWidth = 1024 ;

    // equals 512 when divided by 2 below

int screenHeight = 768 ;

    // equals 384 when divided by 2 below

player.position = ccp(screenWidth / 2 , screenHeight / 2);

A little better right? I'm dividing the width of an iPad (in landscape mode this is 1024) by two and doing the same for the height. Now my image will be right in the middle of the screen. That is good. It could be better though if I didn't even have to worry about entering in the width or height values myself. I can let Cocos2d tell me the size of the screen, so depending on whether the device is held in landscape or portrait mode, I'll have the correct value for placing the image in the center:

CGSize size = [[CCDirector **sharedDirector**] **winSize**];

int screenWidth = size.width;

int screenHeight = size.height;

player.position = ccp(screenWidth / 2 , screenHeight / 2);

Let's break down that block. In the first line, we created a CGSize variable and called it size. **CGSize** is a structure like CGPoint, but instead of an x and y value, CGSize defines a width and height value. This part:

[[CCDirector **sharedDirector**] **winSize**];

will return what a CGSize variable is expecting. Alternately we could have written:

CGSize size = CGSizeMake(1024, 768);

Again though, that hard codes in the value of the width and height. So the best option is to get the values from the [CCDirector **sharedDirector**] using the method **winSize**, which returns a CGSize variable. How does this class know the size of the screen? It doesn't matter. What matters is that it's a useful method that returns what we want.

Once the values are returned to our size variable, we can use them in a really cool way: size actually has two properties, width and height. We access those values using the same dot notation syntax we saw earlier in the section.

int screenWidth = size.width ;

int screenWidth = size.height ;

Then we just set the player.position like before.

You might wonder why I created variables at all for the screenWidth and screenHeight. I really didn't need to once I had the size var. We could have just written:

CGSize size = [[CCDirector **sharedDirector**] **winSize**];

player.position = ccp(size.width / 2 , size.height / 2);

That works just as well now, but later on it's helpful to have variables saved for the width and height.

Let's talk about a practical situation when developing games. You may want to create a CGPoint variable for an **initial starting** position for your player. Then during the game make your player return to the value of that CGPoint after the character dies or restarts a new level. Here's how that would look:

CGPoint startingPosition;

startingPosition = ccp(200, 200) ;

player.position = startingPosition;

Note that my player.position is equal to the startingPosition variable, but I didn't need to write ccp in that line, because the position property expects a CGPoint and I'm giving it a CGPoint variable. Now that I've got that startingPosition variable, you would think I could use it in other methods, like this next example:

-(void) **resetPlayerPosition** {

player.position = startingPosition;

}

How's that code look to you? It would work fine *if* my startingPosition variable (and player too) were visible to other methods in my file. If I had declared the variables in my header file, then this method would be perfectly fine. This is what we will discuss in the next section.

A CGPoint variable and the position property differ slightly in the following examples...

With a CGPoint variable we **CAN** write...
startingPosition.x = 30; // *directly assignable*
startingPosition.y = 50; // *directly assignable*

We **CAN** access the x and y values of both the CGPoint variable and the position property like so...
if (startingPosition.x > 30) // *easily accessible*
if (player.position.x == 30) // *easily accessible*

We **CAN NOT** directly assign a value to the position property's x and y values...
player.position.x = 30; // *not assignable*

Declaring Variables in Header Files

We can't avoid this discussion much longer. I've got to interrupt the fun we could be having with CCSprite variables to talk about something serious. Variables can have a very limited **scope** if we don't explicitly widen the range of where they can be seen or accessed. To do that, we will declare the variable in our header file. Once we do that, the variable can be used throughout the class in any method we write. You might be thinking, "Should we always do this?" Which is a good question, because if you are new to programming, it's not always obvious which variables need declaring and which don't. I'll try to help you there, but first let's just **declare** some variables from our previous example. Using the Cocos2d starting template again:

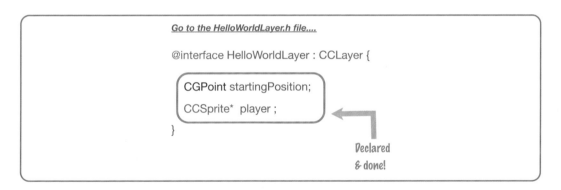

Go to the HelloWorldLayer.h file....

@interface HelloWorldLayer : CCLayer {

CGPoint startingPosition;

CCSprite* player ;

}

Declared & done!

Not hard. All we did was create the variables as usual, without any value in the header file, in this case, **_HelloWorldLayer.h_**.

Now I'll jump over to the HelloWorldLayer implementation, **_HelloWorldLayer.m_**. There's a hot key in Xcode to go from a class's header to implementation file and vice versa: Press **CONTROL + ⌘ + Up.** Let's skip down to the **init** statement and add what I've circled below. As usual, clear out anything else in your **init** statement if you haven't already.

```
-( id ) init {
    if( (self=[ super init ] )) {
        startingPosition = ccp( 200, 200 ) ;
        player  = [ CCSprite spriteWithFile:@"player.png" ];
        [self addChild: player ];
        player.position = startingPosition;
    }
    return self;
}
```

By declaring both player and startingPosition they can be used in the **init** statement or our other methods in the class. If you want to test this project so far, be sure to include an image named ***player.png*** in your Resources folder.

Now let's work entirely outside of the **init** statement, and write a new method.

–(void) **resetPlayerPosition** {

player.position = startingPosition;

}

I can work with both player and startingPosition because their scope has been declared through the entire class. There's that word ***scope*** again. It's a programming term. What isn't in this book though? I won't suddenly start defining farming terms. So if I said, for example, "John was trying to use a variable outside of it's scope," that would mean John was trying to access a variable that hadn't been declared in a particular block of code. Here's an example of a scope issue:

```
-( void ) someMethod {
    int remainingAmmo = 30;
    [ self someOtherMethod ];   // call the method below
}

-( void ) someOtherMethod {
    remainingAmmo = 32; // try to give remainingAmmo a new value
}
```

The problem is that remainingAmmo basically doesn't exist outside of the scope of the method it was created in. So if **someOtherMethod** tries to set the value of remainingAmmo (or do anything with it), you'll get an error. For those of you craving more programming terms, you could say that remainingAmmo was a **local variable** or given **local scope** to that method.

So when do you declare your variables? The obvious answer is when you realize you need to. When I begin a game there's certain variables I almost always know I'll need to declare right away. Variables like level, player, ammoCount are all accessed so frequently and from so many different methods, I'll declare them immediately. Now here's a questionable one: what about the background image of my scene? Suppose I put this in my **init** statement:

CCSprite* background = [CCSprite **spriteWithFile**:@"hills.png"];

[self **addChild**: background];

I've created the background variable and added it to the layer. If I need to do anything else with it (like position it), I'll need to hurry up and do that somewhere else in my **init** statement, because once my **init** statement is done, I won't have an easy way to access it. It won't be impossible to access, but it won't be as easy as just writing background in some other method.

So what's the answer here? Declare it or don't? At this point you could flip a coin. If all you'll be doing with the background is just displaying the same image and never moving it. You're probably fine not declaring it. Of course, if later on you change your mind, all you need to do is head over to your header file and declare it:

in the HelloWorldLayer.h file

@interface HelloWorldLayer : CCLayer {

CCSprite* background ;

}

Then go back to wherever you added the child, probably the **init** statement, and remove the CCSprite* part because you just did that above.

CCSprite* background = [CCSprite **spriteWithFile**:@"hills.png"];
[self **addChild**: background];

If you forget to remove the CCSprite*, you'll get a warning that says:

Local declaration of 'background' hides instance variable

You know some of those terms now. *Local* and *declaration* are familiar. So in plain speak, the warning says that you are declaring a local variable that will hide access to the instance variable already declared. Or in plainer speak, "You're creating the same variable twice, we can't have two! … One fedora per crew, fellas!"

Basic Properties

Back to our little CCSprite class. We only looked at the position property earlier, but we've got quite a few more basic properties we can use to make some changes to how our CCSprite is displayed. Many of these properties can be used for other objects like text labels or entire layers, but for now let's just work with sprites.

```
CCSprite* skeleton = [ CCSprite
spriteWithFile:@"skeleton_in_chains.png"];
[self addChild: skeleton ];

skeleton.position = ccp ( 0 ,0 );

skeleton.rotation = 0 ;
```

// the range is 0 to 360, a value of 180 would rotate this 180 degrees

```
skeleton.scale = 1 ;
```

// a value of 0 would scale this down to 0% (invisible), 0.5 would be 50%, 2 is 200%, and so on ...

```
skeleton.scaleX = 1 ;
```

// uses the same decimal scaling factor as the .scale property but only affects the width.

```
skeleton.scaleY = 1 ;
```

// uses the same decimal scaling factor as the .scale property but only affects the height.

```
skeleton.flipX = NO ;
```

// YES or NO values to flip the object horizontally

```
skeleton.flipY = NO ;
```

// YES or NO values to flip the object vertically

skeleton.visible = YES ;

// YES or NO values to hide the object

skeleton.opacity = 255 ;

// the range is 0 to 255 with 255 being fully opaque, 0 is fully transparent (invisible)

Each of these properties is set to their default value, so setting a CCSprite to any of these values is pointless, but it gives you a baseline to experiment with making subtle changes to each value.

As I mentioned before **some of these properties** can be used on other objects. Since we haven't discussed any other Cocos2d objects yet, see what happens if you just replace the sprite variable name with self and affect the properties of your entire layer.

Some Things You Do <u>Not</u> Need To Know Now

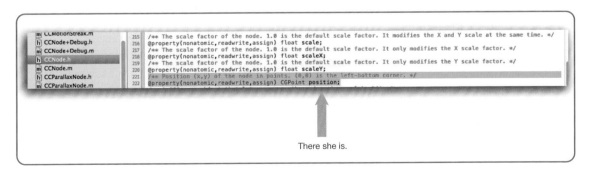

Some of you inquisitive readers might decide to peak into the CCSprite class files (you can find them in the **libs** folder, inside the **cocos2d** subfolder that is included in every project created using the Cocos2d templates). If you do go poking around in the ***CCSprite.h*** or ***CCSprite.m*** file you might expect to find all those basic properties somewhere in there. How else would a CCSprite know what to do with a .position property if it isn't mentioned in the class? Well some of the basic properties on the previous page are actually properties of all CCNode objects. Since a CCSprite is subclassed from CCNode it shares those same properties. I'm not even going to trouble you with a proper definition of "**subclassed**" this early in the book, for now just take what you can from that previous sentence. Or this one: CCSprite gets some properties from being a CCNode. It's that simple. So if you wanted to go on a little fact-finding mission for the position property, you would actually look in the ***CCNode.h*** file.

Here, I'll find it for you, just don't get scared looking at code you don't need to know right now:

```
m CCMotionStreak.m    215  /** The scale factor of the node. 1.0 is the default scale factor. It modifies the X and Y scale at the same time. */
h CCNode+Debug.h      216  @property(nonatomic,readwrite,assign) float scale;
m CCNode+Debug.m      217  /** The scale factor of the node. 1.0 is the default scale factor. It only modifies the X scale factor. */
h CCNode.h            218  @property(nonatomic,readwrite,assign) float scaleX;
m CCNode.m            219  /** The scale factor of the node. 1.0 is the default scale factor. It only modifies the Y scale factor. */
h CCParallaxNode.h    220  @property(nonatomic,readwrite,assign) float scaleY;
m CCParallaxNode.m    221  /** Position (x,y) of the node in points. (0,0) is the left-bottom corner. */
                      222  @property(nonatomic,readwrite,assign) CGPoint position;
```

There she is.

Scheduling Methods

A **scheduled method** is one that performs repeatedly at a certain interval. It could be 1/60th of a second or every 1000 seconds. The interval can be anything. Usually with games you will use 1/60th of a second, which is ideally the app's frame rate, because testing events like collision detection is more accurately perceived at a faster rate. You wouldn't want to trigger the sound effect of a car crashing a quarter of a second after it actually crashed. Someone would notice. Of course, you don't have to use an interval of 1/60, it just depends on the requirements of your game. Also of note, you can schedule multiple methods at once with different intervals.

Below is a method call with a scheduled interval:

[self **schedule**:@selector(**moveSprite**:) **interval**:1.0f/60.0f];

The method that gets called would be written like this:

–(void) **moveSprite**: (ccTime) delta {

> // do stuff approximately 60 times per second.
> // you can even call other methods in here

}

Let's pick apart the **schedule** call:

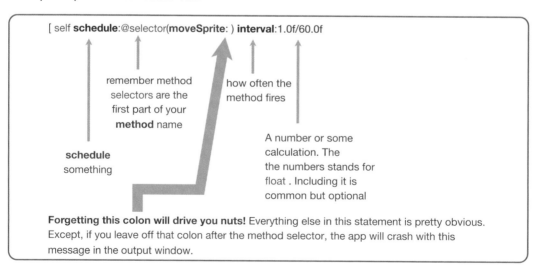

Forgetting this colon will drive you nuts! Everything else in this statement is pretty obvious. Except, if you leave off that colon after the method selector, the app will crash with this message in the output window.

> **Signature not found for selector—does it have the following form?**
> **-(void) name: (ccTime) dt'**

That colon is pretty important. It represents that we are passing the ccTime parameter (the **interval**) into the method. Notice when we wrote the method, we had a **parameter** in there:

-(void) **moveSprite**: (ccTime) delta {

   // do stuff 60 times per second.

}

Did you forget about parameters? Jump back to page 47 if you need a refresher. Just remember that if you call a method expecting a parameter you had better give it one. This is really no different than the methods with parameters we saw before.

Let's talk about the (ccTime) and delta. The delta parameter is the time elapsed since the method was last called. If you wanted to see what the delta equaled every frame, you could write this:

-(void) **moveSprite**: (ccTime) delta {

CCLOG (@"the delta was %f", delta);

}

Then your output window will read something like:

the delta was 0.016731
the delta was 0.016733
the delta was 0.016731

Over and over again. Mind you, 1 divided by 60 equals 0.016666, so hopefully your delta is close enough to that.

To be honest, I rarely ever make use of the delta parameter. Once you get your app on the device, it is worth checking the value of the delta as an indicator of how fast your method is firing, but I haven't made a game where I actually used the delta for something. You might see examples of another author's code that does use it, and since it is a common practice to pass in the time to your scheduled methods, we will too. I don't want you to get caught by surprise one day reading (ccTime) delta.

Stopping a Scheduled Method

Once you get a method going, you had better be ready to stop it if need be. Below are two ways to stop a scheduled method:

[self **unschedule**:_cmd];

[self **unschedule**:@selector(**moveSprite:**)];

// add the colon here too

The first example would need to be called from inside the **current method**, which is what the _cmd stands for. So that line would be called from within the **moveSprite:** method. The second example could be called from anywhere. Notice the colon appears.

Let's look at an easy example of the first way to stop a method. We want something to happen for a short amount of time, but not happen endlessly. So we will create a variable that acts as a counter to end the **schedule** (which moves a CCSprite).

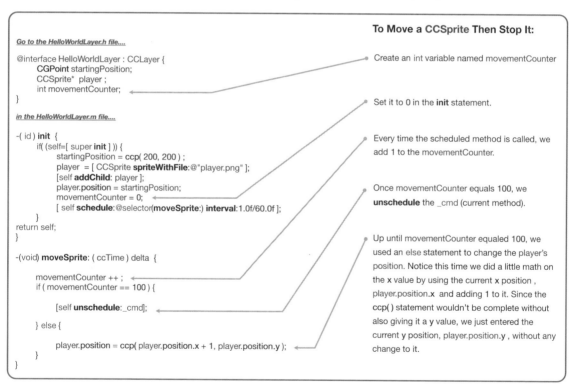

Go to the HelloWorldLayer.h file....

```
@interface HelloWorldLayer : CCLayer {
    CGPoint startingPosition;
    CCSprite*  player ;
    int movementCounter;
}
```

in the HelloWorldLayer.m file....

```
-( id ) init {
    if( (self=[ super init ] )) {
        startingPosition = ccp( 200, 200 ) ;
        player  = [ CCSprite spriteWithFile:@"player.png" ];
        [self addChild: player ];
        player.position = startingPosition;
        movementCounter = 0;
        [ self schedule:@selector(moveSprite:) interval:1.0f/60.0f ];
    }
return self;
}

-(void) moveSprite: ( ccTime ) delta  {

    movementCounter ++ ;
    if ( movementCounter == 100 ) {

        [self unschedule:_cmd];

    } else {

        player.position = ccp( player.position.x + 1, player.position.y );
    }
}
```

To Move a CCSprite Then Stop It:

Create an int variable named movementCounter

Set it to 0 in the **init** statement.

Every time the scheduled method is called, we add 1 to the movementCounter.

Once movementCounter equals 100, we **unschedule** the _cmd (current method).

Up until movementCounter equaled 100, we used an else statement to change the player's position. Notice this time we did a little math on the x value by using the current x position , player.position.x and adding 1 to it. Since the ccp( ) statement wouldn't be complete without also giving it a y value, we just entered the current y position, player.position.y , without any change to it.

Now suppose we wanted to **schedule** this method again, and once again move the same sprite across the scene. One thing you'll need to do is set movementCounter back to 0, or at least a number lower than 100. Then of course re-schedule the method. What I would probably do is take care of both things in one method. For example:

–(void) **startMovingSprite** {

    movementCounter = 0;

    [self **schedule**:@selector(**moveSprite**:) **interval**:1.0f/60.0f];

}

Then call:

[self **startMovingSprite**];

… from inside of my **init** statement (or anywhere else), and then I wouldn't have to worry about the movementCounter again.

You might think, "Yeah, but that seems like more work to create a whole new method just for two lines of code." My response would be, "Is it? Really. Is it?" You aren't paying by the method. Apple isn't charging us here to write extra code. For this particular example, it might seem like it's more trouble than it's worth, but since this is all hypothetical anyway, let's suppose that whenever we wanted to move our sprite, we also wanted to change how the sprite looked. So now our **startMovingSprite** method has one more line of code. The more things that need to occur before and after the sprite moves, the more it makes sense to package up that code in one handy method.

Come to think of it, I'm not paying by the method either in this book, so let's **color** that sprite before we move it (I make simple color changes a lot when I'm testing code because it gives me an easy visual cue that my method is running when it should).

-(void) **startMovingSprite** {

    movementCounter = 0;

    player.color = ccRED;

    [self **schedule**:@selector(**moveSprite**:) **interval**:1.0f/60.0f];

}

Now if you want to return the sprite to it's original color setting we can write the following line when we **unschedule** the method:

[player **setColor**: ccc3(255, 255, 255)];

These two lines are doing the same thing:

player.color = ccRED;

[player **setColor**: ccc3(255, 0 , 0)];

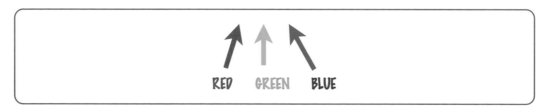

RED   GREEN   BLUE

Both lines are subtracting everything but the red value, so setting the R,G,B values above back to 255 on each, returns full color.

Scheduling with Repeat and Delay Parameters

Take a look at this longer variation of the **schedule** method where two extra parameters have snuck in: **repeat** and **delay**:

```
[self schedule:@selector(someMethod:) interval:1.0/60.0
    repeat:60 delay:5.0f ];

    // this is all one line
```

In this example, **someMethod** gets repeated 60 times at an **interval** of 1/60 with a **delay** of 5 seconds. So really, it only runs for approximately 1 second after a 5 second **delay**, then stops. You do *not* need to **unschedule** this method yourself.

Another delay option is to schedule a method using **scheduleOnce**. As the name implies, the method scheduled will only run once. For example:

```
[self scheduleOnce:@selector( runOnce ) delay:2];
```

For those of you really paying attention, you might recognize that line from the IntroLayer class. It was used to **delay** the transition from the IntroLayer to the HelloWorldLayer class. Notice though, in my example, I'm not including the colon after the method name, **runOnce**. I could, but my method would need to include (ccTime) delta as a parameter. If not, than the colon isn't necessary. Since this example is only calling the **runOnce** method one time, I'm assuming you don't need the delta parameter.

I've saved the simplest update method for last, because to be honest, I forgot about this one. If you wrote this:

[self **scheduleUpdate**];

you'll be calling the method below:

–(void) **update**:(ccTime) delta {

    // gets called every frame

}

That might seem a little odd, because up until now we've been very specific by making scheduled calls using the @selector syntax followed by the exact method name. Well this is the exception to the rule. Cocos2d knows that if you write:

[self **scheduleUpdate**];

it will look for that **update**: method and run it every frame. You don't pass in your own time interval, so this way of updating isn't as flexible as what we saw before, but it is simple.

To stop the update you can write:

[self **unscheduleUpdate**];

Finally, you can stop this type update and any other scheduled methods by calling **unscheduleAllSelectors** like so:

[self **unscheduleAllSelectors**];

The Non-Cocos2d Way

Scheduling isn't the only game in town for running a method after a certain amount of time. Like Yoda said, "No, there is another." We can also write the line below to simply call a method one time (not repeatedly) after a delay:

[self **performSelector**:@selector(**addSpriteWithFileName**) **withObject**:nil **afterDelay**:2.0f];

This would call a method with the selector name of **addSpriteWithFileName** after a 2 second delay. So what's this **withObject**:nil about? We can optionally include an object parameter. In the line above I just wrote nil so we aren't passing anything in. Let's change that:

NSString* myString = @"player.png" ;

[self **performSelector**:@selector(**addSpriteWithFileName:**) **withObject**:myString
   afterDelay:2.0f];

Now notice I said, "object parameter" above. We absolutely have to pass an object type in. So first I created an NSString called myString, then put that after **withObject**. Now we must include the colon after the method selector. Alternatively, I could write this too:

[self **performSelector**:@selector(**addSpriteWithFileName:**) **withObject**:
   [NSString **stringWithFormat**:@"player.png"] **afterDelay**:2.0f];

That block in brackets could be written instead of creating a new variable name. If you want to try this out, here's a method using the call above:

–(void) **addSpriteWithFileName**:(NSString*) theName {

CCLOG(@"the name is %@ ", theName);

   // log the NSString we are passing in to make sure it actually gets passed

CCSprite* player = [CCSprite **spriteWithFile**: theName];

   // set a sprite texture using that file name ...

[self **addChild**: player];

   // add it to the scene

}

This method could be used to add sprites with various file names instead of the same exact image every time it is run. So what if you don't want to pass in an object type and instead just want an int? Remember when I first told you about object and number variables. Here's a case where we want to **convert an int to an NSNumber** object. You'll simply need to do something like this:

[self **performSelector**:@selector(**doSomethingWithNumber:**) **withObject**:
   [NSNumber **numberWithInt**:10] **afterDelay**:2.0f];

Your method could look like:

–(void) **doSomethingWithNumber** : (NSNumber*) theNumber {

CCLOG(@"the NSNumber passed in is %@ ", theNumber);

   // just log the NSNumber to be sure it got passed in

```
int myInteger = [theNumber intValue] ;
```

  // create an integer variable from the NSNumber variable

```
CCLOG(@"myInteger is %i ", myInteger);
```

  // log the integer variable just to make sure it has the same value

```
}
```

Before I forget, I should mention you don't have to delay your method using **performSelector**. You don't have to write **withObject** either. You could simply call a method like so:

```
[self performSelector:@selector( someMethod ) ] ;
```

Of course, if that's all you wanted to do, then you could also just write:

```
[self someMethod ] ;
```

So if you're left wondering which is better **performSelector** or **schedule**, the choice is really up to you. Sometimes I just forget and write **performSelector** when I should probably use **schedule**. Keep in mind that **performSelector** is not actually Cocos2d, it is Objective-C. Which is fine, we'll step outside the Cocos2d framework occasionally to use things like **Gesture Recognizers** or the **Accelerometer**. Sticking with Cocos2d as much as possible has it's benefits though. For example, in Chapter 8 we talk about pushing scenes (keeping one scene in memory and displaying another)—when this occurs Cocos2d will automatically pause all scheduled selectors for you, but it wouldn't know to pause a delayed method called from **performSelector**.

Section 6

Z Depth, Tags, and Constants

Okay!
We get it!

Whoops, I've made it six sections into this chapter without mentioning two key parts to the **addChild** method. You've got two parameters that can be passed in. A **z depth** for arranging the object above or below other objects, and a **tag**, which can identify the object. Let's add both below:

CCSprite* player = [CCSprite **spriteWithFile**: @"player.png"];

[self **addChild**:player **z**:100 **tag**:12345] ;

In our previous examples, we didn't specify a **z** depth, so the object was just being added on top of other objects by default. Whichever child got added last would visually be on top of the previous children. The same thing would be true if we added two objects with the same **z** depth. Below is an example of a child getting added after another, but visually below the first child:

CCSprite* player = [CCSprite **spriteWithFile**: @"player.png"];

[self **addChild**:player **z**: 2 **tag**:12345] ;

CCSprite* enemy = [CCSprite **spriteWithFile**: @"enemy.png"];

[self **addChild**:enemy **z**: 1 **tag**:6789] ;

Make sense? When in doubt, fool with the numbers and build again. I've received emails from students with questions that I know could have been solved by simply changing numbers or variables. You don't get charged money every time you hit the **Run** button in Xcode. Trial and error is your best friend in coding. Build, fail, build, fail, build, fail, build, fail, build, succeed!

Can a **z** depth be negative? You tell me … (it can).

The **tag** parameter was one of my favorite things when I first started with Cocos2d. I can identify a child by tag by writing:

[self **getChildByTag**:12345]

As is, that line doesn't do anything other than find my child with that tag, but watch how I can use it in place of an instance variable name for a CCSprite:

[self **getChildByTag**:12345].position = ccp(500, 200);

That is exactly the same as writing:

player.position = ccp(500, 200);

The cool thing about **getChildByTag** is that I can use it in any method in my class to find the child. So remember how we talked about declaring variables in our header file in Section 4. Well trust me, that discussion was pretty fundamental, but we could have used **getChildByTag** to access the CCSprite variable outside of the local scope where we created it.

So I could do something like this now:

```
-( void ) createEnemy {
    CCSprite* enemy = [CCSprite spriteWithFile: @"enemy.png" ];
    [self addChild:enemy z: 1 tag: 6789] ;

    [ self positionEnemy ]; // call the method below

}

- ( void ) positionEnemy {
    [self getChildByTag: 6789].position = ccp( 400, 200 );
}
```

If I just tried to write enemy.position = ccp(400, 200); in that second method, I would get an error because enemy is outside of that method's scope.

You'll have no problems changing the position and some other properties that are common to all **CCNode** based classes using **getChildByTag**. What if I wanted to change the color property instead? That property is specific to CCSprites, not to every CCNode, so we will run into an issue.

Before we solve that, you might be wondering what a CCNode is. That term leads us into parent classes and subclasses, which I know confuses beginners. So many authors and teachers analogize class concepts, but I'm resisting real hard here ... *must ... resist ... darn, I can't.* **CCNodes are like the lead vampire that creates all the other vampires**. Every sub-vamp gets some common vampire properties like getting burned by the sun and agelessness, but they might pick up their own special properties like super-fast speed or mind reading.

Our CCSprites descend from CCNodes, and have a position property, which is common to all nodes. When I write [self **getChildByTag**:6789] the compiler just assumes I'm referring to a generic CCNode type, not necessarily a CCSprite, so it allows me to change the position property. Since color is a special property of CCSprite (a sub-vampire), the compiler will warn us if we tried writing:

[self **getChildByTag**:6789].color = ccRED;

I'll show you the solution below, and again lets call a method from another method to make this a well-rounded example:

```
-( void ) createEnemy {
    CCSprite* enemy = [CCSprite spriteWithFile: @"enemy.png" ];
    [self addChild:enemy z: 1 tag: 6789] ;

    [ self tintEnemy ]; // call the method below
}

- ( void ) tintEnemy {
    CCSprite* theEnemy = (CCSprite*) [self getChildByTag: 6789];
    theEnemy.color = ccRED;
}
```

This time we created a new CCSprite variable called theEnemy and made it equal to (CCSprite*)[self getChildByTag: 6789]. The important part is obviously this (CCSprite*) in front of [self getChildByTag: 6789] . Notice the asterisk was used after the class, that's a pointer to the data type, which we kind of talked about way back when. So in plain speak, all we're saying to the compiler is, "Listen up, I know this child is a CCSprite. Treat it as such."

Get ready for a big concept. What we did just now is called **casting**. We cast one variable as another. You could think of this like an actor being cast to play the part of a true life person. An actor plays the part so well, you forget that the events actually occurred to someone else.

So when I cast theEnemy to play the part of my original enemy sprite, I didn't create two separate CCSprite variables, one is just acting for the other.

Screech! "Slow up," you're thinking. I introduced a relatively easy concept like **getChildByTag** and suddenly I'm talking about subclasses and casting variables. By now, you're not seeing the forest through the trees. It's tough to imagine putting all this together in a game, because **"all this" is a lot to take in**.

I feel your pain. I'll let you out of this chapter soon with an easy test of what you've learned. Casting won't be on the test. I wanted to bring up this concept now because it's something I wish I had learned to identify in other programmer's examples early on. Even if you won't need to cast one variable as another anytime soon, it's nice to be able to read code you find on help sites and spot casting occur. What you'll probably see though, looks more like this:

CCSprite* theEnemy = (CCSprite*) [self **getChildByTag**: kEnemyTag];

Instead of numbers for the tag, we can **define a constant**. When you're programming a game, you shouldn't even try to remember tag numbers, no matter how easy you make them. Even if you do use numbers like your kid's birth dates or anniversaries, those aren't that easy to remember anyway. Go with something that makes sense to read. You can define constants *anywhere* like this:

#define kEnemyTag 12345 ⟵ No semicolon

The good practice police say you don't just define your constants anywhere in your file. Try to keep them all in one place. At the top of your file, or even better, create a new header file called **Constants.h** and write them all there. In the Xcode menu, go to **File > New > File** ... and find the Empty document option seen in the screenshot. Name it **Constants.h** and you can begin typing your constants in one line at a time.

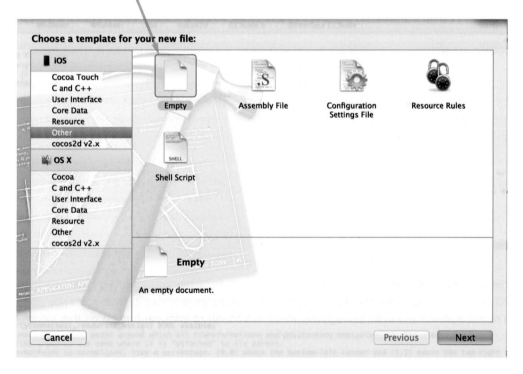

```
#define kEnemyTagRed 121
#define kEnemyTagGreen 122
#define kEnemyTagBlue 123
```

Why name your constants with k as the first letter? You don't have to, but if you choose the same letter for all your constants, it makes it easier on you to toggle through them when Xcode's code suggestions kick in.

This header file isn't a class, it doesn't have a corresponding implementation file (.m file). It's just a solo bad boy, that houses all your constants. **Remember, constants don't change value and you probably don't want any constant that will be used as a tag to have the same value**. Last thing you need to do is import the **Constants.h** file to your other classes. Just write #import "Constants.h" , at the top of either your class's header or implementation files (usually after any other import statements). Again, notice there isn't a semicolon after the line.

#import "Constants.h" ◄━━━━━ No semicolon

Tag Check

After you've assigned a tag to a child, you can check it's value:

if (player.tag == 123)

Or compare it to a constant you defined like so:

if (enemy.tag == kEnemyTag)

If you just want to read the tag in the Output window:

CCLOG(@" the tag is %i ", enemy.tag);

Swapping Depth

I've only swapped depth a couple of times in games, but it is pretty essential when you have a need.

[self **reorderChild**: player z:100];

One great thing about this line of code that us Actionscript 3 coders can really appreciate— your **z** depth can be whatever you want. You don't have to keep it within a range of exactly the top of the stack or lower. So I could have just two children in my scene, and one could be at a **z** depth of 0 and the other at 1000. It doesn't matter how much or how little you buffer the depth between them. This is an important point because if you do just want to keep all your sprites on one CCLayer (and there's nothing wrong with that) you could plan out some wide ranges of **z** depth where certain types of children are layered in at. To make things even easier, you could define their levels in your **Constants.h** file. For example, these definitions could be for a pinball game:

#define kTableBackgroundLayer 0
#define kRampsLayer 75
#define kBallLayer1 150
#define kBumpersLayer 300
#define kBallLayer2 500

So the pinball might have been added to the scene like so:

[self **addChild**: ball **z**: kBallLayer1] ;

Then the ball goes up through some tunnel and needs to reappear on top of everything else:

[self **reorderChild**: player **z**: kBallLayer2];

In my ***Constants.h*** file I'm setting up my definitions with some room to grow, so if later on, I want a group of objects to all be at a **z** depth between the kTableBackgroundLayer and kRampsLayer, I've got plenty of possible values (from 1 to 74).

Getting Z Depth

If you were curious about a child's **z** depth, you could query it with a log statement like so:

CCLOG(@"the depth is %i " , [player **zOrder**]);

If you wanted to **swap the depth of two objects** you could write:

[self **reorderChild**: enemy **z**: [player **zOrder**]];

Since enemy will go on the same depth as player, but added after it, the enemy appears on top.

"Uh, I noticed a few formatting mistakes in the book"

"Oh you did huh?", as the author rolls up his sleeves for a serious tussling. Kidding, I'm sure no matter how well I check this book over, I'll color some type variable wrong or forget to make something bold that should be (and feel free to email me if so). You might notice that sometimes **tag** is bold and sometimes not. This is one of those bits of code that is a Cocos2d property and also a method parameter at times. For example, in the line below, tag is a property of the instance:

if (enemy.tag == 922)

Yet in this next line, **tag** is used as a method parameter in adding the instance to the scene, so I'll make it bold because I've been trying to make all methods and their parameters stand out more in the book:

[self **addChild**: ball **z**: 0 **tag**: 922];

In the next chapter we'll create a class with our own properties and methods, and hopefully the subtle difference will sink in more then.

Removing Children and Child Hierarchy

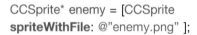

Removing children is even easier than adding them. Suppose we added a child using the code below:

CCSprite* enemy = [CCSprite **spriteWithFile**: @"enemy.png"];

[self **addChild**:enemy **z**: 1 **tag**: kEnemyTag] ;

We can then remove this child using it's tag property:

[self **removeChildByTag**: kEnemyTag **cleanup**: NO];

I set the **cleanup** parameter to NO, because setting this to YES would stop any running actions on the object and since we haven't talked about actions at this point in the book, NO is fine.

We could also remove the child with the instance name, like so:

[self **removeChild**: enemy **cleanup**: NO];

Just assume that enemy is within the scope of where this line occurs, or we have declared enemy in the header file.

We can also go nuclear and wipe every child off the layer with:

[self **removeAllChildrenWithCleanup**: NO];

Using **removeAllChildrenWithCleanup** could be useful if you had multiple layers, or if you added other children to a single CCSprite. Did your jaw just drop thinking, "Whhhhaaaat??"

A CCSprite can act as a container for other objects. Let's strip out the **z** depth and **tag** to make this example easier:

CCSprite* enemy = [CCSprite **spriteWithFile**: @"enemy.png"];

[self **addChild**: enemy] ;

CCSprite* enemyGun = [CCSprite **spriteWithFile**: @"gun.png"];

[enemy **addChild**: enemyGun] ;

Notice where we added the children. First to self, like usual, but then the enemyGun gets added to the enemy, which is *now the parent*. So we've got a little universe-within-a-universe thing going on. Now if I were to move the enemy it would also move the enemyGun. Those are aptly named variables for this example, because if an enemy was holding a gun in their hand, and they moved their body, the gun would go along with them. Now you can imagine why having a child hierarchy saves time coding positions for objects in games. Although before you get too excited and pile everything into a CCSprite, notice how things can get a bit tricky.

First off, we already saw in this chapter that objects get added to the layer at a 0, 0 point, which is in the bottom left of the screen. When you add a CCSprite to another CCSprite, the 0, 0 point is based on the parent sprite. So by default the child sprite would end up at the bottom left corner of the parent node (like the left example below). To center the child right in the middle of the parent, we could add:

CCSprite* enemy = [CCSprite **spriteWithFile**: @"enemy.png"];

[self **addChild**: enemy **z**:0 **tag**: kEnemy] ;

CCSprite* enemyGun = [CCSprite **spriteWithFile**: @"gun.png"];

[enemy **addChild**: enemyGun **z**:0 **tag**: kEnemyGun] ;

enemyGun.position = ccp(enemy.contentSize.width / 2 , enemy.contentSize.height / 2);

   // half the width, and half the height of enemy

This would give you something closer to my example on the right below. Didn't expect a cute enemy pig, did you?

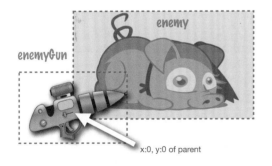

x:0, y:0 of parent

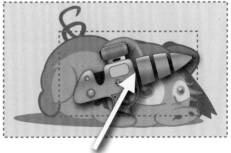

The child enemyGun is approximately centered, using contentSize.width and contentSize.height of the parent.

Another issue you might run into when dealing with children added to children (remember our parent is actually a child of our CCLayer), you need to replace self with the parent when doing things like **getChildByTag**. So using the same example as before, I wouldn't write:

[self **getChildByTag**: kEnemyGun].rotation = 50;

... because self doesn't have a child with that tag, the enemy has a child with that tag. Good news, that's a safe line of code, even though it won't find the child. You might get some feedback in the Output window that says "Child not found," but you shouldn't get a crash. So instead we would write:

[enemy **getChildByTag**: kEnemyGun].rotation = 50;

Or you could even write:

[[self **getChildByTag**:kEnemy] **getChildByTag**:kEnemyGun].rotation = 50;

How tricky is that? First we found the parent by tag, then dug down deeper and found the child by tag as well. Is that practical to go to such extremes to find our child? No, not at all, but it is possible.

Something to be aware of when you see brackets enclosing brackets is that you're calling one method first, then using what's returned from that in the rest of the statement. Similar to working with parenthesis in math. You do what's in the interior parenthesis first, then use the results for the rest of the equation. For example:

$$((5 * 2) + 10) = 20 \quad \text{This part executes first!}$$

I know you are planning out your own game in the back of your head, so let me pump the brakes a little here. We are still just in **Example Land**. If the future game in your mind's eye has enemies with guns don't assume that you need to make a parent sprite with child sprites for weapons. It might make more sense to simply draw the weapon in with the artwork of the enemy character. Honestly, that's probably what I would do, especially if the enemy only carried one or two weapons. It's probably easier to change the texture of a single sprite, then worry about managing two sprites.

A Practical Example

Let's forget about stuffing one object inside of another and look at a great example of how we could add a bunch of children with tags, then remove them all a bit later. I ran into this just recently while creating a slingshot game template called Angry Ninjas. When a ninja flies across the screen, it leaves a trail of white dots behind. The dots are just CCSprites, and they are pretty insignificant as far as the gameplay is concerned. I don't need them to do anything other than be there. I don't want to give them unique instance names to identify one from the other. Plus, since I'm a lazy programmer, I don't want to fuss with making a whole new class out of them either. I just want to see them for a throw, then wipe them out.

For this example, we don't have any ninjas to toss, so we will just start adding dots at a CGPoint and move new ones across the screen. To follow along, first add to your Resources folder a small image of a white circle, named "circle.png". Mine is 16 by 16 pixels, yours can be slightly bigger or smaller.

I highly recommend using a **Constants.h** file, so I'll use one now even though I only have one constant to define.

#define kDotTag 10000

We will use this number as a starting point for our dot child tags. The first tag will be 10001, the next 10002, and so on.

Jump over to your header file, again the HelloWorldLayer class is fine to use, and add the following:

In your HelloWorldLayer.h file

```
#import "Constants.h"

@interface HelloWorldLayer
{
    CGPoint startingPosition
    int dotCount; //  will get added to the kDotTag we defined
    int maxDots;  //  the max number of dots to add
}
```

Now skip over to your ***HelloWorldLayer.m*** file. What I think you should recognize by now, I'll leave uncommented:

```
-(id) init {
    if( (self = [super init])) {

        maxDots = 90;
        CGSize size = [ [CCDirector sharedDirector] winSize ];
        startingPosition = ccp( 0 , size.height / 2 );

        [self startAddingDots];
    }
    return self;          Calls this

-(void) startAddingDots {
    dotCount = 0;
    [self schedule: @selector( addDots: ) interval:1.0f / 10.0f ];


-(void) addDots:(ccTime) delta {

    dotCount ++;  // adds 1, so the first tag we use will be 10001, then 10002, and so on

    CCSprite* whiteDot = [CCSprite spriteWithFile:@"circle.png"];
    [self addChild: whiteDot z:0 tag: kDotTag + dotCount];  // the tag is the kDotTag plus current value of dotCount

    whiteDot.position = ccp( 10 + [self getChildByTag: kDotTag + (dotCount - 1)].position.x ,   startingPosition.y ); // explained here

    if (dotCount % 2 ){ // this is a new bit of code to test if dotCount is an odd number. Remember this, it's very handy!
        whiteDot.scale = 0.5;  // if so, then scale down this dot
    }
```

> For each new whiteDot sprite we place, we position them 10 points apart from the previous dot on the x axis. You can raise or lower that number...
>
> 10 + [self getChildByTag: kDotTag + (dotCount - 1)].position.x
>
> As for the rest, we get the position.x value of the previous dot placed. So if the current dot's tag is kDotTag + dotCount then the previous dot tag is kDotTag + (dotCount -1). The y axis location is constant.

```
if (dotCount == maxDots) {  // if dotCount is equal to maxDots, we unschedule this method and start removing the dots.

        [self unschedule:_cmd]; // stop this method from running again
        [self startRemovingDots];  ◄─────────────────────────

    }
}

        -(void) startRemovingDots {

            dotCount = 0;  // just resets dotCount
            [self schedule:@selector( removeDots:) interval:1.0f / 10.0f ];

        }

        -(void) removeDots:(ccTime) delta {

            dotCount ++; // adds one, so the first tag will be 10001

            [self removeChildByTag: kDotTag + dotCount cleanup: NO];
            // removes dots in the same order we placed them

            if (dotCount == maxDots) {

                [self unschedule:_cmd]; // stop this method from running again
                [self startAddingDots];  // for fun lets loop this!
            }
        }
}
```

Calls the same
method from
the init again

All done? If you want to cheat your way through this example, you can download the example Xcode project by going to **www.focalpress.com/cw/Dike**. While you're there you can also watch a bonus movie on this topic.

Section 8

Your First Real Test!

You probably feel tested enough just getting this far, but now I'm going to make you *try* to code some on your own. I've never liked traditional tests, with questions and answers, and when it comes to programming those type tests hold no place anyway. You'll be tested every day of your coding career because there's always a situation that arises needing some new solution.

Here's the mission:

Program an enemy character that moves a random amount and random direction around the screen

- The enemy should start and stop at intervals.
- The enemy should not go outside of the screen.
- The enemy should face the direction it moves.
- The enemy shouldn't move the same amount every time.
- Change the sprite texture while moving.
- Include a variable for speed (plan ahead for level difficulty).

Watch an example of what I'd like you to program at **www.focalpress.com/cw/Dike**.

Mission accepted? Alright here's some new gear. You can change a CCSprite's texture with the following line:

[enemy **setTexture**:[[CCSprite **spriteWithFile**:@"enemy_walk2.png"] **texture**]];

Don't forget you've already seen how to make a number random:

int diceRoll = **arc4random**( ) % 20;

> // this would give you 0 to 19 as a result

The Answer. Should you be reading this yet?

Like past examples, I'll assume you are using the Cocos2d starting template, so I'll only copy in the code to add:

In your Constants.h file

#define directionLeft 0

#define directionRight 1

#define directionUp 2

#define directionDown 3

In your HelloWorldLayer.h file

#import "Constants.h"

@interface HelloWorldLayer : CCLayer {

CCSprite* enemy;

int screenWidth;

int screenHeight;

```
int walkCounter;

int amountToMoveThisInterval;

int directionToMove;

int speed;

float delay;

}
```

```
-(id) init {
    if( (self=[super init]))
    {
        speed = 2; // feel free to increase this to make the enemy go faster
        CGSize size = [ [CCDirector sharedDirector] winSize ];
        screenWidth = size.width;
        screenHeight = size.height;

        enemy = [CCSprite spriteWithFile:@"enemy_still.png"]; // default pose
        [self addChild: enemy];
        enemy.position = ccp( screenWidth / 2  , screenHeight / 2 ); // place in center of screen

        [self startEnemyMovement ]; // get this party started...
    }
    return self;
}
-(void) startEnemyMovement {

    walkCounter = 0;    // always reset to 0 before moving
    delay = 2.0;    // 2 second delay unless the enemy bumps into the wall
    amountToMoveThisInterval = (arc4random( ) % 100) + 20;      // random range is 0 to 99, plus 20
    directionToMove = arc4random( ) % 4;   // random range is 0 to 3, directionToMove is later used in the switch statement

    [self schedule: @selector( moveEnemy: ) interval:1.0f / 30.0f ]; // runs every 1/30th of a second
}
```
Calls method on the next page

```
-(void) moveEnemy: (ccTime) delta {

   walkCounter ++;

   if ( walkCounter < amountToMoveThisInterval && [self isEnemyWithinBounds] == YES  ) {

      switch (directionToMove) { // handle the actual positioning...
              case directionLeft:
                    enemy.rotation = 90; // facing left
                    enemy.position = ccp( enemy.position.x - speed, enemy.position.y ); // move left
              break;
              case directionRight:
                    enemy.rotation = -90; // facing right
                    enemy.position = ccp( enemy.position.x + speed, enemy.position.y ); // move right
              break;
              case directionUp:
                    enemy.rotation = 180; // facing up
                    enemy.position = ccp( enemy.position.x, enemy.position.y + speed ); // move up
              break;
              case directionDown:
                    enemy.rotation = 0; // facing down
                    enemy.position = ccp( enemy.position.x, enemy.position.y - speed ); // move down
              break;
      }

          if (walkCounter % 2){ // if odd number, show this walk frame..
                 [enemy setTexture:[ [CCSprite spriteWithFile:@"enemy_walk1.png"] texture] ];
          } else { // if EVEN number, show the other walk frame..
                 [enemy setTexture:[ [CCSprite spriteWithFile:@"enemy_walk2.png"] texture] ];
          }

   } else {   // else if moving is done or the enemy went out of bounds...
      [self unschedule:_cmd]; // stop schedule
      [enemy setTexture:[ [CCSprite spriteWithFile:@"enemy_still.png"] texture] ]; // set back to still pose
      [self scheduleOnce:@selector(startEnemyMovement) delay: delay]; // restart using the delay var, note NO color after the method name
   }
}
```

> Two conditions must be true for us to move the enemy: first the walkCounter must be less than the amountToMoveThisInterval AND our method **isEnemyWithinBounds** must return YES. That method handles checking to see if the enemy has walked up to the boundary of the screen.

calls the same method to start movement again

```
-(BOOL) isEnemyWithinBounds {

   if ( enemy.position.x > screenWidth ){ // is enemy's x value greater than screenWidth

      delay = 0.5; // set the delay lower so the enemy tries to move a different direction quicker
      enemy.position = ccp( screenWidth, enemy.position.y ); // put the enemy back within bounds
      return NO ;

   } else if (enemy.position.x < 0) { // is enemy's x value less than 0

      delay = 0.5; // set the delay lower so the enemy tries to move a different direction quicker
      enemy.position = ccp( 0 , enemy.position.y ); // put the enemy back within bounds
      return NO ;

   }else if (enemy.position.y < 0) { // is enemy's y value less than 0

      delay = 0.5; // set the delay lower so the enemy tries to move a different direction quicker
      enemy.position = ccp( enemy.position.x , 0 ); // put the enemy back within bounds
      return NO ;

   }else if (enemy.position.y > screenHeight) { // is enemy's y value greater than screenHeight
```

```
        delay = 0.5; // set the delay lower so the enemy tries to move a different direction quicker
        enemy.position = ccp( enemy.position.x , screenHeight ); // put the enemy back within bounds
        return NO ;

    }else {  // if still within bounds then return YES

        return YES;
    }
}
```

That's it! If you want to download the source files, you can put down this book, switch to your computer and go to … **www.focalpress.com/cw/Dike**.

Create Your Own Class

Are you ready to learn about animation, touches, particles, and all sorts of other awesome topics? Great. That's next chapter. Or maybe the one after that.

This chapter we are going to learn about creating your own classes. I know. I can hear some of you groaning, but a good class is like breathing air. You won't realize how much you need it until you're underwater. Or worse, trapped in a sinking car thinking, "I remember seeing an oxygen tank labeled Chapter 4!"

Put On Your Classes Glasses

We've talked plenty in this book about using classes already. CCSprite is a class, for example. It has properties, like color, and it's own methods, like **spriteWithFile**. We will create our own classes with their own properties and methods too. Follow along and that part is easy. What I want you to really understand is why we do this, so when you're programming your own game you can spot times when building a class makes more sense than going the procedural route. That's a term I was reminded of recently from an emailer that told me his whole company was procedural programmers and no one understood about classes but him. Sadly no one wanted to learn about classes *from* him (maybe he was like Dwight from The Office). Procedural programming follows a pattern of executing code from the top to the bottom of the file. One thing does something,that triggers the next, and so on, in a linear fashion through a program. Traffic lights are probably programmed this way. We need to think bigger.

Object Oriented Programming (or OOP) is what we're embarking on here. Our instances of classes are the objects. Ideally, we create them and they instantly go about their business without much further instruction from us because they contain their own code that tells them how to interact in the universe around them. Take, for example, the roaming enemy we created at the end of the last chapter. Our HelloWorldLayer class told him where to go, how far to go, how fast to walk, and the boundaries to move in. Now imagine if the object itself knew how to do all those things. Then we would just snap our fingers and say, "You exist now, go do your thing." If that was the case, it would make it incredibly easy to not only create one enemy, but an army of hundreds with a simple while statement that adds them to the scene at once. **That's good object oriented programming**.

Before we get started, I'll add that I was a late-in-the-game object-oriented programmer. Since I came from an art background, and not at all classically trained in programming, I was never schooled on the advantages of OOP. I started coding with Actionscript and Flash, a very graphic-heavy programming environment, so it was easy to rely on **Movieclips** to do the work that object-oriented code could do for me. Movieclips in Flash have their own timelines for images and animation, and they can even have their own code contained in them. So when I came over to iOS programming, I still wanted something like Movieclips: a perfect self-contained object of image and code.

Then I finally figured out that, "uh, duh," that's what object oriented programming is all about.

You might be wondering how many classes make up a typical game? Of course that depends on the complexity of the game, but you can expect to at least have some classes like those below:

- **The Player**—what game doesn't have one of these?

- **Enemies**—you might have multiple classes depending on how different each enemy is. If the primary difference is the artwork, then one class might suffice.

- **Scoring/Bonus Objects**, items like coins, magic potions, things that the player collects to earn points or health.

- **Checkpoints**—these could be markers in the game that the player tries to make contact with to level up, or teleport elsewhere on the board.

- **Board objects**—these could be trees or ground planes that don't do much more than block the player or give him something to stand on.

- **Game Scenes**—the classes above would typically all be children of the game engine, which itself would be it's own class (scene). Other scene classes could be a navigation menu, map menu, or level-complete scene.

- **Helper classes**—We haven't looked at CCActions yet, but those could be considered Helper classes: you need help making a player jump, so you use the CCJumpBy or CCJumpTo class.

Don't think that classes always need to be objects, they can be less tangible, simply used to aid in a common task.

Professional Peak In!

Take a look at **just some** of the classes in the Commander Cool App. It's quite a lot, but this project builds an incredibly detailed side scroller game, so having a lot of classes is to be expected.

Create a Class

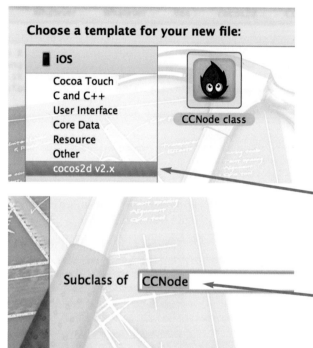

For this section, I'll use the same example project at the end of last chapter.

The first thing we will do is go to **File > New > File**, then find the **Cocos2d v2.x** row of templates and select **CCNode class** (under the iOS section).

When you see a pulldown menu for "Subclass of" chose **CCNode**.

Then for **Save As**, type **Enemy.m**, and press **Create**.

The class has been created with a separate header and implementation file. If your **Enemy.h** file and **Enemy.m** file have another class file between them, that's okay, but I like an organized project, so just drag one of them directly over the other. The class is ready!

We now have four files we should be working in. **HelloWorldLayer.h**, **HelloWorldLayer.m**, **Enemy.h** and **Enemy.m**. So if you see this style writing:

This smaller brown underlined italics text

… just note the file name so you don't write code in the wrong class. First, let's work with the header file of the Enemy class. Since it isn't much, I'll just paste in the entire header below:

In the Enemy.h file

```
#import <Foundation/Foundation.h>

#import "cocos2d.h"

@interface Enemy : CCNode {

}
+( id ) create;                    We are just adding this:

@end
```

That's all for now. What I've done is declared a **class method**. You remember that word declared right? Previously we declared variables so any method in the class could access the variable. Now we are declaring a method, so another class could call the method. Part of the reason we have header files separate from implementation files is so they alone do all this declaring in one place. They act as a gateway to the class. So if a method wasn't declared here, it wouldn't be accessible to another class. Also if another programmer wanted to read a chapter summary basically of your class, they could look at the header file and get an idea of the entire story. If you were to poke around in just the header files of your Cocos2d library classes, you could do the same thing. Try it. In the project you have open now, unfold the **libs** folder, then unfold the **cocos2d** folder, and find a class to explore.

Let's pick apart this method declaration further …

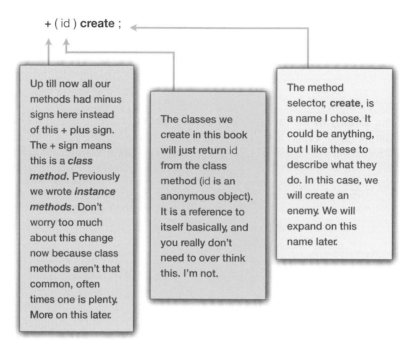

+ (id) **create** ;

Up till now all our methods had minus signs here instead of this + plus sign. The + sign means this is a *class method*. Previously we wrote *instance methods*. Don't worry too much about this change now because class methods aren't that common, often times one is plenty. More on this later.

The classes we create in this book will just return id from the class method (id is an anonymous object). It is a reference to itself basically, and you really don't need to over think this. I'm not.

The method selector, **create**, is a name I chose. It could be anything, but I like these to describe what they do. In this case, we will create an enemy. We will expand on this name later.

Now let's write the code to actually implement the method. I'm also going to go ahead and type in the **init** statement, below the class method. By now these **init** statements should look familiar and this one will be written no different. All I'm including in it is a CCLOG statement for testing:

In the Enemy.m file

#import "Enemy.h"

@implementation Enemy

+ (id) **create** {

    return [[[self **alloc**] **init**] **autorelease**];

    // allocates an autoreleased instance of this class into memory

}

This calls the init method

-(id) **init** {

  if (((self = [super **init**])) {

    // do initialization code here (for now just run the CCLOG statement below)

```
                    CCLOG(@"An instance of this enemy was created (instantiated) ");

        }

    return self;

}

@end
```

That's it for your **Enemy.m** file for now. The **create** method returns itself. Or really, an instance of itself. A copy. When it fires off that return statement, it packs a lot of punch in there with this line … [[[self **alloc**] **init**] **autorelease**] . As I noted above, it is allocating an **autoreleased** instance of this class into memory. It is also calling the **init** method along the way. One great thing about Cocos2d: if you follow this structure for creating your classes, you really don't have to worry much about memory. This child will be autoreleased on it's own, if it's parent is no longer around. So if I removed an entire scene full of layers with children, they should all get released on their own. In my own Cocos2d games I haven't come across an exception to that rule. Although I have read about cases where an object wasn't released because some other object was keeping a reference to it. Hopefully with what I teach you, we can be pretty safe just leaving it up to Cocos2d to release our objects for us.

If you're wondering about if ((self = [super **init**])) ,
I suppose you have a right to by now. You've seen it enough last chapter to be curious, and to be honest it's one of those lines of code that I know goes where it's always supposed to go and I don't think about it really. So since you made me think about it, I had to go Googling for an answer and I found a long one here.
The same code could be written like so...

```
self = [super init];
    if ( self != nil ) {
        // do initialization code here
}
```

The if statement is testing that self does not equal nil. If it did equal nil, meaning nothing got returned from [super **init**] , than the initialization just failed for some reason, and we won't allocate a new instance. So aside from some failure, we get to do the initialization code intended.

Alright, I see you've read a lot, but we haven't written much code. I'm reminded of what the great motivational speaker, Chris Farley, once said, "Dad, I wish you would shut your big **YAPPER!**"

So jump over to your HelloWorldLayer header file, and let's actually create an instance of this new class.

In the HelloWorldLayer.h file

#import "cocos2d.h"

#import "Enemy.h" ◄——————— Be sure to import this

Import the Enemy class first. Then switch over to the **init** statement in your implementation file, and add these two lines:

In the HelloWorldLayer.m file

```
-( id ) init {

        if ( (self = [ super init ] )) {

            // add the enemy ...

                Enemy* theEnemy = [Enemy create];

                [self addChild: theEnemy];

        }

    return self;

}
```

Ding, that class method should appear in the code hinting.

@end

If you were to build this project right now, somewhere in your Output Window would be the CCLOG message:

An instance of this enemy was created (instantiated)

You would see that message for as many times as you added new enemies to the stage. Now let's pick apart this line:

Enemy* theEnemy = [Enemy **create**];

First we have Enemy*, with an asterisk (a pointer to that class). This is the same thing we've done in the past when creating instances from other classes like CCSprite*. Like usual, we give it an instance name of our choice, theEnemy. Something you might have overlooked in the example code where we created white dots: you can give instances the same name. So I could run a while loop and use this same code to create and add many children with the name theEnemy. That's harmless.

Now look at this part [Enemy **create**] , where we call the **class method** that does the work of initializing the class**.** Notice that I'm writing the class name Enemy here instead of the instance name theEnemy. This might seem somewhat obvious at this point, because in calls like [CCSprite **spriteWithFile**:@"file.png"] , we've followed the same pattern by writing the class name there, not instance. Although **after** we've got theEnemy created, we will usually call **instance methods**, not class methods. So keep assuming we are in the **init** statement of ***HelloWorldLayer.m***, some typical method calls after initialization would look more like the last three lines below:

```
                          class name    class method
                             ↓              ↓

         Enemy* theEnemy = [Enemy create];
         [self addChild: theEnemy z:0 tag:123];

         [theEnemy walkAround ];
         [theEnemy setSpeedToLow ];
         [theEnemy tintRedToShowFuriousAnger ];

             ↑              ↑
          instance       instance
           name          methods
```

I've written three example instance methods that should give you an idea of things you might want to do with theEnemy.

Now let's go back to the header file of our Enemy class and declare these same instance methods. Also let's declare a CCSprite instance variable so we can actually see something:

In the Enemy.h file

```
@interface Enemy : CCNode {
    CCSprite* enemySprite;
}
+( id ) create;
- (void) walkAround ;
- (void) setSpeedToLow ;
- (void) tintRedToShowFuriousAnger ;

@end
```

Now let's change the implementation....

In the Enemy.m file

```
-( id ) init {
    if ( (self = [ super init ] ))   {

            enemySprite = [CCSprite spriteWithFile:@"enemy_still.png"];
            [self addChild: enemySprite] ;
        }
      return self;
}

- (void) walkAround {
        CCLOG(@"walk around");
}
- (void) setSpeedToLow {
        CCLOG(@"low speed");
}
- (void) tintRedToShowFuriousAnger {
        CCLOG(@"sunburned Hulk mode");
}

@end
```

Now go back to the **init** statement of HelloWorldLayer:

In the HelloWorldLayer.m file

```
–( id ) init {

    if ( (self = [ super init ] )) {

        CGSize size = [ [CCDirector sharedDirector] winSize];

        // add the enemy ...

        Enemy* theEnemy = [Enemy create];

        [self addChild: theEnemy];

        // position in the center so we can actually see him ...

        theEnemy.position = ccp( size.width / 2, size.height / 2 );
```

```
    // call these methods just to be sure they run ...

    [theEnemy walkAround ];

    [theEnemy setSpeedToLow ];

    [theEnemy tintRedToShowFuriousAnger ];

    }

  return self;

}
```

@end

Build the project again and you should see the theEnemy in the middle of the screen, and in the **Output** window read:

An instance of this enemy was created (instantiated)

walk north

low speed

sunburned Hulk mode

Let's take a breather and make some important notes.

I positioned theEnemy instance variable in the HelloWorldLayer class, instead of positioning the enemySprite in the Enemy class. Why? Let's assume I want to perform some collision tests on theEnemy later against a player. I don't want to compare where the enemySprite is within theEnemy, because that might lead to factoring in some offset amount. It'll be easier if I just leave the enemySprite at the default position of x:0 and y:0 and never change that.

So if enemySprite never moves, and the HelloWorldLayer sets the initial position, then it seems like the HelloWorldLayer would take control of moving the enemy around the scene. If so, doesn't that go against the autonomous principals of object-oriented programming? It would. Fortunately the solution is simple. We can position from within the Enemy class by setting:

self.position

Simple, right? Think about it, writing self from within the Enemy class refers then to that instance. So why did I write:

theEnemy.position = ccp(size.width / 2, size.height / 2);

 ... in the HelloWorldLayer?

I didn't need to. I was just trying to make you think a bit about good OOP. We could also set the initial positioning in the Enemy class itself like so:

CGSize size = [[CCDirector **sharedDirector**] **winSize**];

self.position = ccp(size.width / 2, size.height / 2);

Like nearly everything in programming, you have a lot of options to do the same thing.

So as it is, this is just going to set every copy of the Enemy at the same starting point. Which is okay, but suppose we used a while or for loop to create 20 roaming enemies at once. They would all begin from the same point and that would look pretty strange. Almost like they were multiplying as they spread out. An easy fix is to just set a random position in the **init** statement. For example:

CGSize size = [[CCDirector **sharedDirector**] **winSize**];

int randomX = **arc4random**( ) % (int) size.width;

    // range is 0 to the width

int randomY = **arc4random**( ) % (int) size.height;

    // range is 0 to the height

self.position = ccp(randomX , randomY);

Of course, you could also randomly position them from the HelloWorldLayer too, but I'm trying to emphasize using self here.

Before I forget (and believe me, I **will** forget), let's add a **dealloc** method before the @end in the implementation file.

Before the @end in the Enemy.m file

–(void) **dealloc** {

    [super **dealloc**];

}

@end

When you create your own classes, try to get into the habit of adding this method. Even though we don't have anything to **deallocate**, we should add this. I'll go more into this statement later on in the book.

Recess time! Go brew some coffee, come back and play around a bit using self in your class. You can also set self.rotation , self.scale and some other basic properties. Shucks, I probably shouldn't tell you this, but you can even mess with a child's parent properties by writing self.parent. In my sloppy wilder days of programming Actionscript, I found myself using parent a lot, but in my elder years, I've stayed away from it. Children really shouldn't be telling parents what to do. Right, parents?

Section 3

Initialize with Parameters

Let's keep working with the Enemy class we created last section. We left off pondering the best place to set the initial position of the class. Well, let's settle this for good.

We can initialize an instance of a class with some parameters passed in. This is really no different than passing parameters to methods, which we saw previously.

Last section in our **HelloWorldLayer.m** we wrote:

Enemy* theEnemy = [Enemy **create**];

[self **addChild**: theEnemy];

Now we will write:

Notice the change?

CGPoint somePoint = ccp(400, 300);

Enemy* theEnemy = [Enemy **createWithLocation**: somePoint];

[self **addChild**: theEnemy];

We will pass in a CGPoint to the class on creation. Later on, we will pass in more than just that, but let's start here. So jump over to your Enemy class's header file and change the class method declaration:

In the Enemy.h file

+(id) **createWithLocation**: (CGPoint) thePoint;

So all we are doing is changing **create:** to **createWithLocation:** to make it more human readable. Remember we want to write code that's naturally understandable to us. Then we are just specifying the variable type to pass in with (CGPoint), and finally thePoint will be the variable name we can use once it is passed in.

Now let's make some changes in the implementation file. We will pass the CGPoint around like a hot potato here. First, into the renamed class method **createWithLocation**, then pass it into the renamed instance method **initWithLocation,** where we actually use it with self.position. Follow the arrows below:

In the Enemy.m file

```
+ ( id ) createWithLocation: ( CGPoint ) thePoint {


        return [[[ self alloc] initWithLocation: thePoint ] autorelease];
}


-( id ) initWithLocation: ( CGPoint ) thePoint {
    if ( (self = [ super init ] ))   {


            self.position = thePoint ;
            enemySprite = [CCSprite spriteWithFile:@"enemy_still.png"];
            [self addChild: enemySprite] ;
        }
    return self;
}
```

I've underlined the changes you'll need to make in your project. As a beginner learning this, you might be surprised that the steadfast **init** statement could be written another way, in this case, as **initWithLocation**. Yup, you can do that. Notice that in this line: return [[[self alloc] **initWithLocation:** thePoint] **autorelease**] ... it looks like I'm missing the (CGPoint) part, doesn't it? Keep in mind this is the actual method call, so we don't write the data or object type in parenthesis before the parameters.

Hopefully those arrows illustrate how this variable gets tossed from the class method straight into the instance method. This is a lot like the Telephone Game too, one person tells someone one thing, then that person tells another. Fortunately for us, we are dealing with a machine that won't scramble the message along the way.

Now let's talk **style**. I could make the class method selector and parameters very different from the init method. Like this:

```
+ ( id ) createWithLocation: ( CGPoint ) thePoint {

    return [[[ self alloc] initAtAwesomePlace: thePoint ]autorelease
}

-( id ) initAtAwesomePlace: ( CGPoint ) awesomePlace {
    if ( (self = [ super init ] )) {
            self.position = awesomePlace ;
    ...etc....
```

That example is still doing the exact same thing as the previous one, so it's a harmless change, but it's hard to justify drastically changing those names just for the sake of being different. It is possible to write multiple instance initializer statements, and return different calls from the class method, but for now, let's keep things simple and name these methods similar to one another.

Another parameter worth passing into the class is a base image name. This base name can be an NSString variable that we use to establish different groups of enemy artwork in the Resources folder. In the last project we had these files: *enemy_still.png*, *enemy_walk1.png* and *enemy_walk2.png*. Suppose we also included *troll_still.png, troll_walk1.png* and *troll_walk2.png* . File name-wise, the only difference in the two sets is **"enemy"** and **"troll"** in the beginning. Imagine where a base file name variable could be handy:

// set up these NSString vars .

NSString* baseImage;

NSString* stillFrame;

baseImage = @"troll";

    // set this string to troll

%@ gets replaced by the baseImage, so in this example the full string is *troll_still.png*.

```
// the NSString below will start with troll now
```

stillFrame = [NSString **stringWithFormat**:@"%@_still.png", baseImage] ;

```
// now a sprite image can be set to the NSString above ...
```

enemySprite = [CCSprite **spriteWithFile**: stillFrame];

```
// uses troll_still.png
```

This kind of dynamic string name would give me a lot of flexibility in creating my class. It isn't the only way to make multiple sets of enemies with the same class, but it is easy for a simple class like this.

It's time to fly solo again:

- Create an Enemy class that walks on it's own and roams around within the screen boundaries. Most of that code you already have from the example project at the end of the last chapter, you just need to take what was written in the HelloWorldLayer class and put it in the Enemy class.
- Where appropriate use self to position or rotate the Enemy.
- Include two initializer parameters: a starting point and a base image name.
- Spawn 20 randomly placed Enemy instances from the HelloWorldLayer class.

Watch a bonus movie on this topic at **www.focalpress.com/cw/Dike**.

The Finished Enemy Class

Let's jump right in with the Answer Key for last section's test. Most of this code is the same as the project at the end of Chapter 3, so I've only made comments regarding the changes you should have made.

In your Enemy.h file

#import <Foundation/Foundation.h>

#import "cocos2d.h"

#import "Constants.h" ◄───────────

@interface Enemy : CCNode {

    CCSprite* enemySprite;

    NSString *baseImage;

      // new variable for base image name

    int screenWidth;

    int screenHeight;

    int walkCounter;

    int amountToMoveThisInterval;

    int directionToMove;

    int speed;

    float delay;

}

+(id) **createWithLocation**:(CGPoint) thePoint **andBaseImage**:(NSString*) theBaseImage;

      // passing in two parameters

@end

In your Constants.h file

#define directionLeft 0
#define directionRight 1
#define directionUp 2
#define directionDown 3

```
In your Enemy.m file
#import "Enemy.h"
@implementation Enemy

+ ( id ) createWithLocation: ( CGPoint ) thePoint andBaseImage:(NSString*) theBaseImage {
    return [[[ self alloc] initWithLocation: thePoint andBaseImage: theBaseImage ] autorelease];
}

-(id) initWithLocation:(CGPoint) thePoint andBaseImage:(NSString*) theBaseImage {
    if( (self=[super init]))                    Parameters passed in
    {
        self.position = thePoint;
        baseImage = theBaseImage;
        speed = 2;
         CGSize size = [ [CCDirector sharedDirector] winSize ];
        screenWidth = size.width;
        screenHeight = size.height;
        enemySprite = [CCSprite spriteWithFile: [NSString stringWithFormat:@"%@_still.png", baseImage ]];
        [self addChild: enemySprite];
         [self performSelector: @selector(startEnemyMovement)];
    }
    return self;
}
-(void) startEnemyMovement {   // NO CHANGE from the previous example project
   walkCounter = 0;
   delay = 2.0;
   amountToMoveThisInterval = (arc4random( ) % 100) + 20;
   directionToMove = arc4random( ) % 4;
   [self schedule: @selector( moveEnemy: ) interval:1.0f / 30.0f ];
}
```

Use baseImage for starting pose

```
-(void) moveEnemy: (ccTime) delta {

    walkCounter ++;

if ( walkCounter < amountToMoveThisInterval && [self isEnemyWithinBounds] == YES ) {
    switch (directionToMove) {

    case directionLeft:

        enemySprite.rotation = 90;

        // rotate the enemySprite (not entire class)
        facing left

        self.position = ccp( self.position.x—speed, self.position.y );

        // use self.position move the entire instance left

    break;

    case directionRight:

        enemySprite.rotation = -90;

        // rotate the enemySprite (not entire class) facing right

        self.position = ccp( self.position.x + speed, self.position.y );

        // use self.position to move the entire instance right

    break;

    case directionUp:

        enemySprite.rotation = 180;

        // rotate the enemySprite (not entire class) facing up

        self.position = ccp( self.position.x, self.position.y + speed );

        // use self.position to move the entire instance up

    break;

    case directionDown:

        enemySprite.rotation = 0;

        // rotate the enemySprite (not entire class) facing down

        self.position = ccp( self.position.x , self.position.y—speed );

        // use self.position to move the entire instance down
```

> I'd rather rotate just the enemySprite instead of the entire class object. Suppose I added text over top the sprite like a typical RPG game. I wouldn't want that text to rotate.

```
    break;

}

    if (walkCounter % 2){

        // Converted this to use the baseImage variable

        [enemySprite setTexture:[ [CCSprite spriteWithFile:[NSString

        stringWithFormat:@"%@_walk1.png", baseImage]] texture] ];

    } else {

        [enemySprite setTexture:[ [CCSprite spriteWithFile:[NSString

        stringWithFormat:@"%@_walk2.png", baseImage]] texture] ];

    }

} else {

    [self unschedule:_cmd];

    [enemySprite setTexture:[ [CCSprite spriteWithFile:[NSString

    stringWithFormat:@"%@_still.png", baseImage]] texture] ];

    [self performSelector:@selector(startEnemyMovement) withObject:nil afterDelay: delay ];

  }

}

-(BOOL) isEnemyWithinBounds {

        // just changed enemy.position to self.position below ...

    if ( self.position.x > screenWidth ){

        delay = 0.5;

        self.position = ccp( screenWidth, self.position.y );

        return NO ;

} else if (self.position.x < 0) {

    delay = 0.5;

    self.position = ccp( 0 , self.position.y );

    return NO ;
```

```
}else if ( self.position.y < 0) {

    delay = 0.5;

    self.position = ccp( self.position.x , 0 );

    return NO ;

}else if ( self.position.y > screenHeight) {

    delay = 0.5;

    self.position = ccp( self.position.x , screenHeight );

    return NO ;

}else {

    return YES;

  }

}
```

That does it for the Enemy class. Now return to the HelloWorldLayer class for the following code:

In the HelloWorldLayer.h file

#import "cocos2d.h"

#import "Enemy.h"

    // don't forget to import the Enemy class

In the HelloWorldLayer.m file

```
–( id ) init {

    if ( (self = [ super init ] )) {

CGSize size = [ [CCDirector sharedDirector] winSize ];
```

Use a for loop to iterate through the creation of 20 randomly placed Enemy instances. The first 10 will use *"enemy"* as the base image name, the last 10 will use *"wingthing."*

```
for (int i = 0 ; i < 20 ; i++ ) {

    int randomX = arc4random( ) % (int) size.width;

        // write (int) here to convert size.width to int

    int randomY = arc4random( ) % (int) size.height;

        // write (int) here to convert size.height to int

    Enemy* theEnemy;

        // create this variable outside of the if statement below, otherwise it's
        scope would be local to it/

        if ( i < 10 ){

        // the first 10 will use a different base name then the last 10

        theEnemy = [Enemy createWithLocation: ccp (randomX, randomY)
        andBaseImage:@"enemy" ];

        } else {

        theEnemy = [Enemy createWithLocation: ccp (randomX, randomY)
        andBaseImage:@"wingthing" ];

        }

    [self addChild: theEnemy ];

    }

}

    return self;

}

@end
```

That's it for the HelloWorldLayer **class.** If you'd like to download the example project, from your home Mac go to: www.focalpress.com/cw/Dike.

You can also check out a 6 minute movie overview of the two classes in action while you're there!

Iterating Through Classes

One great thing about having unique classes is that we can cycle through all our children in the scene and only pay attention to certain ones. So keeping with our previous project, in the *HelloWorldLayer.m* file add this after the **init** statement:

In the HelloWorldLayer.m file

–(void) **iterateThroughChildren** {

```
for ( Enemy *opponent in self.children) {

    if ([opponent isKindOfClass: [Enemy class] ] ) {

        // log each time we find an instance of this class

        CCLOG( @"found one!" );

    }

}
```

}

I'll explain the circled code in a moment, but first let's call **iterateThroughChildren** from the **init** statement after you added the Enemy instances. So you have a little extra time to hit Run, then see the results in the Output window—let's add a 4-second delay:

```
[self performSelector:@selector( iterateThroughChildren )
        withObject:nil afterDelay:4.0f ];
```

```objc
-(id) init {

    if( (self=[super init])) {

        CGSize size = [ [CCDirector sharedDirector] winSize ];

        for (int i= 0 ; i < 20 ; i++ ) {

            int randomX = arc4random() % (int)size.width;
            int randomY = arc4random() % (int)size.height;

            Enemy* theEnemy;

            if (i < 10){
                theEnemy = [Enemy createWithLocation:ccp(randomX, randomY) andBaseImage:@"enemy" ];
            } else {

                theEnemy  = [Enemy createWithLocation:ccp(randomX, randomY) andBaseImage:@"wingthing" ];

            }

            [self addChild:theEnemy ];

        }
        // be sure to run this line AFTER the for statement above

        [self performSelector:@selector( iterateThroughChildren ) withObject:nil afterDelay:4.0f];

    }
    return self;
}

-(void) iterateThroughChildren {

    for(Enemy *opponent in self.children)
    {
        if([opponent isKindOfClass:[Enemy class]])
        {

            CCLOG(@"found one!");

        }
    }
}
```

Just so there's no confusion where to write that line, make sure you wrote it outside the for
statement in the **init** (I'll confess I made this mistake myself).

Now, let's pick apart this new code.

```
for ( Enemy* opponent in self.children) {

    // runs code here for each child

}
```

This is a different style for statement than we've seen before, but essentially it is doing the
same thing. We are running the code in the opening and closing brackets for each of the
children in self (the scene's only layer).

Now for each iteration of the for statement, the opponent equals the next child it finds in
self.

We wrote Enemy* above so, when **appropriate**, the opponent variable can have instance
methods called on it that have been created for the Enemy class. For example:

```
for ( Enemy* opponent in self.children) {

    [opponent setSpeedToLow] ;

        // call instance method

}
```

Actually, that example is **not appropriate.** Blazingly calling **setSpeedToLow** could easily lead to a crash, because as is, that method would get called on every child, regardless of whether or not the child actually is an Enemy type. So if the next child in the loop was a CCSprite instead, the program would try to call **setSpeedToLow** and the method wouldn't be found. *Kee-rash!*

So this is obviously why we add an extra if statement to check if the instance is actually that kind of class:

```
if ([opponent isKindOfClass: [Enemy class] ] ) {

    // makes sure the opponent instance REALLY is of that class

    [ opponent setSpeedToLow] ;

    // safe to call now

}
```

You could also use the same iteration loop to examine multiple types of classes. Let's change the for statement to make it a bit more generic and write CCNode instead:

```
for ( CCNode *someChild in self.children) {

    if ([someChild isKindOfClass: [Enemy class] ] ) {

        CCLOG( @"found an enemy!" );

    }

    if ([someChild isKindOfClass: [CCSprite class] ] ) {

        CCLOG( @"found a sprite!" );

    }

}
```

That for statement would run fine, it would tell you in the Output window if it found an Enemy class or CCSprite class. The issue now is that someChild has been cast as a CCNode, instead of a more specific class. You could access basic CCNode properties by writing someChild.position but we would need to recast someChild if we wanted to do something specific to that class. For example:

```
for ( CCNode *someChild in self.children) {

    if ([someChild isKindOfClass: [Enemy class] ] ) {

        CCLOG( @"found an enemy!" );

        Enemy* someEnemy = (Enemy*) someChild;
    // someEnemy now cast as someChild, this time specifically an Enemy type
        [someEnemy setSpeedToLow];
    // since someEnemy is definitely an Enemy type, we can call this method
    }

    if ([someChild isKindOfClass: [CCSprite class] ] ) {

        CCLOG( @"found a sprite!" );

        CCSprite* someSprite = (CCSprite*) someChild;
    // someSprite now cast as someChild, this time specifically a CCSprite
    someSprite.color = ccRED;
    // since someSprite is definitely a CCSprite we can access the color property
    }

}
```

Now sit back and ponder the power of iterating through *all* the children added to your layer, or a specific node. You could have replaced self.children in the for statement with another object like, enemyArmy.children, and then iterated through only the children of that object.

These for loops are a fundamental part of many games when it comes to events like collision detection or simply sorting through objects. Suppose you had a card game, where every card was it's own class called Card. When it was time to clean up after a hand, you could iterate through each Card instance that had been added to the scene, flip it over, and send it flying across the table back to the dealer. Other possible classes, like PokerChips or Drinks, would be left alone.

Class Properties

Our classes can also have their
own properties that other
classes can access. Just like the
instance methods that we
declared in the header file, we
do something similar for properties. Let's keep modifying the Enemy class. This is a three-step process involving both the header and implementation file. First we will declare the variable within the @interface block of the header:

In the Enemy.h file

@interface Enemy : CCNode {

 // leave in what you currently have and add …

 bool canBeDamaged ;

}

That step is no different than what we normally do to declare a variable. Next, outside of that block (above your method declarations), write:

@property bool canBeDamaged;

So we don't lose anyone, see the screenshot on the following page for reference.

Last step, go to your implementation file, and at the top of the file add the @synthesize line below:

In the Enemy.m file

#import "Enemy.h"

@implementation Enemy

@synthesize canBeDamaged;

```
#import <Foundation/Foundation.h>
#import "cocos2d.h"
#import "Constants.h"

@interface Enemy : CCNode {

    CCSprite* enemySprite;
    NSString *baseImage;

    int screenWidth;
    int screenHeight;

    int walkCounter;
    int amountToMoveThisInterval;
    int directionToMove;
    int speed;
    float delay;

    bool canBeDamaged;

}

@property  bool canBeDamaged;

+(id) createWithLocation:(CGPoint)thePoint andBaseImage:(NSString*)theBaseImage;

-(void) walkNorth;
-(void) setSpeedToLow;
-(void) tintRedToShowFuriousAnger;

@end
```

I'll pick apart those last couple steps in a moment, but first let's see the property in action. From your HelloWorldLayer class, you'll add the instance like normal, then you can write:

Enemy* theEnemy = [Enemy **createWithLocation**: ccp(200, 200) **andBaseImage**:@"enemy"];

[self **addChild**: theEnemy];

```
theEnemy.canBeDamaged = YES;

    // notice the simple dot syntax: theEnemy dot canBeDamaged = YES
```

Create Your Own Class

At this point, Xcode should also show you the property in the code hinting that pops up as you type.

We can now set this property, as we are above, or access it as a condition in an if statement:

if (theEnemy.canBeDamaged == NO)

Handy, right? We could achieve the same results by making methods in the Enemy class that do the same thing. For example:

–(bool) **returnValueOfCanBeDamaged** {

return canBeDamaged;

   // would return YES or NO

}

Then rewrite the if statement above to:

if ([theEnemy **returnValueOfCanBeDamaged**] == NO) {

   // don't allow enemy to be hurt

}

Except that's obviously a lot more code to write, so essentially these properties act as a convenience to writing methods to get and set the variable values.

More often than not, you *won't* see properties declared as simply as I just did. When I wrote this line in the header:

@property bool canBeDamaged;

... that is fairly uncommon. Usually you'll see some attributes in parenthesis after the @property, like so:

@property (nonatomic) bool canBeDamaged;

Explaining nonatomic gets into a long discussion on multi-threading, which I'll skip over and just leave you with one word that everyone loves: **performance**. Google "why use nonatomic?" if you want more details.

A more interesting attribute is adding readonly (by default, the property is readwrite). You can comma-separate another attribute, like so:

@property (readonly , nonatomic) bool canBeDamaged;

This makes it so the value of canBeDamaged could be read by another class, but that class can't directly change the value like before. Now the following line would give you an error:

theEnemy.canBeDamaged = YES;

// not valid for readonly property

So why declare that property if all you can do is read the value? Simply put, that might be all that's required from the property. So limiting what another class can do to the property could narrow down possible problems later. Keep in mind, a lot of coding protocols assume that many programmers are working together. You'll probably be developing your games alone in a dank basement, so it's unlikely anyone will ever see your code, and even less likely that someone writes classes that access yours. If that was the case, you might want to put some safety nets up against a free-for-all with your properties.

One last note: when you write @synthesize in the implementation file, you can comma separate multiple properties like so:

@synthesize canBeDamaged, anotherProperty ;

It is also valid to have multiple @synthesize lines. Ready for the short story of what @synthesize does? It takes those properties (with any attributes you specified) and writes the convenience methods to *get* or *set* them, so you can use the simple dot syntax to access the property. You can Google "getters and setters" and find a bazillion programming discussions on those if you like.

Objects as Properties

You can also declare your object type variables as properties as well. Before we used a bool data type, but we also could have made the enemySprite a property in the header, like so:

@property (readonly , nonatomic) CCSprite* enemySprite;

Then we would write the accompanying @synthesize line in the implementation file as well:

@synthesize enemySprite;

Create Your Own Class

Now from another class we could access the enemySprite, like:

if (theEnemy.enemySprite.position.x == 0)

or:

theEnemy.enemySprite.rotation = 120;

theEnemy.enemySprite.color = ccRed;

Whoa, wait! Are those last two lines valid? Didn't I set the enemySprite to readonly above? Oddly enough, that is okay. I can set the readwrite sub-properties of a readonly property. What I couldn't do is set the enemySprite itself to something else.

So this line is **NOT** valid:

theEnemy.enemySprite = [CCSprite **spriteWithFile**:@"enemy_still.png"];

By the way, "sub-properties" isn't really the correct term there. You would probably say, "member properties" or "member variables" instead. Hopefully my simpler terms help get the point across. Remember, I went to art school. Terminology isn't my strong suit.

When to Set Up a Property

Often you won't realize you need something declared as a property until you hit a brick wall without one. In the case of a CCSprite as a property, it might simply be used for collision detection where you need to know the contentWidth and contentHeight of the sprite for a proper test. We'll run into this situation sooner rather than later because testing the contentWidth, contentHeight, or boundingBox values of a parent class containing a CCSprite doesn't return the same values as testing the actual CCSprite.

As for when to declare simple bool variables as properties, I was reminded of a great example in the drive thru for coffee today. The car in front of me had a bumper sticker of one of those venus fly trap-looking plants in Super Mario Bros (they usually rose up out of the pipes). I seem to remember you could get away with just a tad bit of contact with those plants as they were rising up (or maybe lowering down), but as soon as they opened their mouths, you were in trouble. So from a class perspective, the plant must have had some bool variable like canCauseDamage, that changed to YES when the opening animation was finished.

To use this, a game engine class (or any scene class) would first check for a collision between the plant and player. Just assume that is what's happening in the first if statement below. Then you could check the plant instance to see if a variable called canCauseDamage actually equals YES. For example:

```
if ( someCollisionOccured == YES ) {

        // injure the player IF the statement below is also true

        if ( thePlant.canCauseDamage == YES ) {

          // actually injure the player

        }

}
```

Folks, that's it for a somewhat short introduction to creating your own classes! After you learn a bit about collision detection next chapter, we'll revisit creating our own classes for a quick refresher project that tests a player landing on a platform. Yup, like a 2D side scroller game.

Chapter 5

Collisions, Touches, and Gestures

We've all heard this cliched quote before, "You're on a need to know basis ... and you don't need to know." That's true with programming. Don't think that you need to know everything, or use everything you've learned to create your first game. Coding is more of a learn-as-you-go, take-only-what- you need process than you can probably imagine.

So over the next few chapters, I want to give you some excellent self-contained examples that you can easily work into any project as you need them. As I said before, don't try to memorize code, just know where to look for them. One day, I'll be doing the same thing as you, searching this exact section for code I kind of remember writing before.

Collision Detection

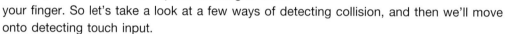

Go geek on me for a moment. Imagine back to all the games you played as a kid. There was almost always an object either avoiding another object or intentionally banging into it. Now with the iOS devices, one of those two objects colliding is often your finger. So let's take a look at a few ways of detecting collision, and then we'll move onto detecting touch input.

First, think about what kind of collision you need. Do you want to test if a very specific point (like the exact center of an object) goes into an object's space or an area of the screen? Or do you want to test if two rectangular areas, like the width and height of an image, cross into each other's space. Or is the shape of your collision object more circular than rectangular? These are some things to consider now, but of course you can always change your code later if you aren't getting the best collision detection for your needs.

Probably the simplest collision for new programmers to understand is to test if a point goes through a rectangle. In this case, the point will be the center of a CCSprite we call bullet, and the rectangular space will be the width and height of another CCSprite called wolf. There are arguably better ways of doing this, but I think you should see this first. The following line is **only** testing if the x location of the bullet crosses within the width of the wolf on the x axis:

```
if ( bullet.position.x > (wolf.position.x — wolf.contentSize.width / 2) && bullet.position.x
      <(wolf.position.x + wolf.contentSize.width /2) )
{

}
```

Subtracting half the width of the image from the x position gives us an x location here to test.

Adding half the width of the image to the x position, gives us an x location here to test.

Test where bullet is on the X axis

x:0   x: 50   x: 100   x: 150

if the bullet is within here, the condition is true

So if that bullet kept traveling toward the wolf, that if statement would obviously ring true for a moment. The bullet would cross inside the width, keep going, and then the if statement would no longer be true again. Since we are only testing along the x axis, if the bullet flew over top the wolf (or below) the statement would still be true. Not good. We should add in another condition for the y axis and image height:

if **(** bullet.position.x > (wolf.position.x—wolf.contentSize.width / 2) **&&** bullet.position.x < (wolf.position.x + wolf.contentSize.width /2) **)**

{

// if the bullet's position on the x axis goes within the width of the wolf, then we also test this …

if **(** bullet.position.y > (wolf.position.y—wolf.contentSize.height / 2) **&&** bullet.position.y < (wolf.position.y + wolf.contentSize.height /2) **)**

{

// DIRECT HIT!!

}

}

y:500

y:400

Now test where bullet is on the Y axis

y:300

y:200

y:100

y:0

Above here isn't a collision

Below here isn't a collision

Phew, that's some bloated code right there. We had four conditions that needed testing, split into two if statements. The main reason I split them was because, **artistically**, I felt it was better to show you what was happening with two. This is a completely valid way to test for a collision, but we can simplify it.

If you want to be really slick, you can just write your own method to do exactly what we just did. We would just pass in the parameters for the CGPoint (in this case, the bullet location), and the CCSprite. If the collision occurs within our method, we will return YES.

```
-( bool ) testCollisionUsingPoint: (CGPoint) thePoint andSprite:(CCSprite*) theSprite {

    if ( thePoint.x > (theSprite.position.x - theSprite.contentSize.width / 2 ) &&
         thePoint.x < (theSprite.position.x + theSprite.contentSize.width / 2 ) &&
         thePoint.y > (theSprite.position.y - theSprite.contentSize.height / 2 ) &&
         thePoint.y < (theSprite.position.y + theSprite.contentSize.height / 2 ) )

    {
        return YES;   // collision occurred , returns YES ( true )
    } else {
        return NO; // collision did not occur, remember you always have to return something even if it's NO ( false )

    }

}
```

One big line of code, this tests all four conditions

Our very own convenience method!

Now to call this **convenience method**, we would write:

if ([self **testCollisionUsingPoint:** bullet.position **andSprite:** wolf]) {

   // collision occurred

wolf.color = ccRED;

   // change the color

} else {

   // optionally we could do something if the collision did not occur

[wolf setColor: ccc3(255, 255, 255)];

   // reset the color

}

For all these collision examples, you could test the if statements from your **init** statement. Of course, to return true, your CCSprites would need to already have been added and be positioned within range of each other. You could also modify the previous chapter's example project, and do your collision detections in a scheduled method. So as the position of an object changes, you can see the results at runtime.

Testing Two Rectangles Colliding

Our first collision method only tested an exact location against a rectangular shape. More often than not, you'll probably want to test two rectangles colliding. Fortunately, there's a convenience method already built into the code library that let's us do this, called **CGRectIntersectsRect**.

So I should properly introduce a **CGRect** huh? We've already seen CGPoint (a structure containing an x and y location) and CGSize (a structure containing a width and height value). CGRect is a structure that combines those two. Imagine a black board.

Draw a dot somewhere. Then using that dot as the center, draw a rectangle around it. That's what a CGRect variable defines. If you had two CGRects, you can test if they entered each other's spaces with **CGRectIntersectsRect**.

Our biggest task is getting two CGRect variables together to test. That's easy if we use the **boundingBox** property of CCSprite which returns a CGRect. Let's keep assuming we have a bullet CCSprite and wolf CCSprite to use:

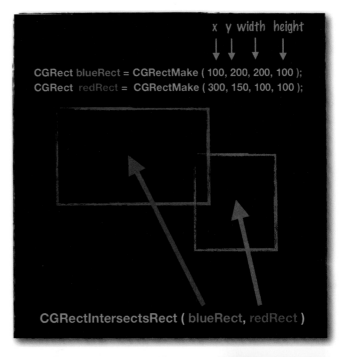

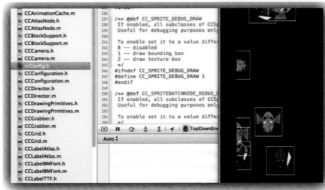

Change your ccConfig.h to show bounding boxes

```
if ( CGRectIntersectsRect ( bullet.boundingBox , wolf.boundingBox ) ) {

    // collision occurred , CGRectIntersectsRect returned YES

}
```

Neat huh. That boundingBox property is pretty handy. Would you believe you can even enable your CCSprites to show you their **bounding boxes** with a simple number change? Yep. Try it out. Unfold your **Libs** folder, then **Cocos2d,** locate ***ccConfig.h,*** and find #define CC_SPRITE_DEBUG_DRAW 0 and change it to 1 instead. Your next build should show white rectangles around each sprite. Of course, you'll want to switch back this variable when you're done testing.

That boundingBox property is a bit too good to be true though. It works great for testing one sprite against another, but it wouldn't test perfectly if we had a similar setup like the project at the end of the last chapter. Remember, we made a custom Enemy class and then had a CCSprite within the class as a child. For this example, let's assume that CCSprite was a declared property called enemySprite. Watch what happens with these log statements:

Enemy *theEnemy = [Enemy **createWithLocation**: ccp(randomX, randomY) **andBaseImage**: @"enemy"];

[self **addChild**: theEnemy];

CCLOG (@"theEnemy width %f", theEnemy.contentSize.width);

    // test the width of the parent class

CCLOG (@"theEnemy.enemySprite width %f", theEnemy.enemySprite.contentSize.width);

    // test the width of the child sprite

In the **Output Window** we would see back:

theEnemy width 0.000000

theEnemy.enemySprite width 64.000000

Ack!?! The contentSize.width amount of theEnemy is 0 but theEnemy.enemySprite is 64 (which is correct, the images are 64 pixels wide). So using either the contentSize property or boundingBox property on the class instance containing the CCSprite is unreliable, which means we need to create a CGRect variable that takes into account the size of the sprite within a class. For example:

CGRect enemyRect;

> // this hungry hippo now wants 4 parameters (x , y , width , height)
> which I'll separate one per line below ...

enemyRect = **CGRectMake(** theEnemy.position.x—(theEnemy.enemySprite.
contentSize.width / 2),
theEnemy.position.y—(theEnemy.enemySprite.
contentSize.height / 2),
theEnemy.enemySprite.contentSize.width,
theEnemy.enemySprite.contentSize.height **);**

Let's pick that previous line apart. To make it a little easier to follow, I'll do some magic with arrows like so:

enemyRect = **CGRectMake** (x , y , width , height)

The x parameter for enemyRect seems easy enough. You would think just entering theEnemy.position.x would do the trick, but I had to subtract half the width of the enemySprite to get the true location. This is one of those cases where we need to factor in that Cocos2d puts children at a 0,0 location within their parent, and the child's center (or anchor) point is in the middle. Thus:

theEnemy.position.x—(theEnemy.enemySprite.contentSize.width / 2)

The y parameter for enemyRect follows the same logic:

theEnemy.position.y—(theEnemy.enemySprite.contentSize.height / 2)

The width of the rectangle is just going to be the contentSize.width property of the enemySprite within theEnemy:

theEnemy.enemySprite.contentSize.width

The height of the rectangle is just the contentSize.height property of the enemySprite within theEnemy:

theEnemy.enemySprite.contentSize.height

If that seems a bit confusing, heck, try it another way. You'll probably *come close* to getting the same result because that's exactly what I did when testing this section of the book. What I was finding though is the true bounding box of the sprites weren't triggering a collision. Close, but no cigar.

Circular Collision Detection

I hope you didn't go too crazy thinking about CGRects because there's one more great way to detect a collision (without using an awesome physics engine like Box2D). Instead of squares, we can test a circular area around an object. This is probably the best of the poor-man's collision detection methods.

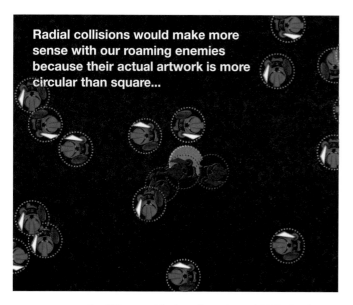

Radial collisions would make more sense with our roaming enemies because their actual artwork is more circular than square...

Why? Well you probably noticed that the area covered by the boundingBox property is actually a bit more than you really want. The corners of sprites often don't contain any pixels of the artwork, because the character is drawn around the middle of the PNG. Even if you crop your sprites as close as possible, those corners don't usually have much in them. Suppose you have two images drawn like that, when the corners of their bounding boxes collide, it doesn't *visually* seem like they are actually colliding at all. This is where a circular or radial collision detection seems so much more accurate. We provide two locations (CGPoints) and corresponding radii, then if the two circular areas collide, we return true. Take a look:

```
-( bool ) collisionWithPoint:(CGPoint) center1 andRadius:(float) radius1 andPoint:(CGPoint) center2 andRadius:(float) radius2 {

        float a = center2.x−center1.x;

        float b = center2.y−center1.y;

        float c = radius1 + radius2;

        float distanceSquared = (a * a) + (b * b);

        if ( distanceSquared < (c * c) ) {

        return YES;

        } else {

            return NO;

        }

}
```

Collisions, Touches, and Gestures

"Whoa, scary math!" Don't worry, real math scares me too. I got kicked out of my high school math class for falling asleep. Kicked out of the building really, because the remedial class was in a trailer outside. On my first day in the **Math Outlands**, the teacher threw an overhead projector across the room because one of the students made a comment about his wife dreaming of Denzel Washington. Which was actually true. She **had** dreamt about Denzel, and the day before I arrived in remedial math somehow that private bit of info got revealed to the class. Who's fault was that?... Anyway, this was when I recognized a math class I could "coast" through easily. As the newly elected Student Body President, I felt I should volunteer to get a new projector bulb from the library. When I came back, I took a nap.... So don't worry about the fancy math you see going on here, all you need to provide is the two locations and radii. Remember, the radius is just half the diameter (half the width of our shapes). **The equation does the rest for us.**

So using this method, we could write an if statement like this:

if ([self **collisionWithPoint**:bullet.position **andRadius**:bullet.contentSize.width/2 **andPoint**:wolf.position **andRadius**:wolf.contentSize.width/2])

{

    // collision occurred

}

You might notice that particular bullet image isn't very circular. Even the wolf image includes a lot of non-ideal collision space around the visible artwork. In cases like this, don't feel like you need to be locked into using contentSize.width/2 for the radius. Dividing by 2 is the same as writing 'contentSize.width * 0.5,' so why not make the radius even smaller by changing 0.5 to a lower decimal value. Adjusting those values could give you a more accurate collision (as depicted on page 136):

if ([self **collisionWithPoint**:bullet.position **andRadius**:bullet.contentSize.width * 0.2 **andPoint**:wolf.position **andRadius**:wolf.contentSize.width * 0.3])

{

    // collision occurred

}

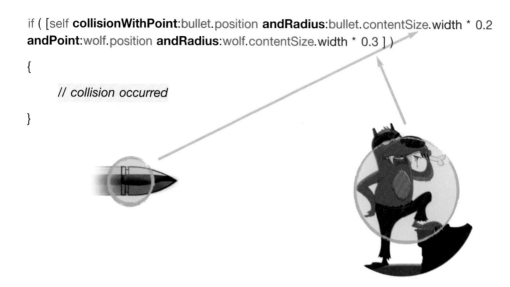

Well, that does it for relatively simple collision detection. If you'd like to experiment with this example project, go to **www.focalpress.com/cw/Dike** and find the folder titled **TopDownEnemy_with_Collisions**.

Finally, I'll let you all in on a secret. There's actually a method already in your code library called **CGRectContainsPoint** that tests almost exactly what we did with this method:

-(bool) **testCollisionUsingPoint**: (CGPoint) thePoint **andSprite**:(CCSprite*) theSprite

So why not just show you that method right away?! While **CGRectContainsPoint** is probably simpler on my part to teach, it doesn't actually *teach* you as much. I think you should get introduced to writing your own convenience methods early on, instead of feeling chained to what's only in your existing library. This book will teach you a small fraction of what Cocos2d offers and an even smaller fraction of the code Apple has created for you to use. That's okay though. As long as you can glue together the code you do know, you'll be an able-bodied programmer.

So if you do want to use **CGRectContainsPoint**, here's an example:

if (**CGRectContainsPoint** (wolf.boundingBox, location)){

    // collision

}

Yeah, that is easier isn't it.

Hiya!! A diversion! If you'd like to play around with collision detection code in the **TopDownEnemy** project, follow the simple changes below to add a square image to the scene your roaming enemies will be detected wandering into:

```
square = [CCSprite spriteWithFile:@"square.png"];
[self addChild:square];
square.position = ccp( size.width/ 2, size.height / 2 );

for (int i= 0 ; i < 60 ; i++ ) {

    int randomX = arc4random() % (int)size.width;
    int randomY = arc4random() % (int)size.height;

    Enemy* theEnemy;

    if (i < 30){
        theEnemy = [Enemy createWithLocation:ccp(randomX, randomY) andBaseImage:@"enemy" ];
    } else {

        theEnemy = [Enemy createWithLocation:ccp(randomX, randomY) andBaseImage:@"wingthing
    }

    [self addChild:theEnemy ];
}

[self schedule:@selector(iterateThroughChildren:) interval:1.0f/60.0f];
}
return self;
}

-(void) iterateThroughChildren:(ccTime) delta {

    for(Enemy *someEnemy in self.children)
    {

        if([someEnemy isKindOfClass:[Enemy class]])
        {

            CGRect enemyRect = [someEnemy getRect];

            if (CGRectIntersectsRect(square.boundingBox, enemyRect )) {

                someEnemy.enemySprite.color = ccBLUE;
            } else {

                [someEnemy.enemySprite setColor:ccc3(255, 255, 255)];
            }

        }

    } //ends for loop
```

Declare a CCSprite named square in your HelloWorldLayer header file, then in the implementation file add it to the scene with any image (mine is name **"square.png"**).

Schedule a selector to iterate through every child. When an Enemy instance is found, call the **getRect** method (which we will write in the Enemy class in a moment). This method will return a **CGRect** similar to the same code in this section used to detect two rectangles colliding.

If an Enemy instance intersects with this **CGRect**, we will tint the enemy blue.

In the *Enemy.h* file just declare this instance method:

-(**CGRect**) **getRect**;

```objc
@interface Enemy : CCNode {

    CCSprite* enemySprite;
    NSString *baseImage;

    int screenWidth;
    int screenHeight;

    int walkCounter;
    int amountToMoveThisInterval;
    int directionToMove;
    int speed;
    float delay;

    bool canBeDamaged;
}


@property ( nonatomic ) bool canBeDamaged;
@property (readonly, nonatomic ) CCSprite* enemySpr

+(id) createWithLocation:(CGPoint)thePoint andBaseI

-(void) walkAround;
-(void) setSpeedToLow;
-(void) tintRedToShowFuriousAnger;
-(CGRect) getRect;
```

```objc
-(CGRect) getRect
{

    return CGRectMake( self.position.x - (enemySprite.contentSize.width /2) ,
                       self.position.y - (enemySprite.contentSize.height /2),
                       enemySprite.contentSize.width,
                       enemySprite.contentSize.height );
}
```

The **getRect** method uses self.position and the contentSize of the enemySprite to return a CGRect variable.

```objc
- ( CGRect ) getRect {

    return CGRectMake(  self.position.x - ( enemySprite.contentSize.width / 2 ),

                        self.position.y - ( enemySprite.contentSize.height / 2 ),

                        enemySprite.contentSize.width,

                        enemySprite.contentSize.height );

}
```

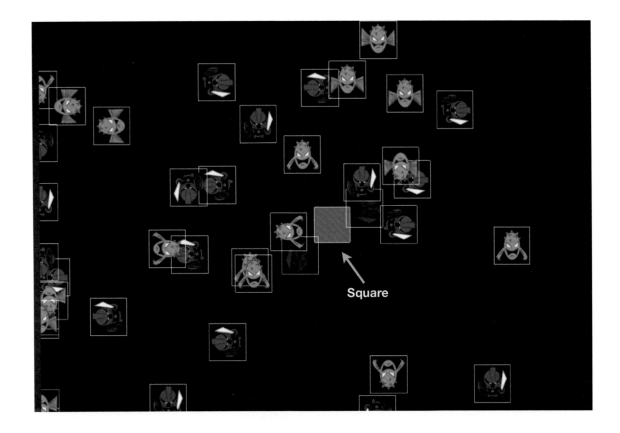

Time to publish! Spawn a ton of enemies and watch them turn blue as they collide with the square CCSprite in the middle of the screen. The bounding boxes are showing because I enabled that option in the **ccConfig.h** file.

Platform Collisions

Without this section, I'll inevitably get an email from someone asking, "How do I keep my character from falling through a platform?" Actually, I already get emails like this.

Everyone loves a 2D side scroller type game. Heck, for my tastes, I don't even need the side scrolling. I love the original Mario Bros, the non-"Super" one. Unfortunately, setting this up right is a topic best left for an entire book on Cocos2d and Box2d, which is an incredible physics engine, but I think we can put together what we already know about collision detection and custom classes to make a decent enough test project where a player gets pulled down by gravity onto a landing platform.

We can even get a bit fancier than that and have the character stop if they run into the side wall of a platform, forcing them to jump over it. This might sound like we're getting ahead of ourselves since we haven't even programmed touch controls for a player, but with a few simple variables for gravity and forward movement, and a CCJumpBy action, we can do this right now.

To get started we'll need two classes, one for a Player and one for a Platform object, and then we'll use the HelloWorldLayer as a bare bones game engine to simply check for collisions.

Following the same steps in the last chapter to create a class, do exactly that for the Player and Platform (both can be subclassed from CCNode).

The Player header file will look like this:

The Player.h file

@interface Player : CCNode {

CCSprite* sprite;

}

@property (readonly, nonatomic) CCSprite* sprite;

+(id) **create**;

@end

We just need to declare a CCSprite aptly named sprite and make this a readonly property (we will only use the contentWidth and contentHeight of it later).

We use the method called **create** to initialize the class. Note that we don't even need any parameters passed in on creation.

Then skip over to your implementation file and write the following. (Don't forget those handy hot keys, **CONTROL + ⌘ + UP** to jump from *.h* to *.m* files and vice versa):

In the Player.m file

@implementation Player

@synthesize sprite;

+(id) **create** {

      return [[[self **alloc**] **init**] **autorelease**];

}

-(id) **init** {

      if ((self = [super **init**])) {

          sprite = [CCSprite **spriteWithFile**:@"farmer.png"];

          [self **addChild**:sprite];

      }

return self;

}

      // we don't really need a dealloc method for an example this simple,
      but it's a good habit to start including these anyway in your custom classes.

-(void) **dealloc** {

[super **dealloc**];

}

@end

As you can see the implementation file is just as simple as the header. All we are doing is adding the CCSprite as a child, we don't even need to position it (the default placement at 0,0 is fine).

Now here's some great news. Get your copy and paste keys ready, because we will do the exact same thing for the Platform class. The only difference will be the file name, use "blocks.png" instead.

Since we don't have many images in this example, if you want to grab them directly from CartoonSmart instead of pulling them from the Resources folder in the example project, you can grab them from CartoonSmart.com.

As usual be sure those are imported to your project preferably in the Resources folder. To critique myself a little, notice that both classes are hard-coding in the file names for **farmer.png** and **blocks.png.**

That keeps my example simple, but in the "real world" the create method might as well at least pass in a parameter with the file name, and be called something like **createWithImage** instead.

Now go to your **HelloWorldLayer.h** file and import in both classes (write these under your other import statements):

#import "Platform.h"

#import "Player.h"

Remember no semi-colon is needed after these lines. Then let's declare the following variables:

@interface HelloWorldLayer : CCLayer {

    Player *player;

    int playerGravity;

    int originalGravity;

    int playerSpeed;

    int originalSpeed;

    int screenWidth;

    int screenHeight;

}

Typically you only ever have one player instance in your class, so declaring it with a name like 'player' just makes sense. You can easily reference it later in any of your code blocks in the implementation file. What doesn't make sense is declaring the instances of the Platform because there could be dozens, maybe hundreds of these. You **do not** want to start declaring platform1, platform2, and so on in the header file.

When we need to do something with these objects we can usually get away with iterating through all the children in the scene and identifying them by class. So in plain speak, *if the child is a platform, then check for such and such condition*. At no point do we need the actual instance name. With that said, when we create the object and add it to the scene, we will name them platform1, platform2, and so on.

In this project I'll do that, but in a later one we will create our objects using a for statement that examines a property list file (basically an xml file) and adds a lot of objects at once. In that example, each instance is just given the exact same name, like someEnemy. So if I didn't emphasize this enough in the section on Iterating Through Classes, then let me do this now: *the instance name is so unimportant at times that hundreds of objects could have the same name*.

Our declared variables for playerGravity and originalGravity will be used to make the player fall down the scene. The playerGravity is what actually affects the position.y of the player. The originalGravity is used to return the playerGravity back to it's original value if it was set to 0 (which it would be when colliding with a platform below the player).

The playerSpeed and originalSpeed function in the same manner to affect the player's position.x value.

The screenWidth and screenHeight just hold onto the size of the screen for us.

Now jump over to your implementation file and add the following to the **init** statement (later on I'll add more than two platforms):

In the init statement of HelloWorldLayer.m

```
-(id) init {
    if( (self=[super init]) ) {
        CGSize size = [ [CCDirector sharedDirector] winSize ];
        screenWidth = size.width;
        screenHeight = size.height;

        player = [Player create];
        [self addChild:player];
        player.position = ccp( 450, screenHeight );

        Platform *platform1 = [Platform create];
        [self addChild:platform1];
        platform1.position = ccp( 500, 400 );

        Platform *platform2 = [Platform create];
        [self addChild:platform2];
        platform2.position = ccp( 650, 300 );
```

```
        originalSpeed = 2;

        playerSpeed = originalSpeed;

        originalGravity = 8;

        playerGravity = originalGravity;

        [self scheduleUpdate];

    }

    return self;

}
```

Everything should read pretty straightforward in the **init** statement. We are creating a Player and two Platform instances with positions. The originalSpeed and originalGravity are both given values and the playerSpeed and playerGravity variables are initially set based on those values.

Finally we're calling **scheduleUpdate** at the end, which runs the **update** method on the next page. That method ends with four closing brackets, which is an eyeful, so to help in picking apart what's what, I'll add some background color to the bracketing.

```
-(void) update:(ccTime) delta {

    if ( player.position.x > screenWidth || player.position.y < 0 ) {
        player.position = ccp (480, screenHeight);
    }
    player.position = ccp( player.position.x + playerSpeed, player.position.y - playerGravity );

    for (Platform* platform in self.children) {
        if ( [ platform isKindOfClass:[Platform class]]) {
            CGRect platformRect = CGRectMake( platform.position.x - (platform.sprite.contentSize.width / 2 ) ,
                                              platform.position.y - (platform.sprite.contentSize.height / 2 ),
                                              platform.sprite.contentSize.width,
                                              platform.sprite.contentSize.height);
            CGRect playerRect = [self returnPlayerRect]; // a convenience method written on the next page
            if ( CGRectIntersectsRect ( platformRect, playerRect ) ) {
                playerGravity = 0;
                while  ( CGRectIntersectsRect ( platformRect, playerRect ) ) {
                    player.position = ccp(player.position.x , player.position.y + 1 );
                    playerRect = [self returnPlayerRect];
                }
            } else {
                playerGravity = originalGravity;
                playerSpeed = originalSpeed;
            }
        }
    }
}
```

Collisions, Touches, and Gestures

Before I explain all that, let me include the convenience method used for setting the playerRect value.

- (CGRect) **returnPlayerRect** {

    CGRect playerRect = **CGRectMake**(player.position.x — (player.sprite.contentSize.width / 2) ,
                                      player.position.y — (player.sprite.contentSize.height /2),
                                      player.sprite.contentSize.width,
                                      player.sprite.contentSize.height);

    return playerRect;

}

Since there are two places (and later there will be more) where I need the CGRect of the player, it's less code to just write this new method which returns it. Now I'll explain what is happening in the rest of the **update** method.

The first four lines in the yellowish block have nothing really to do with the for statement. Primarily we adjust the x and y values with the playerSpeed and playerGravity variables to descend and slide the player across the screen. The if statement checks to see that the player hasn't fallen below 0 or slid past the screenWidth. If either condition is true, then the player is positioned back at ccp(480, screenHeight). As usual, it's good to use a flexible value like the screenHeight whenever possible.

Now for the meat of this. The for statement is going to iterate through all the children in self, and in a sense, temporarily try to say, "Hey, you're a **Platform** class, and I'm gonna call you platform." That name-calling only holds up until the very first if statement which tests **isKindOfClass** on the child. **IF** the child actually is a Platform instance, then we can proceed with some collision detection tests. Prior to testing though, we need to get the CGRect of the platform and of the player.

This is one of those times when using platform.boundingBox or just trying to use platform.contentSize.width will fail us, because it doesn't account for the actual size of the sprite variable within those instances. So in getting a CGRect value we need to factor in this sprite.

Once we're ready to test for the actual collision, we use an if statement with **CGRectIntersectsRect** (platformRect, playerRect), which I've highlighted as our innermost background color (the purplish box). If the collision is a true statement, then the first thing we do is set the playerGravity to 0. Once at 0, there's no descent occurring, so the player will stay at whatever y value it is at. The while statement is included because we can't assume that our player landed perfectly on top of the platform when the collision occurred. He could be split in half, fused into the platform when the condition actually ran. What the while statement does is pretty cool. It keeps checking if **CGRectIntersectsRect** (platformRect, playerRect) is true, with each iteration pushing the player back up in small increments, until eventually the condition is not true and the while loop ceases. Keep in mind that this happens so fast we won't see any kind of pop-up effect when the app is run. The player just lands smoothly on the platform.

Now for the else statement. If the initial **CGRectIntersectsRect** (platformRect, playerRect) is false, then we set the playerGravity back to originalGravity and the playerSpeed back to originalSpeed. Remember though, this for statement could run again right away for the next child and those variables could be back to 0 again in no time. So ultimately every platform must not be touching the player for there to be a successful shift downward or sideways. Although presently we've done nothing to adjust the playerSpeed (that's coming up).

Go ahead and run this code. Cool huh? Now let's have some real fun and add two more platforms in the **init** statement.

Platform *platform3 = [Platform **create**];

[self **addChild**:platform3];

platform3.position = **ccp**(800, 340);

Platform *platform4 = [Platform **create**];

[self **addChild**:platform4];

platform4.position = **ccp**(950, 380);

To see an example movie on this topic go to **www.focalpress.com/cw/Dike** and watch what happens when we collide with Platform instances that are actually above the character … **What!?! He walked up the steps!** That might seem surprising at first, but right now, no matter what part of the player intersects with a platform, the while statement pushes him upwards. Once on top of the platform, playerGravity is still 0 but at no point was playerSpeed ever changed to 0, so the player just keeps right on trucking. Our challenge now is to adjust the collision detection to account for platforms that are actually **above** the player, then the playerSpeed is set to 0. Crowbar in the code below:

```
// replace everything starting with your first CGRectIntersectsRect if statement
if ( CGRectIntersectsRect ( platformRect, playerRect ) ) {
    if ( platform.position.y > player.position.y—(player.sprite.contentSize.height / 2 ) ) {
        //check if platform is higher than player
        playerSpeed = 0;
        player.position = ccp(player.position.x—originalSpeed, player.position.y );
        // bumps the player back some
        playerRect = [self returnPlayerRect ];
    }
```

```
if ( CGRectIntersectsRect ( platformRect, playerRect ) ) {

    // if still intersecting after the adjustment above

    playerGravity = 0;

    while ( CGRectIntersectsRect ( platformRect, playerRect ) ) {

        player.position = ccp(player.position.x , player.position.y + 1 );

        playerRect = [self returnPlayerRect ];

    }

}

}

// <<<< copy from here up, leave in everything starting with the else statement below.

else {
```

So now we still have our primary if statement checking for a collision and if none occurs we set the playerGravity and playerSpeed back to their original values. No change there, but now if a collision is detected, the ***first*** thing we check is if the platform's y position is greater than the player's y position subtracted by half the height of the sprite because we really want to check the bottom of the instance, not the middle (think of it like this, is the platform higher than the feet of the player?). If that's true, then playerSpeed is 0 and we nudge back the player's x position by the amount of the original speed. Finally, we also set the playerRect value to the newest values for the next if statement.

From that point, we have the same code as before to adjust the y value and set the playerGravity to 0. The important thing to note is that this block shouldn't push the player above the platform in front of him because this platform isn't touching him now. We corrected that situation in the if statement prior by nudging him backwards.

Now when I publish the player is stuck. So let's finish this project by making the player try to jump every 4 seconds. At the end of the **init** statement, include:

```
[self schedule:@selector( jumpPlayer:) interval:4.0f];
```

Now let's write the method below called **jumpPlayer**. This will give you a taste of some of the fantastic CCActions later to come in the book:

```
-(void) jumpPlayer:(ccTime)delta {

    CCJumpBy* jump = [CCJumpBy actionWithDuration:1.0f position:ccp(100,0 )
        height:200 jumps:1];

    [player runAction:jump];

}
```

The CCJumpBy variable is initialized with a duration of 1 second, a **position** to jump by of 100 forward on the x and y on the 0 axis, a **height** of 200 points up and the **jumps** parameter is set to 1 (so the player only performs 1 jump over the duration). Finally we apply the jump variable to the player with **runAction**.

To watch a movie that should look similar to your own project, go to **www.focalpress.com/cw/Dike**.

Loyal learners, that's all for this project! You've got the foundation of a side-scroller, which you can build on later with all the code yet to come. If you want the project files for this example, you can download them at: **www.focalpress.com/cw/Dike**.

Section 3

Detecting One Touch

I know you've probably been punching your book waiting for me to introduce touch events. Obviously, touching the screen is pretty essential to any game, so it's about time to make that happen. The first thing you need to do is enable touching in the layer. So in your **init** statement you'll write:

```
-(id) init {
    if( (self=[super init])) {
        self.isTouchEnabled = YES;
        // if you installed an Unstable (beta) version of Cocos2d use ...
        // self.touchEnabled = YES;
    }
    return self;
}
```

That was simple. Assuming you were working in the Cocos2d starting template, and wrote that in the **HelloWorldLayer.m** file, your one and only layer is now listening for touches. The layer is on constant *lookout* for touches, so the methods we write next to handle these events don't need to be called by us. They are always running. So anywhere outside of your **init** statement, write:

```
-(void) ccTouchesBegan:(NSSet *)touches withEvent:(UIEvent *)event
{
    UITouch *touch = [touches anyObject];
    CGPoint location = [touch locationInView:[touch view]];
    location = [[CCDirector sharedDirector]convertToGL:location];
    // do something with the location values
}
```

The **ccTouchesBegan** method handles when a touch begins. If you aren't detecting multiple touches, your code inside the aptly-named **ccTouchesMoved** and **ccTouchesEnded** methods will usually have these same three lines in the beginning. They give us a CGPoint variable called **location**, which is where our first finger touched the screen. The **convertToGL** method is called because the coordinate system for Cocos2d starts at x:0, y:0 on the bottom left of the screen, whereas the UITouch locations are at x:0, y:0 in the top left. Remember that CGPoints are data structures that hold an x and y location. So our location variable holds two values:

Now we can use those values throughout the rest of our **ccTouchesBegan** method. The location variable is local to this method too, so our **ccTouchesMoved**, **ccTouchesEnded** or **ccTouchesCancelled** methods could also have a variable called location.

Before we get into those, let's actually do something with location. Let's continue writing where we left off in that method, and suppose you had already declared a CCSprite called ball:

```
ball.position = ccp ( location.x , location.y );
```

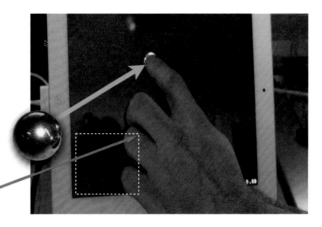

If you didn't want the ball to be exactly centered on your finger you could offset the location with a little addition or subtraction …

ball.position = ccp (location.x + 20 , location.y−20);

Another thing you might want to do is limit where on the screen you do something based on the touch. Suppose you already declared a screenWidth and screenHeight variable in your class and gave them the appropriate size values. You could then write an if statement:

if (location.x < screenWidth * 0.25 && location.y < screenHeight * 0.25) {

    // do something if the touch was in the lower left corner

}

We are checking if the x location of the touch was less than 25 percent the size of the width, *and* if the y location of the touch was less than 25 percent the size of the height (the bottom left corner of the screen). I wrote some code like that recently in an eBook Starter Kit, so anytime the user touched in the corners of the screen, the book would flip a page.

Programmer Meditation Moment
Consider what you have just learned. On the next few pages, I'll show you the code to drag an image from one side of the screen and drop it using the **ccTouchesMoved** and **ccTouchesEnded** methods. Essentially this is the code for a kid's sticker application or dress up game. Just imagine the code in your head before I show it to you …

Watch a bonus movie on this topic at www.focalpress.com/cw/Dike.

For this example project, I'll be using these images: *dressup_bg.png, girl1.png, girl2.png, item1.png, item2.png , item1_sticker.png,* and *item2_sticker.png* . If you want to get an idea of what those look like on their own, or if you want to grab them for your Resources folder, go to www.focalpress.com/cw/Dike. Of course they will also be in the finished source project as well.

So hopefully, you thought a bit about how this will work ahead of time. Here's the gist of it:

Step 1: Our **ccTouchesBegan** method will check to see if we have touched either the hair bow sticker (item1) or belt sticker (item2). If so, it will create a new CCSprite of the corresponding sticker.

Step 2: The **ccTouchesMoved** method will move that sticker around.

Step 3: The **ccTouchesEnded** method will check to see if the sticker was dropped over either girl. If not, then we will turn the sticker red and disallow creation of a new sticker with a bool variable. The whole process can then repeat over and over again.

Step 1: Create an item.   Step 2: Move.

Step 3: Drop and check for collision.

In the HelloWorldLayer.h file

```objc
#import "cocos2d.h"
#import "Constants.h"

@interface HelloWorldLayer : CCLayer
{
    int screenWidth;
    int screenHeight;
    CCSprite* girl1;
        // will be the sprite with the same image name
    CCSprite* girl2;
        // will be the sprite with the same image name
    CCSprite* item1;
        // will be the sprite with the same image name
    CCSprite* Item2;
        // will be the sprite with the same image name
    CCSprite* currentItem;
        // the CCSprite will always be cast as the most recent sticker in play
    bool currentItemWasPositioned;
        // either YES or NO depending on whether the currentItem was dropped over
        // either girl on touch end …
        // …this variable will prevent more than one sticker being added that isn't
        // placed on top of one of the girls.
}
+(CCScene *) scene;
@end
```

In your Constants.h file

```objc
#define tagItem1 1
#define tagItem2 2
```

// or you could define these in your header since it is only two constants

In the HelloWorldLayer.m file (begin with the init statement)

```objc
-(id) init {
    if( (self=[super init])) {
        self.isTouchEnabled = YES;
        // if you installed the Unstable Release of Cocos2d use …. self.touchEnabled = YES;
        CGSize size = [ [CCDirector sharedDirector] winSize ];
        screenWidth = size.width;
```

```
    screenHeight = size.height;

    CCSprite* background = [CCSprite spriteWithFile:@"dressup_bg.png"];
    // set up the background image.
    [self addChild: background];
    background.position = ccp( screenWidth/2, screenHeight/2 );

    girl1 = [CCSprite spriteWithFile:@"girl1.png"];
    // girl1 has already been declared in the header, just give it a file
    [self addChild: girl1];
    girl1.position = ccp( 390, 390 );

    girl2 = [CCSprite spriteWithFile:@"girl2.png"];
    // girl2 has already been declared in the header, just give it a file
    [self addChild: girl2];
    girl2.position = ccp( 685, 400 );

    item1 = [CCSprite spriteWithFile:@"item1.png"];
    // item1 has already been declared in the header, just give it a file
    [self addChild: item1 z:1 tag: tagItem1];
    // we will identify these with the .tag property later, tagItem1 is defined in Constants.h
    item1.position = ccp( 100, 650 );

    item2 = [CCSprite spriteWithFile:@"item2.png"];
    // item2 has already been declared in the header, just give it a file
    [self addChild: item2 z:1 tag: tagItem2];
    // we will identify these with the .tag property later, tagItem2 is defined in Constants.h
    item2.position = ccp( 100, 500 );

    currentItemWasPositioned = YES;
    // setting this to YES initially, so the if statements in the ccTouchesBegan method
    are true on first run.
    }
    return self;
}
```

```
-(void) ccTouchesBegan: (NSSet *)touches withEvent:(UIEvent *)event {

    CCLOG(@"began");
    // I like to see in the output window when these touch events are called
    UITouch *touch = [touches anyObject];
    CGPoint location = [touch locationInView:    [touch view]];
    location = [[CCDirector sharedDirector] convertToGL:location];
    // now we have the location of the touch

for (CCSprite *item in self.children) {
    // iterate through all the children, casting a CCSprite named *item for each child
    switch ( item.tag ) {
    // switch statement to check the value of item.tag
        case tagItem1:
                // in case item.tag is equal to tagItem1 ...
            if ( [self testCollisionUsingPoint: location andSprite: item] &&
                currentItemWasPositioned == YES ) {
                CCSprite* sticker1 = [CCSprite spriteWithFile:@"item1_sticker.png"];
                // add a new CCSprite as a "sticker"
                [self addChild: sticker1 ];
                sticker1.position = ccp( screenWidth/2, screenHeight/2 );
                currentItem = sticker1;
                // casting currentItem as sticker1, so in the other touch methods this sticker will
                be currentItem
                currentItemWasPositioned = NO;
                // this will be NO until the sticker has been released on top of a girl sprite
            }
            break;
        case tagItem2:
        // in case item.tag is equal to
        tagItem2 ...
            if ( [self testCollisionUsingPoint:
                location andSprite: item] &&
                currentItemWasPositioned ==
                YES ) {
                CCSprite* sticker2 = [CCSprite
```

After finding an item with the tag of either tagItem1 or tagItem2, we then test to see if the location of the touch collides within item's width and height using the testCollisionUsingPoint method we created in the last section. Then we are also checking to see if currentItemWasPositioned is equal to YES. The first time this is run, it will be YES.

```
            spriteWithFile:@"item2_sticker.png"];
            // see notes above, just different art
            [self addChild:sticker2 ];
            sticker2.position = ccp( screenWidth/2, screenHeight/2 );
            currentItem = sticker2;
            currentItemWasPositioned = NO;
        }
        break;
    }
  }
}


-(bool) testCollisionUsingPoint: (CGPoint) thePoint andSprite:(CCSprite*) theSprite {
    // see the collision detection code last section for notes
    if ( thePoint.x > (theSprite.position.x—theSprite.contentSize.width /2 ) &&
        thePoint.x < (theSprite.position.x + theSprite.contentSize.width /2 ) &&
        thePoint.y > (theSprite.position.y—theSprite.contentSize.height /2 ) &&
        thePoint.y < (theSprite.position.y + theSprite.contentSize.height /2 )) {
        return YES;
    } else {
        return NO;
    }
}


-(void) ccTouchesMoved: (NSSet *)touches withEvent:(UIEvent *)event {
    CCLOG(@"moving");
        // I like to see in the output window when these touch events are called
    UITouch *touch = [touches anyObject];
    CGPoint location = [touch locationInView:[touch view]];
    location = [[CCDirector sharedDirector] convertToGL:location];
        // now we have the location of the touch
    if ( [self testCollisionUsingPoint: location andSprite: currentItem ] ) {
        // if the touch is overtop the currentItem (sticker)
```

```
    currentItem.position = location;
    // simple code, currentItem's position will be the touch location
    currentItem.color = ccYELLOW;
    // change the color slightly
  }
}


-(void) ccTouchesEnded: (NSSet *)touches withEvent:(UIEvent *)event {
    CCLOG(@"ended");
    // I like to see in the output window when these touch events are called

    UITouch *touch = [touches anyObject];
    CGPoint location = [touch locationInView:[touch view]];
    location = [[CCDirector sharedDirector] convertToGL:location];
    // now we have the location of the touch

  if ( [self testCollisionUsingPoint: location andSprite: currentItem ] ) {
  // once again, let's see if the touch ended overtop the currentItem

  if ( CGRectIntersectsRect(currentItem.boundingBox, girl1.boundingBox) ){
  // then check to see if the currentItem intersects girl1
    [currentItem setColor: ccc3( 255, 255, 255 )];
    // set the color back to normal
    currentItemWasPositioned = YES;
    // this will allow another sticker to be added
    CCLOG(@"current item on girl1");

  } else if ( CGRectIntersectsRect(currentItem.boundingBox, girl2.boundingBox) ){
  // else check to see if the currentItem intersects girl2
    [currentItem setColor: ccc3( 255, 255, 255 )];
    // set the color back to normal
    currentItemWasPositioned = YES;
    // this will allow another sticker to be added
    CCLOG(@"current item on girl2");

  } else {
  // else the currentItem must have been moved off the girls ...
```

```
        currentItem.color = ccRED;
        // set the color red
        currentItemWasPositioned = NO;
        // prevent any other stickers from being added
        CCLOG(@"current item floating in space");
    }
  }
}
```

That's it! This might look like a lot of code with all the notes, but in Xcode it's well under 200 lines. Not much considering this is the basis for countless drag-n-drop sticker or dress-up type games.

Self critique time: This is a great example of an app that does what it's supposed to, and on a small scale, isn't many lines. Except, in my **ccTouchesBegan** method, notice that I have this line twice:

if ([self **testCollisionUsingPoint**: location **andSprite**: item] **&&** currentItemWasPositioned == YES) {

        // ... etc

The lines afterwards in the if statement block are almost identical, except for the file name of the sticker being added. That's okay for now, but if I had twenty items to add, or even hundreds, then this could use some serious tightening up. Anytime you find yourself writing nearly the same lines again and again, consider using a method with parameters to reduce on the same code.

Second, my **ccTouchesBegan** method could be replaced with a CCMenu and actual buttons, but in the order of things, we haven't talked about those yet. Plus, since we just ended a section on collision detection, I wanted to mix that in.

Did we forget **ccTouchesCancelled**? Not really. That method rarely gets called so it's hard to imagine what needs handling there. If you're curious to see when it fires (if ever) you could include the method with a CCLOG statement that tells you in the **Output** window that it ran.

If you want the source for this project, from your home computer go to **www.focalpress.com/cw/Dike** and find the **DressUp** folder.

Detecting Multiple Touches

Detecting multiple touches will only
be a slight modification on the last
section's code. I could have crowbarred this in at the end of that section, but I think a
brand new one will emphasize this crucial step with less chance of you overlooking it:

> **Go to your *AppDelegate.m* file.** Somewhere after this line...
>
> [director_ **setView**: glView];
>
> Write...
>
> [glView **setMultipleTouchEnabled**: YES];

Without that you'll be running around in circles trying to get this section's code to work.
You might be wondering, "Why isn't that enabled by default?" Well, unless you have a very
specific reason for enabling the detection of more than one touch, your game play is
probably improved by leaving this off. Only because if one finger is the primary means of
play, then another finger touching the screen by accident can usually lead to some awkward
results. Plus, since these iOS devices are almost all screen, the chance of a finger slip is
likely. So let's modify our code from before:

```
-(void) ccTouchesBegan: (NSSet *)touches withEvent:(UIEvent *)event {
    // no changes up there, just add ...
    NSArray *touchArray = [touches allObjects];
    if ( [touchArray count] == 2 ) {
        // do something for two touches
    }
}
```

That's the short version of what's ahead. I'll add more inside of the if statement later, but for now let's concentrate on the **NSArray** called touchArray, being created. We haven't talked about arrays yet, and the soft explanation is that they are basically a variable that holds other variables. Or more accurately, an object that *holds* other objects in order. What's interesting about an NSArray is that we could make it contain many different object types. So you could make an NSArray of simple variables like NSNumbers or NSStrings, or more complex objects like CCSprites, or in the case above, **UITouch** objects. I'll show you how to access the contents of an array in a moment, but for now, take a look at this:

[touchArray **count**]

That block calls the **count** method on the touchArray which returns the number of objects it contains. So the statement is asking if the array contains exactly 2 UITouch objects, meaning exactly 2 fingers are touching.

Notice that NSArray begins with "NS" not "CC", which tells us this isn't a Cocos2d type object. We're dealing with some code from Apple so you might get worried now that we have to deal with allocating and deallocating memory because we've stepped out of our perfect little auto-released world of Cocos2d. Well don't worry. We aren't allocating memory for this because we aren't calling **alloc** on touchArray. We are just creating an array, using what we want to from it, then it goes away quietly when the **ccTouchesBegan** handler is done.

So is that block of code even worth writing if we aren't finding out anything about the location of the UITouch objects? **Of course!** One of my first iPad games was a test piece to see if I could program a Peer 2 Peer combat game like Street Fighter. Using some graphics I already had, I made a **cat fighter game** (it's free). Instead of using a virtual gamepad with 3 or 4 buttons like an old Super NES controller, I detected moves based on the amount of fingers touching the screen. Regardless of the location of the touch, punch was 1 finger, jab 2 fingers, and kick 3 fingers. Apparently, people weren't ready for this ground-breaking method of play as one reviewer wrote,

"Ok if u have to play this worst game in app store I think you have to play as Nonie" ... Ouch, but at least he played a few characters.

Next, let's get the location of each touch. I'll keep working within the if statement, because it doesn't make sense to write these new lines elsewhere if I only care about events with exactly 2 touches. Just keep in mind, I could include if ... else if statements to check for 1, 2, 3, 4 finger touches and so on:

```
-(void)ccTouchesBegan:(NSSet *)touches withEvent:(UIEvent*)event{

    NSArray *touchArray = [touches allObjects];

    if ( [touchArray count] == 2 ) {
        // do something for two touches

        UITouch *finger1 = [touchArray objectAtIndex: 0];

        UITouch *finger2 = [touchArray objectAtIndex: 1];
        // we now have two UITouch vars

        CGPoint point1 = [finger1 locationInView:[finger1 view]];

        CGPoint point2 = [finger2 locationInView:[finger2 view]];
        // create CGPoints to store where the UITouches landed

        point1 = [[CCDirector sharedDirector] convertToGL: point1];

        point2 = [[CCDirector sharedDirector] convertToGL: point2];
        // we now have point1.x and point1.y to use
        // we also have point2.x and point2.y to use

    }

}
```

This code is very similar to what we had when we just detected one touch, the obvious difference is that there's twice as much now because we are looking at two touches. Previously we used the following line to setup our UITouch variable:

```
UITouch *touch = [touches anyObject];
```

Instead I'm doing the same thing but writing:

UITouch *finger1 = [touchArray **objectAtIndex**: 0];

First, I'm renaming the variable to
finger1, to be more specific, and I'm
making it equal to **objectAtIndex**: 0
in touchArray. Arrays start numbering
objects at zero instead of one.
So **objectAtIndex**: 0 is the first
finger touching the screen. The next
line:

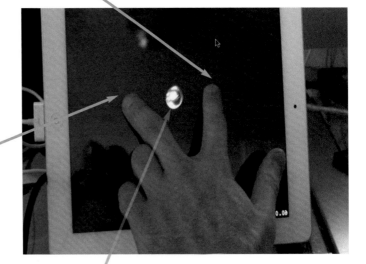

UITouch *finger2 = [touchArray
objectAtIndex: 1];

… is nearly identical, with only a
different variable name and
objectAtIndex value. Next, we
create two CGPoint variables, point1
and point2, for the location of the touches. So what should you do with those? Well two
different objects could each go to a unique location.

sprite1.position = point1 ;

sprite2.position = point2 ;

Or you could split the difference of the two locations and make a single object seem to
levitate between the two touches. This line could be placed inside the **ccTouchesMoved**
method to best simulate that effect:

> // run this after you got your CGPoints …

ball.position = ccp (point1.x—((point1.x—point2.x) / 2) ,
point1.y—((point1.y—point2.y) / 2));

Touch Priority

Writing this section is my own introduction to programming touch priority in Cocos2d. Can you believe I made it this long without ever making one object more **touchable** than another? This gets into a pretty high level of specificity compared to what you need for most games, so don't get too worried thinking you **must** implement any of the following code in your game. Remember recruits, you're operating on a need-to-know-basis! So until you find yourself absolutely having to code a higher or lower priority touch object, you can skip or skim this part. We do look at two interesting new methods, **onEnter** and **onExit**, so keep an eye out for those if you skim this.

Let's suppose for some reason you want to make every instance of a class exclusively touch sensitive. So if you spawn a whole bunch of these instances, only one can be touched at a time. In Cocos2d this is referred to as swallowing touch. We can also set a touch priority for that object, so if the location of the touch encompassed multiple objects the *lower* priority numbered one would swallow the touch. That's a little counter intuitive, because a priority of 0 would swallow touch over a higher number.

This is a good chance to use our previous **TopDownEnemy** project files again. If you want to download those now without the touch priority code already included grab the source files from Chapter 3 at the following link:

www.focalpress.com/cw/Dike

Open those and notice that our Enemy class subclassed a basic CCNode before.

> **In the Enemy.h file**
> @interface Enemy : CCNode {

Which is fine, but if we had tried to set self.isTouchEnabled to YES in the **init** statement, it wouldn't have worked. The IsTouchEnabled property is for CCLayers. I mention this because some of you probably tried adding this already (I did).

Well, we could switch our Enemy class to be a subclass of CCLayer instead of CCNode, and everything will still work fine that we coded in the past, but that doesn't really help us with the task at hand, so let's leave it as a CCNode.

We do need to add a little bit to the Enemy header file though:

In the Enemy.h file

@interface Enemy : CCNode <CCTargetedTouchDelegate>

{

    // etc ...

What we are adding in between the < > symbols is a **delegate class**.

Delegation is a tough concept for beginners, so to keep it simple you can think of it like this: you are *delegating* some of the work to this class. By using this delegate, you are agreeing to some terms, like Lando agreeing to let Vadar torture Han so Cloud City gets left alone. What's required of this delegate is that you include this method in your **Enemy.m** file:

-(BOOL)**ccTouchBegan**:(UITouch *)touch **withEvent**:(UIEvent *)event

Hey, that looks a lot like the methods we saw in the last couple sections. This time around though the method selector is **ccTouchBegan** instead of **ccTouchesBegan**, and instead of returning void from the method, it returns a BOOL value. We actually could have been using **ccTouchBegan** in the first section on touches because we were only looking at one touch there anyway, but I wanted to keep the methods in those two sections as similar as possible.

So why are we returning BOOL here? Well this is pretty cool. If we decide the touch is of value to us, for example, if we detected that the touch was over the top of the sprite in our class, we could return YES, and this would allow our **ccTouchesMoved**, **ccTouchesEnded** or **ccTouchesCancelled** methods to be run. If we return NO, then the object won't even worry about calling those at all.

Keep in mind too, that once this class is listening for touches, it doesn't matter the shape or size of the artwork contained within, everywhere is a possible touch to that class. If you're like me, you mistakenly assumed at first that the touch area of a class was by default limited to the visible area of that class. In a moment, you can see for yourself that touching anywhere can trigger the **ccTouchBegan** method. So go ahead and add in this:

```
-(BOOL)ccTouchBegan:(UITouch *)touch withEvent:(UIEvent *)event
{
    CGPoint location = [touch locationInView:[touch view]];

    location = [[CCDirector sharedDirector] convertToGL: location];

    return YES;

}
```

For now, we won't be picky and just allow any touch to return YES. Later on, we will put an if statement in there so we only care about touches that collide with the sprite within.

Finally I should mention that only the **ccTouchBegan** method is required of the delegate. The other touch handlers are optional.

The last couple of steps involve the **onEnter** and **onExit** methods. Take a look at the code below. Both statements could have been added to our Enemy class prior to this example, we just didn't have a need for them. As they are now, they aren't doing anything really:

```
- (void) onEnter {
    // gets called when the object is added to the scene

    [ super onEnter];
    // be sure to include this

}
- (void) onExit {
    // gets called when the object is removed from the scene

    [ super onExit];
    // be sure to include this

}
```

The **onEnter** method would get called automatically when the child was added to the scene. So that would be *after* we had already initialized the class. For example:

In a class that was adding the Enemy ...

```
Enemy* theEnemy = [Enemy create];        // init would get called here

[self addChild: theEnemy];  ────────▶ // onEnter would get called here
```

When you include the **onExit** method, anything in that block would be called when the object leaves the stage. Now you're probably thinking, "Ah ha, Cocos2d is too good to be true, we finally have to deal with memory." Well you are only half right. Yes, we are including this for performance reasons, but remember I said we could have included these methods in the Enemy class before, but didn't need to. That was true. We still haven't allocated or retained anything that needed explicit deallocation on our part. So just keep in mind, these two methods don't necessarily have to deal with memory or performance. You might simply want to play a sound effect when the child enters or exits the scene.

In this case, we *do* have some important tasks for **onEnter** and **onExit**: tell the Cocos2d **touchDispatcher** about this delegate.

```
-(void) onEnter {
    // the following is one line ...
    [ [ [CCDirector sharedDirector] touchDispatcher]
        addTargetedDelegate: self priority:0
        swallowsTouches: YES];
    [ super onEnter ];
}


-(void) onExit {
    // the following is one line ...
    [ [ [CCDirector sharedDirector] touchDispatcher]
                removeDelegate: self ];
    [ super onExit ];
}
```

Simply put, in our **onEnter** method, the Enemy instance presents his delegate to the almighty **touchDispatcher** who allows the object to **swallowTouches** and have a touch **priority** of zero (which makes this instance high on the chain of command for touching). The **onExit** method just removes the delegate from the dispatcher.

Now, if you want to have some fun with the **TopDownEnemy** project and really test out this touch priority stuff, try setting a different priority for a different image. Remember you have the baseImage variable, which could be used in the **onEnter** statement like so:

```
- (void) onEnter {
    if ( baseImage == @"wingthing" ) {
        [ [[CCDirector sharedDirector] touchDispatcher] addTargetedDelegate: self
        priority:0 swallowsTouches: YES];
    } else {
        [ [[CCDirector sharedDirector] touchDispatcher] addTargetedDelegate: self
        priority:10 swallowsTouches: YES];
    }
    [ super onEnter ];
}
```

In Cocos2d v1, [CCTouchDispatcher **sharedDispatcher**] is used instead of [[CCDirector **sharedDirector**] **touchDispatcher**]

That would let you prioritize touching any of the winged creatures flying around the other enemy. Then let's go back to the **ccTouchBegan** block in the *Enemy.m* file and add some collision detection:

```
-(BOOL) ccTouchBegan:(UITouch *)touch withEvent:(UIEvent *)event {
    CGPoint location = [touch locationInView:[touch view]];
    location = [[CCDirector sharedDirector] convertToGL: location];
    CGRect locationRect = CGRectMake( location.x, location.y, 50, 50 );
```

```
// make a 50 by 50 rectangle around your touch location

if ( CGRectIntersectsRect( locationRect, [self getRect] ) ) {

    // tests locationRect against [self getRect] which is already in this class

    CCLOG( @"touched an enemy or winged thing" );

    return YES;

    // allows a ccTouchMoved, ccTouchEnded or ccTouchCancelled method to be used

} else {

    return NO;

    // no collision, so we don't care about this touch

}

}
```

Alright, I've given you the hard part. You should be able to recreate the example movie at **www.focalpress.com/cw/Dike**. Touch down to move an enemy, then on release, it should continue buzzing around the screen. Give priority to the flying creatures. Then if you want to get real fancy, when you spawn the enemies, make all of one kind visually lower than another. Just for kicks.

If you run into problems, the source code has been uploaded to this chapter's zip file in the folder **TopDownEnemy_Touch_Priority** at **www.focalpress.com/cw/Dike**.

You can also watch a bonus movie while you're there!

Swipes and How to Make a Virtual Joystick

Apple created some nifty **gesture recognition** code for handling common user events like swipes, multiple taps, rotations, and more. Just because we are mostly playing around in the Cocos2d universe, it doesn't mean we can't make use of that code as well.

First, I want to show you a simple way to detect a swipe in a certain direction using the Cocos2d touch methods we've already learned, and in doing so, build a simple joystick.

Create a new project using the Cocos2d starting template (mine is named Virtual_Joystick), and as usual we'll start things off in the *HelloWorldLayer.h* file. All we need to do here is declare a couple int type variables:

In the HelloWorldLayer.h file

@interface HelloWorldLayer : CCLayer {

    int initialTouchX;

    int initialTouchY;

}

All I want from these two variables is to store where the initial location of the touch was on the x axis and y axis when the finger touches the screen in the **ccTouchesBegan** method. We'll then compare those variables to where the finger ends touching the screen in the **ccTouchesEnded** method. This time around, we could care less about the **ccTouchesMoved** method.

Jump over to the HelloWorldLayer implementation file. Modify your **init** statement like so, and add the **ccTouchesBegan** method.

-(id) **init**{

    if((self=[super **init**])) {

        self.isTouchEnabled = YES;

        // self.touchEnabled = YES; if using the Unstable version of Cocos2d

        }

        return self;

}

-(void) **ccTouchesBegan**:(NSSet *)touches **withEvent**:(UIEvent*)event

{

    UITouch *touch = [touches **anyObject**];

    CGPoint location = [touch **locationInView**:[touch **view**]];

    location = [[CCDirector **sharedDirector**]**convertToGL**: location];

```
        initialTouchX = location.x;
            // stores the x value of the first finger touch

        initialTouchY = location.y;
            // stores the y value of the first finger touch

}
```

Now for the **ccTouchesEnded** statement (I'll explain this on the next page):

```
-(void)ccTouchesEnded: (NSSet *)touches withEvent:(UIEvent *)event {

        UITouch *touch = [touches anyObject];

        CGPoint location = [touch locationInView:[touch view]];

        location = [[CCDirector sharedDirector]convertToGL: location];

        int xSwipe;
        // value of the distance moved on the x axis
        int ySwipe;
        // value of the distance moved on the y axis

        xSwipe = abs( location.x—initialTouchX);
        // absolute value ...
        ySwipe = abs( location.y—initialTouchY);
        // ...of the differences

        if ( xSwipe > ySwipe) {
        // the x direction was the greater swipe

            if ( location.x > initialTouchX) {
            // compare initial x to end x

                CCLOG( @"Right Swipe");
                // end touch was greater

            } else {

                CCLOG( @"Left Swipe" );
                // end touch was lesser

            }

        } else {
        // the y direction was the greater swipe
```

```
            if ( location.y > initialTouchY) {
            // compare initial y to end y
                CCLOG( @"Up Swipe" );
                // end touch was greater
            } else {
                CCLOG( @"Down Swipe" );
                // end touch was lesser
            }
        }
    }
}
```

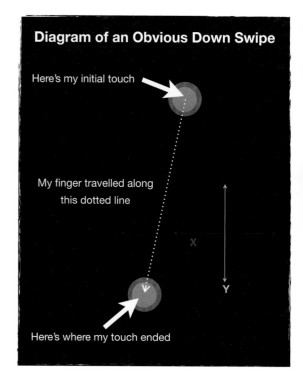

Diagram of an Obvious Down Swipe

Here's my initial touch

My finger travelled along
this dotted line

X

Y

Here's where my touch ended

As usual we are getting a CGPoint location for the end touch. Then I'm creating two int variables, xSwipe and ySwipe. These will each hold the value of the distance moved on their respective axes. To figure this out, I'll subtract the current location by the initial location on each axis. The key part is that I'm using the abs( ) function to give me the **absolute value** of the equation. Forgot what that means? If the equation results in -40, the absolute value is 40.

The reason I'm comparing my xSwipe distance to ySwipe distance is hopefully obvious from the blackboard style diagram on this page. You can see that the distance along the y axis was greater, even though I traveled slightly to the left on the x axis. The math might look like:

```
xSwipe = abs( -20 );
        // travelled left 20 points on the x
```

```
ySwipe = abs( -100 );
        // travelled down 100 points on the y
```

Since we're subtracting the end location from the start, both distances are negative, making ySwipe the greater value when they are converted to absolute values. That's where the if (xSwipe > ySwipe) comes in.

Once that if statement determines if it's the x or the y axis that got the greater swipe, we use our inner if … else statements to see whether the ending x or y axis locations were greater or less than their starting locations. That determines whether we were swiping left, right, up or down.

Collisions, Touches, and Gestures

As you can see I added CCLOG statements to call out the swipe direction, but for the finished project example, I'll change that to call four separate methods instead. This will make the project much cleaner later.

-(void) **rightHandler** {

> *// separate method for handling Right Swipes*

}

-(void) **leftHandler** {

> *// separate method for handling Left Swipes*

}

-(void) **upHandler** {

> *// separate method for handling Up Swipes*

}

-(void) **downHandler** {

> *// separate method for handling Down Swipes*

}

That's all for this example! Download it on your Mac at the usual spot:

www.focalpress.com/cw/Dike.

```objc
-(void)ccTouchesBegan:(NSSet *)touches withEvent:(UIEvent *)event {

    UITouch *touch = [touches anyObject];
    CGPoint location = [touch locationInView:[touch view]];
    location = [[CCDirector sharedDirector] convertToGL:location];

    initialTouchX = location.x;
    initialTouchY = location.y;

}

- (void)ccTouchesEnded:(NSSet *)touches withEvent:(UIEvent *)event
{
    UITouch *touch = [touches anyObject];
    CGPoint location = [touch locationInView:[touch view]];
    location = [[CCDirector sharedDirector] convertToGL:location];

    int xSwipe;
    int ySwipe;

    xSwipe = abs( location.x - initialTouchX);
    ySwipe = abs( location.y - initialTouchY);

    if ( xSwipe > ySwipe ) {  //x direction was the greater swipe
        if (location.x > initialTouchX) {
            [self rightHandler];
        } else {
            [self leftHandler];
        }
    } else { //y direction was the greater swipe
        if ( location.y > initialTouchY) {
            [self upHandler];
        } else {
            [self downHandler];
        }
    }
}
-(void)rightHandler{
    CCLOG(@"Right Swipe");
}
-(void)leftHandler{
    CCLOG(@"Left Swipe");
}
-(void)upHandler{
    CCLOG(@"Up Swipe");
}
-(void)downHandler{
    CCLOG(@"Down Swipe");
}
```

Gestures and How to Rotate a Joystick

Let's take a look at the **gesture recognizers** I mentioned in the last section. Apple gave us programmers an easy way to detect the most common ways users interact with their device, such as tapping, swiping, pressing down, panning, rotating and pinching. I'll discuss the code for all of these, but let's just focus on rotations in this section.

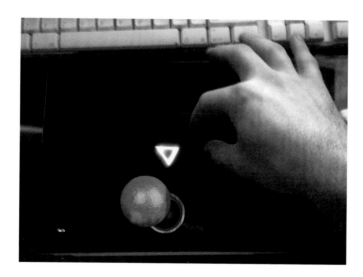

Since we've already got the joystick art to play with from the project files in the last section, let's make it so we can rotate the stick around. To do this I'll set up the **UIRotationGestureRecognizer**, which will enable the view (the screen basically) to detect if my fingers are moving in a rotating manner. It won't matter if I'm actually rotating them over the top of the joystick art, because that might be cumbersome for the gameplay anyway. The joystick is just meant to give players a nostalgia feel. If you don't want to follow along with any of my project's art files, that's fine too. The set up is the same regardless.

Declare your UIRotationGestureRecognizer variable and call it rotationGR:

In the HelloWorldLayer.h file

@interface HelloWorldLayer : CCLayer {

> // leave in anything else you've declared from a past project and add ...

> UIRotationGestureRecognizer *rotationGR;

> // I'll write "GR" in the variable name for "gesture recognizer"

}

Now that rotationGR is declared, I'll jump over to the implementation file and create two methods. One for adding the rotationGR to the view and one for removing it, which will disable listening out for a rotation. Most likely if you're setting up your joystick to spin around, you'll never want to disable that. Like a real arcade machine, you can always fool with the controls, but whether you're actually playing the game is a matter of how many quarters are in your pocket. Since I found enough forums with people asking how to shut off their gesture recognizers, I'll include that code too. Just know the **removeRotationGestures** is optional.

In the HelloWorldLayer.m file[[broen underline end]]

-(id) **init** {

if((self=[super **init**])) {

> // leave in anything from the last project that you want to keep in your init statement

[self **addRotationGestures**];

> // add this. It just call the method below ...

}

}

-(void) **addRotationGestures** {

rotationGR = [[UIRotationGestureRecognizer **alloc**] **initWithTarget**: self **action**:@selector (**handleRotation:**)];

> In Cocos2d v1 **view** was **openGLView**

[[[CCDirector **sharedDirector**] view] **addGestureRecognizer**: rotationGR];

> Any time we move our fingers in a rotation, the handleRotation method gets called.

[rotationGR **release**];

> // rotationGR should be safe to release now, the view retains it

}

```
-(void) removeRotationGestures {

    // will remove the gesture from the view ( optional method, it IS NOT being called)

    [ [ [CCDirector sharedDirector]view]
    removeGestureRecognizer: rotationGR ];

}

-(void) handleRotation:(UIRotationGestureRecognizer
*)recognizer {

    CCLOG( @"rotation in radians is %f", recognizer.rotation );
    // log the value of the rotation in radians

    CCLOG( @"rotation in degrees is %f", CC_RADIANS_TO_DEGREES
    ( recognizer.rotation ) );
    // log the value of the rotation in degrees

    // we will add more to this method later ...

}
```

> Any time we move our fingers in a rotation, the handleRotation method gets called.

The first line in the **addRotationGestures** method allocated the UIRotationGesture Recognizer, initialized it with self, and the really important part is the action taken when the gesture occurs will be the **handleRotation:** method (that's a method name I picked out for us). Don't forget that colon after the method selector name.

The second line is pretty obvious, but you might be curious about the [[CCDirector **sharedDirector**] view] part. Essentially that's just a longer way of writing self.view, which is what we would have written if we weren't using Cocos2d, and using a UIView instead.

Then finally in the **addRotationGestures** method, I'm releasing the rotationGR variable. Since I allocated it, I should release it. Since the view has now taken charge of the gesture, I don't need this variable kicking around anymore. Plus I could call this method again if I needed to bring back the gesture after removing it from the view.

Now let's pick apart the **handleRotation** method with the (UIRotationGestureRecognizer *) recognizer parameter. Oh, we can do a lot with that parameter! For starters, I've included log statements that give you the rotation value of the recognizer parameter (your finger's rotation) in it's raw format of radians, then a second log statement with it converted to degrees using the CC_RADIANS_TO_DEGREES function. Most of us are more familiar with degrees from sporting lingo like, "He did a full 360 degree spin in the air." A 90 degree turn is a quarter turn. 180 is a half turn, and 360 is a complete spin all the way around.

Collisions, Touches, and Gestures

Let's add some more to the **handleRotation** method (you can comment out the log statements if you want). What I'll do now is create an int variable called rotationInDegrees and make that equal to recognizer.rotation (converted to degrees). Then you could use that value to change the rotation of a CCSprite. If I had already declared a CCSprite variable called ship in my header and added it in my **init** statement, then to rotate it I would simply write:

-(void) **handleRotation**:(UIRotationGestureRecognizer *)recognizer {

int rotationInDegrees = CC_RADIANS_TO_DEGREES(recognizer.rotation);

ship.rotation = rotationInDegrees ;

    // this would rotate the graphic

}

Retro Arcade Style Ship
(or a really lazy drawing on my part)

Rotating the Joystick Ball (or any object) Around in a Circle

Here's the part you've been waiting for. This is just one line of code, but we'll need some spice for this formula. If you aren't using the project from last section, go ahead and setup a CGPoint variable for the center point of the joystick. I've already declared one called centerOfJoyStick. This was the starting point location of the CCSprites I used for the joystick ball and base. Now I'll use it once more for the center point of the circular rotation. Next, let's go ahead and create an int variable called length (mine equals 50), which will just save us time writing the same number twice in our equation, but at least you can see on the diagram where the variable comes into play. Increasing or decreasing that length variable determines the size of the circular path. Finally, we work a bit of mathematical magic using the value of the recognizer.rotation and your old friends from high school trigonometry, **sin** and **cosine** (if you forgot what those are, they are in glossary).

centerOfJoyStick

length

Rotate the joystick around a circle

joyStickBall.position = ccp(centerOfJoyStick.x — (cos(recognizer.rotation) * length) ,

centerOfJoyStick.y + (sin(recognizer.rotation) * length));

So as the recognizer.rotation value changes, as does the location of the joyStickBall.position. The length and centerOfJoyStick variables stay the same throughout this example. Of course, they **could** change if you wanted them to, perhaps in a future project that would make more sense. Also too, remember that because the length value is the same for determining the x and y locations, the circular path is a perfect circle. If you varied that amount, your path (and code) could look like this:

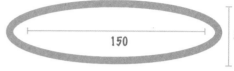

150   50

joyStickBall.position = ccp(centerOfJoyStick.x—(cos(recognizer.rotation) * 150) , centerOfJoyStick.y + (sin(recognizer.rotation) * 50));

There's just one slight problem now. Every time our gesture begins, the recognizer.rotation value starts back at zero. Which would mean that regardless of where our joystick ball had stopped moving, it will always begin at the same spot. Ack! We don't want that at all. I'll ask for a hushed, "awe" from the audience as I present this small but crucial change. Try to follow along before I really explain this:

In the @interface of your header file ...

int degreeOffset;

    // declare this.

Go back to your implementation file ...

-(void) **handleRotation**:(UIRotationGestureRecognizer *)recognizer {

    int rotationInDegrees = CC_RADIANS_TO_DEGREES(recognizer.rotation);

    rotationInDegrees = rotationInDegrees + degreeOffset;

    // add degreeOffset to rotationInDegrees (on first run, degreeOffset will be 0)

    joyStickBall.position = ccp(centerOfJoyStick.x—(cos(CC_DEGREES_TO_RADIANS
                (rotationInDegrees)) * length) ,
                centerOfJoyStick.y + (sin (CC_DEGREES_TO_RADIANS
                (rotationInDegrees)) * length));

    ship.rotation = rotationInDegrees ;

    // if you want to rotate the ship too

    if (recognizer.state == UIGestureRecognizerStateEnded) {

    // this gets called when the user stops the rotation gesture

       CCLOG(@"the gesture ended");

```
    degreeOffset = rotationInDegrees;
    // degreeOffset now equals whatever the value of rotationInDegrees was when
    the gesture stopped
    }

}
```

Did that make sense? All we are doing is saving the final value of rotation (in degrees) in a variable called degreeOffset . So any time we start the gesture, we have the last amount saved so we can add it to the rotation. Thus, picking up where we left off on the circular path.

You'll notice we used this particularly helpful if statement to check the state of the gesture:

if (recognizer.state == **UIGestureRecognizerStateEnded**)

As you can see, we are testing the end state, or when the gesture finished. Here's the complete list of **gesture recognition states** you could test for:

UIGestureRecognizerStateBegan UIGestureRecognizerStateCancelled

UIGestureRecognizerStateChanged

UIGestureRecognizerStateFailed

UIGestureRecognizerStatePossible

UIGestureRecognizerStateRecognized

UIGestureRecognizerStateEnded

You can imagine how testing certain conditions could be quite helpful (thanks, Apple). We'll look at gestures more in the next section—for now, you should feel mighty accomplished if you've created something close to what I have in the example movie, which you can watch at **www.focalpress.com/cw/Dike.**

While you're there you can also find the finished project in the zip file within the folder titled ***Virtual_Joystick_Rotating***.

More Gestures

We have a few more gesture recognizers to look at, so let's dive right in with some examples using the Cocos2d starting template:

In the HelloWorldLayer.h file

@interface HelloWorldLayer : CCLayer {

    // declare swipe gestures

    UISwipeGestureRecognizer *swipeUp;

    UISwipeGestureRecognizer *swipeDownGR;

    UISwipeGestureRecognizer *swipeLeft;

    UISwipeGestureRecognizer *swipeRight;

    // declare tap gesture

    UITapGestureRecognizer *tapGR;

    // declare long press down gesture

    UILongPressGestureRecognizer *longPressGR;

    // declare pan gesture

    UIPanGestureRecognizer *panGR;

    // declare pinch gesture

    UIPinchGestureRecognizer *pinchGR;

}

You can now jump over to your implementation file. I'll create separate methods for adding each of these gestures, so the **init** statement will call each of those methods. This keeps the file a bit cleaner, and if you want to comment out some of the gestures during testing, it will be much easier this way.

```
-(id) init{

    if( (self=[super init])) {

        [self addPinchGesture];

        [self addSwipeGestures];

        [self addPanGesture];

        [self addTapGesture];

        [self addLongPressGesture];

    }

return self;

}
```

Let's be tidy programmers and add a #pragma mark before each method that adds a gesture. You can write this outside of your methods, followed by a note to yourself regarding the code you'll write below. This will help you navigate your code when you pull down where I've indicated in the screenshot.

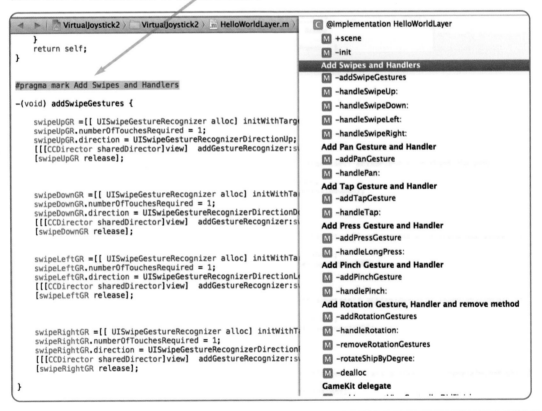

-(void) **addPinchGesture** {

    pinchGR = [[UIPinchGestureRecognizer **alloc**] **initWithTarget**: self **action**:@selector(**handlePinch**:)];

    // NOTE the colon after method!

    [[[CCDirector **sharedDirector**] **view**] **addGestureRecognizer**: pinchGR];

    [pinchGR **release**];

}

> In Cocos2d v1 **view** was **openGLView**

-(void) **handlePinch**:(UIPinchGestureRecognizer *)recognizer {

    CCLOG(@"Pinching with a scale of %f", recognizer.scale);

    // log the scale value in the output window

    // a scale value less than 1 is a pinch inwards, over 1 is a pinch outwards

}

#pragma mark **Add** UISwipeGestureRecognizer **and Handlers**

-(void) **addSwipeGestures** {

    // I'll add all the swipes at once ...

    swipeUp =[[UISwipeGestureRecognizer **alloc**] **initWithTarget**: self **action**:@selector(**handleSwipeUp**:)];

    // colon after method

    swipeUp.numberOfTouchesRequired = 1;

    // have some fun and change this value when testing

    swipeUp.direction = UISwipeGestureRecognizerDirectionUp;

    [[[CCDirector **sharedDirector**] **view**] **addGestureRecognizer**: swipeUp];

    // add swipe up

    [swipeUp **release**];

    swipeDownGR =[[UISwipeGestureRecognizer **alloc**] **initWithTarget**: self **action**:@selector(**handleSwipeDown**:)];

    // colon after method

    swipeDownGR.numberOfTouchesRequired = 1;

    // have some fun and change this value when testing

    swipeDownGR.direction = UISwipeGestureRecognizerDirectionDown;

```
[ [ [CCDirector sharedDirector] view] addGestureRecognizer: swipeDownGR];
// add swipe down
[swipeDownGR release];

swipeLeft =[[ UISwipeGestureRecognizer alloc] initWithTarget: self action:@selector(
handleSwipeLeft:)];
// colon after method
swipeLeft.numberOfTouchesRequired = 1;
// have some fun and change this value when testing
swipeLeft.direction = UISwipeGestureRecognizerDirectionLeft;
[ [ [CCDirector sharedDirector] view] addGestureRecognizer: swipeLeft];
// add swipe left
[swipeLeft release];

swipeRight =[[ UISwipeGestureRecognizer alloc] initWithTarget: self action:@selector(
handleSwipeRight:)];
// colon after method
swipeRight.numberOfTouchesRequired = 1;
// have some fun and change this value when testing
swipeRight.direction = UISwipeGestureRecognizerDirectionRight;
[ [ [CCDirector sharedDirector] view] addGestureRecognizer: swipeRight];
// add swipe right
[swipeRight release];
}


-(void) handleSwipeUp:(UISwipeGestureRecognizer *)recognizer {
    CCLOG(@"Swiped Up");
    joyStickBall.position = ccp( centerOfJoyStick.x , centerOfJoyStick.y + 40);
    // if you want to use the joystick art
}
-(void) handleSwipeDown:(UISwipeGestureRecognizer *)recognizer {
    CCLOG(@"Swiped Down");
    joyStickBall.position = ccp( centerOfJoyStick.x , centerOfJoyStick.y—40);
    // if you want to use the joystick art
}
```

```
-(void) handleSwipeLeft:(UISwipeGestureRecognizer *)recognizer {
    CCLOG(@"Swiped Left");
    joyStickBall.position = ccp( centerOfJoyStick.x−40, centerOfJoyStick.y );
    // if you want to use the joystick art
}
-(void) handleSwipeRight:(UISwipeGestureRecognizer *)recognizer {
    CCLOG(@"Swiped Right");
    joyStickBall.position = ccp( centerOfJoyStick.x + 40 , centerOfJoyStick.y );
    // if you want to use the joystick art
}
```

That takes care of the swipe gestures. Let's move onto the UITapGestureRecognizer:

```
#pragma mark Add UITapGestureRecognizer and Handler
-(void) addTapGesture {
    tapGR = [ [ UITapGestureRecognizer alloc] initWithTarget: self action:@selector
    (handleTap: )];
    // colon after method
    tapGR.numberOfTapsRequired = 3;
    // three fast taps will call the handleTap method
    tapGR.numberOfTouchesRequired = 1;
    // requires exactly 1, no more
    [ [ [CCDirector sharedDirector] view] addGestureRecognizer: tapGR];
    [tapGR release];
}
```

Before we write the **handleTap** method, notice we've got a few more properties now. The numberOfTapsRequired and numberOfTouchesRequired open up a lot of possibilities for interesting gameplay. Imagine a 'Dance Dance Revolution' type game played with your fingers instead of your feet. These tap gestures could be perfect for something like that.

So if you were programming a tap game, you might want to detect exactly where the tap occurred. Here's the code to do that:

```
-(void) handleTap:(UITapGestureRecognizer *)recognizer {
        CGPoint location = [recognizer locationInView: recognizer.view];
        // gets the location of the recognizer
        location = [ [CCDirector sharedDirector] convertToGL: location];
        // convert the location to account for cocos2D starting 0, 0 on bottom left
        CCLOG( @"3 taps detected at x: %f and y: %f", location.x , location.y );
        // log the x and y location of the taps.
}
```

Of course you could then use that location in any of the collision detection methods we've looked at previously. Let's do that with our next gesture as well:

```
#pragma mark Add UILongPressGestureRecognizer and Handler
-(void) addLongPressGesture {
        longPressGR = [[ UILongPressGestureRecognizer alloc] initWithTarget: self
        action:@selector( handleLongPress: )];
        // colon after method
        longPressGR.minimumPressDuration = 3.0;
        // 3 second long press
        [ [ [CCDirector sharedDirector] view] addGestureRecognizer: longPressGR];
        [longPressGR release];
}
```

```
-(void) handleLongPress:(UILongPressGestureRecognizer *)recognizer {
        CGPoint location = [recognizer locationInView: recognizer.view];
        // gets the location of the recognizer
        location = [ [CCDirector sharedDirector] convertToGL: location];
        // convert the location to account for cocos2D starting 0, 0 on bottom left
        CCLOG( @"3 second press detected at x: %f and y: %f", location.x , location.y );
        // log the x and y location of the long press.
}
```

Finally, the panning gesture checks if a finger (or fingers) pan across the screen. I'm setting the minimumNumberOfTouches property to 2 because if I set it to 1, none of the swipe gestures would get recognized. So be careful using these gestures together.

#pragma mark Add UIPanGestureRecognizer and Handler

-(void) **addPanGesture** {

    panGR = [[UIPanGestureRecognizer **alloc**] **initWithTarget**: self **action**:@selector(**handlePan:**)];

    // don't forget the colon

    panGR.minimumNumberOfTouches = 2;

    panGR.maximumNumberOfTouches = 6;

    [[[CCDirector **sharedDirector**] **view**] **addGestureRecognizer**: panGR];

    [panGR **release**];

}

To spice up this last example, let's check the **velocity** of the pan (you could do this with other gestures too):

-(void) **handlePan:**(UIPanGestureRecognizer *)recognizer {

    CGPoint velocity = [recognizer **velocityInView**: recognizer.view];

    // store the x and y velocity variables in a CGPoint

    CCLOG(@"Panning with 2 fingers occurring. Speed on x is: %i and y is: %i", (int)velocity.x ,(int)velocity.y);

    // I'm logging the velocity values as integers because they are easier to read in the output window that way.

    // see if we are moving slowly on the x axis. We use the absolute value, because the velocity could be negative or positive depending on the direction

    if (abs(velocity.x) < 100){

        CCLOG(@"moving slowly");

    // anything under 100 is pretty slow, so let's log it

    }

}

That's it! Not all the gestures affect the joystick in my source project, but I did play around some. Check the log window for statements from each handler. Don't forget what we learned at the end of the last section—you can check the **gesture recognizer states** in your handler methods like so:

```
-(void) handlePan:(UIPanGestureRecognizer *)recognizer {
    if ( recognizer.state == UIGestureRecognizerStateBegan) {
    // limit what you do based on the state
    }
}
```

For the project files go to www.focalpress.com/cw/Dike. Find the folder titled Virtual_Joystick_with_Gestures.

Chapter 6

Accelerometer and Actions

Your test device is probably covered in smudges from all that heartfelt touching in the last chapter. The first thing we'll look at this chapter is using the Accelerometer, which is one of the coolest ways of touch-free interaction with your device. So give your iPad a good wipe down and it should stay that way for a bit.

We'll also spend a long time looking into CCAction classes, which are typically just a couple lines of code that handle animating things like fades, movements, rotations, and even special effects similar to the Filters in Photoshop. Actions can also be composed together to play through a sequence or repeat endlessly. The best part is that they are incredibly easy to set up, so all you day-dreamers can coast through a lot of this chapter!

The Accelerometer

My neck muscles are getting huge like The Rock's

The **accelerometer** is another one of those fantastically simple things to incorporate into your project. If you're totally unfamiliar with that term, then wow, I get to introduce you to something really cool. Your iOS device knows which way it is being tilted via some tiny sensor. You can enable access of the accelerometer and get readings for the degree of tilt on the x, y and z axis. So take a moment to think about how many cool games are still yet to be developed using this sensor as the primary mechanism or "hook" in your game. Did you imagine anything more than marble-rolling and racing apps? Well if not, that's okay. Those are still popular games.

Like enabling touch input, we do the same thing in our **init** statement to get the accelerometer fired up:

```
-(id) init {

    if( (self=[super init])) {

        self.isAccelerometerEnabled = YES;

    }

    return self;

}
```

Next you can begin writing the method below, but it will probably write itself soon after you get started. This is one of those times when the code hinting will fill in exactly what you want right away. Once self.isAccelerometerEnabled is set to YES, the code block below will fire endlessly without you having to call it yourself:

```
-(void) accelerometer:(UIAccelerometer *)accelerometer didAccelerate:(UIAcceleration *)acceleration {

    CCLOG(@"Acceleration Values are, x: %f y:%f z:%f", acceleration.x , acceleration.y, acceleration.z );

}
```

The log statement is there to simply spit out the float values of the acceleration parameter along each axis. Testing in the iOS Simulator really won't do much for you since the Simulator has no accelerometer (don't try tilting your monitor to see a change in the Output window). Let's get you set up with a very small example project to test on an actual device.

We will slide a car across the screen, left or right, and change the image depending on whether we are balanced mid-screen, or tilted strongly to either side. My project is set to landscape mode, which is the default for the Cocos2d template, so even though I'll be tilting horizontally the acceleration.y value is the measurement I care about. Depending on the orientation, the acceleration value could vary from what you assume it to be.

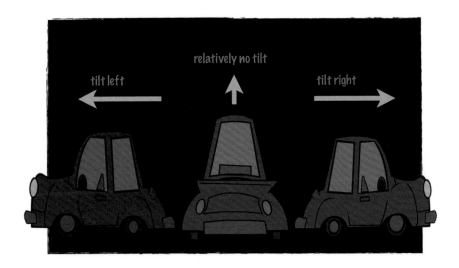

If you want to download the two images I'm using for this example, you can grab them at **www.focalpress.com/cw/Dike**.

So as usual, let's assume you use the Cocos2d template, and start in the header file …

In the HelloWorldLayer.h file

@interface HelloWorldLayer : CCLayer {

    CCSprite* car;

    int tiltHorizontal;
    // variable to store the value of the tilt

}

Then in the implementation file add the car CCSprite and schedule a method to run every 1/60th of a second:

Switch over to HelloWorldLayer.m

```
-( id ) init {

    if( (self=[super init])) {

        self.isAccelerometerEnabled = YES;

        car = [CCSprite spriteWithFile:@"car_backview.png"];

        car.position = ccp( 512 , 200 );

        [self addChild: car ];

        [self schedule:@selector(updateCar:) interval:1.0f/60.0f ];

    }

    return self;

}
```

Now let's return to the **accelerometer:** method. This time I'll use the tiltHorizontal variable declared in the header to keep the current value of the horizontal tilt. You might have noticed when testing before these acceleration values are small decimal numbers, so multiplying them by twenty makes them larger and because tiltHorizontal is an integer type, the values will become whole numbers after multiplication, which I think makes them easier to work with.

```
-(void) accelerometer:(UIAccelerometer *)accelerometer didAccelerate:(UIAcceleration *)acceleration {

        tiltHorizontal = acceleration.y * 20;
        // multiply by 20 to make the number a bit more useable

        CCLOG(@"tiltHorizontal is %i", tiltHorizontal);
        // if you want to see the current value

}
```

Now we will write the method we scheduled in the **init** statement. We are simply checking the value of tiltHorizontal and if it is a low integer in the range of -1 to 1, then the CCSprite texture is returned to the *car_backview.png* image. Otherwise, if the value is greater than 2 or less than -2, we change to the side view image, flip the image, and slide one direction or the other by changing the position.

```
-(void) updateCar:(ccTime) delta {
    if (tiltHorizontal <= 1 && tiltHorizontal >= -1) {
        // Relatively NO TILT
        [car setTexture:[ [CCSprite spriteWithFile:@"car_backview.png"] texture] ];
        // switch to back view of the image
    } else if (tiltHorizontal >= 2) {
        // TILTED LEFT
        [car setTexture:[ [CCSprite spriteWithFile:@"car_sideview.png"] texture] ];
        // switch to side view of the image
        car.flipX = YES;
        // flipped
        car.position = ccp (car.position.x—5, car.position.y );
        // subtract 5 points from the x position of the car
    } else if (tiltHorizontal <= -2) {
        // TILTED RIGHT
        [car setTexture:[ [CCSprite spriteWithFile:@"car_sideview.png"] texture] ];
        // switch to side view of the image
        car.flipX = NO;
        // flip back to normal
        car.position = ccp (car.position.x + 5, car.position.y );
        // add 5 points from the x position of the car
    }
}
```

That's it! You could obviously add a lot to this example, by adding more images for different ranges of the tiltHorizontal value. If you do run a proper test of this on your device, you'll notice you can slide the car right off either side and it won't stop. You could do something more polished with the accelerometer later, this is just a quick test.

Finally, I've been emailed by many students that tell me they have problems using the accelerometer values when an object's position is tied closely to the vertical tilt. For lack of a better term, by "vertical tilt," I mean the tilt toward or away from you when holding the device upright.

To imagine this problem best, suppose we programmed an overhead view labyrinth game with a marble that would move based on the x or y tilt. When the iPad was lying perfectly flat on a table, the acceleration values would be as close to zero as possible, and the marble wouldn't be rolling. Except most people don't ever hold their device perfectly flat, or even close to flat.

For a comfortable gaming experience, we would have to program in an offset for the vertical tilt to account for how most people usually hold their device. This isn't hard, but it's often something that beginners don't think to try. So suppose we did want to include a variable called tiltVertical. In our **accelerometer** method, we could add just a bit to the acceleration.x value before multiplying it:

tiltVertical = (acceleration.x + 0.6) * 20;

offset the tilt

Of course this is something you would need to adjust depending on the game, and how you think most people will be holding the device. As I type this now, I'm slouching to the point that my elbows are about even with my shoulders, so if extreme slackers like myself are your target gamer, then I have no idea what to tell you is a good offset value.

Section 2

Basic CCActions

This seems crazy now, but **CCActions** were not something I used in my first Cocos2d projects. I have a bad habit of *not* looking for easier solutions to things I know I could code with a little time. You'll run into this situation at times too: do you spend 10 minutes programming your own convenience methods, or 10 minutes searching the Internet or documentation for an existing one.

Had I done a little more research prior to starting my first apps (or more thoroughly read my own collection of guide books) I probably would have used CCActions a lot more. Hey, time makes fools of us all, right?

CCActions are classes, but you can think of them more like ***orders*** given to an object (any CCNode really) to do something. So if the order is to, "Get moving!," that object will move, or jump, or scale, and so on. Most of the basic actions have two variations in the class name: "By" and "To." For example, **CCMoveTo** and **CCMoveBy**. Consider the difference if you were on a football field and I ordered you to, "Move forward by 20 yards," versus, "Move to 20 yards." In the first case, you would start running 20 yards from wherever you were. In the second case, you would look down at your current place on the field, locate the 20 yard line, and start running to that spot. In which case, you might be running for a lot longer than just 20 yards, depending on where you started from.

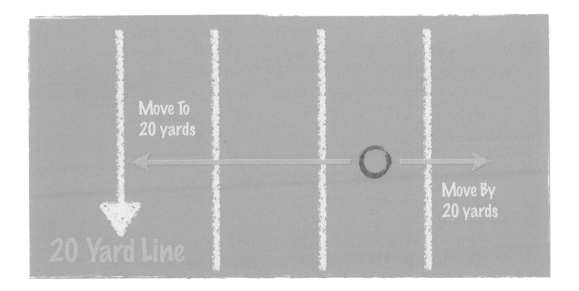

Get used to the difference now, because when prepping the example project for this section, I made the mistake a couple times of using **By** when I meant **To,** and vice versa. It's a harmless problem, but it'll leave you scratching your head at runtime if you mix them up.

Actions typically have a duration parameter, so you can set how long they take to do their action. Duration actions can be paused, resumed, stopped, even reversed. We do have some instant actions as well, which occur immediately.

Multiple actions can be performed in a sequence, or spawned all together. You can even **tag** actions. So you can see we've got a lot to talk about in this section.

Running a Position Action

The basic way to run an action is with two lines of code. The first line has no reference at all to the object we will eventually apply the action to. For example:

CCMoveTo* move = [CCMoveTo **actionWithDuration**:3.0 **position**: ccp (200, 200)];

We're only dealing with the class now. Like any instance of a class we give it a variable name, in this case, move seems appropriate. CCMoveTo, like most other CCAction instances, is initialized with **actionWithDuration**, followed by any other parameters. Your code hinting in Xcode will save you a lot of time if you don't have a nice reference book by your side like this one, because if you just begin writing *"actionWithDuration"* after the class name, you'll see the parameters the class expects.

Then to apply the action to a node you'll write the line below (in this case, just assume ninja is a CCSprite):

[ninja **runAction**:move];

Pretty easy, huh. Let's write it again with a CCMoveBy action instead:

CCMoveBy* move = [CCMoveBy **actionWithDuration**:3.0 **position**: ccp (-100, 0)];

[ninja **runAction**:move];

Aside from the class name change, I only changed the position values. Before I was moving *to* a location value of x:200 and y:200. This time I'm ***moving by* negative 100 on the x, and 0 on the y**. So the object would be moving to the left on the x axis, and the end position on the y axis would be unchanged. Make sense? All the upcoming position actions will run in the same way.

More Position Actions

The **CCJumpBy** and **CCJumpTo** actions are clever ones made with us game programmers in mind. The same **actionWithDuration** and **position** parameters are followed by a **height** parameter that determines how high a jump to the end position will be during the move, and the **jumps** parameter sets how many jumping movements will occur during the action.

CCJumpTo *jumpTo = [CCJumpTo **actionWithDuration**:3.0 **position**: ccp(300, 0) **height**:100 **jumps**: 3];

    // jumps to exact position x:300,y:0

[ninja **runAction**: jumpTo];

```
CCJumpBy *jumpBy = [CCJumpBy actionWithDuration:3.0 position: ccp(300, 0)
height:100 jumps: 3];
    // jumps 300 forward, no y change
[ninja runAction: jumpBy];
```

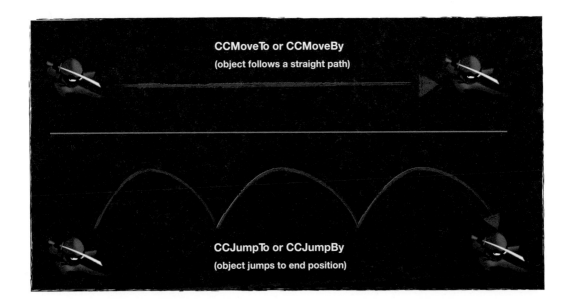

Keep in mind, you could run a CCJumpBy action that leaves the position unchanged using ccp(0 , 0) if all you wanted from the action was to show the object jumping up and down to a certain height. This could come in handy if you wanted to show damage to a character without affecting the end location.

The **CCBezierBy** and **CCBezierTo** actions require a little bit extra work but the payoff is pretty sweet. If you aren't familiar with Bézier curves, to put it simply, they are smooth paths. So our object will travel along in a smooth motion to the end position. To set this up, we first need to define the path.

```
ccBezierConfig path;
path.controlPoint_1 = ccp( 0, 600 );
path.controlPoint_2 = ccp( 600, 0 );
path.endPosition = ccp( 600, 600 );
```

After creating the ccBezierConfig variable, we set positions values for two control points and the end position. Our path variable doesn't need a starting point because that will be determined by the object we run the action on.

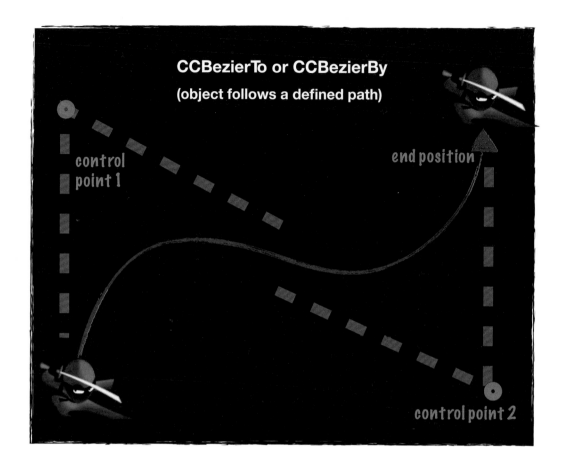

CCBezierTo or CCBezierBy

(object follows a defined path)

control point 1

end position

control point 2

Notice how in my diagram the control points basically tug on the path to bend it. Think of them like little gravitational tractor beams. If you have trouble imagining where your control points should be, well guess what? There's an app for that. Check out the free Sprite Path Designer app. In the app, you can add more than two control points, but our ccBezierConfig only requires two. Next, we just setup the action with the path variable.

CCBezierTo* bezierMove = [CCBezierBy **actionWithDuration**:4.0 **bezier**: path];

[ninja **runAction**: bezierMove];

Again, the same code can be run with the CCBezierBy class where the positions of the curve are relative to the initial starting position. So the endPosition would be 600 to the right and 600 up from the object.

Last up for the position actions, we've got a rather unglamorous one with **CCPlace**. This just moves the object instantly:

CCPlace* place = [CCPlace **actionWithPosition**: ccp(600,300)];

[ninja **runAction**: place];

This action might seem kind of pointless when you consider that you could just change the .position property instead. That's true but CCPlace is useful in an action sequence. You might move and rotate an object then place it somewhere when the first two actions are done running.

Rotation Actions

The **CCRotateBy** and **CCRotateTo** actions are a fantastic way to rotate to a specific degree or rotate a set number of degrees over a duration.

CCRotateTo* rotateTo = [CCRotateTo **actionWithDuration**:1.5 angle:180];

// will end at a rotation value of 180 degrees after 1.5 seconds

[ninja **runAction**: rotateTo];

CCRotateBy* rotateBy = [CCRotateBy **actionWithDuration**:1.5 angle:50];

// will end at a rotation value of 50 degrees MORE than the initial rotation

[ninja **runAction**: rotateBy];

Scale Actions

The **CCScaleTo** and **CCScaleBy** actions work exactly like their class names imply. Remember, your default scale is 1.0, so setting the **scale** to 2.0 would double the size and 0.5 would make the object half it's original size.

CCScaleBy* scaleBy = [CCScaleBy **actionWithDuration**:5.0 **scale**:2.0];

// would double the size, then double again if you ran this twice

[ninja **runAction**: scaleBy];

CCScaleTo* scaleTo = [CCScaleTo **actionWithDuration**:5.0 **scale**: 0.5];

// would go exactly to half the initial size

[ninja **runAction**: scaleTo];

Visibility Actions

The first three of these are **instant actions**, so they perform immediately. They also don't require any parameters. So let's look at all three quickly:

CCShow* show = [CCShow **action**];

> // doesn't need a parameter, you just write
> "action" after the class name in brackets.

[ninja **runAction**: show];

> // will show the object if it's visibility was hidden

CCHide* hide = [CCHide **action**];

[tank **runAction**: hide];

> // will hide the object if it's visibility was on

CCToggleVisibility* toggle = [CCToggleVisibility **action**];

[lightBulb **runAction**: toggle];

> // will toggle the visibility, if it was on before, it will be off now, and vice versa

> These four visibility actions are essentially just affecting the **.visible** property of your CCNodes. So if you set the **.opacity** property to **0**, don't expect the **CCShow** action to have any affect on the opacity. It would still be at **0** affectively keeping your object hidden.

CCShow and CCHide are pretty obvious. They show or hide the object. CCToggleVisibility is an interesting one because it will hide a visible object or show a hidden object depending on the current state. So if you wanted to show a blinking light bulb, you could just repeat this action endlessly. We'll talk more about repeating actions in the next section, but you could do this with what you already have learned, by performing the same delayed method over and over again. In that method you would just run this action. "If only there was an action just for blinking …"

Finally, we've got **CCBlink** which (can you guess) makes a node blink. I use CCSprites a lot for examples, but don't forget these actions can be applied to all CCNodes, so layers or scenes can also have actions applied to them. CCBlink is an interval action, so it has a duration parameter:

CCBlink* blink = [CCBlink **actionWithDuration**: 5.0 blinks:50];

> // will blink 50 times in 5 seconds

[eyes **runAction**: blink];

Opacity Actions

Cocos2d has three opacity actions: **CCFadeTo**, **CCFadeOut**, and **CCFadeIn**. Unlike the visibility actions that toggled the .visible property, these are working with the .opacity property of your CCNode, which has a range of 0 (not visible) to 255 (fully opaque):

CCFadeTo* fadeTo = [CCFadeTo **actionWithDuration**:5.0 **opacity**:125];

    // will fade to an opacity of 125 over 5 seconds

[ninja **runAction**: fadeTo];

CCFadeIn* fadeIn = [CCFadeIn **actionWithDuration**:3.0];

    // fades in after 3 seconds, your object will begin from an opacity of 0

[ninja **runAction**: fadeIn];

CCFadeOut* fadeOut = [CCFadeOut **actionWithDuration**:30.0];

    // fades out after 30 seconds, your object will begin from an opacity of 255

[ninja **runAction**: fadeOut];

Tint Actions

You can tint your objects using **CCTintTo** and **CCTintBy** . The big point to remember here is that your default color values are **red**:255, **green**:255 and **blue**:255 . So lowering that number removes some of that color. Both code blocks below would set the objects tint to full **green** and remove the **red** and **blue** color.

CTintTo* tintTo = [CCTintTo **actionWithDuration**:1.0 **red**:0 **green**:255 **blue**:0];

    // tints to full green by setting red and blue to 0

[drunkDude **runAction**: tintTo];

CCTintBy* tintBy = [CCTintBy **actionWithDuration**: 1.0 **red**:-255 **green**:0 **blue**:-255];

    // tints to full green by setting negative 255 for both red and blue

[sicklyGuy **runAction**: tintBy];

Stopping Actions

Let's get these actions under our iron-fisted control. First, let's stop them. We can do this in a few ways. The easiest thing to do would be to kill every action on a particular object. So if you had more than one running on a ninja sprite, they would all stop with this line:

[ninja **stopAllActions**] ;

> // removes all actions

If we wanted to pick out a specific action to remove, we would either need to use the instance name or identify the action by tag. For this example, I'll write code for both options. In a header file, declare move:

CCMoveTo* move;

> // declare the variable, you know where to write this by now

Now in a method in the implementation file we would write:

move = [CCMoveTo **actionWithDuration**:3.0 **position**: ccp (200, 200)];
move.tag – 12345;

> // give the action a tag to identify it with.

[ninja **runAction**:move];

To stop the action, I could use any of these 3 lines:

[ninja **stopAction**: move];

> // note we could write ninja or self here.

[ninja **stopActionByTag**: 12345];
[ninja **performSelector**:@selector(**stopAction**:) **withObject**: move
afterDelay:2.0f];

> // stops after 2 seconds

Pausing/Resuming Actions

Instead of completely stopping actions on an object we can pause them instead. For this we will call a method on the **CCActionManager** class:

[[CCActionManager **sharedManager**] **pauseTarget**: ninja] ;

To resume all those previously running actions we would simply write:

[[CCActionManager **sharedManager**] **resumeTarget**: ninja] ;

Easing Actions

Your actions that occur over time can also be run with an easing effect to add a little spice or realism to their movement. Think about a car moving, it doesn't start and stop at a constant speed. Below is a list of the easing effects you can add, and we'll add one of these next:

CCEaseBackIn	CCEaseBackOut	CCEaseBackInOut
CCEaseBounceIn	CCEaseBounceOut	CCEaseBounceInOut
CCEaseElasticIn	CCEaseElasticOut	CCEaseElasticInOut
CCEaseExponentialIn	CCEaseExponentialOut	CCEaseExponentialInOut
CCEaseIn	CCEaseOut	CCEaseInOut
CCEaseSineIn	CCEaseSineOut	CCEaseSineInOut

To add an easing effect, we will set up the primary action first, then create the easing action.

CCScaleBy* scaleBy = [CCScaleBy **actionWithDuration**:5.0 **scale**:2.0];

CCEaseBounceIn* bounce = [CCEaseBounceIn **actionWithAction**: scaleBy];

[ninja **runAction**: bounce];

> *// notice after **runAction**: we write **bounce** here instead of **scaleBy***

Pretty easy huh? I'm not going to document every easing effect, because that's way too much typing. Most of them you just need to run to really understand what they do. Although, I will show you one last example because this includes a **rate**: parameter, which effects how noticeable the easing is.

CCScaleBy* scaleBy = [CCScaleBy **actionWithDuration**:5.0 **scale**:2.0];

CCEaseIn* easeIn = [CCEaseIn **actionWithAction**: scaleBy **rate**:10];

[ninja **runAction**: easeIn];

There's more fun actions coming up soon, but I should note before this section ends that another beautiful thing about Cocos2d is that your actions get cleaned up for you. So when an action ends, it is automatically released.

Composing Actions

Time to practice my real love: breaking than repairing violins

The next four actions we'll look at are termed **composition actions** because they allow us to group together a series of actions and run them in sequence, all at once, or repeat them.

For you skim readers, this section is an important one, because it **will** save you time programming down the road. Games are full of small events that happen a lot. A perfect example (which we will code later) is a score that appears over the top of an enemy that has been killed. We've all seen it before, the points float over the top for a second and fade away. That isn't the hardest thing to program without using CCActions, but let's face it, every project has a level of fatigue after a while.

Towards the end of a job, you might not feel like going that extra mile to add the small things that'll really make your game terrific. Instead of programming a nice point score effect, you might be lazy and just tally up the points in the top right corner. I think this is where actions are so useful. They don't take much coding at all, and when you need a quick solution to add something extra, they are perfect.

First up is **CCSequence**, which is simply a list of actions that will be executed one after another in the order you define. For example:

id move1 = [CCMoveBy **actionWithDuration**:0.5 **position**: ccp(0, 50)];

id move2 = [CCMoveBy **actionWithDuration**:0.5 **position**: ccp(0,-50)];

id sequence = [CCSequence **actions**: move1, move2, nil];

[player **runAction**: sequence];

// moves the player up then down 50 points

Whoa! The Matrix has changed all of a sudden. Why do we have id (anonymous object) now instead of CCMoveBy*? Well, it's shorter to write id. The disadvantage is that you couldn't assign the .tag property to the action, but I think tagging your actions is pretty rare. If you ever go searching forums for examples of actions, you'll usually see id. Even the official documentation of Cocos2D uses id. So don't be shocked if you see it used elsewhere. Let's examine the line with our new CCSequence:

id sequence = [CCSequence **actions**: move1, move2, nil];

… it should be pretty obvious what's going on. We list the actions that we want to run in order, then we just write nil at the end. Think of the nil like sealing an end cap on the list.

Finally, we just run the sequence action on player.

Before you have to raise your hand and ask this yourself, I'll do it for you … **What if you want to know when the action has finished?** Great question. That's where the **CCCallFunc** action comes in. It simply allows us to call a function (*ahem*, method) as one of the actions in our composition. Crowbar in the highlighted line below and add callFunc to your actions list.

id move1 = [CCMoveBy **actionWithDuration**:0.5 **position**: ccp(0, 50)];

id move2 = [CCMoveBy **actionWithDuration**:0.5 **position**: ccp(0,-50)];

id callFunc = [CCCallFunc **actionWithTarget**: self **selector**:@selector(**finishSeq**)];

id sequence = [CCSequence **actions**: move1, move2, callFunc, nil];

[player **runAction**: sequence];

    // moves the player up then down 50 points, THEN calls the finishSeq method

Then of course somewhere in your implementation file you'll need to write the **finishSeq** method. To keep it simple, you could just run a log statement that tells you the action finished:

```
-( void ) finishSeq {
        CCLOG( @"finished action!" );
}
```

Give it a test if you want and see that this works before we make a minor change. There's also a **CCCallFuncN** version that passes a sender parameter to the method you call. The sender is who the action was performed on. So in the example above, player was the sender. To use CCCallFuncN instead, note the two minor changes to the nearly identical line above:

id callFunc = [CCCallFuncN **actionWithTarget**: self **selector**:@selector(**finishSeq:**)];

Add "N".   Add a colon.

Now our **finishSeq:** method needs to include the sender parameter. I'll also change the log statement to spit out info on our sender. Right now is a perfect chance to do a little casting, because sender is just passed in as a generic id node. We would need to cast a new CCSprite as the sender if we wanted to do anything to it that was specific to CCSprites, like change the opacity property. Remember casting doesn't create a totally new object, we just have a new instance name that refers to the same object.

-(void) **finishSeq:** (id) sender {

    CCLOG(@"finished action on %@", sender);

    // output info on the sender

    CCLOG(@"the tag of the sender is %i", sender.tag);

    // output only the tag of the sender

    CCSprite* sprite = (CCSprite*) sender;

    // cast a proper CCSprite as the sender

    sprite.opacity = 150;

    // change the opacity for the heck of it

}

So try to imagine for a moment how important this CCCallFuncN action can be. What if instead of changing the opacity, we just removed the sender from the scene (casting wouldn't be necessary in that case). This is partially how we could set up something like a pop-up score that moves upwards, fades out, then removes itself at the end of the sequence.

Finally, there's one more variation of this with **CCCallFuncND** . That final "D" stands for **data** (I'm assuming). So you could pass in a little more **data** if you wanted to. In the line below, myData could be anything really. Another sprite, an integer, whatever.

Add "D"

id callFunc = [CCCallFuncND **actionWithTarget:** self **selector:**@selector
    (**finishSeq:data:**) **data:**(void*) myData];

Add all this exactly as is.

myData is any data you want to pass in.

The **finishSeq** method now looks like this:

```
-(void) finishSeq: (id)sender data:(void*)data {
    // etc ...
```

Just remember, you'll treat the data the same way you did the sender in the previous example. You'll need to do some casting since it came in as a void type.

Let's move on to our next composition action, **CCSpawn** allows us to run a bunch of actions at once.

```
id jump = [CCJumpBy actionWithDuration: 0.5 position: ccp(0, 0) height:100 jumps: 2];
id tint = [CCTintTo actionWithDuration:1.0 red:0 green:255 blue:0];
id spawn = [CCSpawn actions: jump, tint, nil];
[player runAction: spawn];
```

The set up is quite similar to CCSequence. The jump and tint actions will begin at the same time. Note though, the durations don't need to be the same. You could also perform the exact same spawn action by writing the code like so:

```
id spawn = [CCSpawn actions:
    [CCJumpBy actionWithDuration: 0.5 position: ccp(0, 0) height:100 jumps: 2],
    [CCTintTo actionWithDuration:1.0 red:0 green:255 blue:0],
    nil];
[player runAction: spawn];
```

I think for beginners it reads easier to see the code in the first style, so I'll keep writing it like that.

Next up, we've got **CCRepeat**, which as you can guess, will repeat a sequence a set number of times.

```
id fadeIn = [CCFadeIn actionWithDuration:3.0 ];
id fadeOut = [CCFadeOut actionWithDuration:3.0 ];
id sequence = [CCSequence actions: fadeIn, fadeOut, nil];
id repeat = [ CCRepeat actionWithAction: sequence times: 3];
    // repeats sequence 3 times
[ lightBulb runAction: repeat];
```

If you want a sequence to repeat forever, like a vampire stuck on a solar-powered ferris wheel, you can use **CCRepeatForever**. This looks nearly identical to CCRepeat but doesn't include the **times** parameter.

id fadeIn = [CCFadeIn **actionWithDuration**:3.0];

id fadeOut = [CCFadeOut **actionWithDuration**:3.0];

id sequence = [CCSequence **actions**: fadeIn, fadeOut, nil];

id repeat = [CCRepeatForever **actionWithAction**: sequence];

> // repeats sequence forever.

[lightBulb **runAction**: repeat];

Wait. That analogy doesn't really make sense. The vampire wouldn't last a day.

Finally, let's look at **CCDelayTime** and **reverse** . Cocos2D really does have everything. You've even got an action just meant for delaying time for the next action to begin. The handy **reverse** action will rewind the actions that end in "**By**," and some of the ones that end in "**To**" can also be reversed.

Here's an example using both CCDelayTime and **reverse**. The object will move up, stop for a moment, then go back down, and repeat the sequence forever:

id moveUp = [CCMoveBy **actionWithDuration**:2.0 **position**: ccp(0, 100)];

id delay = [CCDelayTime **actionWithDuration**:0.5];

id moveBack = [moveUp **reverse**];

id sequence = [CCSequence **actions**: moveUp, delay, moveBack, nil];

id repeat = [CCRepeatForever **actionWithAction**: sequence];

[boat **runAction**: repeat];

Here's little snippet for you. If you want to delay a random amount of time use this...

id delayRandomTime = [CCDelayTime **actionWithDuration: arc4random**( )% 5] ;

The delay range would be between 0 and 4 seconds.

Repeating Background with Actions

I could have included this in the last section, because we aren't doing much more than using the CCRepeatForever code from before, but I think this topic deserved it's own section for one reason. Every game programmer needs a repeating background at some point or another. Just so you don't have to dig deep to locate this code later, I'll make it easy to find with a dedicated section.

Example Pan: *Since the iPad is 1024 wide, my source image would **usually** be double that at 2048 wide, and include the same artwork on both sides.*

In prepping this example I learned a bit myself too. I've always approached looping backgrounds like an animator. I would group together two copies of the background art (one laying right next to the other) and pan them left or right. When the second background panned all the way across, I would just reset them both back to their initial positions and start panning again.

Hopefully my example images show that, but of course, I wouldn't write text on them, or include a line between the two images. That's just so you get the idea. Once these are moving together it should seem like a nice endless loop. I said "these" but most likely I would just import one image with double the art and animate the position.

We'll do something very similar in our project, but what I just learned is that I don't need my source image to actually include the background art twice. I don't need to use two sprites either.

What I can do is set the size of my CCSprite to be double the size of my image, then set the texture to just repeat in the space that my image doesn't cover. So my source image (which you can download from **www.focalpress.com/cw/Dike**) is 1024 by 1024, and notice in **this line below** the **rect** parameter I'm setting is screenWidth * 2 (or 2048). So exactly half that space would be empty unless we repeated the image. I should mention this example will work best in landscape mode. Follow the notes below, and I'll explain more in a moment:

In the init statement of your implementation file (or anywhere really) ...

CGSize size = [[CCDirector **sharedDirector**] **winSize**];

screenWidth = size.width;

screenHeight = size.height;

> *// set up the background image ...*

CCSprite* clouds = [CCSprite **spriteWithFile**:@"clouds.png" **rect:CGRectMake**
(0, 0, screenWidth * 2, screenHeight)];

ccTexParams params = { GL_LINEAR, GL_LINEAR, GL_REPEAT, GL_REPEAT };

> *// this repeats the image, note those are squiggly brackets*

[clouds.texture **setTexParameters**:&params];

> *// set the texture parameters to those above*

clouds.position = ccp(screenWidth , screenHeight / 2);

> *// x value is set to screenWidth, so this centers the image showing the left half only*

[self **addChild**: clouds **z:**-1];

> *// set up the looping animation ...*

CCMoveBy* move = [CCMoveBy **actionWithDuration**:20.0 **position:** ccp(screenWidth * -1, 0)];

> *// moves BY the negative value of screenWidth*

```
CCPlace* place = [CCPlace actionWithPosition: ccp( screenWidth , screenHeight / 2) ];
    // places the image back where it started
CCSequence* sequence = [CCSequence actions: move, place, nil];
    // set up the sequence
CCRepeatForever* repeat = [CCRepeatForever actionWithAction: sequence];
    // repeat the sequence forever
[clouds runAction: repeat];
    // apply it to the clouds
```

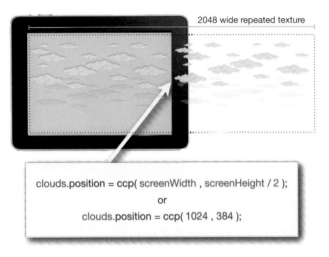

2048 wide repeated texture

clouds.position = ccp(screenWidth , screenHeight / 2);

or

clouds.position = ccp(1024 , 384);

As you can see, a lot of this code is conveniently tied to the screenWidth value. Notice that the initial value of clouds.position and the CCPlace action both use the screenWidth value for the x position. If that's a little confusing, just remember that our clouds sprite is double the size of the screen width. So setting the x position to screenWidth (or 1024 in this case) puts the first half of the image in the viewable area of the screen, as illustrated to the right.

Our CCMoveBy action, moves the sprite *by* negative 1 multiplied by the screenWidth. Note the previous emphasis, I'm not moving it *to* that value. So the action will subtract 1024 on the x axis, and make no change on the y axis.

After the move, we just place the sprite back to the initial position again, and everything repeats from there.

So what if you wanted multiple layers of clouds?

Easy, just duplicate the previous code and change some variable names to protect the innocent. Then to really achieve a nice effect include another image with smaller clouds, and slow down the duration of the move action. Set those smaller clouds behind the initial ones and you'll have a smooth realistic scene. Well, as real as 8-bit style clouds can be.

Download the source project at **www.focalpress.com/cw/Dike**.

Point Score FX
with Actions

Like the repeating background, I'll highlight this bit of code with it's own section because I think it's an important one (and fun). What we'll do here is pass a CGPoint value to a convenience method, which pops up a point score that floats up and fades away from an object. Once faded, the points will be removed from the scene. So this could be useful any time your player killed an enemy. The enemy sprite's location would be the CGPoint we pass into our method.

To add a little extra fun to this example, we'll write two convenience methods, one that uses an image for the point score, and another that uses **CCLabelTTF**, which lets you load a TrueType Font ("**TTF**") and display the score as label instead of an image. In a later chapter, I'll show you how to include custom fonts, but for now this will give you a soft introduction to using the CCLabelTTF class.

First let's work with images for the point scores. Grab these from **www.focalpress.com/cw/Dike** and add them to your Resources ... *100points.png 500points.png 1000points.png 5000points.png* ... then in your implementation file add the two following methods.

```
-(void) pointsWithPosition:(CGPoint) pos andValue:(int) value {

    CCSprite* points = [CCSprite spriteWithFile:[NSString stringWithFormat:
    @"%ipoints.png", value ]];
    // %i gets replaced by value

    points.position = ccp( pos.x , pos.y + 100 );
    // places the sprite above the CGPoint we passed in

    [self addChild: points];

    CCFadeOut* fade = [CCFadeOut actionWithDuration:1.5 ];
    // fades out

    CCMoveBy* move = [CCMoveBy actionWithDuration:1.0 position: ccp( 0, 100 )];
    // moves upwards

    CCCallFuncN* remove =[CCCallFuncN actionWithTarget: self
    selector:@selector(removePoints:)];

    CCSpawn* spawn = [CCSpawn actions: fade, move, nil];
    // runs both the fade and move at once

    CCSequence* sequence = [CCSequence actions: spawn, remove, nil];
    // after the spawn finishes, we remove the sprite

    [points runAction: sequence];

}

-(void) removePoints:(id)sender {

    CCLOG(@"removing sender");
    // unnecessary but if I fade out an object, I like to make sure it is actually being
    removed

    [self removeChild: sender cleanup: NO];
    // removes the sender

}
```

With everything you *should* already know, that code is hopefully easy to read, but let's talk about this line:

```
CCSprite* points = [CCSprite spriteWithFile:[NSString stringWithFormat:
@"%ipoints.png", value ]];
```

Value replaces %i

It might look a little confusing, but it's a great way to show a different image based on the value variable without using a switch or if statement. Keep in mind, our images are named **100points.png, 500points.png** and so on. So if we called our method using this line:

[self **pointsWithPosition:** enemy.position **andValue:** 100 **];**

Then the file used for the points sprite would be **100points.png** . The only danger here is that you end up with a blank image if you pass in a value that doesn't have a corresponding file name. Let's get real though, you fell asleep programming if you let that mistake happen.

Also of note, in the **pointsWithPosition** method, you might have noticed a CCSpawn action is part of my CCSequence action. Since CCSpawn runs multiple actions at once, which could be of varying lengths, the overall duration is determined by the longest action. In this example, the longest duration is 1.5 seconds for the fade action, so in the CCSequence the remove action won't occur until the fade finishes.

Finally, you can see that I'm using the CCCallFuncN instead of the plainer CCCallFunc, which means I'm passing the sender parameter into my **removePoints** method. The sender is the points sprite, so that is what gets removed. Since this method isn't doing much other than removing the sender, on a large project you might want to change the method name to be something more generic, since you could reuse it in other cases where you simply need to remove an object.

Now let's write almost all of this code again, but instead use a CCLabelTTF for the points. The only change other than the method name has been circled:

-(void) **labelWithPosition:**(CGPoint) pos **andValue:**(int) value {

```
CCLabelTTF* points = [CCLabelTTF labelWithString:[NSString
stringWithFormat:@"%i", value] fontName:@"Marker Felt" fontSize: 30];
```

```
    points.position = ccp( pos.x , pos.y + 100 );
    [self addChild: points];
    CCFadeOut* fade = [CCFadeOut actionWithDuration:1.5 ];
    CCMoveBy* move = [CCMoveBy actionWithDuration:1.0 position: ccp( 0, 100 )];
    CCCallFuncN* remove =[CCCallFuncN actionWithTarget: self
    selector:@selector(removePoints:)];
    CCSpawn* spawn = [CCSpawn actions: fade, move, nil];
    CCSequence* sequence = [CCSequence actions: spawn, remove, nil];
    [points runAction: sequence];
}
```

So this time we are using value as the actual text in the label. If you didn't want to use a value at all, then passing in that parameter is pointless, but you could write this instead **labelWithString**:@"good job!". Then **fontName**: is obviously the name of the font. **Marker Felt** is a good comic book type font that is installed on iOS devices. Finally, the **fontSize** is an obvious parameter too.

The advantage to using a label instead of an image is now we can pass in *any* value when we call the method. For example:

[self **pointsWithPosition:** enemy.position **andValue:** 90210 **]**;

You could also set the text of a label at any time by simply calling **setString**, like so:

[points **setString**:@"hi!"];

Test Your Skills

This won't be a difficult test, but it will give you a little something to try this section. Play the movie at **www.focalpress.com/cw/Dike**, and notice how the label behaves. It changes text before fading away. Recreate that, and you'll have made these pixel farmers very happy.

3D and Effects Actions

Are you tired of reading about actions yet? I'm a little tired of writing about them, but that's why I've saved the coolest ones for last. To welcome them in as part of our awesome *Arsenal of Cocos2d*, I've put together a Weapons Board project, so when we tap on one of these nine weapons it will play one or more of these slick actions. I've had this artwork drawn for almost ten years now, so I'll shamelessly keep milking it (and why am I confessing that?).

I realize this screenshot looks a lot like a menu of buttons to press and essentially it is, but there's also a CCMenu class that we'll look at later. For now, this project just tests the touch location against the boundingBox property of each CCSprite weapon icon. They are named weapon1, weapon2 and so on. The background, text, and character are all one image. Since this is a lot of artwork, I won't upload it in pieces to the server, but I'll have the final project linked up at the end of the section and you can pull images from that.

The main focus here isn't on creating a weapons board, instead we just want to see these special actions working. Prior to teaching this section, I hadn't used *any* of these, so I was pleasantly surprised by each one. Other than some scattered YouTube videos, I couldn't find a great repository of each of these actions working well, so I'll add a link to some reference movies of each effect we talk about.

First off, go over to your project's **AppDelegate.m** file and find this block:

// Create an CCGLView with a RGB565 color buffer, and a depth buffer of 0-bits
CCGLView *glView = [CCGLView **viewWithFrame:**[window_ **bounds**]
pixelFormat: kEAGLColorFormatRGBA8
    // previously this was kEAGLColorFormatRGB565

The big change we need to make is switching kEAGLColorFormatRGB565 to kEAGLColorFormatRGBA8. You'll also find a **depthFormat** setting at zero.

Accelerometer and Actions

I've read people suggest upping that for 3D effects, **but** in my testing none of the effects looked better and most looked worse at anything higher than zero. Next make changes to this block if you're using Cocos2d v2.x :

// 2D projection

// [director_ setProjection:kCCDirectorProjection2D];

// delete this line or just comment it out

[director_ **setProjection**: kCCDirectorProjection3D];

// uncomment this line

Be sure that director_ has the underscore after it. Now you're ready to go!

Let's get started with **CCShaky3D**, which animates a shaky effect. For all these examples, I'll run them with a CCRepeatForever action just so they keep playing for a while. Also, I'll write weapon for the object they are running on, but in the example movies, which you can find at **www.focalpress.com/cw/Dike**, I'll change this object to add some variety.

CCShaky3D* shaky = [CCShaky3D **actionWithRange**:10 **shakeZ**: NO **grid**: ccg(20,20) **duration**: 5];

CCRepeatForever* repeat = [CCRepeatForever **actionWithAction**: shaky];

[weapon **runAction**: repeat];

Let's pick apart that first line, **actionWithRange** is basically just the intensity of the effect. Lower that number to 1 and you'll barely notice the effect. Raise it up and you'll see the effect get even crazier. Then **shakeZ** is a bool parameter, which enables the effect on the z axis. I set it to NO because I didn't notice a major change. The **duration** parameter is obviously the number of seconds. If you plan on repeating the action forever you might wonder why you would set the duration very long at all, but when the action loops it is sometimes noticeable, so you might want to set a high duration for that reason.

Finally, the big thing to talk about is the **grid**. Every time I read that, I can hear Jeff Bridges from Daft Punk's TRON: Legacy soundtrack saying "The Grid." So if you want to set the mood for these examples, skip to Track 2 on the album. Most of these actions ask for a grid setting, and I've found 20 by 20 runs smoothly and plays the effect in a believable way. In other words, I don't notice The Grid.

So what is the grid? What does it look like? Ships, motorcycles? Nope. it's just squares. In fact, if you haven't adjusted your **AppDelegate.m** file, you will come face to face with The Grid just like I did when I took this screenshot (see facing page). All those black squares will **not** be there if your **pixelFormat** is kEAGLColorFormatRGBA8.

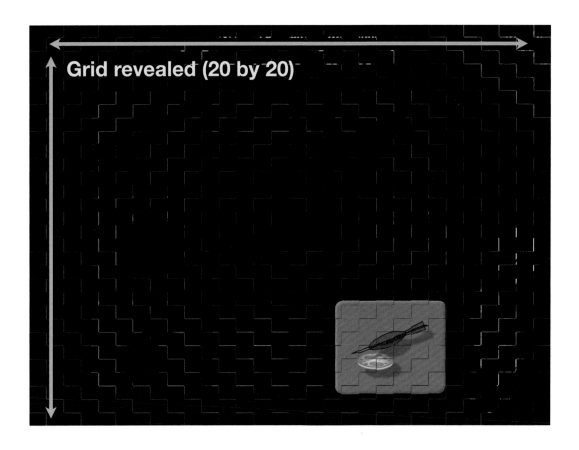

Grid revealed (20 by 20)

Conveniently though, this provides a great example of The Grid. If you were to count the number of squares from left to right and top to bottom it would be twenty and twenty. Most of these actions don't show The Grid as noticeably as this particular tile effect in the screen grab, but they do break the scene down into square chunks to bend and play with. So the fewer squares in your grid the more clunky the effect will be. On the other hand, the more you use, the more resource intensive the action is. So again, I found that 20, 20 is a good starting point, and then you can tweak the effect as you like.

Continuing on, let's look at the **CCWaves** and **CCWaves3D** actions.

CCWaves* waves = [CCWaves **actionWithWaves**:5 **amplitude**:20
                horizontal:YES **vertical**:NO **grid**: ccg(20,20)
                duration: 5.0];

repeat = [CCRepeatForever **actionWithAction**: waves];

[weapon **runAction**: repeat];

```
CCWaves3D* waves = [CCWaves3D actionWithWaves:5
                    amplitude:25 grid: ccg(20, 20)
                    duration: 2.0];
repeat = [CCRepeatForever actionWithAction: waves];
[weapon runAction: repeat];
```

As you can see these are pretty similar. Adjust the **actionWithWaves** or **amplitude** parameters to change the number of waves in the duration and intensity. The CCWaves3D action appears much smoother to me and more like a waving flag.

Next, let's look at **CCFlipX3D** and **CCFlipY3D**, these are so similar I'll just show you the x axis version. In the example code below (and movie example on the website) , I'm running a **reverse** action in the sequence to send the weapon icon back in place. Then it repeats endlessly.

```
CCFlipX3D* flip = [CCFlipX3D actionWithDuration:3.0];
CCSequence* sequence = [CCSequence actions: flip,
[flip reverse], nil];
CCRepeatForever* repeat = [CCRepeatForever actionWithAction:
sequence];
[weapon runAction: repeat];
```

Next up, is **CCRipple3D**, my favorite because it looks like the heat signature from something really hot if the effect is subtle enough.

```
CCRipple3D* ripple = [CCRipple3D actionWithPosition:
weapon.position radius:
weapon.contentSize.width waves:3 amplitude:15 grid: ccg(40,40)
duration:8.0];
CCRepeatForever* repeat = [CCRepeatForever actionWithAction:
ripple];
[weapon runAction: repeat];
```

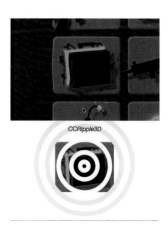

CCRipple3D

Since this action is creating a ripple and bending the object around that, it is asking for an **actionWithPosition** and **radius** for the ripple. You could use any location or size **radius**, in this example, I'm using the weapon.position and weapon.contentSize.width (approximately illustrated in the diagram). The other parameters are similar to the previous actions, but I changed the grid to 40 by 40 for a smoother effect.

Ready to get dizzy? Let's look at **CCTwirl**:

CCTwirl* twirl = [CCTwirl **actionWithPosition**:
weapon.position **twirls**:1 **amplitude**:3

grid: ccg(20, 20) **duration**:3.0];

CCRepeatForever* repeat =
[CCRepeatForever **actionWithAction**: twirl];

[weapon **runAction**: repeat];

Again, I'm using the center of the weapon icon for the **actionWithPosition** parameter. The **twirls** parameter is how many times the object will twirl in the given duration and the **amplitude** changes the intensity as usual. In the example movie, you can see the **amplitude** set to 0.5 then again at 3. The **grid** becomes a bit more noticeable at 3.

My second favorite, **CCLiquid** creates a fun watery effect.

CCLiquid* liquid = [CCLiquid **actionWithWaves**:5 **amplitude**:
20 **grid**: ccg(20,20) **duration**:3.0];

CCRepeatForever* repeat = [CCRepeatForever **actionWithAction**:
twirl];

[weapon **runAction**: repeat];

Experiment with the **actionWithWaves** and **amplitude** values to your liking.

Next, let's combine a few actions to save time. As you can see in the bonus movie (at **www.focalpress.com/cw/Dike**), the object moves like a wave, shakes at three different settings, then does two fade-out effects:

CCWavesTiles3D* tileWaves = [CCWavesTiles3D **actionWithWaves**:3 **amplitude**:15
grid:ccg(20,20) **duration**:5]

CCShakyTiles3D* shaky = [CCShakyTiles3D **actionWithRange**:4 **shakeZ**: YES
grid:ccg(20,20) **duration**:1.0];

CCShakyTiles3D* shaky2 = [CCShakyTiles3D **actionWithRange**:10 **shakeZ**: YES
grid:ccg(20,20) **duration**:1.0];

CCShakyTiles3D* shaky3 = [CCShakyTiles3D **actionWithRange**:20 **shakeZ**: YES
grid:ccg(20,20) **duration**:1.0];

CCFadeOutBLTiles* tileEffect = [CCFadeOutBLTiles **actionWithSize**: ccg(20,20)
duration:2.0];

    // tiles fade from the Bottom Left "BL"

id reverseTiles = [tileEffect **reverse**];

  // *reverse the previous action*

CCFadeOutTRTiles* tileEffect2 = [CCFadeOutTRTiles
actionWithSize: ccg(20,20) **duration**:2.0];

  // *tiles fade from the Top Right "TR"*

id reverseTiles2 = [tileEffect2 **reverse**];

  // *reverse the previous action*

CCSequence* sequence = [CCSequence **actions**: tileWaves,
shaky, shaky2, shaky3, tileEffect, reverseTiles, tileEffect2,
reverseTiles2, nil];

CCRepeatForever* repeat = [CCRepeatForever **actionWithAction**:
sequence];

[weapon **runAction**: repeat];

Finally, I've prepared one more sequence of tiled actions. This time you'll see a jump effect, quick shattering, shuffle (which moves the tiles across the screen and back again using the **reverse** action), column split, row split, and two more fade effects (which look like window blinds closing).

CCJumpTiles3D* jump = [CCJumpTiles3D **actionWithJumps**:3 **amplitude**:10 **grid**:
ccg(30,30) **duration**:5];

CCShatteredTiles3D* shatter = [CCShatteredTiles3D **actionWithRange**:20 **shatterZ**: NO
grid: ccg(20,20) **duration**:0.2];

CCShuffleTiles* shuffle = [CCShuffleTiles **actionWithSize**: ccg(20,20) **duration**:2];

id reverse = [shuffle **reverse**];

CCSplitCols* split = [CCSplitCols **actionWithCols**:30 **duration**:2.0];

CCSplitRows* split2 = [CCSplitRows **actionWithRows**:30 **duration**:2.0];

CCFadeOutDownTiles* fade = [CCFadeOutDownTiles **actionWithSize**: ccg(20,20)
duration:4.0];

CCFadeOutUpTiles* fade2 = [CCFadeOutUpTiles **actionWithSize**: ccg(20,20) **duration**:4.0];

CCSequence* sequence = [CCSequence **actions**: jump, shatter, shuffle, reverse, split,
split2, fade, fade2, nil];

CCRepeatForever* repeat = [CCRepeatForever **actionWithAction**: sequence];

[weapon **runAction**: repeat];

There's a couple more actions I'll let you explore on your own. **CCLens3D**, which I couldn't get to animate, and **CCTurnOffTiles**, which makes the tiles disappear.

When stopping these type actions you'll probably want to keep the object visible and return it to it's original non-transformed state. Just stopping the action can still leave the grid visible, so you'll need to call **setGrid** with a value of nil. Here's the complete reset code:

[self **stopAction**: repeat];

> // first stop the action .... You'll probably need to declare the **CCRepeatForever*** **repeat** in your header

[weapon **setGrid**: nil];

> // set the grid to nil and the object will go back to it's original non-transformed state

That brings us to the end of Chapter 6. Do you feel like an Action Hero now? If so, I salute you. You can grab the source files for this project at **www.focalpress.com/cw/Dike**, just look for the *Actions_3D_SpecialFX* folder.

Chapter 7

Animation and Particle FX

We've come to this chapter at last!

Animation, and the icing on the cake, Particle FX! Both can add a TON of life to your application. Particles are incredibly easy to use, and they look really impressive for just a few lines of code. For you skim readers, don't miss the movie examples of those, which you can find at **www.focalpress.com/cw/Dike**. Even if you just add a glowing sun to the background of your game, it'll be worth it.

As for animation, I can hear some of you non-animators groaning, "Ugh, I can barely draw one frame, and now you want more!" While others of you might be thinking "Aww, great, I have to buy some Sprite Sheet software to work with." Nobody panic. I'll try my best this chapter to keep everyone happy. Animation is NOT a big deal.

Animation Pep Talk

Animation is not difficult. Whoops, I hear people screaming at me. **Great** animation is very difficult. Just **okay** animation is not hard. I started my career as a Flash animator. One of the first. Stop laughing, I really was. This was a LONG time ago. The Internet was going crazy over this new thing called Flash Player, it came pre-installed in absolutely nothing, but it could make lengthy animations at sizes that even dial-up Internet users could handle. I was hired by a toy company that wanted to make weekly 2 to 3 minute cartoons featuring their products. Yeah, weekly. What our rag-tag little crew of Flash animators realized early on was: (1) it was impossible; (2) we had to cut a lot of corners to get anything done on time. Oddly enough though, the less-is-more approach to animation often looked as good or better than when we pushed ourselves to do things we really couldn't at the time.

For an example of what I mean, take a look at the example movie for Chapter 7 at **www.focalpress.com/cw/Dike**. Does the character convey a sense of shadiness? Do those shifty eyes make you think he's up to no good? Well keep in mind, this is only four different frames. One blink, and three changes of the eyes. Yet for a few seconds, these four frames accomplished all I needed. Obviously, it's not difficult to move around some eyeballs.

Now, take a look at the next movie at the same URL and tell me if the situation for our little green-haired punk has got any better:

Looks pretty bad for him, huh? The character hasn't changed, I've only added four circles in the background. They are just blurry red and blue circles moving like police siren lights.

This is the type of corner-cutting we would rely on at my old animation studio. It looks good and it took 10 minutes to make. Even if you aren't a trained animator, you can do this. It just takes one piece of primary artwork, and the rest is easy.

Game animations are even better suited to this style of animation for a few reasons. People don't expect Disney-quality animation in their mobile games (unless Disney made the game). Most folks are still happy with Pac-Man and that had almost no animation other than Pac-Man's mouth moving up and down. It's the quality of the gameplay that matters most. From a resources perspective, if you can make do with a handful of graphics to get the mood across in your game, you'll cut down on the app's file size and use less system memory. Let's talk real quick about those two things and maybe set your mind at ease before we really get started.

First off, **IF** you can make your app's file size be less than 20Mb, it means users can download the app without Wifi. That's great, I just don't think it's absolutely necessary. So if the app of your dreams is looking to be 50Mb, then fine. You're going to go way over the 20Mb mark anyway, so what the heck, don't sweat it. If you're seeing your app just barely at 20Mb or slightly over, then you should try to trim the fat if you can. I'll always err on the side of not sacrificing the vision you have for the game.

Now about memory, Apple has been doing amazing things recently with pushing these devices to their fullest. With updates of the OS, older devices are running graphics faster than ever. I have a hard time now pushing the devices I own to their peak. I usually test on an iPad 1, 2, and 3, my iPhone 3GS and iPhone 4S. Obviously the 3GS is the slowest and oldest, but even that can run through a series of animated images at sixty frames per second very well. Later on this chapter, we can play around with an animated smoke effect I used in one of my pinball games. The sequence was about fifty frames long and each PNG had a lot of transparency data, since smoke is obviously fairly see-through. There was no way fifty frames of smoke was going to fit on one sprite sheet, so I would just have to load each image separately. That scared me. I really wanted to include this effect because I knew it was going to look fantastic. Instead of the plunger hitting the pinball, it would enter the board with a loud gunshot and smoke.

I decided, "I don't care how lousy this runs on the lesser breed of iOS devices, I'm making this for me!". Perhaps that's an elitist way of thinking, but there's something to be said for

staying ahead of the curve too. Turns out, I had nothing to worry about. The effect ran fine on all my test devices. I was worrying about how things were years before, when the first iPhone would crash from playing a short animated sequence. Those days are gone, and they aren't coming back. The next iOS device is inevitably going to run as good or better than the last.

So the point is, be fearless. Disregard what you think you know about programming for the iPhone and iPad. You can push it pretty darn far nowadays. Worst case, your app slows down and you take a step back to examine what you did to make it slower. If you need to run your animation at 30fps instead of 60fps, you do that. Or maybe you just toss out a few frames. There's no harm in testing the limits. The only cost is your time.

Animating Sprite Textures

I know some of you want to work with sprite sheets to run your animations, but hear me out a little before you skim the next two sections. With larger images, creating sprite sheets just isn't that practical. They are great for "spritely" little game characters, but I trust there's some real animators out there wanting to fill the screen at times with animation. In which case, we could just change a CCSprite's texture and hopefully you won't notice a performance difference. That doesn't mean there isn't one, but you probably won't **notice** it. Sprite sheets put all the frames of an animation on to one image file, which is loaded with the data of where each individual image is on the sheet. For many of my projects, I like to just use separate image files for each frame and skip making a sprite sheet. The recent iOS devices are all getting to a point where they can rip through most animations at sixty frames per second using either method. Performance reasons aside, I like to work fast and make subtle changes on the fly, so I prefer exporting out a new sequence of animated frames, and seeing the results without having to generate a new sprite sheet every time I tinker with a file or two.

Even if you go the sprite sheet route later (and you probably will), give these next two sections a good read. I'll show you how to make a custom class for animation, and most of you could use more practice making your own classes anyway.

If you've been reading this book from the beginning, you might remember that we've already seen the code to change the texture of a sprite. It looks like this:

[sprite setTexture:[[CCSprite **spriteWithFile**: @"file.png"] **texture**]];

In that line, sprite is a CCSprite that's already been added to the scene, we are simply changing the image being displayed from whatever it was before to *file.png*.

The Texture Cache

Let's pick apart the line above a little more. This interior bracketed part … [CCSprite **spriteWithFile**: @"file.png"] … we've seen before. Every time we've created a CCSprite with an image file name we've used exactly that. What I haven't mentioned before though is what's happening behind the scenes in that line. Cocos2d is checking with it's texture cache to see if that image is already stored, and if not, it will add this image to the cache and display it. If it already exists in the cache, it will save on some processing and display the image from the cache as the texture. How nice is that? You don't have to concern yourselves with managing the texture cache yourself. If the texture cache gets full, Cocos2d will dump out unused textures to free up memory. In which case, if you pay attention to the Output window when you test your games on your device, you'll get messages telling you about memory warnings and textures being dumped to free up memory. That's all fine. Let Cocos2d do it's thing. It's very good at taking care of it's own business. If your app isn't crashing, and running smoothly then you probably don't need to overly concern yourself with the texture cache.

With that said, you could preload an image to the cache with the following line:

[[CCTextureCache **sharedTextureCache**] **addImage**:@"logo.png"];

You could clean out the **CCTextureCache** with this line:

[[CCTextureCache **sharedTextureCache**] **removeUnusedTextures**];

I'm introducing you to the cache now before we get started animating, partially for good measure, but also because I think one of the few times you'll want to dump the cache is early on in the game if you include a **splash animation**. Splash animations are typically a little extra fluff to the introduction menu of your game. This could be your main character doing somersaults into a brick wall which shatters to reveal the logo of the game. The images you use for this animation will probably never be seen again if they are highly stylized and not in-game graphics. So here's an opportunity where a series of larger sized textures could be tossed from the cache to free up memory for later. Now granted, Cocos2d will eventually toss those images from memory on it's own if it needs to, but you could lend a hand in this case.

Squished Images!

If you're going to animate by swapping out textures, keep your images in the sequence the same dimension sizes. So if the first frame is going to be 100 pixels wide by 400 tall, all the images afterwards should be sized the same. Otherwise you get into a world of pain, that you don't want to deal with. For example, the zombie sprite below is 128 by 256, if I tried to re-texture it with the CartoonSmart logo, it will get squished into that 128 by 256 space.

Most likely, any program you export out a series of animated images from will create them all with the same dimension sizes, so this shouldn't be a major issue.

Powers of 2

Cocos2d works with powers of 2 when it comes to textures in memory. **Powers of 2** go like this … **2, 4, 8, 16, 32, 64, 128, 256, 512, 1024, 2048**. So if possible, try to work with those numbers when creating your images. Reason being, a 120 by 250 pixel image gets loaded into memory as if it were 128 by 256, while a slightly bigger image at 130 by 260 will take up the same amount of memory as the next powers up, which is 256 by 512. So *if* you can work with your images at those dimensions, you should. If you forget, and use an image that's 33 pixels by 66, you'll be no different than all us other developers that do the same thing from time to time.

Time to Animate!

I know you're chomping at the bit by now, so let's get you started with some images for your project's Resources folder, just go to **www.focalpress.com/cw/Dike.**

You will find a folder with three animated sequences which you can also preview there. Each one loops a few times in the preview.

Let's begin with the shortest animated sequence of the zombie walking. It's only nine frames long and the images are named *walking1.png*, *walking2.png*, and so on. In your project's header file, declare a CCSprite to use for this example called walker, and while you are there go ahead and declare a couple more called smoke and explosion. Also we'll want an int variable to keep track of the current frame of the animation.

In the header file

@interface HelloWorldLayer : CCLayer {

        CCSprite* walker;

        CCSprite* smoke;

        CCSprite* explosion;

        int frame;
        // frame will be equal to 0 by default

}

Now in your implementation file we will add the walker sprite to the scene in the **init** statement, then **schedule** a method and frame rate of our choosing which will ultimately change the texture of the sprite with new frames.

In the implementation file

-(id) **init** {

   if((self=[super **init**])) {

      frame = 1;
      // start frame at 1 instead of 0

      walker = [CCSprite **spriteWithFile**:@"walking1.png"];

      walker.position = ccp(400, 300);

      [self **addChild**: walker];

      [self **schedule**:@selector(**updateAnimation:**) **interval**:1.0/10.0];
      // 1 divided 10 will be 10 frames per second

   }

   return self;

}

Now we need to write the method we scheduled.

```
-(void) updateAnimation:(ccTime) delta {

    frame ++;
        // add 1 to what frame equals
    [walker setTexture:[ [CCSprite spriteWithFile:[NSString stringWithFormat:
    @"walking%i.png", frame] ] texture ] ];
    if (frame == 9) {
        frame = 0;
        // set frame back to 0 if the last image
        // in the sequence has been reached
    }
}
```

%i gets replaced by whatever frame equals at the time.

That's all it takes to create an endless looping animation. The first time the **updateAnimation** method runs, frame will get incremented by one, so since it started at one, frame now equals two. In the next line, we call **setTexture** for the walker, using **stringWithFormat** for the file name which replaces **%i** in between the strings "walking" and ".png," to form a completed string of "walking2.png." The first eight times this method is run the if statement will get ignored until finally it is true, and we set frame to 0. Keep in mind, the method will keep running, and once called again frame will increment to 1 before we set the texture. Thus creating an endless loop.

You can play around with setting a different frame rate for the animation by changing the **interval** parameter when you **schedule** the **updateAnimation** method.

Your if statement could also be used to stop the method (and animation) from repeating, like so:

```
if (frame == 9) {
    [self unschedule:_cmd];
        // _cmd is the current method
}
```

Another way of stopping the animation is to schedule the method with a preset limit to the number of times it will repeat, like so:

```
[self schedule:@selector(updateAnimation:) interval:1.0/60.0 repeat: 18 delay: 0 ];
        // runs 18 times, optionally you can delay the start
```

After eighteen iterations (or two complete walk cycles), it will stop. Your if statement does not need to call [self **unschedule:**_cmd];

Dealing with Leading Zeros

You might have noticed the other two sets of images I included in the zip file have leading zeros in their file numbering. The set of gun smoke images start with an entirely unnecessary three zeros (*gunsmoke0001.png*) and the explosion set has two zeros in the first image (*explosion001.png*). I can't even remember why now, but I used to like leading zeros. Now that I'm a programmer, I don't like them as much. Fortunately, other programmers greater than thou, figured out how to deal with them in cases exactly like ours today. Before I show you the solution, you *could* add them yourself in the **stringWithFormat** and test what frame equals before setting the texture:

```
-(void) updateAnimation:(ccTime) delta {
    frame ++;
    if (frame <= 9 ) {
        [smoke setTexture:[ [CCSprite spriteWithFile:[NSString stringWithFormat:
        @"gunsmoke000%i.png", frame]] texture] ];
    } else if (frame <= 99 ) {
    [smoke setTexture:[ [CCSprite spriteWithFile:[NSString stringWithFormat:
    @"gunsmoke00%i.png", frame]] texture] ];
    }
        etc ...
```

> Add the zeros
> yourself in the string.

That's not the worst solution, but our trusty **%i** integer replacement syntax has some variations that will automatically **append zeros**. So for example, using **%04i** will always make the integer be four places long. Keep in mind, it isn't adding four zeros. If frame was equal to 131, the integer inserted in the string would be **0131**. Or if frame was equal to 2345, then a zero wouldn't be added at all.

So for the gun smoke set of images all we need to do is write:

[smoke **setTexture**:[[CCSprite **spriteWithFile**:[NSString

stringWithFormat:@"gunsmoke%04i.png", frame]] **texture**]];

    // use %04i instead of %i

Syntax	Example number ...
%04i	file**0001**.png
%03i	file**001**.png
%02i	file**01**.png
%i	file**1**.png

Do-It-Yourself Animation Class

Take aim. I want to punch out a couple of things in this section: first, introduce you to my own little class for animating sprite textures and second, remind you how to write your own class. Or more importantly, remind you *why* you should write your own classes. Writing your own classes is a little bit like working hard to buy a La-Z-Boy recliner. You're investing time now to make life easier later.

Here's some of the things I considered when building this class:

- I want the option to show the first frame of the animation before playing it.
- I want to set a property to optionally loop the animation.
- If looping is enabled, I want the option to loop back to a random frame.
- I want the animation to be able to remove itself from the scene if it doesn't loop.
- I want to set a property that specifies the number of leading zeros to account for.
- I want to be able to pause and resume the animation.
- I want to be able to start the animation from a specific frame.
- I want the option to preload images in the texture cache.
- I want a property to set the frame rate.
- I want to be able to scale, rotate and apply actions to the entire animation (this is a no-brainer because anything subclassed from CCNode can do that).

Does it sound like I'm asking too much? Oddly enough, it's really not that much code. The implementation file is under 200 lines and easily half of those are blank. Hopefully this project will give you some interesting comparisons next section when we look into using sprite sheets and Cocos2d's own classes for animation.

Anytime you plan out a custom class try to dream big. How awesome can you make it? If you program a great shortcut for yourself, others could benefit from it too. If it's worth sharing with the rest of the community of **Cocos2d** programmers, blog about it or post the code on a forum. You might even get back some feedback to make it even better!

As usual, you can work with a new project using the Cocos2d starting template. The project could be named **AnimationTest** or anything else you want. Again, you can grab the zip file I uploaded to www.focalpress.com/cw/Dike with three sequences of animations:

Add those images to your project's resources, then let's create a new class file. **Go to File > New > File ...** and choose **CCNode** class, then **Subclass of CCNode**, and finally call the class **CSAnimatedSprite.m**

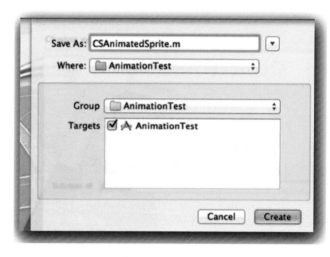

Now let's add a few lines to our HelloWorldLayer header file.

In HelloWorldLayer.h file

#import "cocos2d.h"

#import "CSAnimatedSprite.h"

> Don't forget to #import the classes you write.

@interface HelloWorldLayer : CCLayer {

    CSAnimatedSprite* smoke;

    CSAnimatedSprite* walker;

    CSAnimatedSprite* explosion;

> Once the #import statement is written, you can declare variables of that class type.

}

+(CCScene *) **scene**;

@end

Now jump over to your HelloWorldLayer implementation file. I'll go ahead and show you some of the code we could write here, but if you want to hold off on including it in your project, that's a good idea. Until we finish our CSAnimatedSprite class, this code will do nothing but pop up warnings. Regardless, I'd like you to see it now because it illustrates how simple it will be to run an animation once the CSAnimatedSprite class is done. Below are two sequences that animate right away, but you don't have run them immediately. You can optionally preload the images, or show just the first frame of the animation and play the rest later.

```
-(id) init {

    if ( (self=[super init] ) ) {
```

```
        // set up the walking animation sequence. Frames are named
        walking1.png through walking9.png
        walker = [CSAnimatedSprite animateWithBaseName:@"walking"
        andFrames:9];
        [self addChild: walker];
        walker.position = ccp( 100, 300 );
        walker.doesTheAnimationLoop = YES;
        // change the does TheAnimationLoop property to YES so it loops
        walker.frameRate = 10;
        // zombies move slow so let's lower the frameRate property a tad,
        the default value is 60 (meaning 60fps)
        [walker animate];
        // that's it! just call the animate method on the object
```

```
        // set up the gunsmoke animation sequence. Frames are named
        gunsmoke0001.png through gunsmoke0053.png
        smoke = [CSAnimatedSprite animateWithBaseName:@"gunsmoke"
        andFrames:53];
        [self addChild: smoke];
        smoke.position = ccp( 400, 300 );
        smoke.leadingZeros = 3;
        // change the leadingZeros property because the sequence has
        3 leading zeros on the first frame
        [smoke animate];
        // that's it! just call the animate method on the object
    }
    return self;
}
```

Now let's go over to our CSAnimatedSprite header file. I'll paste in the entire file below (which will span a couple of pages). I'm going to leave this relatively un-commented and instead highlight the broader points to pay attention now. We'll get into the details later.

In the CSAnimatedSprite.h file ...

#import <Foundation/Foundation.h>

#import "cocos2d.h"

```
@interface CSAnimatedSprite : CCNode {
    CCSprite *sprite;
    NSString *baseName;
    int framesToAnimate;
    int frameRate;
    int framesBeginAt;
    int currentFrame;
    int leadingZeros;
    int preloadCount;
    bool doesTheAnimationLoop;
    bool useRandomFrameToLoop;
}
@property (nonatomic, readwrite) int framesBeginAt;
@property (nonatomic, readwrite) int currentFrame;
@property (nonatomic, readwrite) int leadingZeros;
@property (nonatomic, readwrite) int frameRate;
@property (nonatomic, readwrite) bool doesTheAnimationLoop;
@property (nonatomic, readwrite) bool useRandomFrameToLoop;


+( id ) animateWithBaseName:(NSString*)name andFrames:(int)num;
-(void) showFirstFrame;
-(void) animate;
-(void) animateFrom:(int)startFrame;
-(void) pause;
-(void) resume;
-(void) restart;
-(void) preload;
-(void) showFirstFrameAndPreload;

@end
```

All the stuff we're declaring that gets used by the class to run the animation. Note that most of the int and bool variables are also declared as properties below ...

Have you forgotten why we declare some variables as properties? ... The variables will all have default values set up in the **init** statement. When we create our instance of the class, we might want to switch these variables to other values. If we didn't declare these as properties they wouldn't be directly assignable by another class. For example, from **HelloWorldLayer.m** we might write ...

smoke.frameRate = 30 ;

The first line is our **class method** (notice the plus symbol in the beginning) for creating the instance. We are only passing in two parameters, an NSString base name and int value for the number of frames in the sequence. By default, the animation does **NOT** play or even display the first frame. Which is why we are declaring the other **instance methods** so we can do things like run the animation, stop it, etc., from the HelloWorldLayer class (or any other class).

Now let's jump over to the CSAnimatedSprite implementation file, synthesize our properties, then hack away at all these methods we need to write. The first couple will be our class and **init** methods. Again, we just want a base name and number of frames to get our instance started, so we'll pass those same parameters from the **animateWithBaseName:** class method to the **initWithBaseName:** method:

In the CSAnimatedSprite.m file ...

#import "CSAnimatedSprite.h"

@implementation CSAnimatedSprite

@synthesize doesTheAnimationLoop, useRandomFrameToLoop, currentFrame, framesBeginAt, leadingZeros, frameRate;

+(id) **animateWithBaseName**: (NSString*) name **andFrames**: (int) num {

    return [[[self **alloc**] **initWithBaseName**: (NSString*) name **andFrames**:(int) num] **autorelease**];

}

-(id) **initWithBaseName**:(NSString*)name **andFrames**:(int)num {

    if ((self = [super **init**])) {

        baseName = name;

        framesToAnimate = num;

        framesBeginAt = 1;

        currentFrame = 1;

        leadingZeros = 0;

        frameRate = 60;

    }

  return self;

}

Aside from baseName and framesToAnimate, the rest of the variables will get default values here in the **init** statement. I think most animation programs export out sequences with 1 as the first frame, so I'm setting framesBeginAt to 1, currentFrame logically matches that for now, leadingZeros will be 0 (or none), and the frameRate will be 60. These int variables are all properties which can be set to something else before the animation runs. Notice too, we aren't even adding our CCSprite to the node at this point. We are just prepping the instance basically. Which is a perfect lead-in to our next method:

```
-(void) showFirstFrame {

    currentFrame = framesBeginAt;

    sprite = [CCSprite spriteWithFile:[self formatName: currentFrame]];
    // formatName method will return an NSString for the file name

    [self addChild: sprite];

}
```

When another class calls this method on the instance, we first make sure that currentFrame equals framesBeginAt, just in case framesBeginAt was changed after initialization. Then our sprite goes through the usual routine of being added as a child, with one major exception, we haven't seen this part before … [self formatName: currentFrame] … because that's a method we need to create next.

This method will return a formatted NSString with leading zeros. So **IF** you knew with 100 percent certainty that you'll never use leading zeros in your animations, then you could remove this method, but let's go ahead and include it for our examples. You can see the familiar **stringWithFormat**: method we've been using so much in this book. The format asks for the baseName string and frame integer, which we passed into the method when we called it. It combines those two and adds ".png" to form a complete file name. Like the last section, we're using the syntax %02i, %03i, or %04i to append zeros if needed.

```
-(NSString*) formatName:(int) frame {

NSString* fileName;
    switch (leadingZeros) {
    // cases for how many leading zeros your first frame has …
        case 0:
        fileName = [NSString stringWithFormat:@"%@%i.png", baseName, frame];
        // no appending of zeros
        break ;
    case 1:
        fileName = [NSString stringWithFormat:@"%@%02i.png", baseName, frame];
        break ;
    case 2:
        fileName = [NSString stringWithFormat:@"%@%03i.png", baseName, frame];
        break ;
```

```
        case 3:
            fileName = [NSString stringWithFormat:@"%@%04i.png", baseName, frame];
            break ;
        }
    return fileName;
}
```

Next, let's actually animate the sprite. Write the following method:

```
-(void) animate {
    if ( sprite == nil ) {
        CCLOG(@"oops sprite hasn't been added, let's add it first");
        [self showFirstFrame];
    }
    [self schedule:@selector( runAnimation: ) interval: 1.0 / frameRate ];
}
```

The if statement checks to see if sprite equals nil, in which case, it hasn't been added to the node yet so we should call [self showFirstFrame]. Then we schedule the runAnimation method below, with the frameRate variable used in the equation for the interval:

```
-(void) runAnimation:(ccTime) delta {
    currentFrame ++;
        // adds 1 to currentFrame
    if (currentFrame <= framesToAnimate) {
        // if there's still more frames to animate, we just set the texture of the next image ...
        [sprite setTexture:[[CCSprite spriteWithFile:[self formatName:currentFrame]] texture] ];
    } else if ( doesTheAnimationLoop == YES && useRandomFrameToLoop == NO) {
        // else loop and go back to the first frame to begin at
        currentFrame = framesBeginAt−1;
    } else if ( doesTheAnimationLoop == YES && useRandomFrameToLoop == YES) {
        // else loop with a random frame to go back to
        currentFrame = arc4random( ) % framesToAnimate;
        // you'd get a range of 0 to whatever framesToAnimate is
    } else {
        // else if the animation doesn't loop and all frames have been run, we delete the
        // sprite and entire node
```

```
        [self unschedule:_cmd];
        [self removeChild: sprite cleanup: NO];
        [self removeFromParentAndCleanup: NO];
    }
}
```

The **runAnimation** method is really pretty simple. If the currentFrame is less than the total number of framesToAnimate, then we show the image associated with the current frame. If that's not the case, we have three other possible scenarios: (1) the animation loops back to the framesBeginAt value; (2) the animation loops back to a random frame in the sequence; (3) the animation is done for good and we remove the instance. Keep in mind, I'm not calling [[CCTextureCache **sharedTextureCache**] **removeUnusedTextures**] when I remove the object because clearing the cache should be done only when you really need to. You can remove the CSAnimatedSprite instance, but bring a new one back later and still make use of the textures that were already cached from before.

Now we can add some extra levels of control to the class. Two aptly-named methods are **pause** and **resume**:

```
-(void) pause {
        [self unschedule:@selector(runAnimation:)];
}
-(void) resume {
        [self animate];
}
```

Calling **pause** on the instance has no effect on the value of the currentFrame variable, so if you **resume** later, the animation will just continue from whatever value currentFrame was before. Now let's write methods to restart or start animating from a specific frame:

```
-(void) restart {
        [self unschedule:@selector(runAnimation:)];
        // stops the animation if already running
        currentFrame = framesBeginAt − 1;
        // we subtract 1 because the runAnimation method always adds 1 right away
        [self animate];
}
```

```
-(void) animateFrom:(int)startFrame {

    [self unschedule:@selector(runAnimation:)];

    // stops the animation if already running

    framesBeginAt = startFrame – 1;

    // we subtract 1 because the runAnimation method always adds 1 right away

    currentFrame = framesBeginAt;

    // make currentFrame equal framesBeginAt

    [self animate];

}
```

Next, let's write a method that preloads the images by adding the sequence to the CCTextureCache. We talked a little about this last section, the only thing worth noting is that we finally get to use a while loop again. In the condition of the loop, I'm using the preloadCount variable which starts at the value of framesBeginAt plus 1. This somewhat assumes that you'll be viewing the first frame and preloading the rest. If you want to just make the preloadCount equal to exactly framesBeginAt, that's fine too.

```
-(void) preload {

    preloadCount = framesBeginAt + 1;

    while( preloadCount <= framesToAnimate) {

        [[CCTextureCache sharedTextureCache] addImage:[self formatName:
        preloadCount]];

        preloadCount ++;

    }

}
```

One thing to be aware of: if you have a long enough sequence of images, they might fill up the cache and start deleting previously cached images to make room for new ones. If that were to happen, you should get some indication in the Output window. If this were the case, you might not want to preload at all, and just see how the animation plays on it's own. Or you might need to consider slowing down the frame rate, and unfortunately dropping some of the images in the sequence. On my first iOS game, Zombie Air Strike, that was my solution when I wanted to push through an animation that the device couldn't process fast enough.

Finally, this method just shows the first frame and preloads the rest.

```
-(void) showFirstFrameAndPreload {
    [self showFirstFrame];
    [self preload];
}
```

That's it for the CSAnimatedSprite class! If you want to download the example project, go to **www.focalpress.com/cw/Dike**.

Remember too, your CSAnimatedSprite instances are subclassed from CCNode so you can do things like change the scale property, rotation, assign them tags, z-depth, or run actions on them. So for example, to make our animated zombie walk across the screen, we could write:

In HelloWorldLayer.m file

```
-(id) init {
  if ( (self=[super init] ) ) {
      CGPoint startLocation = ccp( 0, 300 );
      // where the walker will start at and go back to in the Action sequence
      walker = [CSAnimatedSprite animateWithBaseName:@"walking" andFrames:9];
      [self addChild: walker];
      walker.position = ccp( 100, 300 );
      walker.doesTheAnimationLoop = YES;
      walker.frameRate = 10;
      [walker animate];
```

> Apply an Action sequence to move the walker 1024 points to the right, over 30 seconds, and then return to the original position and start walking again.

```
      CCMoveBy* move = [CCMoveBy actionWithDuration:30.0 position: ccp(1024,0)];
      CCPlace* place = [CCPlace actionWithPosition: startLocation];
      CCSequence* sequence = [CCSequence actions: move, place, nil];
      CCRepeatForever* repeat = [CCRepeatForever actionWithAction: sequence];
      [walker runAction: repeat];
  }
  return self;
}
```

Sprite Sheet Generation

Sprite sheets, or **texture atlases** as they are also called, are textures that contain more than one image. Typically you'll have a rather large **.png** file with an accompanying **.plist** file, which tells Cocos2d where each frame is on the **.png** file. The program you use to create the sprite sheet is doing a lot of work for you in assembling all the frames onto one image and then generating that **.plist** file with all the data about each frame. In other words, it's worth investing a few bucks in the sprite sheet software you settle on. Most have a free trial period before a purchase.

```
○ ○ ○                    hanksheet_poses.plist
<?xml version="1.0" encoding="UTF-8"?>
<!DOCTYPE plist PUBLIC "-//Apple//DTD PLIST 1.0//EN" "http://www.apple.com/DTDs/
PropertyList-1.0.dtd">
<plist version="1.0">
<dict>
        <key>frames</key>
        <dict>

            <key>hank_crouchattack0.png</key>
            <dict>
                    <key>aliases</key>
                    <array>

                    </array>
                    <key>spriteColorRect</key>
                    <string>{{41, 90}, {98, 127}}</string>
                    <key>spriteOffset</key>
                    <string>{15, -41}</string>
                    <key>spriteSize</key>
                    <string>{98, 127}</string>
                    <key>spriteSourceSize</key>
                    <string>{150, 225}</string>
                    <key>spriteTrimmed</key>
                    <true/>
                    <key>textureRect</key>
                    <string>{{920, 0}, {98, 127}}</string>
                    <key>textureRotated</key>
                    <false/>
            </dict>
```

If you aren't familiar with a **.plist** file, here's your chance to meet one. With lots of opening and closing tags, it looks a bit like XML, doesn't it? Fortunately, you won't need to create this **.plist** yourself.

The picture to the right is a sprite sheet we'll use later. The actual size is 1024 by 1024 for the standard images and 2048 by 2048 for the Retina display images. Notice that's a lot of frames crammed onto one image. Forget about the fact that your sprite sheet generation software creates a *.plist* file, just imagine trying to lay out all those images in Photoshop on your own. For this section, I'll be using Zwoptex, but another favorite is Texture Packer, and even Adobe Flash CS6 now makes sprite sheets.

Before we begin, let me just address a common misconception. Sprite sheets aren't only for animations. You could include **ALL** your game's artwork on a single image if it fit within the max texture size (to be safe for all iOS devices assume that is 2048 × 2048 pixels). Or you could have a couple of sprite sheets for all the artwork in the game. It's up to you how you want to divide up your game's resources and load them in.

From my experience, I've yet to see a noticeable performance lag by loading a separate image file for the static (non-animated) objects. In a pinball game for example, most objects like the bumpers, walls, ramps, etc., are going to load up initially and stay on the layer for the duration of the gameplay without change. From a workflow perspective, I like to keep that artwork in a separate file, export or replace an existing copy, and not worry about replacing an entire sprite sheet because I made subtle changes to a single bumper image (I tweak artwork constantly). For animations, you see an image for a fraction of a second, and then it's gone. So you do want a fast load time. When animating, if you change one frame in the sequence you'll often affect a few more to follow, which softens the blow of having to replace your entire sprite sheet if multiple images need updating. Plus, making a new sprite sheet really isn't that hard at all, and to prove that point, let's actually get started.

Let's suit up. You'll need images. Lots of them. Go to www.focalpress.com/cw/Dike, and find the subfolder named **"hank_images"** in the **"other"** folder.

That folder contains two folders, called **hank_SD** and **hank_HD** . Each has seventy-three different poses for zombie Hank (as much as I want to, I can't take credit for drawing Hank, he was illustrated by my friend and fellow CartoonSmart instructor, Justin Cook, from SeenCreative.co.uk). The SD folder houses the non-Retina display versions and the HD folder obviously has the higher resolution ones. An important thing to note though is the images are named the same. I haven't included the **-hd.png** or **-ipadhd.png** name add-on's for the higher resolutions. Normally we would do that, but sprite sheets are an exception. Ultimately we'll have four files to bring into our Retina display enabled iPad-only project:

- *hanksheet_poses.plist*
- *hanksheet_poses.png*
- *hanksheet_poses-ipadhd.plist*
- *hanksheet_poses-ipadhd.png*

Notice it's the **.plist** and **.png** files that get the **-ipadhd** name change. If you were working with an iPhone-only app, then your name change would just be **-hd.** Or if you wanted to go Universal, then you should make sprite sheets with **-hd**, **-ipad**, and **-ipadhd**. Since my example project (which I'll give you later) is set to iPad-only, the standard non-HD images don't need to be named with **-ipad**. That's only for Universal projects. As usual, if you want to include HD images, don't forget to enable Retina display in the **AppDelegate.m** file.

Now onto Zwoptex. I'll save two separate projects for the SD and HD images. Both projects I'll name **hanksheet.zwd** (*.zwd* is the Zwoptex file format extension so if you're using a different texture atlas program, you'll have a different name obviously). Since both projects have the same exact name, I'll save them in different folders so one doesn't overwrite the other (as evidenced by the Date Modified timestamps in my image below, this book will forever record an 80 minute lunch break).

▼ 📁 hanksheet_HD	Today 3:16 PM
📄 hanksheet.zwd	Today 3:15 PM
▼ 📁 hanksheet_SD	Today 4:35 PM
📄 hanksheet.zwd	Today 4:35 PM

Now you just need to dump all seventy-three images from each folder into the corresponding HD/SD project. Drag them into either the middle panel or the **Library** window.

Hit the **Layout** button in the top menu, and your images should all line up neatly apart from one another, but not necessarily in the sequence order.

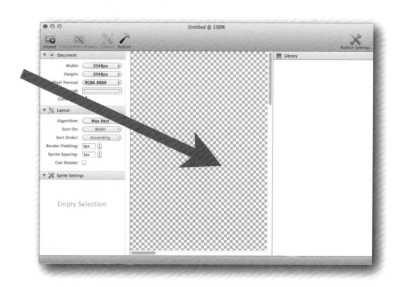

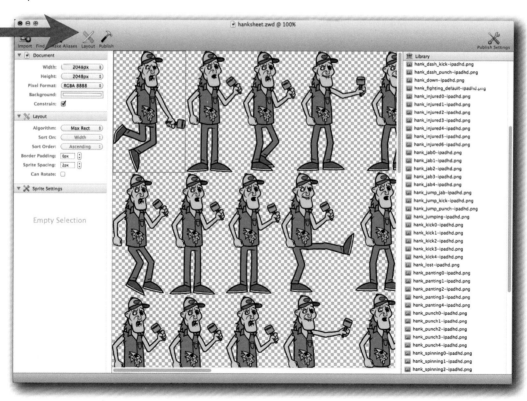

The program will arrange them as tight as possible as it sees fit. You can even toggle on an option to rotate them if that helps to get them into a smaller space. Your SD images should all fit onto a 1024 by 1024 document and the HD images will need a 2048 by 2048 document. The width and height settings are in the top right in Zwoptex and they should be easy to find in any other program. If you play around with different size documents, you'll need to hit the **Layout** button again to recalculate their positions.

We're almost ready to export the *.png* and *.plist* file, but first I should point out something very cool the program is doing.

Most of Hank's source images all have a lot of unnecessary transparent space above the main character. This was to account for the character jumping in some poses, but you can see in the screenshot on the previous page, that extra transparent space has been removed. Every Hank is right on top of each other. The *.plist* file will note with an offset variable where the character was in relation to the bottom of the image in the original files.

Time to visit **File > Publish Settings**. In our SD project, go to Targets, and click the **Plus Sign**. Call the new Target profile "**poses**." You can delete the existing Target profile called "*default*." Now under **Texture > Format** pulldown **Portable Network Graphics (.png)** and under **Coordinates > Format** choose **cocos2d (.plist)**. Then press **Done**.

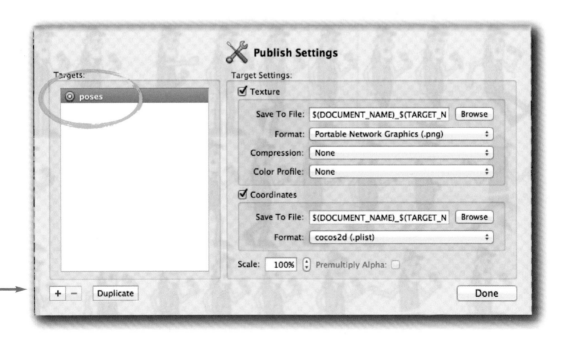

Finally, go to **File > Publish** and your SD project should now have two new files next to the **hanksheet.zwd** file.

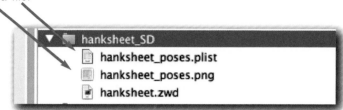

We'll do the same thing for our HD project, but our Target profile will be called **"poses-ipadhd."** Set the rest, and hit **File > Publish**.

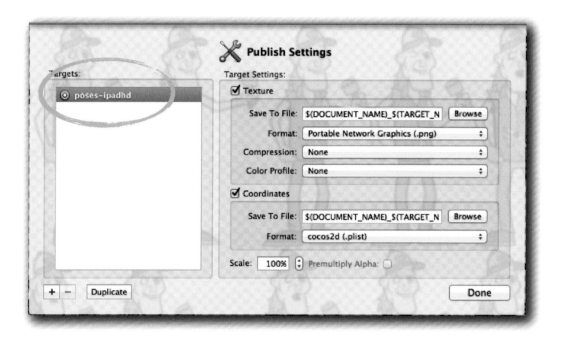

If you want to see the final HD sprite sheet on your iPad, I've uploaded the PNG file of all seventy-three poses to www.focalpress.com/cw/Dike.

That's it for Zwoptex! If you use a different texture atlas program, just be sure to format the **.plist** file for Cocos2d and you should be fine.

Sprite Sheet Animation

In your Xcode project, add the two
.plist files and two *.png* files into
your Resources folder that you created in the last section. If you didn't bother with creating
those sprite sheets yourself, you can find them in the source projects folder for this chapter.
As usual you can use the Cocos2d starting project, so in the HelloWorldLayer header file,
we need to declare a couple things. First, the CCSprite, which will display the animation,
and then we need to declare the CCRepeatForever action, which will basically house the
CCAnimate and CCAnimation actions we write later.

In the HelloWorldLayer.h file ...

@interface HelloWorldLayer : CCLayer {

       CCSprite* zombie;

       // a CCSprite like usual

       CCRepeatForever* walk;

       // the action we can start and stop

}

@property (nonatomic, retain) CCRepeatForever * walk;

Before we forget, synthesize walk in the implementation:

At the top of HelloWorldLayer.m file

@implementation HelloWorldLayer

@synthesize walk ;

       // don't forget to do this!

Now the one thing out of the ordinary here is that we're setting up the walk action as a
property, but not so another class can access it, rather so that we explicitly **retain** it.
Otherwise the action will get autoreleased after the **init** method **IF** we were to stop and try
to start it again. Queue drumroll. ... We have to actually do something in our **dealloc
method**! That's why the slack-jawed yokel in this section's header is running away terrified
of his sprite sheet.

Jump over the implementation file and add the highlighted line to the existing **dealloc** method. It best to do this now, otherwise we might forget to release it entirely.

At the bottom of the HelloWorldLayer.m file …

- (void) **dealloc** {

> self.walk = nil;
>
> *// sets the object to nil and releases it*

> *// don't forget to call "super dealloc"*

[super **dealloc**];

}

A Short Diversion Into Deallocation...

We haven't talked much about the **dealloc** method because so far we haven't really needed to. Our children have been auto-releasing themselves and Cocos2d has been doing all the cleanup work for us. I know a lot of programmers (myself included) get anxious when it comes to memory-related issues because the fear is that you'll program an app that hogs memory until it finally crashes. I haven't actually seen that happen, but the idea is scarier to me than any of the Paranormal Activity movies.

Some of you familiar with iOS programming previously, might be tempted to write this line as well in the **dealloc** method...

[walk **release**]; *// release the retained object*

I tried adding that, but when I tested this project in **Instruments** (a program you also have for checking memory/performance), I didn't notice a difference with or without the [walk **release**] call. Which made me do some actual research and from what I read on the old internet, setting properties to nil that include the self. part in front, are released from that line alone.

So if you declared @property (nonatomic, retain) on an object, then calling these two circled blocks below in the **dealloc** method are the same.

> self.object = nil;

> [object **release**];
> object = nil;

One thing to remember, our **dealloc** method wouldn't get called unless we replaced the HelloWorldLayer scene with another one or removed it. So if we forgot to set the self.walk action to nil, it would be pretty harmless in this project because we aren't ever removing HelloWorldLayer. Imagine though, if your Enemy class from a few chapters ago had a retained property, the game spawned 100 Enemy instances, and you forgot to **dealloc** properly when they got removed. That's a lot of retained objects hanging around. You don't have to try this yourself, but if you ever wanted to test your **dealloc** method, a simple way is to replace a scene with itself...

[[CCDirector **sharedDirector**]replaceScene:[HelloWorldLayer **scene**]];

You could call a scheduled method with that line to run every few seconds and replace your current scene over and over again. We'll talk more on transitioning scenes in a later section, but since we're two pages into talking about sprite sheet animations, and way off topic, let's get back on track...

If you took that dealloc detour, you are a true learner. Gold stars for you today. Now let's actually use this sprite sheet.

In the HelloWorldLayer.m file ...

```
-(id) init {
    if( (self=[super init])) {
        [[CCSpriteFrameCache sharedSpriteFrameCache]
        addSpriteFramesWithFile:@"hanksheet_poses.plist"];
        //add sprite from .plist
        zombie = [CCSprite spriteWithSpriteFrameName:@"hank_fighting_default.png"];
        // loads the image with this name as the key
        [self addChild: zombie];
        zombie.position = ccp( 300, 300 );
    }
    return self;
}
```

Wah-lah! You're now displaying a single image from the sprite sheet. Not difficult at all right? We just load in our sprite frames from the property list file, and then instead of using the usual **spriteWithFile:** parameter we write **spriteWithSpriteFrameName:** and follow that up with the source file name from the original set of images we dropped into the sprite sheet software we used.

Mind you, hank_fighting_default.png is just a **Key** in the *.plist* file used to look up data about where that particular image is on the large sheet of all the zombie Hank poses. When I showed you the *.plist* file last section, I used a text editor to open it which showed you all the mark-up tags.

I'll admit I meant it to look a little confusing just to give you some appreciation for the software generating that file. Now look at the screenshot of the same *.plist* file after I double-clicked it and let Xcode open it. This makes it a lot easier to read, and you can see the **Key** column shows you the original file names of each image followed by their properties.

Next we'll use an **NSMutableArray** variable to store some of the sprite frame names. This array eventually gets used later in our next block of code, but for now let's just focus on creating the NSMutableArray and giving it some values.

An array is a variable containing multiple objects. So you could think of it like a list or a collection, where one object gets added, then another, and so on. Since this is a **mutable** array, we could remove/add objects at any time, but in this case we won't need to.

We'll initialize our array with a capacity of nine, meaning the array will be able to store nine objects. In this case, the objects being collected in the array are CCSpriteFrames.

So continue writing where we left off in the **init** statement:

```
NSMutableArray *walkingFrames = [NSMutableArray arrayWithCapacity:9];

for (int i = 1; i <= 9; ++i ) {
    NSString* file = [NSString stringWithFormat:@"hank_walkforward%i.png", i ];
    CCSpriteFrame* frame = [[CCSpriteFrameCache sharedSpriteFrameCache]
    spriteFrameByName: file ];
    [walkingFrames addObject: frame];
}
```

This for statement saves us a lot of coding. Since we are adding similarly named frames (**hank_walkforward1.png**, **hank_walkforward2.png**, etc.) it just makes sense to loop through a for statement 9 times and get the names that way. Eventually each frame gets added to the walkingFrames array with the **addObject** method.

Alternatively, we could have done the same exact thing without a for statement, but take a look at how much more code that is:

```
NSMutableArray *walkingFrames = [NSMutableArray arrayWithCapacity:9];

CCSpriteFrame* frame;

frame = [[CCSpriteFrameCache sharedSpriteFrameCache] spriteFrameByName:@"hank_walkforward1.png"];
[walkingFrames addObject:frame];
frame = [[CCSpriteFrameCache sharedSpriteFrameCache] spriteFrameByName:@"hank_walkforward2.png"];
[walkingFrames addObject:frame];
frame = [[CCSpriteFrameCache sharedSpriteFrameCache] spriteFrameByName:@"hank_walkforward3.png"];
[walkingFrames addObject:frame];
frame = [[CCSpriteFrameCache sharedSpriteFrameCache] spriteFrameByName:@"hank_walkforward4.png"];
[walkingFrames addObject:frame];
frame = [[CCSpriteFrameCache sharedSpriteFrameCache] spriteFrameByName:@"hank_walkforward5.png"];
[walkingFrames addObject:frame];
frame = [[CCSpriteFrameCache sharedSpriteFrameCache] spriteFrameByName:@"hank_walkforward6.png"];
[walkingFrames addObject:frame];
frame = [[CCSpriteFrameCache sharedSpriteFrameCache] spriteFrameByName:@"hank_walkforward7.png"];
[walkingFrames addObject:frame];
frame = [[CCSpriteFrameCache sharedSpriteFrameCache] spriteFrameByName:@"hank_walkforward8.png"];
[walkingFrames addObject:frame];
frame = [[CCSpriteFrameCache sharedSpriteFrameCache] spriteFrameByName:@"hank_walkforward8.png"];
[walkingFrames addObject:frame];
```

Finally, our last block of code will get this zombie walking.

CCAnimation* walkAnimation = [CCAnimation **animationWithSpriteFrames**: walkingFrames **delay**:0.1f];

    // delay is 1/10 of a second

CCAnimate* animate = [CCAnimate **actionWithAnimation**: walkAnimation];

self.walk = [CCRepeatForever **actionWithAction**:animate];

[zombie **runAction**: walk];

We end up using three CCAction classes above. The **CCAnimation** action will use the walkingFrames array, and set the time **delay** between each frame. The second action, **CCAnimate**, will just ask for the CCAnimation action (I know it doesn't seem like this action is doing much, but there's some other parameters we *could* add, we just aren't). Finally, self.walk is our CCRepeatForever action, which we already declared and retained as a property in the header file. This action is just running the CCAnimate over and over again. Remember, we retained this action so we could stop and restart it later without it getting auto-released on us. Normally with our declared variables we haven't had to write self. when referencing them, but this is slightly different since it was set as a property and retained.

That's it! If you want to run a quick test to start and stop the animation, add these two methods:

At the bottom of your **init** statement, schedule the action to stop:

```
-(void) stopTheWalkAction:(ccTime) delta {
    [zombie stopAction: walk];
    [self unschedule:_cmd];
    [self schedule:@selector(restartTheWalkAction:) interval: 2.0f];
}
```

```
-(void) restartTheWalkAction:(ccTime)delta {
    [zombie runAction: walk];
    [self unschedule:_cmd];
    [self schedule:@selector(stopTheWalkAction:) interval:2.0f];
}
```

[self **schedule**:@selector (**stopTheWalkAction**:) **interval**:2.0f];

Alternatively, you could use:

[zombie **pauseSchedulerAnd Actions**];

[zombie **resumeSchedulerAnd Actions**];

Instead of:

[zombie **stopAction**: walk];

[zombie **runAction**: walk];

If you didn't want to pause **all** actions and scheduled methods on the zombie then **pauseSchedulerAndActions** is not your best option.

Test Time!

I want you to make Hank **jump**, **punch** and **kick** based on the gesture recognizers we've already learned. Which gesture is up to you. Also, this project won't be too impressive if Hank doesn't walk around some so I'll also leave that up to you. He could follow your finger location, move based on the accelerometer tilt, or walk from left/right swipe gestures. The project, as it is now, has been uploaded to **www.focalpress.com/cw/Dike**, and saved in the folder ***SpriteSheets_HankWalking***.

Sprite Sheet Animated Fighter

Good, I've been looking for a fight ever since I had to rewrite that entire Customs form at the post office.

I don't want to brag too much, but this test project was an easy one. Right? What. No one agrees?! Okay, maybe it was a little easier for me because it's very similar to one of my first games I got in the App Store. That wasn't programmed in Cocos2d though, and this time around it was much easier using CCActions to control the character's movements and animation. The last time I programmed a Street Fighter type game, I was writing all my own methods for jumping and moving. Being able to do the same thing with CCJumpBy and CCMoveBy was quite nice.

Watch a bonus movie on this topic at **www.focalpress.com/cw/Dike**.

As you can see from the movie, I went with gesture recognizers to control all of the movement. One of the only problems I ran into was allowing one gesture's method to run before another had finished. All in all, this was only about 300 lines of code (mostly double spaced), which isn't much for, what I would consider, the foundation of a decent fighting game.

Let's get started recreating it. We will begin with the same project I uploaded at the end of the last section, so let's dive right in with the changes we need to make to the HelloWorldLayer header.

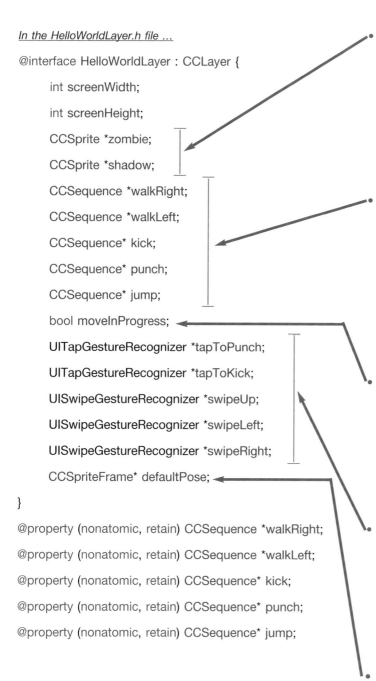

In the HelloWorldLayer.h file ...

@interface HelloWorldLayer : CCLayer {

    int screenWidth;

    int screenHeight;

    CCSprite *zombie;

    CCSprite *shadow;

    CCSequence *walkRight;

    CCSequence *walkLeft;

    CCSequence* kick;

    CCSequence* punch;

    CCSequence* jump;

    bool moveInProgress;

    UITapGestureRecognizer *tapToPunch;

    UITapGestureRecognizer *tapToKick;

    UISwipeGestureRecognizer *swipeUp;

    UISwipeGestureRecognizer *swipeLeft;

    UISwipeGestureRecognizer *swipeRight;

    CCSpriteFrame* defaultPose;

}

@property (nonatomic, retain) CCSequence *walkRight;

@property (nonatomic, retain) CCSequence *walkLeft;

@property (nonatomic, retain) CCSequence* kick;

@property (nonatomic, retain) CCSequence* punch;

@property (nonatomic, retain) CCSequence* jump;

We can use the same zombie CCSprite as before. I'll add a new CCSprite called shadow which will do nothing more than constantly follow the x location of the zombie. The y location will be constant. If the zombie jumps up, obviously the shadow stays on the ground plane.

All of my retained actions will be CCSequence actions. In the previous version of the project, walk was retained as a CCRepeatForever action. This time I need to use a CCSequence which will play a CCSpawn of the animation and whatever action we are using to move the zombie, either CCMoveBy or CCJumpBy.

Each CCSequence will always end by calling a method that switches the bool variable moveInProgress to NO. So when a move starts, we'll switch it to YES. This will be a part of how we prevent two moves occurring at once.

Then we've got two UITapGestureRecognizers and three UISwipeGestureRecognizers. We'll be able to copy most of the code we used last time we added these gestures, so if you have that project from before, open it up.

Finally our **CCSpriteFrame** called defaultPose will be used to set the zombie to the default image after each move (and in the **init** statement).

That's it for the header file, now jump over to the implementation file and add the new properties that need synthesizing:

In the HelloWorldLayer.m file …

@synthesize walkRight, walkLeft, punch, kick, jump;

Let's also add these to the **dealloc** method too:

- (void) **dealloc** {

    self.walkRight = nil;

    self.walkLeft = nil;

    self.punch = nil;

    self.kick = nil;

    self.jump = nil;

    [super **dealloc**];

}

Until I tell you otherwise, the code I'll be writing over the next few pages will go in the **init** statement. I'll make note of some key points, but most of this code you've seen before, so I'm not going to over-explain it unnecessarily:

-(id) **init** {

  if((self=[super **init**])) {

    CGSize size = [[CCDirector **sharedDirector**] winSize];

    screenWidth = size.width;

    screenHeight = size.height;

    CCSprite* background = [CCSprite **spriteWithFile**:@"background.png"];

    [self **addChild**: background **z:**-2];

    background.position = ccp(screenWidth /2, screenHeight/ 2) ;

    [[CCSpriteFrameCache **sharedSpriteFrameCache**] **addSpriteFramesWithFile:**@"hanksheet_poses.plist"];

    // same as before

defaultPose = [[CCSpriteFrameCache **sharedSpriteFrameCache**] **spriteFrameByName**:@"hank_fighting_default.png"];

zombie = [CCSprite **spriteWithSpriteFrame**: defaultPose];

    *// slight change, now using a CCSpriteFrame called **defaultPose** for the starting image*

```
[self addChild: zombie];

zombie.position = ccp( 300, 300 );

shadow = [CCSprite spriteWithFile:@"shadow.png"];
    // download the SD or HD version.

[self addChild: shadow z:-1];

shadow.position = ccp( zombie.position.x – 10, zombie.position.y – 100);
    // set initial position based on where the zombie is

    // Set up the walkRight and walkLeft CCSequences, the first few lines should look
    // identical from the last section ...

NSMutableArray *walkingFrames = [NSMutableArray arrayWithCapacity:9];
    for (int i = 1; i <= 9; ++i ) {
        NSString* file = [NSString stringWithFormat:@"hank_walkforward%i.png", i ];
        CCSpriteFrame* frame = [[CCSpriteFrameCache sharedSpriteFrameCache]
        spriteFrameByName: file ];
        [walkingFrames addObject: frame];
    }

CCCallFunc* moveDone = [CCCallFunc actionWithTarget: self selector:@selector(
allowAnotherMove )];
    // we'll write this method later,
    // ALL of our CCSequences include this same CCCallFunc

CCAnimation* walkAnimation = [CCAnimation animationWithSpriteFrames: walkingFrames
delay:0.1f ];

CCAnimate* animateWalk = [CCAnimate actionWithAnimation: walkAnimation];

CCMoveBy* moveRight = [ CCMoveBy actionWithDuration:1 position: ccp( 50, 0 )];
    // move 50 points to the right

CCSpawn* spawnWalkRight = [CCSpawn actions: animateWalk, moveRight, nil];
    // spawn the moveRight and animateWalk actions to play at once

self.walkRight = [CCSequence actions: spawnWalkRight, moveDone , nil];
    // when spawnWalkRight finishes then the moveDone actions runs,
    // which is what calls allowAnotherMove

CCMoveBy* moveLeft = [ CCMoveBy actionWithDuration:1 position: ccp( –50, 0 )];
    // moves left 50 points

CCSpawn* spawnWalkLeft = [CCSpawn actions: animateWalk, moveLeft, nil];
```

```objc
    // uses the same animateWalk action that spawnWalkRight used
self.walkLeft = [CCSequence actions: spawnWalkLeft, moveDone , nil];
    // use the same CCCallFunc moveDone action written before
[self addSwipeToMoveGestures];
    // we'll write this method later.
    Ultimately swiping will call either [zombie runAction:walkLeft]; or [zombie runAction:
    walkRight ];

    // set up punch CCSequence ...
NSMutableArray *punchFrames = [NSMutableArray arrayWithCapacity:5];
    for (int i = 0; i <= 4; ++i ) {
        NSString* file = [NSString stringWithFormat:@"hank_punch%i.png", i ];
        // these files start with zero, for example ... hank_punch0.png
        CCSpriteFrame* frame = [[CCSpriteFrameCache sharedSpriteFrameCache]
        spriteFrameByName: file ];
        [punchFrames addObject: frame];
    }
CCAnimation* punchAnimation = [CCAnimation animationWithSpriteFrames: punchFrames
delay :0.1f ];
CCAnimate* animatePunch = [CCAnimate actionWithAnimation: punchAnimation
restoreOriginalFrame: YES];
CCMoveBy* moveWithPunch = [ CCMoveBy actionWithDuration:0.3 position:ccp( 10, 0 )];
CCEaseOut* easeWithMovePunch = [CCEaseOut actionWithAction: moveWithPunch
rate:5];
    // use easing for the punch, looks much better!
CCSpawn* spawnPunchMoves = [CCSpawn actions: animatePunch,
easeWithMovePunch, nil];
self.punch = [CCSequence actions: spawnPunchMoves, moveDone, nil ];
[self addTapToPunchGesture];
    // we'll write this method later.

    // set up kick CCSequence ...
NSMutableArray *kickFrames = [NSMutableArray arrayWithCapacity:5];
    for (int i = 0; i <= 4; ++i ) {
        NSString* file = [NSString stringWithFormat:@"hank_kick%i.png", i ];
```

```
    CCSpriteFrame* frame = [[CCSpriteFrameCache sharedSpriteFrameCache]
    spriteFrameByName: file ];

    [kickFrames addObject: frame];

}

CCAnimation* kickAnimation = [CCAnimation animationWithSpriteFrames: kickFrames
delay:0.1f ];

CCAnimate* animateKick = [CCAnimate actionWithAnimation: kickAnimation
restoreOriginalFrame: YES];

CCMoveBy* moveWithKick = [ CCMoveBy actionWithDuration:0.3 position: ccp( –10, 0 )];

CCEaseOut* easeMoveWithKick = [CCEaseOut actionWithAction: moveWithKick rate:5];

CCSpawn* spawnKickMoves = [CCSpawn actions: animateKick, easeMoveWithKick, nil];

self.kick = [CCSequence actions: spawnKickMoves, moveDone, nil];


[self addTapToKickGesture];

    // we'll write this method later.


    // set up jump CCSequence ...
NSMutableArray *jumpFrames = [NSMutableArray arrayWithCapacity:4];

    // only four frames this time

  for (int i = 0; i <= 3; ++i ) {

    NSString* file = [NSString stringWithFormat:@"hank_spinning%i.png", i ];

    CCSpriteFrame* frame = [[CCSpriteFrameCache sharedSpriteFrameCache]
    spriteFrameByName: file ];

    [jumpFrames addObject: frame];

}

CCAnimation* jumpAnimation = [CCAnimation animationWithSpriteFrames: jumpFrames
delay:0.05f ];

CCAnimate* animateJump = [CCAnimate actionWithAnimation: jumpAnimation
restoreOriginalFrame: YES];

CCRepeat* repeatAnimation = [CCRepeat actionWithAction: animateJump times: 2];

// repeat the spinning frames twice

CCJumpBy* jumpBy = [ CCJumpBy actionWithDuration: 0.5 position: ccp(10,0)
height:100 jumps:1];

CCSpawn* spawnJump = [CCSpawn actions: repeatAnimation, jumpBy, nil ];

self.jump = [CCSequence actions: spawnJump, moveDone, nil];
```

```
    [self addSwipeToJumpGesture];
    // we'll write this method later.

    [self scheduleUpdate];
    // we'll write this method later.
    }
return self;
}
```

That's it for the **init** statement! Moving on, let's take care of the moveDone action, which appeared in all of our CCSequences. This CCCallFunc action will call **allowAnotherMove,** which sets moveInProgress to NO and changes the zombie sprite to the defaultPose.

```
-(void) allowAnotherMove {
    moveInProgress = NO;
    // when each move starts this will be set to YES
    [zombie setDisplayFrame: defaultPose ];
}
```

It's worth nothing that **setDisplayFrame** is a new method we haven't seen yet. The parameter it requires is a CCSpriteFrame, which we already saw in the **init** statement to set the zombie to the default image.

Now let's add our gesture recognition code and accompanying handler methods which get called each time the gesture is detected.

```
-(void) addTapToPunchGesture {
    tapToPunch = [[ UITapGestureRecognizer alloc] initWithTarget:
    self action:@selector ( handleTapToPunch:)];
    tapToPunch.numberOfTapsRequired = 2;
    // two taps to punch
    tapToPunch.numberOfTouchesRequired = 1;
    // only one finger required
    [ [[CCDirector sharedDirector]view] addGestureRecognizer:
    tapToPunch];
    [tapToPunch release];
}
```

```
-(void) handleTapToPunch:(UITapGestureRecognizer*) recognizer {
    if ( moveInProgress == NO) {
        moveInProgress = YES;
        [zombie stopAllActions];
        [zombie runAction: punch];
        } else {
        CCLOG(@"move already in progress");
        // unnecessary, just adding this to see that it works.
    }
}
```

Time to cram a little logic in your noggin. As is, the gestures will **always** be recognized, but we can make the handler methods they trigger do almost nothing if moveInProgress equals YES. That will prevent us from calling many actions on the zombie at once. Suppose you called a CCMoveBy while another, counter direction, CCMoveBy was already in progress. That's like trying to throw away a trash can, it may or may not get picked up. I'm also calling **stopAllActions** on the zombie before running the punch action. This way if the zombie was running a walkLeft or walkRight action at the time, that would get cancelled.

What you'll see happen is that the attack actions can all cancel walking actions, but walking actions can't cancel attack actions. Think about it in terms of the gameplay and that makes total sense. Moving onto the kick gesture. This isn't much different at all:

```
-(void) addTapToKickGesture {
    tapToKick = [[ UITapGestureRecognizer alloc] initWithTarget: self action:@selector
    ( handleTapToKick:)];
    tapToKick.numberOfTapsRequired = 2;
    // two taps to punch
    tapToKick.numberOfTouchesRequired = 2;
    // two fingers required
    [[[CCDirector sharedDirector]view]
    addGestureRecognizer: tapToKick];
[tapToKick release];
}

-(void) handleTapToKick:(UITapGestureRecognizer *)
recognizer {
    if ( moveInProgress == NO) {
    moveInProgress = YES;
```

```
    zombie stopAllActions];

    [zombie runAction: kick];

} else {

    CCLOG(@"move already in progress");

}

}
```

> Once this project is ready to test, go back and play around with these two lines in the **init** statement...
>
> CCAnimation* kickAnimation = [CCAnimation **animationWithSpriteFrames**: kickFrames **delay**:0.1f];
>
> CCMoveBy* moveWithKick = [CCMoveBy **actionWithDuration**:0.3 **position**: ccp(-10, 0)];
>
> You can have some fun changing the **delay** and **actionWithDuration** parameters, as well as the end location of the CCMoveBy.

Now let's add our swipe up gesture. This will trigger the jump action:

```
-(void) addSwipeToJumpGesture {

    swipeUp =[[ UISwipeGestureRecognizer alloc] initWithTarget: self action: @selector
    (handleSwipeUp:)];

    swipeUp.numberOfTouchesRequired = 1;

    swipeUp.direction = UISwipeGestureRecognizerDirectionUp;

    [[[ CCDirector sharedDirector ] view] addGestureRecognizer: swipeUp];

    [swipeUp release];

}

-(void) handleSwipeUp:(UISwipeGestureRecognizer *)recognizer {

    if ( moveInProgress == NO) {

        moveInProgress = YES;

        [zombie stopAllActions];

        [zombie runAction: jump ];

    } else {

        CCLOG(@"move already in progress");

    }

}
```

To add the swipe to move left and swipe to move right gestures, I will include them together in the following code:

```
-(void) addSwipeToMoveGestures {
    swipeRight = [[ UISwipeGestureRecognizer alloc] initWithTarget: self
    action:@selector( handleSwipeRight:)];
    swipeRight.numberOfTouchesRequired = 1;
    swipeRight.direction = UISwipeGestureRecognizerDirectionRight;
    [[[CCDirector sharedDirector]view] addGestureRecognizer: swipeRight];
    [swipeRight release];
    swipeLeft =[[ UISwipeGestureRecognizer alloc] initWithTarget: self
    action:@selector(handleSwipeLeft:)];
    swipeLeft.numberOfTouchesRequired = 1;
    swipeLeft.direction = UISwipeGestureRecognizerDirectionLeft;
    [[[CCDirector sharedDirector]view] addGestureRecognizer: swipeLeft];
    [swipeLeft release];
}

-(void) handleSwipeLeft:(UISwipeGestureRecognizer *)recognizer {
    if ( moveInProgress == NO) {
        [zombie stopAllActions];
        [zombie runAction: walkLeft];
    }
}

-(void) handleSwipeRight:(UISwipeGestureRecognizer *)recognizer {
    if ( moveInProgress == NO) {
        [zombie stopAllActions];
        [zombie runAction: walkRight];
    }
}
```

Notice anything different in the if statements on the previous page? Neither of them include moveInProgress = YES;. This means moves will still be allowed if the walkLeft or walkRight actions are running. Yet, we still check to make sure moveInProgress == NO before running a walk action.

Animation and Particle FX

Finally, at the end of our **init** statement we wrote [self **scheduleUpdate**]; so let's add that **update** method, which simply positions the shadow and prevents the zombie from leaving the screen area.

```
-(void) update:(ccTime) delta {
     // runs at the frame rate
   shadow.position = ccp( zombie.position.x –10 ,
   shadow.position.y );
   if ( zombie.position.x < 0 ) {
      [zombie stopAllActions ];
      [self allowAnotherMove ];
      zombie.position = ccp( 1 , zombie.position.y );

   }
else if( zombie.position.x > screenWidth) {
      [zombie stopAllActions ];
      [self allowAnotherMove ];
      zombie.position = ccp( screenWidth – 1 , zombie.position.y );

   }
}
```

The shadow will always stay at the same y position, but follow the zombie.position.x minus 10 (slight offset). Then we just check to make sure the zombie stays on screen. If it exceeds the stage bounds, we **stopAllActions**, then call **allowAnotherMove**, and change the position to be back within the stage boundary max or minimum.

Folks, that is it for this project! You can download it at the usual spot and find it in the folder named ***SpriteSheets_Fight_Character***.

Particles

Particle systems can make a dull level or character action suddenly look amazingly detailed with explosive effects or subtle ambience like snow falling. Wait till you see just how little code is involved. Hold on, you don't need to wait at all! Write this in the **init** statement of any of your existing projects:

CCParticleSystem* system = [CCParticleSnow **node**];

[self **addChild**: system];

Watch a bonus movie on this topic at **www.focalpress.com/cw/Dike**.

That was easy, right? If you hit build now, you'll see a snowy wave of squares slowing descending down your screen. It's cool but very blocky. What your project needs is a file called **fire.png** (and **fire-hd.png** or **fire-ipadhd.png** for Retina display devices) which Cocos2d will automatically use to replace each one of those squares.

In all my past projects, including the Ninjits app, I'm simply using a blurry circle. Your **fire.png** file can be any graphic you want, but since the particle system is usually spawning *a lot* of these, the source file size shouldn't be larger than 64 × 64 pixels. Your particle will be tinted and transparent based on the presets of the particular system you choose. For example, with a CCParticleSnow type system, the particles will all be white and various degrees of transparency. I'll show you how to alter some of those presets later.

My fire.png file, the background is transparent, not grey.

Particle systems are a lot like every other node we've seen. We can declare them in the header, add them, remove them, scale them, position them, give them z depth and tags, etc. So let's run a few CCActions on a system. Again, you can just add this code to the **init** statement of any project:

CCParticleSystem* system = [CCParticleSun **node**];

    // I'll call the instance "system" but you can name it anything

[self **addChild**: system **z**:0 **tag**:12345];

// the z depth and tag aren't necessary, just showing you can add those

system.position = ccp(0, 100);

system.scale = 1;

// not necessary to set as 1, but if you change this to another number you'll get some neat effects.

CCJumpBy* jump = [CCJumpBy **actionWithDuration**: 5 **position**: ccp(1000, 0) **height**:300 **jumps**:2];

// over 5 seconds will jump twice

id reverse = [jump **reverse**];

// reverse the previous action

CCSequence* sequence = [CCSequence **actions**: jump, reverse, nil];

CCRepeatForever* repeat = [CCRepeatForever **actionWithAction**: sequence];

// repeats the sequence forever

[system **runAction**: repeat];

The bonus movie at **www.focalpress.com/cw/Dike** shows you exactly what happens when the code above runs. Pretty cool, eh? You get a nice trailing fireball. Which would be a sweet effect for a game that actually involved flaming fireballs. Play with changing **CCParticleSun** to **CCParticleFire** for a similar effect.

A particle system could follow your finger as well. I'll use a CCParticleGalaxy in this example, but if you're getting curious to test more of these, use any of the system names in the table to the right.

In the HelloWorldLayer.m file ...

-(id) **init** {

    if ((self=[super **init**])) {

    self.isTouchEnabled = YES;

    //or just ... self.touchEnabled = YES;

    CCParticleSystem* system = [CCParticleGalaxy **node**];

    [self **addChild**: system **z**:0 **tag**:12345];

    // tag is needed this time IF I didn't declare "system" in my header file.

    }

  return self;

}

Try them all out ...	CCParticleFireworks
CCParticleSun	CCParticleGalaxy
CCParticleFlower	CCParticleMeteor
CCParticleSpiral	CCParticleExplosion
CCParticleSmoke	CCParticleSnow
CCParticleFire	CCParticleRain

```
-(void) ccTouchesMoved:(NSSet *)touches withEvent:(UIEvent *)event {
    UITouch *touch = [touches anyObject];
    CGPoint location = [touch locationInView:[touch view]];
    location = [[CCDirector sharedDirector] convertToGL: location];
    // just make the system follow the exact position of the touch
    [self getChildByTag:12345].position = location;
}
```

Run this example and you'll get a similar effect with the system trailing behind your touch location and fading off. **CCParticleGalaxy** is a clever one because it is constantly rotating "in space" as you can see from the movie at **www.focalpress.com/cw/Dike**.

Stopping and Restarting Emitting

If you were to add a particle system and then delete it using the usual **removeChild** method, you would notice the system immediately goes away. Which looks a bit odd because the viewer will probably expect the particles to fade away. Fortunately there's a great way to stop your system from emitting new particles and easing it's way out of existence:

[system **stopSystem**];

Then if you wanted to restart the system again, you would write:

[system **resetSystem**];

If you play the movie on the website **www.focalpress.com/cw/Dike**, you'll see I added a CCParticleMeteor system that follows the zombie character around. When I initially add it to the scene, I stopped the system from emitting right away. Whenever one of the attack moves occurs I just reset the system, then when the move is finished, stop it again. The system stays positioned with the character in the same **update** method that keeps the shadow's x position locked into the character's x location. The CCParticleMeteor system is a good one for what appears like a short burst of energy coming from the character. What if the character was facing the opposite direction though? You could just flip the entire system so the particles reverse the direction they fade off to using: system.scaleX = −1;

Increasing or Decreasing the Life of Particles

The lifetime of each particle in your system is easily changed with two properties, life and lifeVar. Many of the properties of particle systems have a corresponding property of the same name ending with "Var," which acts as a variance. So for example if we set:

system.life = 5.0 ;
system.lifeVar = 8.0 ;

... the particles would randomly live for anywhere between 5 seconds and 8 seconds. Each system also has a property called totalParticles, which is your max particle count. The longer particles live, the more likely the max is reached, at which point new particles won't be emitted until others have died off. The preset systems each have their own max number of particles, so for example, the CCParticleMeteor is 150 but a **CCParticleFireworks** system is 1500. You can lower the number of particles in each system by setting:

system.totalParticles = 100;

> *// or any number lower than the max*

If you are ever curious what the max is, use:

CCLOG(@"total Particles %i" , system.totalParticles);

You can also set the duration the entire system will run for, using:

system.duration = 20.0;

> *// after 20 seconds the system will stop*

Changing Particle Colors and Sizes

The preset systems are a great starting point for customizing the effect you *really* want, and often the only thing that needs tweaking is the color. So let's take a look at this using the **CCParticleSpiral** system, which by default uses a full range of colors.

CCParticleSystem* system = [CCParticleSpiral **node**];

[self **addChild**: system];

system.startColor   = (ccColor4F){ 0, 1, 0, **1** };

> *// r, g, b, alpha*

system.startColorVar = (ccColor4F){ 0, 0.8, 0, **1** };

system.endColor   = (ccColor4F){ 0, 1, 0, 0 };

system.endColorVar   = (ccColor4F){ 0, 0.8, 0, 0 };

The startColor and endColor properties (and their accompanying variance properties) obviously set a start color and end color. The ranges are from 0 to 1 for setting the red, green, blue and **alpha** (color coded the same above). So in this example I'm setting green to full and red and blue to none for the start and end colors with a variance of 0.8. So new particles could start and end anywhere from 0.8 to 1 for their green value.

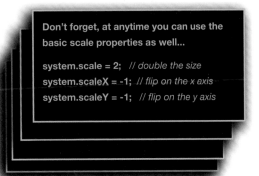

Don't forget, at anytime you can use the basic scale properties as well...

system.scale = 2; *// double the size*
system.scaleX = -1; *// flip on the x axis*
system.scaleY = -1; *// flip on the y axis*

The example movie, which you can find at **www.focalpress.com/cw/Dike**, also changes the endSize and endSizeVar properties. There's also a startSize and startSizeVar but I left those settings at the default.

system.endSize = 64;

    // in points

system.endSizeVar = 50;

Changing Gravity and Angle

Particles can be affected by gravity and we can change the starting degrees of each particle's emission angle. This example let's use **CCParticleSmoke** because by default it slowly moves straight upward and isn't all that exciting. We can make it appear that wind is blowing the smoke, which gives it a more realistic effect. First though, run a couple log statements on the gravity and angle values:

CCParticleSystem* system = [CCParticleSmoke **node**];

[self **addChild**: system];

CCLOG(@"angle %f", system.angle);

CCLOG(@"gravity X: %f , gravity Y: %f" , system.gravity.x , system.gravity.y);

You should see that the angle is 90. These values are in degrees with 90 angling particles upward, 0 to the right, −90 downward and 180 to the left. The float values from system.gravity.x and system.gravity.y are both 0. When we set a gravity position, which will be a CGPoint like usual, the particles will be pulled in that direction. The greater the values, the greater the pull. For example:

system.gravity = ccp (20, 0) ;

    // slight pull to the right

system.gravity = ccp (−200 , 0) ;

    // negative 200, so heavy pull to the left

system.gravity = ccp (−100 , 200) ;

    // pull to the left AND heavier pull up

system.gravity = ccp (0 , −300) ;

    // pull straight down

In the example movie, at **www.focalpress.com/cw/Dike**, for this system I've set the angle to 45 so the particles will try to move to the right, but the gravity is ccp (−25, 50) which pulls them left and up, overpowering the angle.

Emission Rate and Texture

We've got a few more notable properties to talk about. You can raise or lower the emissionRate of the system, which will change how many particles are added per second.

system.emissionRate = 50;

> // 50 particles added per second

If you have multiple systems in your app, and want a different particle image to be used in each, you don't have to settle for the default **fire.png** file for all of them. The two lines below will create a CCTexture2D called tex and assign that as the system.texture property. All you would need to change in your code is the file name.

CCTexture2D* tex = [[CCTextureCache **sharedTextureCache**] **addImage**:@"particle.png"];

system.texture = tex;

> // uses particle.png

Phew! That's all I have to say about particles. I hadn't planned on detailing **every** property of CCParticleSystem when I thought to write this section, but I got through most of them. I'll give you a link to the programming guide on Cocos2d-iPhone.org for a few more settings you can explore. If you really want to program your own particle effect without starting with one of the predefined systems, check out this nifty Particle Designer app at **www.71squared.com**.

Chapter 8

Menus, Sounds, Scenes, and Text

We've got to a group of topics that I think most game developers tackle after a few levels have already been coded. Players, on the other hand, experience a game in the reverse of the development order. They hear audio and see the intro scene or game menu before playing the first level. For us developers, that's usually the work we've saved for last. For good reason though, I like to know if the idea in my head is actually worth building a game around. The first few levels are a prototype, and probably 80 percent of my development time is spent testing an app without sound that skips to level one as soon as I build it.

So this chapter covers that other 20 percent of stuff that is no less important, but is probably not what you want to do right away.

Scene Basics

If you're at the point where you've got a nice little prototype of your game together, you might start thinking about changing scenes. Perhaps to create a new level, or to just show a series of title cards before your app. We've been hiding within the shelter of the HelloWorldLayer scene for quite a while, but I know you can't stay at home forever. All you little Nemos must swim out to sea and get lost eventually. So let's talk about some scene-related basics now and then, in Chapter 9, we will talk more about scenes and classes with regards to structuring your game. I know many of you are pining to learn how to create a singleton class, game data class, multiple game levels, etc. I promise we're getting there, but for now let's keep it basic with some scene transitions.

Most of you are probably using the Cocos2d version 2 templates to work along with the code in this book, so you've got an introduction to transitioning scenes early on in the IntroLayer class. If you remember, it runs this line of code to replace itself with the HelloWorldLayer class:

[[CCDirector **sharedDirector**] **replaceScene**:[CCTransitionFade **transitionWithDuration**:1.0 **scene**:[HelloWorldLayer **scene**] **withColor**: ccWHITE]];

My preference is to run the same code above in two lines, by writing the following:

CCTransitionFade *transition=[CCTransitionFade **transitionWithDuration**:1 **scene**: [HelloWorldLayer **scene**] **withColor**: ccWHITE];

[[CCDirector **sharedDirector**] **replaceScene**: transition] ;

This code could actually be run from your ***HelloWorldLayer.m*** file to replace itself with itself. Now why would you ever do that? Well, one good reason would be to simply restart the same level over again. Suppose, your character dies ten paces into the level by some enemy turtle, perhaps you ran head-on into him instead of jumping on his shell, and you're dead. Is the game over? Probably not, you simply want to restart the same level. The value of a variable called lives might be the only difference between the scene you were just playing and the scene you're playing now. I think most of us remember that every level of Mario Bros reset with each enemy back in the same position again.

Before I reveal a long list of possible scene transitions, I want to introduce you to a **static variable** in Objective-C. I won't dare call this a class variable because every time I run into a discussion about static variables on the Internet, someone chimes in that Objective-C doesn't really have class variables. So how about I tell you what a static variable can do, and I'll leave it up to you to decide what to make of it.

We can create a new static variable, by writing this:

static int theCount = 0;

… in a place we don't usually create variables. For example, that line could be written above the @implementation line.

static int theCount = 0;

@implementation HelloWorldLayer

Curious, eh? Now here's the really interesting part: in the **init** statement of **HelloWorldLayer.m** I could increment theCount variable up by 1, by simply writing:

theCount ++;

… then every time I replaced the HelloWorldLayer scene with itself, essentially resetting it, theCount will keep it's value from before. **It won't be reset to 0!** You might be thinking, "Ah-ha, so that's how to store variables for things like the game's score or the number of lives a player has."

No, slow down. Next chapter we will create a singleton class to maintain all our variables that will persist through multiple levels or scenes.

So if I'm not suggesting using a static variable for such things, why are we even discussing them? Well, I think this is a perfect place to bring them up because we can use them in a little scene transition project without putting too much emphasis on using them for your really crucial data.

If you want to follow along, go through the same steps on this page for creating a static int called theCount in your **HelloWorldLayer.m** and incrementing it in the **init** statement. Also add a CCSprite of your choice to the scene too, preferably an image large enough to cover most of the screen. When we start transitioning the scene, you want to be able to see the effect occurring over the image instead of empty black space. Then include this line at the end of the **init** statement:

[self **schedule**:@selector(**replaceWithMyself**) **interval**:5.0f];

The HelloWorldLayer class will initialize, then 5 seconds later it will perform a method called **replaceWithMyself.** I chose 5 seconds because I want to be sure the scene doesn't try to replace itself in less time than it takes to transition the new one in again. Each scene transition will take 2 seconds to run, so relatively speaking the difference between 2 seconds and 5 seconds is more than enough time to safely transition over and over again (I ran into this issue when testing). Now we need to actually write that method called **replaceWithMyself,** which will choose from three possible scene transitions based on the value of theCount. Prior to choosing a transition we will make sure theCount goes back to equaling 1 again, if it equals 4, thus creating an endless loop of these three transitions:

```
-(void) replaceWithMyself {

    if (theCount == 4) {

        theCount = 1;

    }

    CCLOG(@"theCount is ... %i", theCount);

    if (theCount == 1) {

        CCTransitionFadeTR *transition1 = [CCTransitionFadeTR transitionWithDuration:2
        scene:[HelloWorldLayer scene] ];

        [ [CCDirector sharedDirector] replaceScene: transition1];

        // transitions tiled effect from the bottom left to top right ( TR )

    } else if (theCount == 2) {

        CCTransitionSplitCols *transition2 = [CCTransitionSplitCols transitionWithDuration:2
        scene:[HelloWorldLayer scene] ];

        [ [CCDirector sharedDirector] replaceScene: transition2];

        // transitions with spliced column effect

    } else if (theCount == 3) {

        CCTransitionMoveInB *transition3 = [CCTransitionMoveInB transitionWithDuration:2
        scene:[HelloWorldLayer scene] ];

        [ [CCDirector sharedDirector] replaceScene: transition3];

        // transitions full screen in from the bottom

    }

    CCLOG(@"transitioning scene over 2 second transition");

    [self unschedule:_cmd];

    // not really needed, but we might as well unschedule this method now

}
```

Run that and hopefully you can see that a static int is an easy way to keep a running count over many instances of the same class. It shouldn't be overlooked that we are creating and removing an instance of the HelloWorldLayer class each time we transition in and out.

Menus, Sounds, Scenes, and Text

So to really drive that point home, add some log statements to the **init** method like these:

CCLOG(@"theCount is … **%i**", theCount);

CCLOG(@"new instance initialized");

```
new instance initialized
transitioning scene over the next 2 seconds
removing instance
theCount is... 2
new instance initialized
transitioning scene over the next 2 seconds
removing instance
theCount is... 3
new instance initialized
transitioning scene over the next 2 seconds
removing instance
theCount is... 1
new instance initialized
transitioning scene over the next 2 seconds
```

Then in the **dealloc** method, write:

CCLOG(@"transitioning scene over the next 2 seconds");

CCLOG(@"removing instance");

Your log window should be spitting back something like this screenshot. Notice in the order of things, we initialize a new instance, then transition for 2 seconds, then an instance is removed. So for 2 seconds there, we have both scenes in memory. Cocos2d is good at handling that brief usage spike, but if you notice your app constantly crashing at this point, you might need to retool what occurs in the **init** statement of the incoming class. Also, if you ever notice your **dealloc** method isn't firing after a transition, that's an indication of a memory leak.

Okay, I've made you wait too long already, here's a list of all the possible scene transitions you can play with.

Transition List

CCTransitionCrossFade
CCTransitionFade
CCTransitionFadeBL
CCTransitionFadeDown
CCTransitionFadeTR
CCTransitionFadeUp
CCTransitionFlipAngular
CCTransitionFlipX
CCTransitionFlipY
CCTransitionJumpZoom
CCTransitionMoveInB
CCTransitionMoveInL
CCTransitionMoveInR
CCTransitionMoveInT
CCTransitionPageTurn
CCTransitionProgress
CCTransitionProgressHorizontal
CCTransitionProgressInOut
CCTransitionProgressOutIn
CCTransitionProgressRadialCCW
CCTransitionProgressRadialCW
CCTransitionProgressVertical
CCTransitionRotoZoom
CCTransitionScene
CCTransitionSceneOriented
CCTransitionShrinkGrow
CCTransitionSlideInB
CCTransitionSlideInL
CCTransitionSlideInR
CCTransitionSlideInT
CCTransitionSplitCols
CCTransitionSplitRows
CCTransitionTurnOffTiles
CCTransitionZoomFlipAngular
CCTransitionZoomFlipX
CCTransitionZoomFlipY

Each of those transitions can run with the same method parameters seen in the previous examples: **transitionWithDuration** and **scene**. In a few cases you can optionally add an extra parameter, for example:

CCTransitionPageTurn *transition = [CCTransitionPageTurn **transitionWithDuration**:2 **scene**:[HelloWorldLayer **scene**] **backwards**:NO];

CCTransitionFlipX *transition = [CCTransitionFlipX **transitionWithDuration**:2 **scene**:[HelloWorldLayer **scene**] **orientation**: kOrientationDownOver];

Other options for the orientation parameter are: kOrientationLeftOver, kOrientationRightOver, kOrientationUpOver .

All these examples assume you are just replacing HelloWorldLayer with itself, otherwise don't forget to include your import statement for the class you want to replace the current one:

#import "YourClassWithAnotherScene.h"
> // write this in the header file of the class

Pushing Scenes (or Pausing Scenes)

If the children in your scene to be replaced had some early warning of their imminent doom you might hear their tiny little voices screaming about the end of the world. You've signed their death warrant and there's no turning back now. Instead though, if you want to temporarily pause your primary scene, keeping all the inhabitants alive and well, to put another scene on top of them, you can use **pushScene** :

[[CCDirector **sharedDirector**] **pushScene**: [Preferences **scene**]];

In the example above, the class is appropriately named Preferences, because for most games you'll find using **pushScene** for your preferences or options menu makes sense. Cocos2d even pauses all scheduled selectors in your main scene, so your game essentially has a **Pause Button** without much extra programming on your part. Particles will freeze in place, and touch events will be swallowed by the pushed scene. To return to the main scene you simply call **popScene** from the pushed scene.

[[CCDirector **sharedDirector**] **popScene**];
> // in this case, the Preference class would call this line to remove itself

Using **pushScene** and **popScene** for a preferences menu is just one example. You could use them to display a simple pop-up message with gameplay instructions for your app. The tricky thing to keep in mind is that it *is* possible to pile up these pushed scenes, in which case **popScene** will only remove the uppermost one. So try not to confuse yourself (or your user) by overdoing it.

Creating a New Class with a Scene

Way back in Chapter 4 we started creating our own custom classes, but we haven't actually made a new class with a scene and layer. Many of you might have tried this already, by simply copying most of the same code from the HelloWorldLayer class, and if so, I salute you. That's exactly what I would do too. So let's create a Preferences class to simply test the **pushScene** and **popScene** code. Later on, in Chapter 9, we will actually program some communication between a game data class, preferences menu class, and your main game class.

We've done this before, but I'll explain it again. First go to **File > New > File**, choose the Cocos2d template called CCNode class, subclass of CCLayer is fine, then name it **Preferences.m** (the header file gets created as well).

This is a pretty bare bones class file right now. What we want to do is declare a class method called **scene** in the header file. We are only adding one new line, but so we are all on the same page, I'll paste in the entire header file below:

The Preferences.h file

#import <Foundation/Foundation.h>

#import "cocos2d.h"

@interface Preferences : CCLayer {

}

+ (CCScene *) **scene**; ← ⎯⎯⎯⎯⎯⎯⎯⎯⎯⎯ Class Method,
note the plus sign
in front.

@end

You might have overlooked this before, but when we were replacing scenes or pushing them with snippets like this:

pushScene: [Preferences **scene**]

... the **scene** here refers to the class method we are writing now. Just in case you didn't connect that dot previously.

Now onto our **Preferences.m** file. If you want to type a bit less (and what good programmer doesn't) you can copy the same **scene** method from the **HelloWorldLayer.m** file. The only change we will need to make is replacing a couple of occurrences of the word HelloWorldLayer with the word Preferences. I'll copy in below the entire top portion of my file:

```
#import "Preferences.h"

@implementation Preferences

+(CCScene *) scene {
    // 'scene' is an autorelease object.
    CCScene *scene = [CCScene node];
    // 'layer' is an autorelease object.
    Preferences *layer = [Preferences node];
    // add layer as a child to scene
    [scene addChild: layer];
    // return the scene
    return scene;
}
```

To me, these **scene** methods are a bit like those stereograms that were so popular in the 1990s. If I stare at this code long enough, I'll figure it out, but I really don't care to. To sum it up with Twitter-style brevity, our Preference class now has a method that returns a CCScene called scene containing a layer that is actually an instance of our Preferences class. I know, it seems like a "which came first, the chicken or the egg?" type situation, but it doesn't matter because, from here on out, we don't even need to give it a second thought. It's ready.

Let's move onto the **init** statement. This statement won't look any different than usual. So we have something to show when our Preferences class appears, let's add an image to the scene. I'm also enabling touch so we can tap the screen in the upper right corner to remove the scene later.

```
-(id) init {
    if( (self=[super init]) ) {
        CGSize size = [[CCDirector sharedDirector] winSize];
        CCSprite *background = [CCSprite spriteWithFile:
        @"Preferences.png"];
        // any image will do
        background.position = ccp(size.width/2, size.height/2);
        [self addChild: background];
        self.isTouchEnabled = YES;
        // if using the Unstable version of Cocos2d switch to
```

```
        // self.touchEnabled = YES;
    }
    return self;
}
```

Before we forget, let's add in a **dealloc** method:

```
- (void) dealloc {
        CCLOG( @"removing preferences instance" );
        [super dealloc];
}
```

To finish off the Preferences class, let's add a simple **ccTouchesBegan** method to pop the scene when a touch is detected in the top right corner of the screen:

```
-(void) ccTouchesBegan:(NSSet *)touches withEvent:(UIEvent *)event
        UITouch *touch = [touches anyObject];
        CGPoint location = [touch locationInView:[touch view]];
        location = [[CCDirector sharedDirector]convertToGL: location];
        // if touching the top right corner
        if ( location.x > 950 && location.y > 700) {
        [[CCDirector sharedDirector] popScene];
    }
}
```

Then jump over to your HelloWorldLayer class and we'll do the same thing but detect the touch in the top left corner of the screen.

The HelloWorldLayer.m file

```
-(void) ccTouchesBegan:(NSSet *)touches withEvent:(UIEvent *)event
        UITouch *touch = [touches anyObject];
        CGPoint location = [touch locationInView:[touch view]];
        location = [[CCDirector sharedDirector]convertToGL: location];
        // if touching the top left corner
        if ( location.x < 100 && location.y > 700) {
        [[CCDirector sharedDirector] pushScene[ Preferences scene ] ];
    }
}
```

Now you need to write:

#import "Preferences.h"

… in your HelloWorldLayer class. Last, don't forget to include:

self.isTouchEnabled = YES;

… in your **init** statement.

That's all folks! You should be able to hit Run and push and pop your Preferences class as much as you like.

If you want to download the source files for this project, they are saved in the zip file at www.focalpress.com/cw/Dike, in the Folder named **ScenesAndMenus_Transitions**.

Section 2

Menus and Buttons

I've been waiting for an easy section to come along, and this could be the one! How hard can building a menu be, right? Well, the code to make a menu (or simply a button) with Cocos2d is very easy. Since you're probably reading this before you've created a menu for your game, let me plant some thoughts in your head before you undertake this.

Think about who will be using your app. Is your typical player able to read? That sounds like a joke, but I play games with my three-year-old every night before bed. He's memorized the order of the buttons to press in the games we play, but one navigation curveball could lead to him getting distracted and before I can grab the phone back, it's crushed underneath a keyboard shaped like a cat's head (doe-ray-meow-ouch, broken screen). I just so happen to have an app installed on my phone that illustrates this well: Ms. PAC-MAN. To be clear, **not** the sacred arcade version (a moment of silence please). This app is a good example of what-not-to-do with a menu:

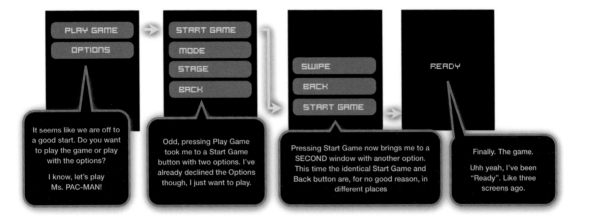

It seems like we are off to a good start. Do you want to play the game or play with the options?

I know, let's play Ms. PAC-MAN!

Odd, pressing Play Game took me to a Start Game button with two options. I've already declined the Options though, I just want to play.

Pressing Start Game now brings me to a SECOND window with another option. This time the identical Start Game and Back button are, for no good reason, in different places

Finally. The game.

Uhh yeah, I've been "Ready". Like three screens ago.

Three big notes on what went wrong there:

- **If your button describes one thing, make it do that thing.** "Play Game" plays the game. "Options" gives you options. Imagine if pressing the options button also started playing the game in the background.

- The third screen shifted where the identical **Start Game** and **Back** buttons were on the previous screen. This is massive user interface error to me. **Returning players will want to step through a navigation as quick as possible**, so if we are going to be forced to see two options screens, then at least let us power through them by fast-tapping the same spot onscreen. This shift in buttons makes me feel like I'm being warned *not* to play. Like I need to get my second-in-command to turn nuclear keys with me to ensure I really want to do this.

- **Use the available space you have.** The second screen had more than enough space to include another option, thus making the third screen even more unnecessary. As a user this wastes time.

As for a good example, Lego has some excellent games in the App Store that not only take into account the age of their typical player but also that those kids don't all speak the same language. So the navigation doesn't even have words in some of their games, and it is very intuitive even for someone young enough to be interested in Duplo blocks (those are the ones big enough to not be swallowed).

Whether you're building a menu with ten buttons or just one, you can use the **CCMenu** class. Depending on how you want your buttons to be arranged on screen you might find it necessary to use more than one CCMenu at a time. Before creating your CCMenu, you'll first need to setup a **CCMenuItem** (or items). These are the buttons your user will press, which can be images or text-based. Images are always more interesting to me, so let's begin there:

```
CCMenuItem *button1;
button1 = [CCMenuItemImage
    itemWithNormalImage: @"button1_normal.png"
    selectedImage: @"button1_selected.png"
    target: self
    selector:@selector( buttonMethod1 )];
    // runs on press
```

That second line and everything after is all one line of code. The images are obviously your choice. The **selectedImage** could be the same as the normal image, but I would suggest making at least a small change to the normal image so users have some indication they are pressing a button. To avoid a crash, be sure to write the **buttonMethod1** now. Even if you just write:

```
-(void) buttonMethod1 {
    CCLOG(@"button 1 pressed");
}
```

Forgetting to write that method is an easy mistake to make, and you will crash the app if you test without it.

Now we can add this lonesome CCMenuItem to a CCMenu:

```
CCMenu *menu = [CCMenu menuWithItems: button1, nil ];
    // always add nil at the end
[menu alignItemsHorizontallyWithPadding:20];
    // 20 points of padding if there was another item. You can also use alignItems
    VerticallyWithPadding
menu.position = ccp( 400, 400 );
    // position like usual
[self addChild: menu ];
    // added like usual, z depth and tag it if you want
```

That's it! You've created your first CCMenu. To add more items/buttons, simply comma-separate them like so:

```
CCMenu *menu = [CCMenu menuWithItems: button1, button2, button3, button4, nil ];
```

Just don't forget to add nil at the end. In case it isn't obvious, you can name your instances of CCMenuItem anything you want, if you want something more descriptive than button1, like BackButton, go for it.

Menu from Fonts

If you've been using the Cocos2d v2 starting templates, you've had a sneak peak at the code I'm about to show you. The HelloWorldLayer class creates a leader board and achievement board with similar code. Again our CCMenu is composed of CCMenuItems, this time those items are created with a Font instead:

[CCMenuItemFont **setFontSize**:28];

> *// you have the option to set the default size prior to creation*

[CCMenuItemFont **setFontName**:@"Arial"];

> *// you can also set the default font*

CCMenuItem *button1 = [CCMenuItemFont **itemWithString**:@"My Button" **target**: self **selector**:@selector(**buttonMethod1**)];

CCMenuItem *button2 = [CCMenuItemFont **itemWithString**:@"My Other Button" **target**: self **selector**:@selector(**buttonMethod2**)];

The code to add those buttons to the CCMenu is the same as before. Notice the font size and font name have been set to a default value in the CCMenuItemFont class itself. So the text in both buttons will have the same look. That's a good thing. If you arranged a menu (either stacked or side-by-side) with a different font and text size, it's going to look bad. Even the greasiest restaurant you've ever eaten at probably had a menu designed with enough sense not to make this mistake. For good measure though, I'll show you how you **could** (not should) do this with some variation using a CCLabelTTF:

CCLabelTTF *label1 = [CCLabelTTF **labelWithString**:@"Go Back" **fontName**:@"Marker Felt" **fontSize**:64];

CCLabelTTF *label2 = [CCLabelTTF **labelWithString**:@"Play Game" **fontName**:@"Arial" **fontSize**:30];

Now we have two labels with different sizes using different font names. So each CCMenuItem will use **itemWithLabel** instead:

CCMenuItem *button1 = [CCMenuItemLabel **itemWithLabel**: label1 **target**: self **selector**: @selector (**buttonMethod1**)];

CCMenuItem *button2 = [CCMenuItemLabel **itemWithLabel**: label2 **target**: self **selector**: @selector (**buttonMethod2**)];

CCMenu *menu = [CCMenu **menuWithItems**: button1, button2, nil];

[menu **alignItemsVerticallyWithPadding**: 20];

> *// stacked vertically with 20 points of padding between*

[menu **setPosition**: ccp(400, 400)];

[self **addChild**: menu];

Calling the Same Method for All Your Menu Items

You could have each of your CCMenuItems call the same method when pressed and identify who was pressed by the sender. To do this, the method that gets called needs to expect the sender as a parameter like so:

-(void) **methodAllButtonsCall**:(id) sender {

CCLOG (@"Pressed by —- %@", sender);

> // this will output something like ... Pressed by —- <CCMenuItemLabel = 0x195c630 | Tag = -1>

}

Before you test that out, make a slight change to your CCMenuItem setup:

CCMenuItem *button1 = [CCMenuItemLabel **itemWithLabel**: label1 **target**:   Call the same
self **selector**: @selector (**methodAllButtonsCall**:)]; ⟵   method.

CCMenuItem *button2 = [CCMenuItemLabel **itemWithLabel**: label2 **target**:
self **selector**: @selector (**methodAllButtonsCall**:)];   Add a colon!

button1.tag = 12345;

> // tag the CCMenuItem with whatever

button2.tag = 67890;

> // continue with the same CCMenu code on the previous page

Don't forget to add the colon after the method selector above or you will crash the app. Only thing left to do is include an if ... else if statement in the **methodAllButtonsCall** to test which tagged item was pressed.

-(void) **methodAllButtonsCall**:(id) sender {

    CCMenuItem* touchedItem = (CCMenuItem*)sender;

    // first cast touchedItem as the sender

    if (touchedItem.tag == 12345) {

        // test the tag

        CCLOG(@"button 1 was pressed");

    } else if (touchedItem.tag == 67890) {

        CCLOG(@"button 2 was pressed");

    }

    // do more code that is common to pressing either button

}

There you have it. Before or after your if statement you could perform more code that is common to pressing all your buttons. This could be a sound effect or a huge block of code. Don't think you have to use one method for all your buttons though, it's perfectly fine to create a separate method for each (and that's probably what I would do).

Okay, it's critique time. I did some Pac-slamming early in this section, now it's time to put my money where my mouth is. For your consideration, the image on this page is from one of my iPhone Pinball games (it's free). Call it lazy, call it streamlined, but the app opens directly into the game. It is pinball though. Everyone knows how to play, and the flipper controls are easily guessed at by simply pressing either the entire right side of the screen or the left side. There is one button, called **Menu**, which opens what you see here. Scores, game options, sound FX options, table styles, even ads are all in one place. Is it tight? Maybe. Or maybe it's just cozy. I think it works.

Emphasizing the Button Selected

The main reason I'm showing this image is because of these menus. The last icon selected stays selected. An obvious nicety for your players since they don't have to fumble around trying to remember which option they are currently using. This took a little time to set up, but worth the extra effort. We'll replicate this exact menu, which involves removing the CCMenu each time an option is selected and immediately rebuilding it. Don't worry, no one will even notice. There won't be a flicker effect to indicate the menu was ever removed. Then we'll use a static int so the class remembers the last selection.

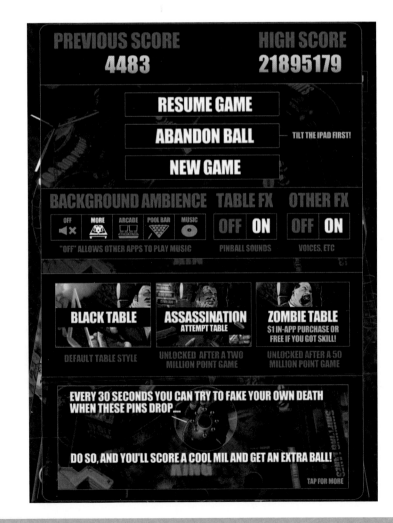

If you want to follow along, you'll need to suit up. You can use the same project from the end of last section, but you'll need some images to work with. Grab them from www.focalpress.com/cw/Dike.

Contained inside that zip are images for the menu bar background, then four icon sets, each with an "on" image (solid white) and "off" image (solid grey). I chose to make the menu bar a separate image because if each icon contained a portion of the bar, it would just be trickier to line them up perfectly.

We'll do all our work inside the Preferences class from the previous project. First off, go over to the header file and declare instances of the CCMenu and four CCMenuItems. Include as well a CGPoint variable for the position of the menu, this way we can do all our positioning in the **init** statement even though we won't create the CCMenu until later. I just find it easier to adjust positions when they are altogether.

In the Preferences.h file

```
@interface Preferences : CCLayer {
    CCMenu *menu;
    CCMenuItem *muteItem;
    CCMenuItem *musicItem;
    CCMenuItem *barItem;
    CCMenuItem *arcadeItem;
    CGPoint menuPosition;
}
```

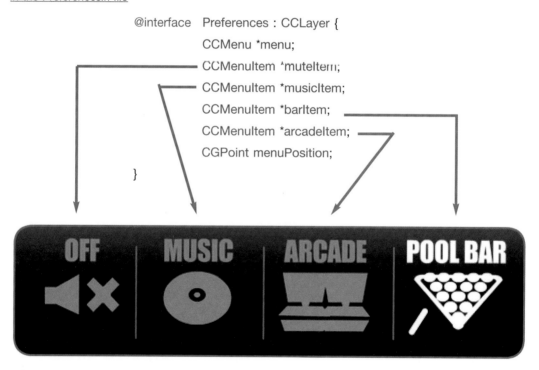

Now jump over to the Preferences implementation file and create a static variable and define some constants. I'll be lazy and not worry about creating a **Constants.h** file this time.

Menus, Sounds, Scenes, and Text

```
#import "Preferences.h"

#define kMuteSelected 0

#define kMusicSelected 1

#define kArcadeSelected 2

#define kBarSelected 3

static int selection = kMusicSelected;
```

Next in our **init** statement we will set the CGPoint position and add the background of the menu bar, both of which are centered in the middle of the screen. Then we will write a switch statement to test the value of selection. The four possible case conditions are the defined states above. Depending on the condition, we will call a different method for creating the menu. For example, on the first run, selection = kMusicSelected, so we will call the method that creates the menu with the music icon selected. Then if the user presses a different button, we simply remove the entire menu and call one of the other menu creation methods. Each of those methods has some code in common, so I've added a method called **addMenuItems**, which takes that shared code and puts it in one place. It should be easy to follow when you see it:

```
-(id) init {
    if( (self=[super init ]) ) {
        self.isTouchEnabled = YES;
        // or use self.touchEnabled = YES; if using the Unstable release of Cocos2d
        CGSize size = [[CCDirector sharedDirector] winSize];
        menuPosition = ccp( size.width/2, size.height/2 );

        // code from before ...
        CCSprite *background = [CCSprite spriteWithFile:@"Preferences.png"];
        background.position = ccp(size.width/2, size.height/2);
        [self addChild: background];

        CCSprite *menuBar = [CCSprite spriteWithFile:@"menu_bar.png"];
        menuBar.position = ccp( size.width/2, size.height/2 );
        [self addChild: menuBar];

        switch (selection) {
            case kMuteSelected:
                [self createMenuWithMuteSelected];
```

```
            break;
        case kMusicSelected:
            [self createMenuWithMusicSelected];
            break;
        case kArcadeSelected:
            [self createMenuWithArcadeSelected];
            break;
        case kBarSelected:
            [self createMenuWithBarSelected];
            break;
    }
  }
  return self;
}
```

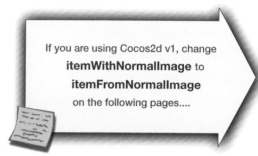

If you are using Cocos2d v1, change **itemWithNormalImage** to **itemFromNormalImage** on the following pages....

```
-(void) createMenuWithMuteSelected{
    selection = kMuteSelected;
    muteItem = [CCMenuItemImage itemWithNormalImage:@"icon_mute_on.png"
        selectedImage:@"icon_mute_on.png"
    target: self selector:@selector(createMenuWithMuteSelected)];
    musicItem = [CCMenuItemImage itemWithNormalImage:@"icon_music_off.png"
        selectedImage:@"icon_music_on.png"
    target: self selector:@selector(createMenuWithMusicSelected)];
    arcadeItem = [CCMenuItemImage itemWithNormalImage:@"icon_arcade_off.png"
        selectedImage:@"icon_arcade_on.png"
    target: self selector:@selector(createMenuWithArcadeSelected)];
    barItem = [CCMenuItemImage itemWithNormalImage:@"icon_bar_off.png"
        selectedImage:@"icon_bar_on.png"
    target: self selector:@selector(createMenuWithBarSelected)];
    [self addMenuItems];
    // calls the method containing common code for all these menu creation methods
}
```

```
-(void) createMenuWithMusicSelected{

        selection = kMusicSelected;

        muteItem = [CCMenuItemImage itemWithNormalImage:@"icon_mute_off.png"
              selectedImage:@"icon_mute_on.png"

        target: self selector:@selector(createMenuWithMuteSelected)];

        musicItem = [CCMenuItemImage itemWithNormalImage:@"icon_music_on.png"
              selectedImage:@"icon_music_on.png"

        target: self selector:@selector(createMenuWithMusicSelected)];

        arcadeItem = [CCMenuItemImage itemWithNormalImage:@"icon_arcade_off.png"
              selectedImage:@"icon_arcade_on.png"

        target: self selector:@selector(createMenuWithArcadeSelected)];

        barItem = [CCMenuItemImage itemWithNormalImage:@"icon_bar_off.png"
              selectedImage:@"icon_bar_on.png"

        target: self selector:@selector(createMenuWithBarSelected)];

        [self addMenuItems];

        // calls the method containing common code for all these menu creation methods

}
```

```
-(void) createMenuWithArcadeSelected{

        selection = kArcadeSelected;

        muteItem = [CCMenuItemImage itemWithNormalImage:@"icon_mute_off.png"
              selectedImage:@"icon_mute_on.png"

        target: self selector:@selector(createMenuWithMuteSelected)];

        musicItem = [CCMenuItemImage itemWithNormalImage:@"icon_music_off.png"
              selectedImage:@"icon_music_on.png"

        target: self selector:@selector(createMenuWithMusicSelected)];

        arcadeItem = [CCMenuItemImage itemWithNormalImage:@"icon_arcade_on.png"
              selectedImage:@"icon_arcade_on.png"
```

target: self **selector**:@selector(**createMenuWithArcadeSelected**)];

barItem = [CCMenuItemImage **itemWithNormalImage**:@"icon_bar_off.png"
    selectedImage:@"icon_bar_on.png"

target: self **selector**:@selector(**createMenuWithBarSelected**)];

[self **addMenuItems**];

// calls the method containing common code for all these menu creation methods

}

-(void) **createMenuWithBarSelected**{

    selection = kBarSelected;

    muteItem = [CCMenuItemImage **itemWithNormalImage**:@"icon_mute_off.png"
        selectedImage:@"icon_mute_on.png"

target:self **selector**:@selector(**createMenuWithMuteSelected**)];

    musicItem = [CCMenuItemImage **itemWithNormalImage**:@"icon_music_off.png"
        selectedImage:@"icon_music_on.png"

target:self **selector**:@selector(**createMenuWithMusicSelected**)];

    arcadeItem = [CCMenuItemImage **itemWithNormalImage**:@"icon_arcade_off.png"
        selectedImage:@"icon_arcade_on.png"

target:self **selector**:@selector(**createMenuWithArcadeSelected**)];

    barItem = [CCMenuItemImage **itemWithNormalImage**: @"**icon_bar_on.png**"
        selectedImage:@"icon_bar_on.png"

target:self **selector**:@selector(**createMenuWithBarSelected**)];

[self **addMenuItems**];

// calls the method containing common code for all these menu creation methods

}

-(void) **addMenuItems** {

    // all the createMenu methods call this ...

    [self **removeChild**: menu **cleanup**: NO];

    // remove the old menu first

```
menu = [CCMenu menuWithItems: muteItem, musicItem, arcadeItem, barItem, nil];
// create the menu again
[menu alignItemsHorizontallyWithPadding:0];
[menu setPosition: menuPosition];
[self addChild: menu z:10];
}
```

That's it! Since we set the selection variable to a new value each time we create the menu, the class will always initialize itself with the same menu selected as before. You can see this occurring in the example movie at **www.focalpress.com/cw/Dike**. Later in Chapter 9 we will use a singleton class to do something similar but for now the static int is doing a fine job.

Watch a bonus movie on this topic at **www.focalpress.com/cw/Dike**.

While you're there you can also download the finished example files.

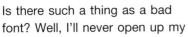

Section 3

Text and Custom Fonts

Is there such a thing as a bad font? Well, I'll never open up my **Font Book** app to find a territorial font has murdered some newly installed font for stepping on his turf: letters lying everywhere, detective fonts are drawing chalk outlines around the remains, saying things like "Back in the day, the kerning in this part of town was tight." Won't happen, but that would be cool to see.

I'll argue though that there **are** bad fonts out there. Not every font looks good at a certain size, or with outlining, or has perfect spacing between characters (that's the kerning). Or dog-gone-it, I'll come right out and say this: the author made an ugly font. I have ugly fonts installed on my computer. I've even used them to make something intentionally look ugly.

Now is the time to be picky. You've spent countless hours programming your game, so don't settle on **Arial** or **Helvetica** because those are easy choices. Those are good fonts, but probably not for your game. Think **style**. Be fabulous, honey.

Blambot.com is my go-to site any time I need a new font or just some inspiration. If you haven't heard of the site before, believe me, you've seen the author's work somewhere. When you need a logo for your game or some very prominent in-game text, check out his site. A lot of the Blambot fonts are free too.

Another favorite of mine is FontsForFlash.com. Which is an ironic domain name today if your font won't be for Flash, but it's got a nice ring to it anyway. They have a ton of great pixel fonts that are especially good for labels that will be sized relatively small in your game. This could be for scores, or tiny in-game prompts like "Open Door" or "100 XP Gained." Pixel fonts are terrific for messages that you want the user to half-hear in a sense. If they want to ignore it, they can. If your character is battling five enemies, and one dies, you're still engaged in combat with four more, so you don't want to distract the player with too much emphasis on the points or rewards gained from killing the first enemy.

I think that's an important point to consider when planning out how your game communicates with the user. At what point are you telling the player too much? We've all known someone that talked too much. Or told us the same thing in three different ways every conversation. It's annoying. If an app does that, we stop playing. Or worse, we hold down the app icon and wiggle it to death (next time you do that, imagine they are all shaking with fear and say things like, "who *vill* be next to *vitness* my power").

So let's get started. Just as a reminder, we've already seen the code to add a CCLabelTTF with text from a **TrueType font** (that's the "TTF" in the class name). What we'll be doing now is using the **CCLabelBMFont** class which refers to a **Bitmap Font**. This is a font defined from an image that contains all the letters, numbers, or other characters. When creating a Bitmap Font, you don't have to include more than you need. So for a point score label, you might only want numbers, like the image here.

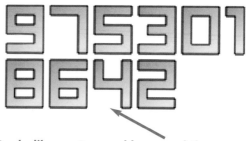

Looks like my 3-year-old arranged these in "numerical" order.

You would think that using an image instead of one of the **TrueType** fonts already installed on the device, like **Arial**, would be slower to render in a fast-paced game, but that's not the case. In fact, you might have noticed that the Cocos2d starting templates all include files called ***fps_images.png***, which are used in displaying the frame rate of the game.

./0123456789

Re-rendering the texture of a CCLabelTTF is very slow, so if this was occurring every single frame, the frame rate would suffer and you wouldn't get a true representation of the frames per second. So a CCLabelBMFont is the way to go for labels that need fast updating.

Menus, Sounds, Scenes, and Text

Here's the downside. To change the size, there's not a pretty way to do this like [label **setFontSize**:28] . We could scale the label up or down, but of course scaling it up would eventually cause some pixellation because that's what happens with any image when it gets viewed larger than it should be. So if you need to use the same font at different sizes, you'll want to create some variations of the **Bitmap Font**.

The yellow-to-orange outlined font on the opposite page is one I used in a Starter Kit Template. The program you'll use to create the **Bitmap Font** will figure out the tightest way to arrange the characters to squeeze them into the smallest image possible. It will then export out the image file along with an accompanying *.fnt* file, which is just a text file that tells the compiler where each of those characters is on the image.

```
info face="hooge 05_55" size=64 bold=0 italic=0 charset="" unicode=0 stretchH=100 smooth=1 aa=1
padding=0,0,0,0 spacing=0,0
common lineHeight=74 base=58 scaleW=256 scaleH=128 pages=1 packed=0
page id=0 file="hooge2-ipadhd.png"
chars count=10
char id=48 x=154 y=2 width=36 height=44 xoffset=0 yoffset=12 xadvance=42 page=0 chnl=0
char id=49 x=192 y=2 width=20 height=44 xoffset=0 yoffset=12 xadvance=26 page=0 chnl=0
char id=50 x=116 y=48 width=36 height=44 xoffset=0 yoffset=12 xadvance=42 page=0 chnl=0
char id=51 x=116 y=2 width=36 height=44 xoffset=0 yoffset=12 xadvance=42 page=0 chnl=0
char id=52 x=78 y=48 width=36 height=44 xoffset=0 yoffset=12 xadvance=42 page=0 chnl=0
char id=53 x=78 y=2 width=36 height=44 xoffset=0 yoffset=12 xadvance=42 page=0 chnl=0
char id=54 x=40 y=48 width=36 height=44 xoffset=0 yoffset=12 xadvance=42 page=0 chnl=0
char id=55 x=40 y=2 width=36 height=44 xoffset=0 yoffset=12 xadvance=42 page=0 chnl=0
char id=56 x=2 y=48 width=36 height=44 xoffset=0 yoffset=12 xadvance=42 page=0 chnl=0
char id=57 x=2 y=2 width=36 height=44 xoffset=0 yoffset=12 xadvance=42 page=0 chnl=0
```

The contents of the *.fnt* file looks pretty scary, but if you don't want to look inside those files, you never have to. The only thing you need to do is import that file into your project Resources along with the image file, which is most likely a *.png* file. As usual, Cocos2d will be smart enough to use an alternate *.fnt* and *.png* file for the correct device, you just need to include those alternates as well. So for example, your point score label might need four different Bitmap fonts (eight files total) for a Universal app.

blambot.png and *blambot.fnt*

blambot-hd.png and *blambot-hd.fnt*

blambot-ipad.png and *blambot-ipad.fnt*

blambot-ipadhd.png and *blambot-ipadhd.fnt*

Once you've got everything in the project, the code to get you started is incredibly simple. Declare the label in your header file:

CCLabelBMFont * scoreLabel ;

> *// declare in your header*

Then in your implementation file, write:

scoreLabel = [CCLabelBMFont **labelWithString**:@"0000" **fntFile**:@"blambot.fnt"];

> *// the score would be 0000 to start*

[self **addChild**: scoreLabel];

scoreLabel.anchorPoint = ccp(1.0 , 0.5);

> *// anchors at right edge instead of the middle which by default is (0.5f, 0.5f)*

Optionally, you can set the anchorPoint property to the far right by setting 1 above. Previously the alignment was in the middle. I think this looks much better for doing something like updating the score values in a game. You'll see the difference later in the final example movie. At any time now you could use the following line to change the value of the string:

[scoreLabel **setString**:@"12345"];

> *// note that numerical digits are also considered string characters*

In the next example, I'll show you how to use a variable there instead. Keep in mind, if your **Bitmap Font** ONLY includes numbers, you would not want to set the string to a character that wasn't included in the font. If you did, you'll crash.

Using bmGlyph

I know some of you are about to pound your head against the wall because you can't test this without a **Bitmap Font** to use. You can use the source files referred to at the end of this section and dig out the *.fnt* and *.png* files from the Resources folder of that project, but to be true Cocos2d Warriors today, I think you should invest in some new software to create your own Bitmap Fonts. For the price of ten $0.99 apps, you can get **bmGlyph**, the very same Bitmap Font generator I'm using. Is that an endorsement or what? You can find it on the Mac App Store.

I'll step you through a quick export of a font called Armor Piercing 2.0 by Blambot. Select the font in the **Fonts Panel** and adjust the size. You can see I've set this to 205, which will appear rather large on your screen, but I'm creating this for the retina iPad so it will appear half this size but with double the resolution. When we publish later, **bmGlyph** will automatically create the HD and SD versions as well.

Next step is define the characters we want to include in our Bitmap Font. As you can see I've included only numbers and a decimal point, just in case we choose to use that. After entering those, you might need to hit Return on the keyboard to see them in the preview window.

Go ahead and save your **bmGlyph** project file. It's a good idea to save your project someplace you'll remember later, because trust me, recreating these fonts again is much easier with the original project. When the iPad 3 was released I had to revisit some old font projects to make **-ipadhd** versions.

Now for the fun part. You can add color, textures, fill gradients, strokes, stroke gradients, and shadows to your font.

This comes at no extra cost to the app because no matter how jazzed up your text is, it's always going to be derived from an image anyway.

Next, scroll down to the Publish Settings panel. You'll want to set the Format to **Cocos2d / BMFont**. If you're creating an iPad retina-enabled game, set the **Auto SD Level** to **Full HD (@4x)**. I've checked off **Redraw when downscaling** because, for some reason, it just sounds like I should. Choose a

Directory to publish to, and choose a **Font Name**. My recommendation would just be to publish to wherever you've saved the **bmGlyph** project, and give the font name the same name as whatever you called the project. Again, if you need to update these fonts later or create a variation, you can search and find them easily.

So I called my project, **nuclear_horizon.bmGlyph**, and when I hit **Publish** it will create:

nuclear_horizon.png and *nuclear_horizon.fnt*

nuclear_horizon-hd.png and *nuclear_horizon-hd.fnt*

nuclear_horizon-ipadhd.png and *nuclear_horizon-ipadhd.fnt*

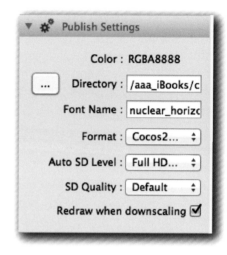

Hmmm. What's missing there? What about the *-ipad* version for the SD iPads?. Well essentially that's what the *-hd* version is, because this variation is exactly half the size of the **Full HD (@4x)** version. If you want, you can duplicate the *-hd* versions, name the files with *-ipad* instead, then simply open the *-ipad.fnt* file in Text Editor, and after you see "file=" change "-hd" to "-ipad" instead. Except, get this: the SD iPads should use the *-hd* version anyway before resorting to the default name, if there's no *-ipad* version (your **AppDelegate.m** lists these fallback suffixes).

Once you've got your Bitmap Font file sets, dump them all into your Xcode project, and let's give this a real test run. I'm going to create a CCLabelBMFont which updates at 60 fps with a variable called score.

In the header file ...

```
@interface HelloWorldLayer : CCLayer {
    CCLabelBMFont* scoreLabel;
    int score;
}
```

In the Implementation file ...

```
-(id) init {
    if( (self=[super init]) ) {
        scoreLabel = [CCLabelBMFont labelWithString:@"0" fntFile:@"nuclear_horizon.fnt"];
        scoreLabel.position = ccp( 400, 400 );
```

Menus, Sounds, Scenes, and Text

```
    [self addChild: scoreLabel];
    scoreLabel.anchorPoint = ccp( 1.0 , 0.5 );
    // keep the numbers aligned right
    [self schedule:@selector(updateLabel:) interval:1/60];
}
return self;
}


-(void) updateLabel:(ccTime)delta {
    score = score + 101;
    // adds 101 each frame
    NSString* scoreString = [NSString stringWithFormat:@"%i", score];
    // %i gets replaced by the value of the score integer
    [scoreLabel setString: scoreString];
    // set the string to the scoreString variable
}
```

Test that and you'll see a number counter add up pretty quickly. Don't feel like you need to make this modification to your own test project, but just so you can see the difference the anchorPoint value makes, I'll add two more labels with alignments to the right, left, and middle. Watch a bonus movie on this topic at www.focalpress.com/cw/Dike.

The top example is obviously not the way to go. The default anchorPoint at 0.5, 0.5 (in the middle) doesn't shift too wildly, but as you can see the bottom example (anchored right) keeps the lowest digits in the same place throughout most of the movie.

If you'd like to build this example, or just pull out the *.fnt* and *.png* files for this font you can do so at www.focalpress.com/cw/Dike.

NSUserDefaults and an Easy Score Board

This section title is too long!

Since we were just discussing score labels, I have a loose tie-in to talk about how to build a locally-saved high-score/leader board using **NSUserDefaults**. By local, I mean, the board will pull data saved to a special location for *only* the app you are building, and *only* on the user's device. So the scores won't be saved to an external server, or data-handler like Game Center. This is a perfectly fine way to save high scores or other variable data, if you simply don't care about doing anything fancier.

Of course a high-score board is definitely something that could be better left to **Game Center** because that's one of the things **Game Center** was made to do, but the NSUserDefaults are also an easy way to store basic user preferences like: bool variables to determine whether or not the sound should be muted in the game, an NSString variable to remember the user's name from the previous game, or an int variable to track the last level the player completed. Those are just a few examples, and with the common variables like int, float, bool or NSString, you can restore endless game state possibilities.

The upside of using NSUserDefaults is that even if the app quits (perhaps the device restarted) those variables are still saved. The downside is that if the app is ever deleted, the data is gone for good. So all that precious high-score data (ahem, sarcasm) will never be looked at in awe by yourself or your teenage cousins that want to rub their greasy fingers on your screen and best your scores. If you're wondering "WWJD?" ("what would Justin do?"), I love using NSUserDefaults. They are a quick and easy way to save insignificant data. Let's be real here, most game data is pretty insignificant.

In the header file of whatever class you want to use here, declare your defaults:

@interface ... *etc*

NSUserDefaults* defaults;

Now in our implementation file's **init** statement, write:

defaults = [NSUserDefaults **standardUserDefaults**];

That's all you need to do to get started.

Typically your next step will be to retrieve back some variable data that was stored before. For example, you might continue writing in your **init** statement with:

int lastLevelComplete;

lastLevelComplete = [defaults **integerForKey**:@"lastLevel"];

Ah, but wait. What if this is the first time the app has ever been run? Nothing would have been saved previously so lastLevelComplete will equal what? Zero. Which is perfect because zero levels have been completed anyway. So just keep in mind, it's okay for your defaults to equal nothing on first run.

Let's pick apart **integerForKey**. The variable type we want to pull from the defaults is an integer because lastLevelComplete is an integer. That part is pretty obvious. The **"ForKey"** part of **integerForKey** is what might sound unfamiliar (hence, troubling) to some of you. Just think of the Key as a variable name. So basically we are saying, "Yo, defaults, go get me the integer value from this variable name." That name is @"lastLevel." Which is an aptly named Key of our choosing to fit this example.

Keeping with our hypothetical level-saving scenario for just a moment longer, whenever progress needs storing in the defaults, all we need to write is:

[defaults **setInteger**: 2 **forKey**:@"lastLevel"];

Now the next time this app is run (even after fully quitting), our code in the **init** statement gives lastLevelComplete the value of whatever amount was saved last. It's that easy.

You can save some pretty complex object types in the NSUserDefaults, but for now let's just go over some other common ones besides int.

Save and retrieve an NSString value:

[defaults **setObject**:@"Justin" **forKey**:@"myName"];

    // save

NSString* name = [defaults **stringForKey**:@"myName"];

    // return

Save and retrieve a bool value:

[defaults **setBool**: YES **forKey**:@"mutePref"];

    // save

bool muteSound = [defaults **boolForKey**:@"mutePref"];

    // return

Save and retrieve a float value:

[defaults **setFloat**:123.45 **forKey**:@"cashMoney"];

    // save

```
float bills = [defaults
floatForKey:@"cashMoney"];

        // return
```

Quick High-Score Board

Let's record some high scores for other
players to bow down before. This is
really not much code, but then again,
I'm only saving the top three scores. If

In my games, I usually save int data, which I define in my *Constants.h* file.
So I might have ...
#define weaponAxe 0
#define weaponSword 1
#define weaponNinjaStars 2

Then I can just save...
[defaults **setInteger**:weaponSword **forKey**:@"lastWeaponUsed"];

you want more, you'll pick up on the set up pretty quick. In the header file below, our
NSUserDefaults are declared with a variable name of defaults. We have int variables for the
scoreBoardFirstPlace, scoreBoardSecondPlace, and scoreBoardThirdPlace slots. Another int
variable called newScore will be our hypothetical end-of-game point total. In actuality, it will
just be a random number. Then we have CCLabelBMFont variables to display each score.
Finally, a CGPoint variable, just to set up the initial location of the entire score board (the
labels will be incrementally positioned based on this initial location).

In the HelloWorldLayer.h file

@interface HelloWorldLayer : CCLayer {

    NSUserDefaults* defaults;

    int scoreBoardFirstPlace;

    int scoreBoardSecondPlace;

    int scoreBoardThirdPlace;

    int newScore;

    CCLabelBMFont* scoreLabelFirst;

    CCLabelBMFont* scoreLabelSecond;

    CCLabelBMFont* scoreLabelThird;

    CGPoint scoreBoardPosition;

}

Now go over to our implementation file's **init** statement. First, let's add in a CCSprite so we
have something other than a black background. Then we will try to get any previously saved
scores from the defaults and equate them to their appropriate variables. Next, we'll set the
scoreBoardPosition location. Then, we call a method named **createScoreBoard**. Instead of
creating the board now by adding the CCLabelBMFont variables to the scene in the **init**

statement, I'm putting that code in a separate method so I can conveniently call this same method later whenever we need to re-create the board with different scores. Finally, we will schedule a method called **generateRandomHighScores,** which as you can guess, will give newScore a random value every 3 seconds:

In the HelloWorldLayer.m file

```
- ( id ) init {
    if ( ( self= [super init] ) ) {
        CGSize size = [[CCDirector sharedDirector] winSize];
        CCSprite* background = [CCSprite spriteWithFile:@"background.png"];
        // add in some background art
        background.position = ccp( size.width / 2, size.height / 2 );
        [self addChild: background];
        defaults = [NSUserDefaults standardUserDefaults];
        scoreBoardFirstPlace = [defaults integerForKey:@"firstPlace" ];
        // these will all be zero on first run ...
        scoreBoardSecondPlace = [defaults integerForKey:@"secondPlace" ];
        scoreBoardThirdPlace = [defaults integerForKey:@"thirdPlace" ];
        scoreBoardPosition = ccp( 210, 680 );
        // set any position you want, this one matches up to my background art
        [self createScoreBoard];
        // we will call this method again every time a new score is set
        [self schedule: @selector( generateRandomHighScores: ) interval:3.0f ];
        // every 3 seconds generate a new score to test
    }
    return self;
}
```

Now let's write the **createScoreBoard** method. The only thing that might seem tricky is that I'm removing each CCLabelBMFont before adding a new one. On the first run, the game won't have a CCLabelBMFont to remove, but we can safely call this code anyway.

```
-(void) createScoreBoard {
    // remove scoreLabelFirst (in case we are recreating the score board),
    then create a new one
    [self removeChild: scoreLabelFirst cleanup: NO];
```

```
scoreLabelFirst = [CCLabelBMFont labelWithString: [NSString
stringWithFormat:@"%i", scoreBoardFirstPlace] fntFile: @"green_arcade.fnt"];

scoreLabelFirst.position = ccp( scoreBoardPosition.x, scoreBoardPosition.y );

[self addChild: scoreLabelFirst];

scoreLabelFirst.anchorPoint = ccp(1.0f, 0.5f );

// remove scoreLabelSecond (in case we are recreating the
score board), then create a new one

[self removeChild: scoreLabelSecond cleanup: NO];

scoreLabelSecond=[CCLabelBMFont labelWithString:[NSString
stringWithFormat:@"%i", scoreBoardSecondPlace] fntFile:@"green_arcade.fnt"];

scoreLabelSecond.position = ccp( scoreBoardPosition.x, scoreBoardPosition.y – 40);

[self addChild: scoreLabelSecond ];

scoreLabelSecond.anchorPoint = ccp(1.0f, 0.5f );

// remove scoreLabelThird (in case we are recreating the score board),
then create a new one

[self removeChild: scoreLabelThird cleanup: NO];

scoreLabelThird = [CCLabelBMFont labelWithString:[NSString
stringWithFormat:@"%i", scoreBoardThirdPlace] fntFile: @"green_arcade.fnt"];

scoreLabelThird.position = ccp( scoreBoardPosition.x, scoreBoardPosition.y – 85 );

[self addChild: scoreLabelThird ];

scoreLabelThird.anchorPoint = ccp(1.0f, 0.5f );

}
```

> You can pull this font from the source files or use your own.

Now we generate a random score to test against the best of the best. The if … else if statement below should be pretty easy to follow, but here goes: if the random newScore is higher than the first place score variable, we make the third place score equal the second place score, then the second place score equals the first place score and the first place score now equals the newScore variable. We then call a method named **saveNewDefaults** (which you'll see on the next page) and call the **createScoreBoard** method. We do the same thing in the else if statements to check against the lesser place values. I added an else statement just to see when a new high score isn't made.

```
-(void) generateRandomHighScores:(ccTime) delta {
    newScore = arc4random( ) % 10000;
        // range is 0 to 9999
        if (newScore > scoreBoardFirstPlace ) {
```

```
// if a new 1st place is set, shift all scores down, save new defaults,
recreate the score board
        scoreBoardThirdPlace = scoreBoardSecondPlace;

        scoreBoardSecondPlace = scoreBoardFirstPlace;

        scoreBoardFirstPlace = newScore;

        [self saveNewDefaults];

        [self createScoreBoard] ;

} else if (newScore > scoreBoardSecondPlace ) {

// if a new 2nd place is set, shift scores down, save new defaults,
recreate the score board
        scoreBoardThirdPlace = scoreBoardSecondPlace;

        scoreBoardSecondPlace = newScore;

        [self saveNewDefaults];

        [self createScoreBoard];

} else if (newScore > scoreBoardThirdPlace ) {

// set new 3rd place score, save new defaults, recreate the score board
        scoreBoardThirdPlace = newScore;

        [self saveNewDefaults];

        [self createScoreBoard] ;

} else {

        CCLOG(@"no new high scores, the random number was only: %i", newScore);

    }

}
}
```

Finally, we create a method to save all the default values if the scoreboard shifted values.

```
-(void) saveNewDefaults {
        [defaults setInteger: scoreBoardFirstPlace forKey: @"firstPlace"];

        [defaults setInteger: scoreBoardSecondPlace forKey: @"secondPlace"];

        [defaults setInteger: scoreBoardThirdPlace forKey: @"thirdPlace"];

        [defaults synchronize];

        // see notes above ...

}
```

The only new code you are seeing above is [defaults **synchronize**], which is optional here and arguably not recommended. Depending on how often you set your defaults to something new, you should use that line sparingly. Reason being, by calling **synchronize** it will write the changes to a *.plist* file (which is what the defaults dictionary is saved in) and this can be slightly resource intensive, slowing down the device. The app will **synchronize** on it's own when it closes and at other times periodically, without you explicitly calling this. So why does Apple even give us the option to **synchronize**? They just do. If you want to be in absolute control and make sure those defaults get saved when you think they should, you can.

Ready for the source files? Dig in. **www.focalpress.com/cw/Dike**.

Sound FX and Background Audio

Playing sound is incredibly easy with Cocos2d. Actually, I should say, playing sound is incredibly easy with CocosDenshion, to give credit where it's due. The CocosDenshion sound framework comes included with your bundle of Cocos2d goodies, and the class files are copied into your project any time you begin with a Cocos2d template. The only thing you need to do is import in the header files wherever you'll be playing audio. So assuming you're working in the HelloWorldLayer class, add the two circled lines underneath the import statements already in your file:

In the HelloWorldLayer.h file (or any class you need to use audio with) ...

#import <Foundation/Foundation.h>

#import "cocos2d.h"

#import "SimpleAudioEngine.h"
#import "CDAudioManager.h"

Many of you will only need to import the SimpleAudioEngine class but I'm going to show you some settings in the CDAudioManager as well, that I found worth knowing in the past. Plus, there's really not a lot of code to explain in the SimpleAudioEngine so I might as well give you a little more in this section. The line you'll probably want first is how to play a simple effect for some action in your game.

```
[ [SimpleAudioEngine sharedEngine] playEffect:@"flipper1.caf"];
```

Incredibly easy right?! Of course, you need to include a sound file called **flipper1.caf** in your project, or you won't hear a darn thing. If you aren't familiar with **.caf** file types, we'll talk about those later. You can test this with other sound files as well, like **.mp3** or **.wav**. Now take a stab in the dark at the next method name for playing background music. Just guess:

```
[ [SimpleAudioEngine sharedEngine] playBackgroundMusic:@"smokers_section.mp3" loop:
YES];
```

Pretty easy to remember right? Just remember that you can only play one background track at a time. So if you wanted to play music for a level, but also include an ambient rain sound the entire time as well, you'll be better off mixing those tracks together in an audio editor so you have one **.mp3** file instead of two.

Those two lines of code are all most of you will require for your games to blast some funky background music and play an effect every time an enemy gets hacked to death. For the rest of you, here's some extra lines to play with.

```
[ [SimpleAudioEngine sharedEngine] stopBackgroundMusic ];
        // stops background music
[ [SimpleAudioEngine sharedEngine] pauseBackgroundMusic ];
        // pauses background music ( use this if you want to resume it vs stopping it )
[ [SimpleAudioEngine sharedEngine] resumeBackgroundMusic ];
        // resume background music ( from wherever you paused it )
[ [SimpleAudioEngine sharedEngine] rewindBackgroundMusic ];
        // rewinds the background music to the beginning
```

You can test whether or not the SimpleAudioEngine is currently playing background music like so:

```
if ( [[SimpleAudioEngine sharedEngine] isBackgroundMusicPlaying ] == YES ) {
        // do something if it is
}
```

You can preload your sound effect files and background music with the following two lines:

```
[ [SimpleAudioEngine sharedEngine] preloadEffect:@"flipper1.caf"];
    // will preload this file to play later
[ [SimpleAudioEngine sharedEngine] preloadBackgroundMusic:@"smokers_section.mp3" ];
    // will preload this file to play later
```

In a fast-paced game, preloading some of your sound effects is a good idea. You might notice a slight lag right before a non-preloaded effect plays, and in a game like pinball, where the ball is hitting many different objects right away, each causing different sound effects, a repeated stutter in the beginning of a game can be very distracting.

You can unload effects (but not background music) with this line:

```
[ [SimpleAudioEngine sharedEngine] unloadEffect:@"flipper1.caf"];
    // unloads a preloaded or already played effect of that same name
```

That could be useful if you played an effect once, but knew it wouldn't be used again.

You can also lower the effect volume and background volume separately with the following lines:

```
[ SimpleAudioEngine sharedEngine].backgroundMusicVolume = 0.5;
    // 50% normal volume
[ SimpleAudioEngine sharedEngine].effectsVolume = 0.2;
    // 20% normal volume
```

The range for both of those is 0 to 1, with 1 being 100 percent volume (which is the default).

Without getting too complicated, that's it for the SimpleAudioEngine. Let's take a look at one setting in the CDAudioManager class. You might want your app to disable or enable music that is already playing from another app. Now think carefully on this one, because I'm sure many of you have been pleasantly listening to your Music library, then started a game and realized you can't listen to your music anymore. Dude, not cool. Below is the code to choose how your app handles audio (one of the first three is probably what you want):

```
[[CDAudioManager sharedManager] setMode: kAMM_FxOnly ];
    // other apps will be able to play their audio
[[CDAudioManager sharedManager] setMode: kAMM_FxPlusMusic ];
    // only this app will play audio ( shuts down other apps playing music )
[[CDAudioManager sharedManager] setMode: kAMM_FxPlusMusicIfNoOtherAudio ];
```

// if another app is playing audio at start up then allow it to continue and don't play music (GOOD CHOICE)

[[CDAudioManager **sharedManager**] **setMode**: kAMM_MediaPlayback];

// this app takes over audio like a music player app

[[CDAudioManager **sharedManager**] **setMode**: kAMM_PlayAndRecord];

// app takes over audio and has input and output

Audio File Types

Prior to reading Steffen Itterheim's excellent book on Cocos2d Game Development, I hadn't heard of a *.caf* audio file, granted, I'm not exactly a sound guru either. Steffen suggested using *.mp3* files for background audio and *.caf* files for sound effects, and I can't argue with a good thing. I feel like my Cocos2d apps all handle audio very smoothly with those files.

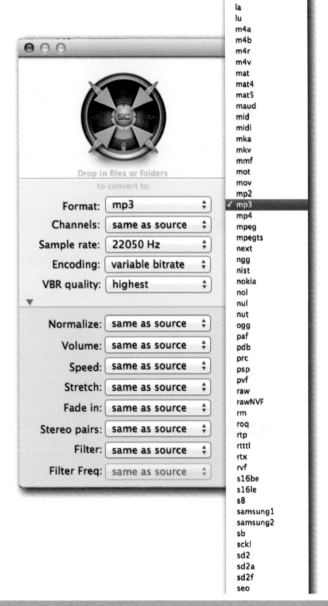

If you don't have an audio conversion program, but you do have a few bucks to pony up for one, check the Mac App Store for SoundConverter by Stephen Dekorte. You just drag and drop your audio files into the app, and it does it's best to convert them. I've found that occasionally this great little app can't make every conversion with every file, but take a look at the list of file formats it will attempt to convert in the screen grab to your right. You can't please everyone (evidenced from a few one-star ratings in the Store), but I've found this app to be great (and I'm giving it five stars now).

Alternatively, you can convert audio files with the **Terminal** window with a line like the one below (change directories to where *soundFile.aif* is).

```
/usr/bin/afconvert -f caff -d LEI16 soundFile.aif soundFile.caf
```

I'll let you google more on how to do that if you run into trouble, because for the sake of your own workflow, I highly suggest doing things the easy way.

Randomizing Your Sound Fx

To give your game a more realistic feel, you might want to play slightly different sound if an event is triggered often. For example, a flipper in a pinball game. Whenever a flipper would go up, I would call this method:

[self **flipperSound**];

Which would then call:

```
-(void) flipperSound {
    if ( soundFXTurnedOff -= NO ) {
        // make sure the audio isn't muted before going any further
        int randomNum = arc4random ( ) % 4;
        // this gives me a random int from 0 to 3
        switch ( randomNum ){
        // do one of the cases below based on the randomNum value
            case 0:
                [ [ SimpleAudioEngine sharedEngine] playEffect:@"flipper1.caf"];
                break;
            case 1:
                [ [ SimpleAudioEngine sharedEngine] playEffect:@"flipper2.caf"];
                break;
            case 2:
                [ [ SimpleAudioEngine sharedEngine] playEffect:@"flipper3.caf"];
                break;
            case 3:
                [ [ SimpleAudioEngine sharedEngine] playEffect:@"flipper4.caf"];
                break;
        }
    }
}
```

In my games, I actually had thirteen different flipper sounds. They were all pretty similar, but for my own sanity at least, I didn't notice a specific effect being over-played. Trust me, if you get tired of your app's audio while testing it, you've got a rough road ahead with your customers.

Audio is something many developers leave for the end and throw together in a mad rush to get their app into the store. Don't make that mistake.

In this section you've seen how easy it is to add audio, so my suggestion is that you work with sound effects during your entire development process. If you've just finished programming your character walking, then take the time *that same day* to find some good audio for the action. There are plenty of cheap, royalty-free audio FX merchants and probably hundreds of thousands of free audio clips just floating around the Internet. Sorting through all that isn't the quickest job in the world, but this is why if you leave your audio work to the end of the project, you might just think "Do I *really* need to play a sound effect for the character walking?" Cut to two weeks later, and you find yourself with a low-rated app in the store.

Chapter 9

Game Structure

I feel like I've given you a tool kit so far. A handyman's work chest of sorts. The projects have been relatively small, and mostly focused on demonstrating a handful of methods to show off the best of Cocos2d. A larger project can sometimes obscure the details. That way of doing things will end this chapter. We have to go big, or go home.

I'll build an example game which, unfortunately, you might have no interest in because it seems light-years different from the game you *really* want to build. Bear with me, though. My goal is that by the end of this chapter you can take that project, strip out minor parts of it, and be left with what is essentially an Empty Starter Kit Template. By that I mean you've got a starting project you can build anything from that already has some of the work done for you, at least in terms of the basic structure.

Property Lists

Let's take a look at using a **Property List**, or **.plist** file, to handle setting important values in our game. Now I know we haven't even made a game yet, but setting up a **.plist** is something you should think about early on because it can make building and testing your game a lot easier later. For example, if all your game's most important variable values were in one document, completely separated from your main code, don't you think you would test your app more times with minor tweaks if it was easier to make those changes? Just look at the **.plist** file below, nothing is easier than changing rows of values:

PlayerSpeed	⊕ ⊖	Number	11
EnemySpeed		Number	7
EnemiesToKill		Number	200
HasGravity		Boolean	YES
Gravity		Number	56
BackgroundArt		String	clouds.png
Music		String	FeelMyHeat.mp3

As a programmer you have to be able to step back from the canvas like every good artist knows to do. Get a fresh take on your creation. When coding, you'll sometimes feel that your first or second pass at setting an important variable was good enough. Especially once you get accustomed to that value. The danger is that your mind essentially locks in settings because you can't imagine changing them.

I made this exact mistake when programming my first pinball game. The flipper speed was horribly slow. I love pinball, but I hadn't actually played pinball in forever. If I had just gone to one bar that had a machine, I would have instantly seen how terribly slow my flippers were. So can you imagine the comments I got when my app first came out? Pretty bad. To finally get it right (I won't say "perfect"), it took submitting a few versions to Apple, and finally watching the pinball documentary "Special When Lit."

Experiment with how sweeping changes affect the game environment. For example, change your gravity, player speed, enemy speed, bullet range, etc., all at once just to get a feel for how different the game can be. Using a *.plist* for "experimentation" is the artist in me talking. The programmer in me will clue you into an even better reason for using them by the end of this section.

Property lists are just XML files, but inside of Xcode they look a lot more readable than they do in a text editor, where you would see tags like *<integer>3</integer>*. Like XML, you can have groups (arrays) of properties. For example:

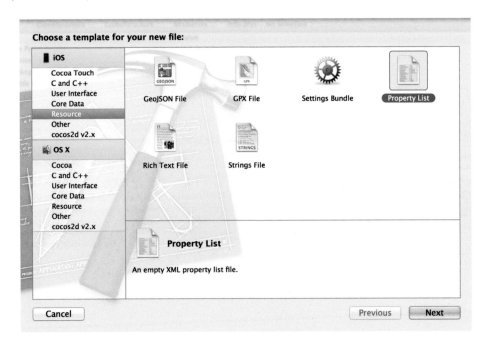

Key	Type	Value
▼ Root	Dictionary	(1 item)
▼ Levels	Array	(2 items)
▼ item 0	Dictionary	(7 items)
PlayerSpeed	Number	6
EnemySpeed	Number	4
EnemiesToKill	Number	200
HasGravity	Boolean	YES
Gravity	Number	56
BackgroundArt	String	forest.png
Music	String	RealUltimatePower.mp3
▼ Item 1	Dictionary	(7 items)
PlayerSpeed	Number	11
EnemySpeed	Number	7
EnemiesToKill	Number	200
HasGravity	Boolean	YES
Gravity	Number	70
BackgroundArt	String	clouds.png
Music	String	FeelMyHeat.mp3

Notice how in the Key column (the first column) I have an item called Levels, that unfolds to show **Item 0** and **Item 1**, which also both unfold to show the same set of properties (**PlayerSpeed**, **EnemySpeed**, etc.). So each level in the game could have the same properties, but with different values which are setup here in the *.plist* file. Neat eh?

So let's build one called *GameData.plist*. You can create a new Property List file by going to **File > New > File. ...** Then under the **iOS** section, find **Resource** then select **Property List** (shown below).

Choose a template for your new file:

iOS
- Cocoa Touch
- C and C++
- User Interface
- Core Data
- **Resource**
- Other
- cocos2d v2.x

OS X
- Cocoa
- C and C++
- User Interface
- Core Data
- Resource
- Other
- cocos2d v2.x

GeoJSON File   GPX File   Settings Bundle   **Property List**

Rich Text File   Strings File

Property List

An empty XML property list file.

Cancel   Previous   Next

This will create an empty file. It has a **Root** Key dictionary, which we will add a **New Item** to by pressing the plus icon in the **Root** row, like so:

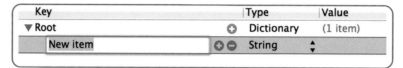

Change the name of the **New Item** to **Difficulty**, leave the type as **String** and give it a value of **Easy**. Add two more items, a **Boolean** type named **SoundEnabled** with a value of YES, then a **Number** type named **LevelsPerSection** with a value of 3. Your **GameData.plist** file should look like this now:

Key		Type	Value
▼ Root		Dictionary	(3 items)
LevelsPerSection		Number	3
SoundEnabled	⊕ ⊖	Boolean	YES
Difficulty		String	Easy

Before we get fancy and set up variables on a per-level basis, let's simply read in these common data types. For our hypothetical game, you can imagine that these aren't level-specific variables anyway, because just by their names alone you could see how they might apply to the entire game.

So in the header file of HelloWorldLayer (or any class), declare some variables to hold onto the values we get from the **GameData.plist** file.

In the header file

@interface HelloWorldLayer : CCLayer {

      int LevelsPerSection;

      bool SoundEnabled;

      NSString* Difficulty;

}

Notice that the variable names I'm declaring are exactly the same as the **Key** names in the **.plist** file. This is completely optional. They don't need to be, but you won't have any conflict if they are. Next let's jump over to the implementation file for the real work.

In my example project, I'll add the lines below to the **init** statement, but you could write these in any method. The first two lines create an NSString variable that is simply a path to the **.plist** file. This path is then used to create an NSDictionary which contains the data (the keys and values) of the **.plist** file.

```
NSString *path = [[NSBundle mainBundle] bundlePath];
// this is just the "main bundle" of stuff you've packaged up with the app
NSString *finalPath = [path stringByAppendingPathComponent:@"GameData.plist"];
// the name of our file
NSDictionary *plistData = [NSDictionary dictionaryWithContentsOfFile: finalPath];
// create an NSDictionary with the contents
```

Next we make our instance variables equal to their corresponding keys in the NSDictionary variable called plistData. In all three lines below, we use **objectForKey** to look up the value. The only tricky thing here is that for LevelsPerSection and SoundEnabled we need to convert the object returned to an int and bool value because the data retrieved is an **NSObject**, which is not exactly the data type we want. This is why we include **integerValue** and **boolValue** in the exterior brackets, which converts the object value.

```
Difficulty = [plistData objectForKey:@"Difficulty"];
// NSString is an object, so no conversion is needed
LevelsPerSection = [ [plistData objectForKey:@"LevelsPerSection"] integerValue];
// converts the object to integer
SoundEnabled = [ [plistData objectForKey:@"SoundEnabled"] boolValue];
// converts the object to bool
```

Finally, I'll just test that those variables equal what they should with some CCLOG statements:

```
CCLOG(@"Levels per section is: %i", LevelsPerSection);
if ( SoundEnabled == YES) {
// remember you could also write if ( SoundEnabled == 1)
    CCLOG(@"sound is on");
}
CCLOG(@"The Difficulty is: %@", Difficulty );
```

Note, if you had a float value instead of int, you could use **floatValue** in place of **integerValue** above.

Property List Arrays

Now let's create some high scores for the app with an Array type property. Except wait, should we really add in high scores to an app that won't have been played yet when the user first installs it? Well, that hasn't stopped game developers in the past! I can remember Atari games that had pre-programmed high scores. Players gotta have a goal to beat, right?

▼ HighScores	Array	(3 items)
Item 0	String	123456000
Item 1	String	234567
Item 2	String	6087

So in your *.plist* file, click the plus sign on the **Root** row, and create an item named **HighScores** and set the Type to **Array**. Then on the **HighScores** row, click the plus sign three times, making **Item 0**, **Item 1**, and **Item 2**. Don't try to rename those. The data types can be **String** because for this example we will just feed the values straight into a CCLabelBMFont anyway, and labels are initialized from NSStrings. If you want to convert the value to an integer later, we just saw how to do that on the previous page. Next our first three lines from before can be used again:

> NSString *path = [[NSBundle **mainBundle**] **bundlePath**];
>
> NSString *finalPath = [path **stringByAppendingPathComponent**:@"GameData.plist"];
>
> NSDictionary *plistData = [NSDictionary **dictionaryWithContentsOfFile**: finalPath];

Then we just create an NSMutableArray called theScores, which is equal to the Array object named HighScores in the file:

> NSMutableArray* theScores = [NSMutableArray **arrayWithArray**:[plistData **object ForKey**:@"HighScores"]];

To steal some code from our section on labels, you could then use the **objectAtIndex:** 0 , which is **Item 0**, in a label like so:

> CCLabelBMFont* firstPlaceLabel = [CCLabelBMFont **labelWithString**:
> [theScores **objectAtIndex**:0] **fntFile**:@"blambot.fnt"];

Property Lists Organized by Level

Now that you've got the hang of this, let's add more to the *GameData.plist* file and organize it by level because most games have more than one level with similar properties. On the **Root** row, click the plus sign and create a **Key** named **Levels** set as an Array type. Then on the **Levels** row, click the plus sign and you'll get a new item called **Item 0**.

Don't try to rename that, just change it's type to **Dictionary**. Now you can start creating the same keys and values you see below. You can leave in the Keys you previously had, they are just cut off in the following image.

Key		Type	Value
▼ Root		Dictionary	(1 item)
▼ Levels		Array	(2 items)
▼ Item 0		Dictionary	(7 items)
PlayerSpeed		Number	6
EnemySpeed		Number	4
EnemiesToKill		Number	200
HasGravity		Boolean	YES
Gravity		Number	56
BackgroundArt		String	forest.png
Music		String	RealUltimatePower.mp3
▼ Item 1	⊕ ⊖	Dictionary	(7 items)
PlayerSpeed		Number	11
EnemySpeed		Number	7
EnemiesToKill		Number	200
HasGravity		Boolean	YES
Gravity		Number	70
BackgroundArt		String	clouds.png
Music		String	FeelMyHeat.mp3

Now before you create a second **Dictionary** item and start clicking a bunch of plus signs again, let me show you how to speed things up. First off, you can simply copy and paste the first item by right-clicking on it, hitting **Copy**, then selecting the **Levels** key, right-clicking again and hitting **Paste**. That's the easiest thing to do, but you could open your *p.list* file in any text editor and make the changes by copying and pasting blocks of tags.

▼ Root		Dictionary	(5 items)
SoundEnabled		Boolean	YES
LevelsPerSection		Number	3
Difficulty		String	Easy
▼ Levels		Array	(2 items)
▶ Item 0	⊕ ⊖	Dictionary ↕	(7 items)
▶ Item 1		Dictionary	(7 items)
▶ HighScores		Array	(3 items)

So let's bring in some data from the items in our **Levels** Array. If you want to test this out too, you don't really need to declare anything in your header file. Since my main purpose now is just showing you how to retrieve the data, we'll use CCLOG statements to check that it's coming in okay and not worry about declaring variables in the header.

Just remember, since this data isn't being saved to a variable it won't persist past the **init** statement or method you're running this code in. Again, your first three lines from before should stay in:

```
NSString *path = [[NSBundle mainBundle] bundlePath];

NSString *finalPath = [path stringByAppendingPathComponent:@"GameData.plist"];

NSDictionary *plistData = [NSDictionary dictionaryWithContentsOfFile: finalPath];
```

Then let's create a variable called currentLevel. Most likely when you bring in data specific to a level, you *only* care about one level at a time. If you're playing level 3, we really don't need the variable values for level 4, do we? The player might never make it there anyway, so why bother holding onto those values now if we can just get them as we need them later. So we'll use the value of currentLevel to determine which **Item** we pull from in the **Levels Array**. Here goes:

```
int currentLevel = 1;

// in a real app, you'd probably have this declared in the header first

NSMutableArray* levelArray = [NSMutableArray arrayWithArray:[plistData objectForKey:@"Levels"] ];

NSDictionary* levelDict = [NSDictionary dictionaryWithDictionary:[ levelArray objectAtIndex: currentLevel - 1 ]];

// subtract 1 !
```

So in the second line above, levelArray was created to equal the **Array** value from the **objectForKey**:@"Levels". Then on the next line, we just create another NSDictionary called levelDict, which is equal to one of our items in the levelArray. Which one is determined by **objectAtIndex**, and that's where we use currentLevel. Just remember that arrays start counting their items at zero, not one. So that's why we subtract one from the value of currentLevel. In other words, the first level is using the values from **Item 0** in the **.plist.** That's all it takes. You've sorted through more data from the **.plist** file. Now keep in mind, you aren't using any of it. So let's at least check some of it with a CCLOG statement. The line below should output, "Level 1- Background Art File is: forest.png" …

```
CCLOG(@"Level %i – Background Art File is: %@", currentLevel, [levelDict objectForKey:@"BackgroundArt" ] );
```

Feel free to test that with any of the other values in levelDict. Also try changing currentLevel to 2, just to make sure you get different values for the other level's properties.

By now, I hope you are getting a glimpse of the **structure** of things to come. Think of the **GameData.plist** (or really any game data) like the fuel for an engine. That engine could be a class file appropriately named GameEngine. Without the fuel, the engine doesn't work.

It doesn't know how many enemies to spawn, or the time limit to pass a level, the number of health units the player starts with, the starting locations of land mines, and so on.

Think about how many things a property list could be used for to fuel your game engine, which in many apps is essentially just a template for every possible level. The point here is that you probably don't need separate class files for Level1, Level2, Level3, etc. Not if you can make a reload-able GameEngine class that sucks in data and spits out a unique level.

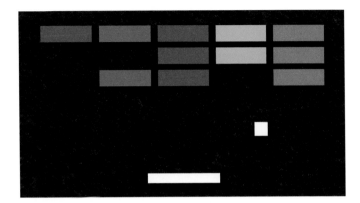

I think you "get it", but just to train your mind some, think about programming aspects of a **Brick Breaker** game and consider what parts could be handled by the level engine and what is just level data.

- Brick locations.
- How breakable a brick is (does one ball touch break it?).
- Detecting brick and ball collisions.
- Detecting paddle and ball collisions.
- Ball speed.
- User interaction with the paddle.
- The current level.
- Paddle sliding speed.
- Physics, like momentum loss, angles, etc.
- The points scored for breaking each brick.
- The running score for all levels.
- How many balls you start with (lives).
- Testing if the ball goes below the screen (death).

Did you meditate on those? If so, then you've done well my grasshopper. Hit the sauna. Exercise is over for the day. Try not to cry yourself to sleep thinking about those tricky bullet points that are best handled by neither the engine or pulled in as *.plist* data.

To download the source project for this section, you can find it at **www.focalpress.com/cw/Dike**. We'll continue working this same project progressively through the entire chapter. The project as it is now has been saved in a folder called ***GameStructure_plists***, which you can find at the same website.

Singleton Classes

Setting up a **property list**, or simply coding initial values into your class, gives your variables a starting point. Many of those variables will never need to change value after that. Once your game engine (or level template) has gotten the initial value for say, gravity on a particular level, it will probably stay constant and it won't need to be remembered on the next level. Yet there are usually some variables that need to persist throughout level changes. If you remember, we already looked at creating static variables on page 275, which got that job done on a smaller scale. Creating a **Singleton** class takes this concept one step further.

The idea here is that we create a single class made for sharing data to other classes. As the name "Singleton" implies, there's **only ever one instance** of this class. So when our app first runs it initializes this class, and that class stays initialized for the life of the app. Whereas, a class like our GameEngine (just assume we name it that later), could get wiped from memory and reloaded each time we start a new level or restart the same level after losing a life. When the GameEngine reloads it can't go back and pull in a value for a variable like numberOfLives from **GameData.plist** because that was only appropriate for the initial starting amount. If your player just lost a life, we need to keep track of that loss.

Your singleton class, let's call it AppData, can also pull values from your **GameData.plist** just like your game engine, but it can be a little pickier about what it needs to store. It probably doesn't need the specifics of each level, it is better off getting those initial starting variables that apply to the entire game, like the number of lives to begin a new game with. Here's an important point to remember—**the AppData singleton can hold both the starting values for something, and current values for something**.

So in your AppData **init** statement, you might have a variable like numberOfLives equal to the amount from **GameData.plist,** but then a second variable called currentLivesLeft which equals numberOfLives initially, but then changes over time. The numberOfLives variable shouldn't change because we need that value to fall back to when the entire game resets. For example, when you start a new game of Pac-Mac, you get all your lives back. That amount must come from somewhere. So our AppData class can manage sharing data like currentLivesLeft to other classes *and* do massive resets for the entire game like making currentLivesLeft equal to numberOfLives again.

So even though your AppData singleton could access a *GameData.plist* as often as you like, it probably doesn't need to. Once it has those initial values to reset the game back to, it can hold on to them for good. Unlike the GameEngine, which might access the *GameData.plist* every time it reloads or reinitializes.

Most likely, your GameEngine will load variable values from the AppData singleton as well as a *GameData.plist*. So it draws a bit from both sources. Usually it will need to get info from the singleton first, before retrieving a property list. For example, to get the value of a variable like currentLevel, the AppData class will provide the GameEngine with the currentLevel, which is then used to fetch the level info from the *GameData.plist*. We saw how that worked in our project last section.

Speaking of which, let's keep building on that project. First create a new class, **File > New > File**. Pick the CCNode template as usual, but this time it can be a subclass of CCNode instead of CCLayer. Why the change of heart? Well we don't need to visibly show anything with this class. It's just going to handle data, we won't ever ask it to show a CCSprite. We could, but we won't.

Name that class AppData, so our project should now have an *AppData.h* and *AppData.m* file. Perhaps more so than any of our other classes, the header file of AppData is putting herself out there. Pretend our lovely lady Singleton is the only "single" female in town, which is essentially true because as a Singleton there can only be one instance of AppData around at a time. She will have a lot of other interested classes checking her out, so she's only going to reveal what she needs to (in the header file). If you forgot why we declare methods in a header file, now is a good time to refresh your memory (see page 99), but to sum it up, other classes will be able to call these methods on AppData.

The Class Method of Your Singleton

The most interesting of those declared methods is the **class method** (remember those start with a **+** sign). In the AppData header file, go ahead and add this line below:

@interface AppData : CCNode {

}
+ (AppData*) **sharedData**;
@end

Now switch over to your AppData implementation file, and add the following code circled below:

@implementation AppData

static AppData *sharedData = nil;

We've already seen a static variable in the last chapter working with Scenes and Menus, but back then our static variable was pretty simple because it was just an int type. To jog your memory, because we made it static, we didn't lose the count (the variable value) when the scene was removed from memory. So now that our static variable type is AppData, the class itself, what can you assume will happen here? **The class stays in memory**. If we refer to it later, we know we're referring to the same instance.

Below that, continue writing by finishing the class method we declared in the header:

```
+ ( AppData* ) sharedData {
    if (sharedData == nil) {
        sharedData = [[AppData alloc] init] ;
    }
    return sharedData;
}
```

This class method gets called every time we need to do something with the AppData class, but the only time that if statement gets run is the first time this method gets called. At which point it will be true that sharedData == nil, so then we allocate and initialize the class, which calls the **init** statement that we need to write next:

```
-(id) init {
    if( (self = [super init] ) ) {
        sharedData = self;
    }
    return self;
}
```

That **init** statement looks the same as every other one we've written before, we've just added sharedData = self, which I can't describe any better than just simply saying the static variable called sharedData now equals itself (and no longer is nil).

So when we call the class method named **sharedData** it just returns a reference to itself, by giving us back the static sharedData variable. In other words, we get returned the **one and only instance** of the AppData class.

Instance Methods in Your Singleton

The question on your mind now is probably, "When do we call the Singleton's class method?" The answer is, whenever we want to **also** call one of the Singleton's instance methods. So the class method just gives us access to the rest of the methods we will declare.

I think the instance method names in the exterior brackets below should give you an understanding of how the Singleton is used by other classes. Keep in mind, other classes would be the ones making these calls below:

[[AppData **sharedData**] **isGamePaused**];

    // returns a bool value for other classes to know if the game is paused

[[AppData **sharedData**] **returnLevel**];

    // returns an int for the value of the current level

[[AppData **sharedData**] **resetGame**];

    // performs a lot of code that sets the game to it's original state on level 1

[[AppData **sharedData**] **saveState**];

    // performs code to save NSUserDefaults

[[AppData **sharedData**] **advanceLevel**];

    // performs code to increment to the next level

[[AppData **sharedData**] **isSoundMuted**];

    // returns a bool value so other classes that are about to play audio, check with AppData to verify IF they actually should or not.

[[AppData **sharedData**] **turnOffMusic**];

    // performs code to mute the music, but doesn't affect other sound FX

Notice a pattern? In every line, we had an interior method call of [AppData **sharedData**] , which just returned to us the AppData instance to use for the method call in the exterior brackets. Those hypothetical methods would have been declared as instance methods in the header of AppData (remember instance methods begin with a – sign, instead of **+** sign like class methods).

All those instance method names (like **returnLevel , isSoundMuted,** etc.) were ripped from past projects of mine. I included some examples where other classes would be calling a method to return something (basically asking AppData a question about the state of the game) and in other cases making a command (telling AppData to change the state of the game). So just because AppData is our all-knowing, all-seeing class, that doesn't mean it won't be told what to do by other classes.

Before we actually add an instance method to AppData and call it, let's just take a moment to search this book for past occurrences of the word "shared." Why? Well just to prove how many times you've already accessed a **Singleton** class with Cocos2d**.**

Here's what I've found searching:

[[CCDirector **sharedDirector**] etc. … **]**

[[CCActionManager **sharedManager**] etc. … **]**

[[CCTextureCache **sharedTextureCache**] etc. … **]**

[[CCSpriteFrameCache **sharedSpriteFrameCache**] etc. … **]**

Most of those searches had to do with [CCDirector **sharedDirector**], as that's a very commonly used one, but obviously you can see that you haven't been a stranger to accessing a **Singleton** class throughout the book.

Okay, let's get back to the project. In the AppData header file, let's declare some instance variables and instance methods.

In the AppData.h file

@interface AppData : CCNode {

     int levelsPassed;

     int currentLevel;

     int numberOfLives;

     int currentLivesLeft;

}

Add the methods below after the class method:

+ (AppData* **) sharedData;**

- (int **) returnLevel ;**

- (void **) advanceLevel ;**

- (int **) returnLives ;**

- (void **) subtractLife ;**

- (void **) resetGame ;**

Now before we get some complaints from Xcode about not implementing those, let's jump over to the implementation file and add what we can about those methods:

In the AppData.m file

-(int) **returnLevel** {

     return currentLevel;

}

```
-(void) advanceLevel {
        currentLevel ++;
        // increment up 1
}
-(int) returnLives {
        return currentLivesLeft;
}
-(void) subtractLife {
        currentLivesLeft = currentLivesLeft − 1;
        if ( currentLivesLeft == 0 ) {
                [ self resetGame ];
        }
}
-(void) resetGame {
        currentLivesLeft = numberOfLives;
        currentLevel = 1;
        // or this could return to last level passed
}
```

There's some work left to do in the **init** statement, namely making our instance variables actually equal something other than their default values, but I'll do that in a moment with the *GameData.plist* file and NSUserDefaults. For now, I'd like you to just focus on these instance methods. One thing that might stand out to you is how simplistic they are. Even though I'm trying to give you simple examples, many of these aren't that different then finished methods I've used in my own games. You might have assumed your AppData class would be this complex entity, but it doesn't need to be at all.

Before you test this out, remember any class that wants to access AppData needs to include this line in either the header or implementation:

#import "AppData.h"

So perhaps HelloWorldLayer would like to access the currentLevel of AppData. In any method you could write:

int level = [[AppData **sharedData**] **returnLevel**];

Another example would be to test a returned bool value like so:

```
if ( [ [AppData sharedData] isGamePaused ] == YES ) {
    // game is paused
} else {
    // game is not paused
}
```

You don't actually have to write == YES above, the if statement would run the same without it.

Now notice what would happen if you called:

```
[ [AppData sharedData] subtractLife ];
```

… assuming that currentLivesLeft equaled one before you made that call, the if statement would be true, and AppData would then call [self resetGame], in a sense, taking over some control of itself by pausing the game and resetting a bunch of variables.

By declaring resetGame as an instance method, other classes can also call it directly, for example, if a GameMenu class had a button labeled "Start Game Over" it might call:

```
[ [AppData sharedData] resetGame ];
```

An important thing to consider here is that your AppData class can unify the end result of many things occurring in your game. So if your GameEngine had ten different ways of killing your main player, be it pitfalls, spikes, charging turtles, or just a time clock ticking down to zero, all those events could call the same subtractLife method in AppData.

Also since AppData is one single instance, you can occassionally get away with some sloppy programming. For example, suppose when the subtractLife method tested that all lives were lost, it scheduled a game reset like so:

```
[ self schedule:@selector( resetGameInThreeSeconds: ) interval:3.0f ];
```

Then "whoops!", somehow your subtractLife method got called again. Fortunately because the method above is already scheduled, it wouldn't get scheduled again. That's a bad example for a lot of reasons, mostly because, if your player lost all their lives the GameEngine should also be aware of this, and cease running code that could call [[AppData sharedData] subtractLife]. I'm just trying to give you an example of how you can play with the *singularity* of your singleton class.

I'm in danger now of letting a bad example lead to some bad ideas, because my Spidey-sense is telling me some of you might be thinking of using your **Singleton** for scheduling methods like game timers. I really can't say "No! No! No!" to this, but I don't think I can say, "Sure go for it" either. I can't even muster an, "I dunno, try it." I think your AppData class needs to stay away from the duties of the GameEngine. For something like a running game timer, in my mind, that's GameEngine territory. Let's work toward a strict division of labor with our classes. Your AppData class *might* be accessed almost every frame for some reason or another while the GameEngine is running a level, but I don't think the AppData class should be sending messages to the GameEngine constantly as well. If you did that, you basically have two fast talking people trying to talk to each other at once. It's better to just have one fast-talker, and the other person is simply nodding their head sporadically saying, "uh huh … uh huh … yup … nope … I don't agree … okay, shut up now."

Using the GameData.plist, NSUserDefaults, and Singleton Together

Exciting sub-section title, eh? Well let's do one more thing first. Create a GameEngine class. We've talked about a hypothetical one forever, so let's actually add one. This way we can test the AppData values from the GameEngine, and the code you already have inside of your HelloWorldLayer class can stay locked in. We won't use HelloWorldLayer after this, so all the **GameData.plist** parsing you did before can stay there as reference for later.

In Xcode, go to **File > New > File** … Select the CCNode template, but set the sub-class as CCLayer. Save it as **GameEngine.m**, and let's get it ready for the big game. Modify the header file to look like this:

In the GameEngine.h file

#import <Foundation/Foundation.h>

#import "cocos2d.h"

#import "AppData.h"

@interface GameEngine : CCLayer {

    int lives;

    int level;

}

(CCScene *) **scene**;

@end

Don't overlook the #import statement for **AppData.h**. Without that we'll have some big problems testing the two int variables we are declaring. I know, I know … we aren't testing much now, but in the next section we'll continue to modify the GameEngine and keep building on this same project. Now go over to your GameEngine implementation file. You can save time by copying the **scene** method below from your HelloWorldLayer class and just replacing in "GameEngine."

@implementation GameEngine

```
+(CCScene *) scene{
        CCScene *scene = [CCScene node];
        GameEngine *layer = [GameEngine node];
        [scene addChild: layer];
        return scene;
}
```

Then in your **init** statement we will just set lives and level to the returned values from AppData.

```
-(id) init {
    if( (self=[super init])) {
            lives = [[AppData sharedData] returnLives];
            level = [[AppData sharedData] returnLevel];
            CCLOG( @"The lives left is: %i , and the level is %i", lives, level);
    }
    return self;
}
```

That does it for the GameEngine class for now. Switch over to your **_IntroLayer.m_** file (or the **_AppDelegate.m_** file if you're using a Cocos2d v1 template). You can do a **Find and Replace** for the text "HelloWorldLayer" replacing it with "GameEngine." That would take care of changing it in both the #import statement and **replaceScene** method. If you were to build your app now, it should run the GameEngine instead of HelloWorldLayer.

Now let's get back to our AppData class. In the header file, declare your NSUserDefaults:

In the AppData.h file

@interface AppData : CCNode {

NSUserDefaults* defaults;

> *...etc. leave in the rest from before.*

Then in the **init** of your implementation file, add the following code below where you already have written, sharedData = self;

```
-(id) init {
    if( (self=[super init])) {
        sharedData = self;
        // USE THE DEFAULTS TO CHECK THE LEVELS PASSED
        defaults = [NSUserDefaults standardUserDefaults];
        levelsPassed = [defaults integerForKey:@"levelsPassed"];
        // by default this will be 0
        currentLevel = levelsPassed + 1;
        // if 0, then currentLevel will be 1, if the first level is passed, then currentLevel will
        be 2
        // USE THE PROPERTY LIST TO CHECK THE NUMBER OF LIVES TO START WITH
        NSString *path = [[NSBundle mainBundle] bundlePath];
        NSString *finalPath = [path stringByAppendingPathComponent:@"GameData.plist"];
        NSDictionary *plistData = [NSDictionary dictionaryWithContentsOfFile: finalPath];
        numberOfLives = [[plistData objectForKey:@"LivesAtGameStart"] integerValue];
        currentLivesLeft = numberOfLives;
    }
    return self;
}
```

So, by using the NSUserDefaults the app initially loads with the currentLevel value at one more than the levelsPassed. So if you've passed five levels, your next starting level is six. Or if you've passed zero levels, you'll be at level one. Consider too, that you might want your game to always start players back at level one, but you can still save the levelsPassed value and use it to keep track of the levels the player has unlocked if you want to let them skip forward from an Options/Level Menu. I can think of a popular labyrinth game that does exactly that.

Now we're using the NSUserDefaults for the levelsPassed, we need to actually save that value when we advance a level. So add a bit to your **advanceLevel** method:

```
-(void) advanceLevel {
    levelsPassed = currentLevel;
    // be sure to do this before incrementing currentLevel
    [defaults setInteger: levelsPassed forKey:@"levelsPassed"];
    // save it
```

currentLevel ++;

// increment the currentLevel

[defaults **synchronize**];

// optional, but saving a new level passed is probably a fine time to force-save the defaults since this occurs infrequently

}

That's it for now! If you wanted to test this, in the **init** statement of ***GameEngine.m*** (or elsewhere), you could call:

[[AppData **sharedData**] **advanceLevel**];

… to check that the value is actually advancing/saving when you return to publish the game again. Of course, I checked this in my project and all seems A-okay! If you want to download the source files (as they are now), you can find them in the folder titled ***GameStructure_Singletons*** at **www.focalpress.com/cw/Dike**.

Section 3

The Game Engine

In the last section we created a class called GameEngine to test as a hypothetical level template and pull in data from our AppData singleton class. We didn't do much more than the initial setup, so this section we will continue with those project files and really populate the GameEngine class with the fundamentals. Which are what exactly?

Well, I can't foresee every game you'll want to create, but most games have some things in common.

- A **main player** or object under control of the user.
- **Enemies/Obstacles** the player shouldn't collide with.
- **Points** for colliding with "good" objects or simply staying alive.
- **Lives** to make multiple attempts to pass a level.
- **An end goal** to advance to the next level.

Consider the list above, and think about a marble game. The main player is the marble, which you have three of, to attempt to pass the level. Enemies could simply be holes on the board you want to avoid. Points could be given for rolling over certain spots. The end goal could also just be a spot on the board you want to roll over.

Now imagine a second game using the same list. The player is a bird flying up and down. Enemies are thorns you want to avoid. Points are attained by colliding with floating feathers. The end goal is making it back to a nest, or simply a position on the level.

Visually and conceptually the two games are completely different, but under the hood they are very similar. The marble game could feel very static, like nothing is moving but the marble. The bird game could have the "illusion of movement" by simulating a side scroller where the enemies move toward the bird (which actually stays in place). That's a very minor difference code-wise. The entire set up is nearly identical to the first game.

In both games we could use a property list organized by level to position the player, enemies/obstacles, scoring objects and end goal. The GameEngine mostly just handles control of the player and collision detections. Separate classes, like the one we created in Chapter 4, can handle the specifics of what certain objects do. We'll see how all that works again to give you a bit of a review.

So yes, **we will** create a small game this section, but I don't want you to lose interest in this rather long section, if you're not into the type of game we are making. I don't want you thinking, "Meh, I don't want to program a side scrolling flying bird game". You don't have to. *This code IS NOT specific at all to any one game*. I really want to emphasize that. It's very generalized and could be used in countless other games.

Our GameEngine class will be in charge of the following:

- **Setting up the level**—mostly by using the *.plist* to place the Player, Enemy and any other classes we create.
- **Running a main game loop**—used for handling collisions by seeing what kind of class is touching another, checking for objects to remove or add to the scene, and detecting a conclusion to the level or a player death, which might restart the same level or entire game.
- **Handling control of the player**—in this game, we'll just use the accelerometer.
- **Managing information** of what is going on—for example, the score or health of the main character.

Setting up the GameData.plist (for real this time)

Let's go back to our *GameData.plist* and make some slight changes. We can keep our **Levels** array from before, but you might as well delete all but one item, because we have a lot of changes to make.

Key		
▼ Root		s)
LivesAtGameStart	Number	3
▼ Levels	Array	(1 item)
▼ Item 0	Dictionary	(7 items)
▶ ScoreObjects	Array	(2 items)
▶ Enemies	Array	(4 items)
▼ PlayerProperties	Dictionary	(8 items)
SpriteSheetName	String	fatbird_sheet
BaseImage	String	fatbird_default.png
BruisedImage	String	fatbird_bruised.png
PlayerLocation	String	{300,500}
IsAnimated	Boolean	YES
AnimationBaseName	String	fatbird_flying
FramesToAnimate	Number	20
Gravity	Number	1
ScrollingArt2	String	clouds_red.png
ScrollingArt1	String	thorns.png
BackgroundArt	String	sky_green.png
Music	String	level1.mp3
▶ HighScores	Array	(3 items)

PlayerProperties

I've highlighted **Item 0** under the **Levels** Array and only unfolded the **PlayerProperties** Dictionary so we can focus on that first. Take a look at the properties I've created within **PlayerProperties**. Some of them like **SpriteSheetName**, might seem like they could be used throughout every level of the game, so why specify this on a per-level basis? I think it's easier to plan for all possible situations now. It's true that for this simple example I don't plan on making more than one sprite sheet for the main character, but when you start making a "real" game, you might want different clothes on your character for each level. Maybe over time the character's armor increases. Since we're just going to copy and paste *all* of **Item 0's** properties for the next level anyway, it's really no problem to make this flexible for later (even if only one level were to use a different sheet).

The entire **PlayerProperties** Dictionary will be passed into the Player class we create later. If you remember back in Chapter 4, our Enemy class was created with a location and base image. This will be a similar set-up, passing in the NSDictionary as a parameter when we initialize the class. So our GameEngine class will not have to do anything with these properties. It simply needs to get the information, create the Player instance, and pass it on. We will talk about those specific **PlayerProperties** later.

Key		Type	Value
▼ Root		Dictionary	(3 items)
LivesAtGameStart		Number	3
▼ Levels		Array	(1 item)
▼ Item 0		Dictionary	(7 items)
▶ ScoreObjects		Array	(2 items)
▼ Enemies	⊕⊖	Array ⬍	(2 items)
▼ Item 0		Dictionary	(8 items)
BaseImage		String	thorns1.png
FlipY		Boolean	NO
FlipX		Boolean	NO
EnemyLocation		String	{2000, 100}
EnemySpeed		Number	3
PlaceThisManyMore		Number	5
XPaddingOfMultiples		Number	200
ZDepth		Number	6
▼ Item 1		Dictionary	(8 items)
BaseImage		String	thorns1.png
FlipY		Boolean	NO
FlipX		Boolean	NO
EnemyLocation		String	{1500, 100}
EnemySpeed	⊕⊖	Number	3
PlaceThisManyMore		Number	3
XPaddingOfMultiples		Number	200
ZDepth		Number	6
▶ PlayerProperties		Dictionary	(8 items)
ScrollingArt2		String	clouds_red.png
ScrollingArt1		String	thorns.png
BackgroundArt		String	sky_green.png
Music		String	level1.mp3
▶ HighScores		Array	(3 items)

*(Callout label: **Enemies** pointing to the Enemies Array row)*

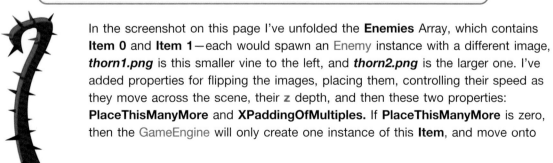

In the screenshot on this page I've unfolded the **Enemies** Array, which contains **Item 0** and **Item 1**—each would spawn an Enemy instance with a different image, **thorn1.png** is this smaller vine to the left, and **thorn2.png** is the larger one. I've added properties for flipping the images, placing them, controlling their speed as they move across the scene, their **z** depth, and then these two properties: **PlaceThisManyMore** and **XPaddingOfMultiples.** If **PlaceThisManyMore** is zero, then the GameEngine will only create one instance of this **Item**, and move onto the next **Item** in the **Array**. If **PlaceThisManyMore** is a value higher than zero, it will start creating duplicates using the same values in the NSDictionary (so the same image will be used), and the **XPaddingOfMultiples** value will be used to space each clone apart from one another.

So if **PlaceThisManyMore** is two, and the **XPaddingOfMultiples** value is 1000, and the **EnemyLocation** property is { 700, 350 } then the GameEngine would place them as they are in the image below.

Each new instance would be separated by 1000 points. So this would be an easy way to add a few clones of the same object, all at once. Our ScoreObjects class will be set up similarly, and a good example would be a row of ten coins to pick up.

Again, this is another case where our GameEngine will mostly just be parsing the information from the *.plist* and putting the Enemy class in charge of itself with the data.

Since you're getting a hint of the game backdrop in the image below, let's talk about that real fast. Each **Item** in the **Level** Array will have a property called **BackgroundArt** (non-moving), **ScrollingArt1**, and **ScrollingArt2**. We will scroll and repeat those exactly the same way we did back in Section 4 of Chapter 6.

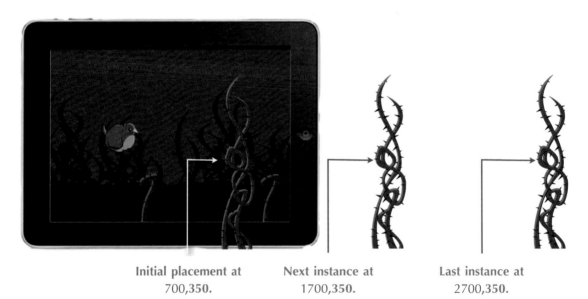

Initial placement at
700,**350.**

Next instance at
1700,**350.**

Last instance at
2700,**350.**

I'll give you a break on property list editing in one moment, we have just one more big set to look at with **ScoreObjects**. These will be anything that scores points, and you can see the first property in **Item 0** is **Points**. Other than that, the rest is similar to the same properties we will pass into each Enemy instance, but there will be one difference in how we scroll them across the screen.

I want to give you two examples of how our objects can scroll across the screen. Enemy instances will each have an internal scheduler which adjusts their position based on the speed. Our project in Chapter 4 was similar in that each instance moved on it's own. ScoreObjects are a bit simpler. They don't have an internal scheduler, instead they will get added as children to a class called ScoreNodes, which somewhat assumes you'll be adding many objects at once to each ScoreNodes (notice ScoreNodes is plural). This way the group moves together as the entire ScoreNodes instance gets moved. This will also

Key		Type	Value
▼ Root	*ScoreObjects*	Dictionary	(3 items)
LivesAtGameStart		Number	3
▼ Levels		Array	(1 item)
▼ Item 0		Dictionary	(7 items)
▼ ScoreObjects		Array	(2 items)
▼ Item 0		Dictionary	(9 items)
Points		Number	300
BaseImage		String	feather.png
FlipY		Boolean	NO
FlipX		Boolean	NO
ObjectLocation		String	{500, 650}
Speed		Number	2
PlaceThisManyMore		Number	3
XPaddingOfMultiples		Number	50
ZDepth		Number	1
▼ Item 1		Dictionary	(9 items)
Points		Number	300
BaseImage		String	feather.png
FlipY		Boolean	NO
FlipX		Boolean	NO
ObjectLocation		String	{2000, 450}
Speed		Number	3
PlaceThisManyMore		Number	3
XPaddingOfMultiples		Number	50
ZDepth		Number	1
▶ Enemies		Array	(2 items)
▶ PlayerProperties		Dictionary	(8 items)
ScrollingArt2		String	clouds_red.png
ScrollingArt1		String	thorns.png
BackgroundArt		String	sky_green.png
Music		String	level1.mp3
▶ HighScores		Array	(3 items)

give us a great opportunity to look at how the GameEngine's main loop will convert an object's position inside of another object to "world space". The method is appropriately called **convertToWorldSpace**, and is an important one for game developers.

Surely by now some of you are concerned about the playback speed of this game, since we are spawning *all* of these objects defined in our *.plist* and scrolling them toward that fat bird. We could get away with twenty or so just fine, but after that the device will get sluggish. We have two ways to keep our app running at a smooth 60 fps: **any object or object group that passes out of view is removed, and any object that is coming into view won't be added until right before we need to see it**. Object groups are the items in our property list where we have specified a **PlaceThisManyMore** value greater than zero. So once the first object is within the screen's view, it will get added with all the rest. For that reason, you probably wouldn't want to set the **PlaceThisManyMore** value too high and try to populate your entire level with the same object group. Since all the objects are made with the identical artwork anyway, the board would look pretty lame if you did this. So that's the game plan for now. Let's get into it.

To get started, my header file for the GameEngine class has these variables declared below. I'll explain more in the notes:

#import <Foundation/Foundation.h>

#import "cocos2d.h"

#import "AppData.h"

#import "Player.h"

> *// to avoid warnings, go ahead and create an empty class for this now, subclass it from CCNode*

@interface GameEngine : CCLayer {

> int lives;
>
> *// number of lives to start with*
>
> int level;
>
> *// the current level*
>
> int tilt;
>
> *// this variable is used to store the value of the tilt of the device*
>
> int ticker;
>
> *// used for determining when to add new enemies / objects to the screen, initial value will be the screenWidth*
>
> int screenWidth;
>
> *// always useful*

```
int screenHeight;
// always useful
NSString* backgroundString;
// stores the value from the plist file for the non-moving background art file name
NSString* scrollingBgString1;
// stores the value from the plist file for the scrolling background art file name
NSString* scrollingBgString2;
// stores the value from the plist file for the 2nd scrolling background art file name
Player* player;
// the actual player, there's only one of these, so it's always easy to declare the
instance in the header
NSMutableArray* scoreObjArray;
// we will hold onto some of the data from the plist file to add scoring objects
only as needed
NSMutableArray* enemyArray;
// we will hold onto some of the data from the plist file to add enemy objects
only as needed
}
@property (retain, nonatomic) NSMutableArray* scoreObjArray;
    // we need to retain this data so it sticks around
@property (retain, nonatomic) NSMutableArray* enemyArray;

+(CCScene *) scene;
@end
```

Now scoot over to the implementation file for the GameEngine class. First, be sure to synthesize the enemyArray and scoreObjArray, by adding the following line below the @implementation:

```
@implementation GameEngine
@synthesize scoreObjArray, enemyArray;
```

Now let's look at the **init** statement. This will take a couple pages to paste in, so I'll explain some points throughout the code:

```
-(id) init {
    if( (self=[super init])) {
        CGSize size = [ [CCDirector sharedDirector] winSize ];
```

```
screenWidth = size.width;

screenHeight = size.height;

ticker = screenWidth;
```

The ticker will equal the screenWidth initially because this variable will be used to determine when new objects or enemies should be added to the scene. So on first run, any object in the **.plist** file with a starting position less than the ticker will be added. Then as the game continues we add one to the ticker every frame and check if the ticker has exceeded the starting positions of any objects that haven't yet been added. If so, we add those objects. Continuing on:

```
lives = [[AppData sharedData] returnLives];

level = [[AppData sharedData] returnLevel];

self.isAccelerometerEnabled = YES;
```

The lives and level variables get their values from the AppData singleton exactly like we set them up last section, so there's no change there. The accelerometer is enabled because that's our primary method of moving the character.

```
NSString *path = [[NSBundle mainBundle] bundlePath];

NSString *finalPath = [path stringByAppendingPathComponent:@"GameData.plist"];

NSDictionary *plistData = [NSDictionary dictionaryWithContentsOfFile: finalPath];

NSMutableArray* levelArray = [NSMutableArray arrayWithArray:[ plistData
objectForKey:@"Levels"]];

NSDictionary *levelDict = [NSDictionary dictionaryWithDictionary:[ levelArray
objectAtIndex: level − 1 ]];
```

Everything above should look familiar from the end of Section 1 of this chapter. We are just sorting through the data in the **.plist** file based on the current value of level (subtracted by one).

```
scoreObjArray = [[NSMutableArray alloc] initWithArray:[levelDict
objectForKey:@"ScoreObjects"] ];

enemyArray = [[NSMutableArray alloc] initWithArray:[levelDict objectForKey:@"Enemies"] ];
```

Next, we're paying special attention to our scoreObjArray and enemyArray by actually allocating them, which has been rare this book. We will need to release them later in the **dealloc** method because of this. The reason we call **alloc** is because we don't want these arrays getting automatically released from memory before we are done with them. These two arrays will store the **.plist** data for all the enemies and objects, some of which won't immediately be placed on screen. When an object or enemy does get added though, we don't need that info in the array anymore, so we can remove it (which will prevent us from adding the same object twice).

```
NSDictionary* playerDict = [NSDictionary dictionaryWithDictionary:[levelDict
objectForKey:@"PlayerProperties"]];

player = [Player createWithDictionary: playerDict];

[self addChild: player z: kPlayerLevel ];
```

Above we set up our player instance. You can go ahead and type in the lines above, but until your Player class includes the method createWithDictionary, you'll get a warning. As I mentioned earlier this section, we will create the Player instance by passing in the entire contents of the Dictionary from the .plist file. This way we really don't have to do much other than add the child. For the z depth value I'll use a value from the Constants.h file called kPlayerLevel, but if you just want to enter a number like five, that's fine too. Continuing on:

```
backgroundString = [levelDict objectForKey:@"BackgroundArt"];

scrollingBgString1 = [levelDict objectForKey:@"ScrollingArt1"];

scrollingBgString2 = [levelDict objectForKey:@"ScrollingArt2"];

[self setupBackground ];
        // write this later
```

Next, I'm just storing the file names for each of the pieces of background art as NSString variables, which will get used later in the method named setupBackground that I'm calling above. To keep things simple in the init statement, I'm just putting all that background code elsewhere. If you want to write this method now, you can skip ahead a few pages where I've included the code to do so. Otherwise, just create an empty method for setupBackground, so when you test the project you'll call a method that exists. Finally, in the line below, I'm scheduling a method called mainLoop, which runs every frame. The "engine" is essentially turned on once this starts firing: our ticker will increment, new objects will appear on screen, collision detection is active, and our player will fly around:

```
        [self schedule:@selector(mainLoop:) interval:1.0f/60.0f];

    }

    return self;

}
        // end of the init statement
```

Let's go ahead and release the scoreObjArray and enemyArray in the **dealloc** statement before we forget:

- (void) **dealloc** {

    [scoreObjArray **release**];

    [enemyArray **release**];

    enemyArray = nil;

    scoreObjArray = nil;

    [super **dealloc**];

}

Go ahead and include your Accelerometer code as well:

-(void) **accelerometer**:(UIAccelerometer *)accelerometer **didAccelerate**:(UIAcceleration *)acceleration {

    tilt = (acceleration.y * 20);

}

Similar to when I first showed you how to access the Accelerometer, I'm multiplying the value of acceleration.y so it is a bit more of a substantial number. Since this game is set up to be in landscape mode, the acceleration.y is basically the tilt from left to right. Left will make the bird fly higher, right will make the bird drop lower. All we need to do above is set the value of the tilt variable. In the **mainLoop** method, we will actually use the tilt value to reposition the bird.

One thing you might have noticed missing in the **init** statement is that we didn't actually create any of our scoring objects or enemies. I've saved that for the **mainLoop** too. We will add a bit more to the **mainLoop** in the next section, but I'll break down what it's primarily doing below.

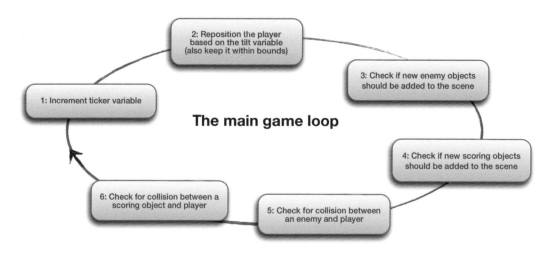

The main game loop

1: Increment ticker variable

2: Reposition the player based on the tilt variable (also keep it within bounds)

3: Check if new enemy objects should be added to the scene

4: Check if new scoring objects should be added to the scene

5: Check for collision between an enemy and player

6: Check for collision between a scoring object and player

Unfortunately we can't begin to do much with the **mainLoop** method until we get our other classes set up. Also we can't test the project, as is, without crashing until we at least define the **mainLoop** method. So for now, you can just add in:

-(void) **mainLoop**: (ccTime) delta {

   ticker ++;

      // 1: Increment ticker variable

      // 2: Reposition the player based on the tilt variable (also keep within bounds)

      // 3: Check if new enemy objects should be added to the scene

      // 4: Check if new scoring objects should be added to the scene

      // 5: Check for collision between an enemy and player

      // 6: Check for collision between a scoring object and player

}

If it helps you to get your mind around the tasks ahead, create a little to-do list inside of the method.

Creating the Player Class

If you haven't already, create a class called Player which is subclassed from CCNode. Let's take a closer look at the Dictionary called **PlayerProperties,** which is getting passed into the Player class instance. We have an item called **SpriteSheetName** that is

PlayerProperties		Dictionary	(8 items)
SpriteSheetName		String	fatbird_sheet
BaseImage		String	fatbird_default.png
BruisedImage		String	fatbird_bruised.png
PlayerLocation		String	{300,500}
IsAnimated		Boolean	YES
AnimationBaseName		String	fatbird_flying
FramesToAnimate		Number	20
Gravity		Number	1

the name of the PNG file and corresponding .plist file for the sprite sheet I've created for the player art. The **BaseImage** is the initial frame to show, or if the player wasn't going to be animated, then this would be the main frame to default back to after the player got injured. The **BruisedImage** is the image frame to show if the player is injured. The **PlayerLocation** is the initial starting point. Notice the value is in squiggly brackets { } here. This is a special formatting used in *.**plist*** files for CGPoints. The **IsAnimated** item determines whether to run an animated sequence for the player. **AnimationBaseName** defines the frame names for the animated images (excluding the frame number). **FramesToAnimate** is the number of frames in that sequence. Finally, **Gravity** is used to make the player descend on screen.

So let's get the header file of the Player class setup:

```objc
@interface Player : CCNode {
    CCSprite* playerSprite;
    // the animated or at times non-animated sprite within the instance
    CCRepeatForever *flying;
    // declared and later retained CCRepeatForever variable
    CCSpriteFrame* bruisedPose;
    // we will show this frame when the player is injured / loses health
    CCSpriteFrame* defaultPose;
    // default frame
    bool isAnimated;
    // optionally we can make the player non-animated and just flip between the default
    and bruised frames
    NSString* animationBaseName;
    // base name for the animated images in the sprite sheet
    int framesToAnimate;
    // the number of frames to animate in sequence
    int gravity;
    // variable used to make the player slowly descend
    bool isBruised;
    // whether or not the player is currently injured
}
@property (nonatomic, retain) CCRepeatForever *flying;
    // if we don't retain this, it won't stay in memory to use again
+(id) createWithDictionary:(NSDictionary*)theDictionary;
    // the class method to create the instance with the dictionary
-(void) showBruisedState;
    // instance method which gets called if the mainLoop of the GameEngine
    detects a collision.
@end
```

Now jump over to your implementation file for the **Player** class. First let's synthesize the flying variable, then write the class method:

@implementation Player

@synthesize flying;

```
+(id) createWithDictionary:(NSDictionary*)theDictionary {

    return [[[self alloc] initWithDictionary:(NSDictionary*) theDictionary ] autorelease];
        // calls the init statement, passing in theDictionary

}
```

Now let's write the **initWithDictionary** statement, and I'll go over the code:

```
- (id) initWithDictionary:(NSDictionary*) theDictionary {
    if ((self = [super init])) {
        self.position = CGPointFromString( [theDictionary objectForKey:@"PlayerLocation"] );
        NSString* spriteSheetName = [theDictionary objectForKey:@"SpriteSheetName"];
        NSString* plistName = [NSString stringWithFormat:@"%@.plist", spriteSheetName ];
        [[CCSpriteFrameCache sharedSpriteFrameCache] addSpriteFramesWithFile:
        plistName ];

        NSString* bruisedImage = [theDictionary objectForKey:@"BruisedImage"];
        bruisedPose = [[CCSpriteFrameCache sharedSpriteFrameCache]
        spriteFrameByName: bruisedImage];
        NSString* defaultImage = [theDictionary objectForKey:@"BaseImage"];
        defaultPose = [[CCSpriteFrameCache sharedSpriteFrameCache]
        spriteFrameByName: defaultImage];

        playerSprite = [CCSprite spriteWithSpriteFrame: defaultPose];
        [self addChild: playerSprite];

        gravity = [[theDictionary objectForKey:@"Gravity"] integerValue];
        isAnimated = [[theDictionary objectForKey:@"IsAnimated"] boolValue];
            if ( isAnimated == YES ) {
                animationBaseName = [theDictionary objectForKey:@"AnimationBaseName"];
                framesToAnimate = [[theDictionary objectForKey:@"FramesToAnimate"]
                integerValue];
                [self setUpAnimation];
            }
```

```
        [self schedule:@selector(movePlayerDown:) interval:1.0f/60.0f ];
    }
    return self;
}
```

We have some new code right off the bat in the **init** statement:

self.position = **CGPointFromString**([theDictionary **objectForKey:**@"PlayerLocation"]);

That **CGPointFromString** function converts the string text in the **.plist** file to a CGPoint. In this case, the string was { 300, 500 } and notice I'm writing self.position so the entire instance is being positioned at 300, 500 as opposed to moving the playerSprite within this instance. The playerSprite will **always** stay at 0, 0. Any position changes will occur on the entire instance, not just the sprite.

The next few lines should look familiar from back in Chapter 7 when we created an animated fight character using a sprite sheet. We're getting the spriteSheetName from the **GameData.plist** file, using it to determine the **.plist** for the bird sprite sheet which is of course added as a Resource in the project already. We are then filling the **sharedSpriteFrameCache** with frames from the sheet. If you want the sprite sheet I'm using, the project files are available at **www.focalpress.com/cw/Dike** and you can copy **fatbird_sheet.plist** and **fatbird_sheet.png** (and the **-ipadhd** versions) to your project.

The two CCSpriteFrame variables declared as bruisedPose and defaultPose get set up next. The **.plist** file defines the names of these frames, which we then find in the **sharedSpriteFrameCache** with the **spriteFrameByName** method.

Next, we make the playerSprite equal to the defaultPose with this line:

playerSprite = [CCSprite **spriteWithSpriteFrame**: defaultPose];

Then we add it to the instance, but I'm not setting a position, so it will just default to 0, 0 which is what we want anyway.

Next, we give gravity a value from the **.plist** file. Then we determine if isAnimated is YES or NO. If it is, then animationBaseName and framesToAnimate need corresponding values from the **.plist** file. We will then call this method ... [self **setUpAnimation**] ... which we will look at in just a moment.

Finally, we schedule a method called **movePlayerDown**, which will make the player move down over time. This is an easy method to set up, so let's go ahead and take care of this first:

```
-(void) movePlayerDown:(ccTime) delta {
    self.position = ccp( self.position.x, self.position.y – gravity );
    // changes the y location, the x is unaffected
}
```

Obviously if gravity is zero this method does nothing. In fact, if gravity is zero this method wouldn't even need to run. Next, let's write the animation method. This should also look familiar from Chapter 7, so I won't over explain it:

-(void) **setUpAnimation** {

    NSMutableArray *flyingFrames = [NSMutableArray **arrayWithCapacity**: framesToAnimate];

    for (int i = 1; i <= framesToAnimate; ++i) {

        NSString* file = [NSString **stringWithFormat**:@"%@%i.png", animationBaseName, i];

        CCSpriteFrame* frame = [[CCSpriteFrameCache **sharedSpriteFrameCache**] **spriteFrameByName**: file];

        [flyingFrames **addObject**: frame];

    }

    CCAnimation* flyingAnimation = [CCAnimation **animationWithSpriteFrames**: flyingFrames **delay**:1.0/15.0];

    CCAnimate* animate = [CCAnimate **actionWithAnimation**: flyingAnimation];

    self.flying = [CCRepeatForever **actionWithAction**: animate];

    [playerSprite **runAction**: flying];

    // the playerSprite appears to fly

}

Now that we actually have something needing to deallocate it's a good time to include this method:

-(void) **dealloc** {

      self.flying = nil;

      [super **dealloc**];

}

Our last bit of business in the Player class is to write methods to toggle between a bruised state and the normal state. The normal state could simply be the defaultPose or if the player is usually animated, then we will return the player to it's animation sequence.

-(void) **showBruisedState** {

    if (isBruised == NO) {

        // if the player was already in a bruised state we don't need to run this code twice

        isBruised = YES;

        // if the player wasn't bruised before, than he officially is now

```
    if ( isAnimated == YES ) {

        [playerSprite stopAction: flying];

        // stop the animation if it is usually on

    }

    [playerSprite setDisplayFrame: bruisedPose];

    // set the playerSprite to the bruisedPose

    [self performSelector:@selector(showNormalState) withObject: nil afterDelay:0.5f ];

    // after half a second, return to the normal state

    }

}
```

Now for the method that returns the player back to normal:

```
-(void) showNormalState {

    if ( isAnimated == YES ) {

        [playerSprite runAction: flying];

        // if the player is usually animated then we restart the flying sequence

    } else {

        [playerSprite setDisplayFrame: defaultPose];

        // otherwise if the player is not usually animated, just show the defaultPose

    }

    isBruised = NO;

    // switch this back to NO

}
```

That does it for the Player class. It might seem like a lot of code, but it really isn't (my implementation file is under 150 lines with generous spacing between lines). You'll probably be happy to know, our Enemy and ScoreObject classes require even less to set up.

Creating the Scrolling Background

Now that you've got your player ready, you might be itching to test how it looks with the background scrolling by. Add this method:

- (void) **setupBackground** {

CCSprite* background = [CCSprite **spriteWithFile**: backgroundString];

// *this is the non-moving background image*

background.position = ccp(screenWidth / 2 , screenHeight / 2);

[self **addChild**: background **z**: kSkyLevel] ;

// *kSkyLevel is defined in a Constants.h file, add this now or enter a number*

CCSprite* scrollingArt = [CCSprite **spriteWithFile**: scrollingBgString1 **rect**: **CGRectMake**(0, 0, screenWidth* 2, 512)];

ccTexParams params = {GL_LINEAR,GL_LINEAR,GL_REPEAT,GL_REPEAT};

// *repeat the image horizontally*

[scrollingArt.texture **setTexParameters**:&params];

scrollingArt.position = ccp(screenWidth , 255);

[self **addChild**: scrollingArt **z**: kLandscapeLevel];

// *kLandscapeLevel is defined in a Constants.h file, any number higher than the sky will do*

CCMoveBy* move = [CCMoveBy **actionWithDuration**:15.0 **position**: ccp(screenWidth * - 1, 0)];

CCPlace* place = [CCPlace **actionWithPosition**: ccp(screenWidth , 255)];

CCSequence* scrollingArtSequence = [CCSequence **actions**: move, place, nil];

CCRepeatForever* repeatSequence = [CCRepeatForever **actionWithAction**: scrollingArtSequence];

[scrollingArt **runAction**: repeatSequence];

// *run the sequence that scrolls this image*

CCSprite* scrollingArt2 = [CCSprite **spriteWithFile**: scrollingBgString2 **rect**: **CGRectMake**(0, 0, screenWidth* 2, screenHeight)];

ccTexParams params2 = {GL_LINEAR, GL_LINEAR,GL_REPEAT,GL_REPEAT};

// *repeat the image horizontally*

[scrollingArt2.texture **setTexParameters**: &params2];

scrollingArt2.position = ccp(screenWidth , screenHeight / 2);

```
[self addChild: scrollingArt2 z: kCloudsLevel];
```
// z:kCloudsLevel is defined in a Constants.h file, any number lower than the previous image is fine

```
CCMoveBy* move2 = [CCMoveBy actionWithDuration:40.0 position: ccp( screen Width * -1, 0 )];
CCPlace* place2 = [CCPlace actionWithPosition: ccp( screenWidth , screenHeight /2) ] ;
CCSequence* scrollingArtSequence2 = [CCSequence actions: move2, place2, nil];
CCRepeatForever* repeatSequence2 = [CCRepeatForever actionWithAction: scrollingArtSequence2];
[scrollingArt2 runAction: repeatSequence2];
```
// run the sequence that scrolls this image

```
}
```

Creating the Enemy Class

Let's review the Dictionary that gets passed into each Enemy class instance. The **BaseImage** property is the one and only image for each enemy. If the game you plan to build calls for animated frames for each enemy, then you should use the exact same set-up as the Player class as an example. **FlipX** and **FlipY** obviously get used if we want to flip the artwork. The **EnemyLocation** isn't used within the instance at all. The ticker in the GameEngine will be used to determine when/where to create each enemy. The initial x location we set for each Enemy could be far off screen, but that x value won't actually be where we place it. Remember we only add the instance as needed, and when the object is needed is right before it is visible on the right side of the screen. So the location it actually gets placed at on creation is right at the edge of the screen, not the value set in the *.plist*. **EnemySpeed** is how fast the object moves towards the left. Setting a variety of speed values for enemies obviously makes the game a bit harder because it isn't a constant,

Enemies	Array	(4 items)
▶ Item 0	Dictionary	(8 items)
▶ Item 1	Dictionary	(8 items)
▼ Item 2	Dictionary	(8 items)
BaseImage	String	thorns2.png
FlipY	Boolean	NO
FlipX	Boolean	NO
EnemyLocation	String	{1300, 350}
EnemySpeed	Number	2
PlaceThisManyMore	Number	0
XPaddingOfMultiples	Number	1,000
ZDepth	Number	5
▶ Item 3	Dictionary	(8 items)

making dodging one enemy more difficult than another. Finally, we already talked about the **PlaceThisManyMore** and **XPaddingOfMultiples**, and the **ZDepth** is optional. None of those properties get used inside of the class instance anyway, these are all used by the GameEngine.

The header file is pretty simple for the Enemy class (create this class now if you haven't already):

@interface Enemy : CCNode {

    CCSprite* enemySprite;

    int speed;

}

@property (readonly, nonatomic) CCSprite* enemySprite;

+(id) **createWithDictionary**:(NSDictionary*) theDictionary;

@end

I'm making the enemySprite a property because the GameEngine will need to check the contentSize.width and height of this sprite when it does collision detection against the player. By making enemySprite a readonly property, it can do that. So at the top of the implementation file, be sure to synthesize it, then let's go ahead and write the **createWithDictionary** method, similar to the Player class:

@implementation Enemy

@synthesize enemySprite;

+(id) **createWithDictionary**:(NSDictionary*)theDictionary {

    return [[[self **alloc**] **initWithDictionary**:(NSDictionary*)theDictionary] **autorelease**];

}

Now we can write the **init** statement. There isn't much to do here. We will add the enemySprite with an image determined by the file name set in the **.plist** file. We will flip it on the x or y depending on the **.plist** settings. The speed value is also set, and finally, we schedule a method called **moveEnemy** to run at 60 frames per second.

-(id) **initWithDictionary**:(NSDictionary*)theDictionary {

  if ((self = [super **init**])) {

    enemySprite = [CCSprite **spriteWithFile**: [theDictionary **objectForKey**:@"BaseImage"]];

    [self **addChild**: enemySprite];

    enemySprite.flipY = [[theDictionary **objectForKey**:@"FlipY"] **boolValue**];

    enemySprite.flipX = [[theDictionary **objectForKey**:@"FlipX"] **boolValue**];

    speed = [[theDictionary **objectForKey**:@"EnemySpeed"] **integerValue**];

```
        [self schedule:@selector(moveEnemy:) interval:1.0f/60.0f ];
    }
    return self;
}
```

The **moveEnemy** method basically has a self-destruct switch in it. It subtracts the enemy's x position by the speed (which moves it left) and when the position is less than −100, it removes itself from the scene with the **removeFromParentAndCleanup** method. I went with −100 instead of 0 because the center point of the Enemy instance would hit 0 leaving the right side of the enemy still visible on screen. So −100 should keep a portion of the enemy from suddenly disappearing, but depending on the artwork you use, you might want to set this number lower, like −200.

```
-(void) moveEnemy:(ccTime) delta {
    self.position = ccp( self.position.x − speed, self.position.y );
    if ( self.position.x < -100) {
        [self unschedule:_cmd];
        // unschedule this selector
        [self removeFromParentAndCleanup: YES];
        // setting cleanup to yes, should also unschedule this as well.
    }
}
```

Finally, we need to include our **dealloc** statement. We don't actually need to write anything else inside of it, but I think it's a good idea to add a CCLOG statement, just so we know for sure that these enemies are getting removed off screen when we think they are. Since we won't actually see them be removed, this is a safe way of knowing they are gone. CCLOG statements can be left in your project without slowing down the final app you submit to Apple.

```
-(void) dealloc {
    CCLOG(@"removing enemy");
    [super dealloc];
}
@end
```

That's it! Before you forget, go back to your GameEngine header file and import this class … #import "Enemy.h"

The ScoreObject Class

The ScoreObject, whatever that may be: coins, mushrooms, etc., won't have autonomous control of itself like the Enemy class, which has it's own scheduler incrementing the self.position value offscreen. Instead, I want to give you a second option because giving every instance of a class control of it's movement might be overkill, especially if every instance is moving at a constant speed. This time we will group together the ScoreObject instances into a parent class called ScoreNodes, which will handle moving the entire group. It's not a major change from what we did before, now we just have two classes each doing some of the work.

Let's create the ScoreObject class. As usual, create a new class file, subclassed from CCNode. Below is the header file:

```
@interface ScoreObject : CCNode {
        CCSprite* objectSprite;
        int pointValue;
}

@property (readonly, nonatomic ) CCSprite* objectSprite;
@property (readonly, nonatomic ) int pointValue;
+(id) createWithDictionary:(NSDictionary*)theDictionary;
@end
```

Again we are passing in the Dictionary data from the *.plist* file, but you might notice I'm not declaring a speed variable. We'll save that for the ScoreNodes class. The ScoreObject class mostly just displays the sprite and holds onto the pointValue—both of which are declared as readonly properties so the GameEngine class can access these later.

Below is the entire implementation file for the ScoreObject class. As you can see, there isn't much to it. The **initWithDictionary** statement simply adds the objectSprite to the instance with the appropriate image file, flips it on the x or y depending on the bool properties of the *.plist*, and the pointValue variable is set from the *.plist* as well. The **dealloc** method has a CCLOG statement because I want to be sure these objects get removed when we assume they should be.

```
@implementation ScoreObject
@synthesize objectSprite, pointValue;

+(id) createWithDictionary:(NSDictionary*)theDictionary {
    return [[[self alloc] initWithDictionary:(NSDictionary*)theDictionary ] autorelease];
}
```

```
-(id) initWithDictionary:(NSDictionary*)theDictionary {
    if ((self = [super init])) {
        objectSprite = [CCSprite spriteWithFile: [theDictionary objectForKey:@"BaseImage"]];
        [self addChild: objectSprite];
        objectSprite.flipY = [[theDictionary objectForKey:@"FlipY"] boolValue];
        objectSprite.flipX = [[theDictionary objectForKey:@"FlipX"] boolValue];
        pointValue = [[theDictionary objectForKey:@"Points"] integerValue ];
    }
    return self;
}

-(void) dealloc {
    CCLOG(@"removing score object");
    [super dealloc];
}
@end
```

The ScoreNodes Class

Hooray! This is our last class to create before we can move back to our GameEngine and put all the pieces together. The ScoreNodes class just has one job, house it's children, which will be the ScoreObject instances and move at the speed we pass in. The speed will come from the plist file, but because this class only needs this one bit of data we won't pass in an entire Dictionary object like we've done with the other classes. Below is the header file:

```
@interface ScoreNodes : CCLayer {
    int moveSpeed;
}
+(id) createWithSpeed:(int) speed ;
@end
```

Then jumping over to the implementation file, our **initWithSpeed** method mostly just schedules a method called move (listed on the following page), which uses the moveSpeed variable. Again, I'm including a CCLOG statement in the **dealloc** method.

```
@implementation ScoreNodes

+(id) createWithSpeed:(int)speed {
    return [[[self alloc] initWithSpeed:(int)speed ] autorelease];
}
```

```
-(id) initWithSpeed:(int)speed {
    if ((self = [super init])) {
        moveSpeed = speed;
        // moveSpeed equals the speed value passed in
        [self schedule:@selector(move:) interval:1.0f/60.0f ];
    }
    return self;
}
-(void) move:(ccTime) delta {
    self.position = ccp(self.position.x – moveSpeed, self.position.y );
}
-(void) dealloc {
    CCLOG(@"removing score group");
    [super dealloc];
}
@end
```

That's it for the ScoreNodes class. Let's go to our **GameEngine.h** file and review all the import statements we have.

```
#import "AppData.h"
#import "Player.h"
#import "Enemy.h"
#import "ScoreObject.h"
#import "ScoreNodes.h"
#import "Constants.h"  ─────────────►
#import "SimpleAudioEngine.h"
```

```
#define kSkyLevel -10
#define kCloudsLevel -5
#define kLandscapeLevel -3
#define kScoreObjectsLevel 1
#define kPlayerLevel 5
#define kEnemiesLevel 10
```

You can go ahead and import in the SimpleAudioEngine class, since you'll probably want to play sound eventually. Also if you didn't already create a **Constants.h** file, go ahead and do that. All the code in my **Constants.h** file, is shown above. I'm simply defining the **z** depth I want objects to be created at. I find it easier to define depths as constants in case I want to rearrange them later.

The Main Game Loop—Controlling the Player

Head back over to the **GameEngine.m** file and let's add this line to the **mainLoop** statement you started writing oh so long ago:

```
- (void) mainLoop: (ccTime) delta {
        ticker ++;
        [ self adjustPlayerPosition ];
}
```

Instead of typing all the code to control the player inside of the **mainLoop** method, let's peel out of it and work in a separate method. We'll do this for all the main tasks of the loop, for the simple reason that it's cleaner code. Also if we wanted to rearrange the order of what occurs in the loop, or comment out a portion for debugging, it's much easier this way.

```
-(void) adjustPlayerPosition {
    if ( player.position.y < screenHeight + 10 && player.position.y > 0) {
    // if within the screen bounds
        player.position = ccp( player.position.x, player.position.y + tilt );
    } else if ( player.position.y >= screenHeight + 10) {
    // if too high
        player.position = ccp( player.position.x, screenHeight );
    } else if ( player.position.y <= 0 ){
    // if too low
        player.position = ccp( player.position.x, 2 );
    }
}
```

We're checking three conditions above. First, if the player's y position is lower than the screenHeight (plus ten, so he can fly a tad higher) and greater than zero (the bottom of the screen), then in that case, the y position is added to by the tilt variable (the tilt is set by the accelerometer). Else if the player is greater than the screenHeight (plus ten), then we bump the player's y position down to the screenHeight. The last else if statement does the same thing, keeping the player from flying below the bottom of the screen.

The Main Game Loop—Setting Up Enemies

In your **mainLoop**, add in this next method call [self **setupEnemies**]; and let's pick it apart below. I'm going to write this method first without the option to add multiple copies using the **PlaceThisManyMore** item in the plist file. Hopefully once you understand this code without that extra part, it will make it easier to follow when I do add it.

```
-(void) setupEnemies {
    for ( int i = 0; i < [enemyArray count]; i++ ) {
        NSDictionary *enemyDict = [NSDictionary dictionaryWithDictionary:[ enemyArray
        objectAtIndex: i ]];
        CGPoint startPosition = CGPointFromString( [enemyDict
        objectForKey:@"EnemyLocation"] );
        if (startPosition.x < ticker ) {
        // time to add a new instance!
            [enemyArray removeObjectAtIndex: i ];
            // remove this enemy data from the array, so we won't add it twice to the scene
            Enemy* someEnemy = [Enemy createWithDictionary: enemyDict];
            [self addChild: someEnemy z: kEnemiesLevel ];
            if ( startPosition.x > screenWidth){
            // if the position was originally greater than the screenWidth, we adjust it below ...
                startPosition = ccp( screenWidth + (someEnemy.enemySprite.contentSize.width /
                2) , startPosition.y );
            }
            someEnemy.position = startPosition;
            // someEnemy's position is now the startPosition which may or may not have
            been adjusted
        break;
        }
    }
}
```

The for statement is going to iterate through the enemyArray. This array contains the info on every enemy in the plist file that has **not** yet been created. So on first run, the enemyArray has the most data it ever will. We can find out how many enemies were defined in the plist file by calling [enemyArray **count**], which you see used in the for statement's signature. So every time **setupEnemies** is called, we go back through the array, and check to see if an enemy's start location is within range to add to the scene. We create the CGPoint startPosition to hold onto those start location values through each iteration. If the startPosition.x is less than the ticker value, then we know we need to add a new Enemy instance. Remember too, the ticker initially starts at the value of the screenWidth. So within a few frames of the app initially loading, any enemies defined to start on screen will be there.

Within the if statement to create a new instance, the first thing we do is call:

[enemyArray **removeObjectAtIndex**: i];

This will remove the current dictionary data from the array so we never have to worry about adding the same enemy data again. The only tricky thing here is that we're removing an item from the array, while our for statement is still iterating through that same array. Think of this like stacking cups on top of each other. Each cup is an item in the array. If we remove the bottom cup, the stack falls. So notice at the bottom of this first if statement, I've written a break; statement. This will stop the for statement from iterating any further and it's a safe way to prevent any problems from removing that item from the array. Keep in mind too, our **mainLoop** runs every frame of the game, so this same for statement will get restarted again 1/60th of a second later, and continue adding enemies as needed.

So after we remove the object from the array, we write Enemy* someEnemy = [Enemy **createWithDictionary**: enemyDict]; Then add the child. You can use kEnemiesLevel from the **Constants.h** file or if you want to use the **z** depth from the plist file swap in [[enemyDict **objectForKey**:@"ZDepth"] **integerValue**] instead.

The interior if statement checks if the startPosition.x is greater than the screenWidth, which would mean that the Enemy instance wasn't originally viewable when the game opened, and the screen has scrolled a bit (the ticker has increased) until it was necessary to add it. In which case, we make the startPosition.x value equal to the screenWidth, plus a little something extra. If we created the enemy at exactly the screenWidth, it's the center point which would be located there, thus immediately revealing the left half of the enemy. We want the entire enemy to scroll in, not just the back half. So we add half the contentSize.width of the enemySprite within the instance.

Then finally, we set the position with someEnemy.position = startPosition;

That's it. You should have Enemy instances scrolling toward your player now.

If you want to crowbar in a little bit more to include the option to place clones with the same enemy data, I'll show you where to add that below. Between the two existing lines below, add the highlighted yellow portion:

someEnemy.position = startPosition;

```
int multiples = [[enemyDict objectForKey:@"PlaceThisManyMore"] integerValue];
if ( multiples > 0 ) {
    int count = 1;
    int padding = [[enemyDict objectForKey:@"XPaddingOfMultiples"] integerValue];

    while ( count <= multiples) {
        Enemy* someEnemy = [Enemy createWithDictionary: enemyDict];
        [self addChild: someEnemy z: kEnemiesLevel ];
        someEnemy.position = ccp( startPosition.x + ( count * padding ), startPosition.y );
        count++;
    }
}
```

break;

The first thing we do is create an int called multiples and make it equal to the value of the **PlaceThisManyMore** item in the enemyDict. Then if multiples is anything greater than zero we know we need to add some. We create an int var called count just for use in the while statement and we create an int called padding, which will be used to offset the starting x position of each multiple we add.

The while statement just iterates through the number of multiples, each time adding a new Enemy instance. You can see the x position is based on the value of startPosition.x + (count * padding). If that's confusing, just run through it in your head. If count = 1, then 1 multiplied by the padding, is just the original padding value again, which is added to the startPosition.x . Then if count = 2, the padding is doubled, and that is added to the startPosition.x, and so on, and so on, spacing them out by the padding amount each time.

The Main Game Loop—Setting Up Score Objects

In your **mainLoop**, add in this next method call: [self **setupScoreObjects**]; and prepare to breathe it all in below.

-(void) **setupScoreObjects** {
    for (int i = 0; i < [scoreObjArray **count**]; i++) {
        NSDictionary *scoreObjDict = [NSDictionary **dictionaryWithDictionary**:[scoreObjArray **objectAtIndex**: i]];
        CGPoint startPosition = **CGPointFromString**([scoreObjDict **objectForKey**:@"ObjectLocation"]);

```
if (startPosition.x < ticker) {

    [scoreObjArray removeObjectAtIndex: i ];

    ScoreNodes* someGroup = [ScoreNodes createWithSpeed:[[scoreObjDict
    objectForKey:@"Speed"] integerValue] ];

    [self addChild: someGroup z: [[scoreObjDict objectForKey:@"ZDepth"]
    integerValue]];

    ScoreObject* someObject = [ScoreObject createWithDictionary: scoreObjDict];

    [someGroup addChild: someObject ];

    // NOTE the child is added to someGroup instead of self

    if (startPosition.x > screenWidth){

    startPosition = ccp( screenWidth + (someObject.objectSprite.contentSize.width / 2) ,
    startPosition.y );

    }

    someObject.position = startPosition;

    int multiples = [[scoreObjDict objectForKey: @"PlaceThisManyMore"] integerValue];

    if ( multiples > 0 ) {

        int count = 1;

        int padding = [[scoreObjDict objectForKey:@"XPaddingOfMultiples"]
        integerValue];

        while ( count <= multiples) {

            ScoreObject* someObject = [ScoreObject createWithDictionary:
            scoreObjDict];

            [someGroup addChild: someObject];

            // NOTE the child is added to someGroup instead of self

            someObject.position = ccp( startPosition.x + ( count * padding ),
            startPosition.y );

            count ++;

        }

    }

    break;

    }

}

}
```

Most of that method is identical to the previous one for adding Enemy instances. The main exception is these four lines:

ScoreNodes* someGroup = [ScoreNodes **createWithSpeed**:[[scoreObjDict **objectForKey**:@"Speed"] **integerValue**]];

[self **addChild**: someGroup **z**: [[scoreObjDict **objectForKey**:@"ZDepth"] **integerValue**]];

ScoreObject* someObject = [ScoreObject **createWithDictionary**: scoreObjDict];

[someGroup **addChild**: someObject];

// NOTE the child is added to someGroup instead of self

We first create a ScoreNodes instance called someGroup, where we initialize it with the **Speed** value from the plist. We add it to the scene, this time I'm using the **z** depth from the plist. I'm being a little wishy washy about using **z** depths defined in the *Constants.h* file vs ones set up in the plist. You can decide which is best for your project, I'm just giving you both options.

Then we create the ScoreObject instance called someObject. This will get added as a child of someGroup instead of added directly to the scene with self. Can you tell I don't put much weight in instance names by the way I call them "some" every time? Saying, "some object gets added to some group," doesn't sound too fancy, but the fact is, the actual instance names really don't matter when we are populating the board with a bunch at once like this. Eventually all I need to know is what kind of class they are, not their names.

So that's the main difference. Of course, any multiples of this same object also get added to someGroup instead of the usual self.

That should do it for spawning all your enemies and score objects. The enemy objects are already set up to self destruct when they get far enough off screen. Our ScoreObject and ScoreNodes will require a little extra work to delete because I'll use the **mainLoop** to check that every child in the ScoreNodes instance has been removed before I get rid of the parent. Even without that, you can test the app at this point. You'll just end up leaving some objects in existence unnecessarily. If you ever have a hunch that some of your objects are still "around" when they shouldn't be, take a look at the **draw calls** number in the display stats in the bottom left corner of the screen. The draw calls is the top number in the stack. If an object hasn't been removed, it's probably still being added to that number.

Once we have our app finished, that draw calls number should stay relatively low, because even though we're adding a lot of objects, we're constantly removing them too. You might have noticed in this screen grab my frame rate is a frighteningly low at 5.5fps and that's only because I captured the image from the Simulator. The iOS Simulator will rarely give you an accurate frame rate. *Always test on your iOS device!*

The Main Game Loop—Checking for Enemy Collisions

Let's check in with our **mainLoop**, and add another method to the mix:

- (void) **mainLoop**: (ccTime) delta {

    ticker ++;

    [self **adjustPlayerPosition**];

    [self **setupEnemies**];

    [self **setupScoreObjects**];

    [self **checkEnemyCollisions**] ;

}

This is a relatively simple method. We iterate through all the children in the scene, checking each one to see if it is an Enemy class, and if so, we then create a CGRect called enemyRect using the position and contentSize values of the enemySprite within the instance, and compare that to the player.position value in another if statement using **CGRectContainsPoint**. If a collision is detected, we call a method inside of the player instance, [player **showBruisedState**]; In the next section, we'll add a bit more when the player is injured.

-(void) **checkEnemyCollisions** {

    for (Enemy* enemy in self.children) {

      if ([enemy **isKindOfClass**:[Enemy **class**]]) {

        CGRect enemyRect = **CGRectMake**(enemy.position.x – (enemy.enemySprite.contentSize.width / 2) ,

        enemy.position.y – (enemy.enemySprite.contentSize.height / 2),

        enemy.enemySprite.contentSize.width,

        enemy.enemySprite.contentSize.height);

      if (**CGRectContainsPoint**(enemyRect, player.position) {

      // collision detected!

        [player **showBruisedState**];

      }

    }

  }

}

The Main Game Loop—Checking for Score Object Collisions

Add one last method to the **mainLoop** method: [self **checkScoreObjectCollisions**];

This one is a whooper, so I'll paste it in over the next couple pages and step you through it afterwards. This is very similar to the method checking for Enemy collisions, but we have some extra code to delete the group nodes when they aren't needed any longer.

-(void) **checkScoreObjectCollisions** {

    for (ScoreNodes* group in self.children) {

  // the first for statement

      if ([group **isKindOfClass**:[ScoreNodes **class**]]) {

  // check for ScoreNodes

        for (ScoreObject* object in group.children) {

  // and another for statement checking the children in the group

          if ([object **isKindOfClass**:[ScoreObject **class**]]) {

  // checks for ScoreObject classes

            CGPoint worldCoord = [group **convertToWorldSpace**: object.position];

  // convert coordinates to world space

            CGRect objRect = **CGRectMake**(worldCoord.x − (object.objectSprite.
                              contentSize.width / 2) ,
                              worldCoord.y − (object.objectSprite.
                              contentSize.height / 2),
                              object.objectSprite.contentSize.width,
                              object.objectSprite.contentSize.height);

          if (**CGRectContainsPoint**(objRect, player.position)) {

  // if a collision is detected

  // ADD TO THE SCORE (WE WILL DO THIS NEXT SECTION)

            [group **removeChild**: object **cleanup**: NO];

            // remove it

          if ([group.children **count**] == 0){

          // if group has no more children then remove it

            [self **removeChild**: group **cleanup**: YES];

            break;

          }

        else if (worldCoord.x < -100) {

  // else if the object has travelled significantly off stage

```
        [group removeChild:object cleanup:NO];
        // remove it
        if ([group.children count] == 0){
        // if group has no more children then remove it
            [self removeChild:group cleanup:YES];
            break;
        }
    }
  }
 }
}
}
}
// Yep, that's seven closing brackets at the end. Sometimes you just gotta go big
or go home
```

So you probably noticed we have two for statements being used in this method. The first goes through all the children in the scene and finds any ScoreNodes types. If so, we refer to that object as group and use a second for statement to pick out any ScoreObject types in group.children . When a ScoreObject is found we create a CGPoint called worldCoord (short for world coordinates) and make it equal to [group **convertToWorldSpace**: object.position]. This handy function converts the position of the object (which is our ScoreObject) from it's local value inside of the ScoreNodes instance to the position it would currently be at if it were a child of the main scene. This is the position value we need to properly test a collision between the ScoreObject and the player. Once we have that, we use it in creating a CGRect called objRect, and use this with the if statement testing **CGRectContainsPoint** (objRect, player.position).

If a collision is detected, we remove the object from the group. Although before doing so, we would want to grab the score value property that the object is holding onto. I'm saving the actual scoring aspect of this game for next section, so just make a mental note that we will come back and insert a method in there later.

After removing the ScoreObject instance from the ScoreNodes group, we should check to see if that was the only child in the parent. An if statement tests [group.children **count**] == 0 … and if so, we remove the group from the scene and break out of the for statement since we obviously don't need to do any further testing.

Watch a bonus movie on this topic at **www.focalpress.com/cw/Dike**.

Game Structure

The else if statement on the previous page is run if a collision between the player and ScoreObject did not occur, and here we are testing to see if the worldCoord.x value of the object has got low enough to be considered off screen. I'm using −100, but if your images are pretty wide, you might want a lower number. Again we remove the object, then test to see if the group is empty. If so, we remove the group and break from the for statement.

Finally, you can see we have quite a few closing brackets at the end. That's never fun to look at, but it's a necessary evil. Okay, maybe it's a little fun to look at.

Congrats! Your core game engine is complete. What's missing? Well, a running score, a health meter, a finishing point to the level, some sort of reset for the level if you don't pass it, and a menu to pause the action and set preferences. All that is yet to come! In the meantime, feel free to download my version so far, in the ***GameStructure_GameEngine*** folder at **www.focalpress.com/cw/Dike**.

Section 4

Points, Health, Lives, and Level Advances

If the GameEngine in the last section seemed a little too unlike anything you plan to build in your dream game, this section will hopefully come across as a bit broader. We'll still need to work with the previous project, but tallying points, decreasing health, dealing with lives and leveling up are all common aspects of nearly every game. They all lend themselves to some interface aspect of the game so this section will mostly deal with the stats and other parts that surrounds the actual play.

Points

Let's start with adding up points since this is an easy topic. The GameEngine class has an obvious place to include this code too, since we've already got the collision detection between the player and our scoring object. We just didn't deal with the scoring aspect last section. So let's create a new method with one parameter: thePoints to add to the overall score.

```
-(void) addToScore: (int) thePoints {
        CCLOG(@"the points are %i", thePoints);
}
```

That method can be written anywhere in your GameEngine implementation file. Then in the existing method named **checkScoreObjectCollisions,** find this if statement:

```
if ( CGRectContainsPoint( objRect, player.position) ) {
```

… and within it, call **addToScore** using the point value property of the ScoreObject as the parameter.

```
[self addToScore: object.pointValue];
```

Hopefully you haven't already forgotten that our ScoreObject class has a pointValue property (given value from the *GameData.plist* file on creation).

Now the question is, what to do with this value inside of the **addToScore** method? We can all assume a label should be displayed on screen with the overall score, but who's job is this? Well, there's no reason our GameEngine can't include these general statistical type elements, but we should also tell the AppData class that the score is being added to, because whenever our GameEngine reloads with either the same level or a new level, the overall score will still be added to. So when we create our label we should populate it initially with a value from the AppData class. Then when a new score occurs we can add to the AppData class and update the label. To get this set up, first go over to your *GameEngine.h* file and declare a couple of new variables:

```
CCLabelBMFont* scoreLabel;
int score;
```

Now go to the **init** statement of the GameEngine and let's add the following lines (anywhere should be fine, but in my project I added them towards the end of what I currently had):

```
scoreLabel = [CCLabelBMFont labelWithString:@"0" fntFile:@"green_arcade.fnt"];
scoreLabel.position = ccp( screenWidth − 100, screenHeight − 30);
// screen height minus 30
[self addChild:scoreLabel];
scoreLabel.anchorPoint = ccp(1.0f, 0.5f);
```

That should all look familiar from the last chapter's section on Labels. If you need to, refresh your memory by glancing back at page 293.

```
score = [[AppData sharedData] returnTotalScore];
NSString* scoreString = [NSString stringWithFormat:@"%i", score];
[scoreLabel setString: scoreString];
```

Now add those next three lines above. You'll get a warning regarding the first line because our AppData singleton doesn't yet have a method called **returnTotalScore**, but when it does it will return an integer value giving the score variable in the GameEngine class an initial value of whatever the AppData class has for the total score. On first run, this will be zero by default, which is fine since there's no score. So let's go back to our almost-forgotten AppData class and declare a totalScore variable and two new methods in the header file:

Declare these in the AppData.h file …

int totalScore;

-(int) **returnTotalScore**;

-(void) **addToTotalScore**: (int) theScore;

Now jump over to your implementation file, and let's write those two methods.

-(void) **addToTotalScore**: (int) theScore {

    totalScore = totalScore + theScore;

    // add to the total score with the points passed in

}

-(int) **returnTotalScore** {

    return totalScore;

    // return the total score

}

Easy and easier, right? Now we can go back to our GameEngine class, and finish the **addToScore** method:

-(void) **addToScore**: (int) thePoints {

    score = score + thePoints;

    // add to the score for this class

    [[AppData **sharedData**] **addToTotalScore**: thePoints];

    // add to the score for the AppData class

    NSString* scoreString = [NSString **stringWithFormat**:@"%i", score];

    [scoreLabel **setString**: scoreString];

    // update the score

}

So with those first two lines, our **addToScore** method is keeping both the GameEngine and AppData classes up to speed on the total score. Then we simply update the scoreLabel with the score value. Alternatively, in that third line inside the method, you could write:

NSString* scoreString = [NSString **stringWithFormat**:@"%i", [[AppData **sharedData**] **returnTotalScore**]];

Except, I don't see much need to trouble the AppData class since it's pretty easy to maintain a total score in both classes.

That does it for scoring. Right? Well, we really don't have any way to thoroughly test if this is working. The label should be updating any time you run into a ScoreObject (so that works), but we can't really test yet if the AppData is *actually* keeping a total score. There's an easy way to fix that. Let's just replace the GameEngine scene with itself. We won't worry about advancing the level variable yet, we will just reload the same level over again and we should see the previous score in the label. Add this to the GameEngine implementation file:

-(void) **reloadLevel** {

    CCTransitionFadeTR *transition = [CCTransitionFadeTR **transitionWithDuration**:2 **scene**:[GameEngine **scene**]];

    [[CCDirector **sharedDirector**] **replaceScene**:transition];

}

Then in the **init** statement call the **reloadLevel** method after a delay. Give yourself enough time to collide with some ScoreObject instances. Obviously this line won't make the final cut in the project, but for testing purposes, it'll do the trick:

    [self **scheduleOnce**:@selector(**reloadLevel**) **delay**:20.0f];

    // 20 second delay

Health Meter

What game doesn't have one of these? Okay, plenty don't, but for a game development book, this is a staple element that can't be ignored. Even if your dream app doesn't need a running health bar, this same set-up could easily be converted to a bar indicating how much time is left to complete the board, or show how much fuel is left in the player's gas tank. In both cases, the bar would probably be set to

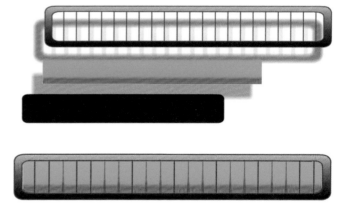

automatically decrease over time with a scheduled method. In our case, we will decrease the health bar when the player contacts one of the Enemy objects. The health bar will be comprised of three pieces of art. A top overlay, a middle green portion (the only part that actually gets scaled as health decreases) and then a bottom layer so we have something other than the background of the board showing through when the health meter isn't full. These will all be stacked on top of each other to form our meter.

Let's go the extra mile and create a custom class for the health meter. Create a new Cocos2d class subclassed from CCNode, and name it HealthMeter. The **HealthMeter.h** file will look like this after the usual import statements:

@interface HealthMeter : CCNode {

    CCSprite* scaleMeter;

}

+(id) **createWithPercentage**:(float)percent ;

-(void) **adjustPercentage**:(float)percent ;

@end

We don't need to declare any CCSprites other than the artwork that represents the health (which in my version is the middle green part). I'll call that sprite the scaleMeter.

Then I've declared a class method called **createWithPercentage**, which will initialize the class with one parameter—the percentage the meter is full. Most likely you'll always create the class with a float value of 1 (or 100 percent) but this will give you the option to make it less full.

We also have an instance method called **adjustPercentage**, which will take in a float value to set the scaleMeter to a new percentage.

The HealthMeter class doesn't need to know anything other than the percentage it should be at. It doesn't control anything—for example, it doesn't call a method in another class if the percentage drops to zero. It is simply a graphical representation of the health percentage in the GameEngine class. I'm not selling this class short, it just doesn't make much sense to have it do more than it needs.

Jump over to the implementation file of HealthMeter and write the rest of your class method:

+(id) **createWithPercentage**:(float)percent {

    return [[[self **alloc**] **initWithPercentage**:(float)percent] **autorelease**];

}

That will call our **initWithPercentage** method passing in the same percent value. Then we will set up the artwork, all of which will initially be positioned at 0, 0 except our scaleMeter will get a quick readjustment after we factor in the percent full it should be:

-(id) **initWithPercentage**:(float)percent {

    if ((self = [super **init**])) {

        CCSprite* backing = [CCSprite **spriteWithFile**:@"health_meter_base.png"];

        // the base

        [self **addChild**:backing **z**:0];

        // set at a z depth of 0

        scaleMeter = [CCSprite **spriteWithFile**:@"health_meter_green.png"];

        // the green part

        [self **addChild**:scaleMeter **z**:1];

        // set at a z depth of 1

        CCSprite* overlay = [CCSprite **spriteWithFile**:@"health_meter_overlay.png"];

        // the top layer

        [self **addChild**:overlay **z**:2];

        // set at a z depth of 2

        scaleMeter.scaleX = percent;

        // a percent of 1 is 100%, so the scaleMeter would not be scaled, a percent of 0.5 would scale it by half

        scaleMeter.position = ccp((-1 * scaleMeter.contentSize.width / 2) + (percent *
                    (scaleMeter.contentSize.width / 2)) ,
                    scaleMeter.position.y);

        // this equation does nothing to affect the y position, it only recalculates the x position

    }

    return self;

}

Everything above should read pretty straightforward until that very last line. We're doing a lot of work to reposition the x value of the scaleMeter. Let's look at just that part of the line:

> (-1 * scaleMeter.contentSize.width / 2) + (percent * (scaleMeter.contentSize.width / 2))

In the first parenthesis, I'm just subtracting half the width from it's current value. Then I'm adding half the width back multiplied by the percent. So if the percent was 1, we're not adjusting the x value at all because I'm subtracting the same amount I'm adding back. If the percent was 0.5, then I'm only adding back half of what I subtracted. That offset keeps the health bar draining toward the left side.

I'm sure there's another way of doing this by adjusting the anchorPoint, but a while back I figured out that nifty little equation and it's worked well for me before. This way you don't have to mess with the anchor at all. Next up, let's write the **adjustPercentage** method:

-(void) **adjustPercentage**:(float)percent {

    if (percent >= 0) {

// if the percent is greater than 0, otherwise we don't need to do anything. The level has probably already reset anyway.

      if (percent < .2){

// if the percent is low, like under 20 percent, you can optionally tint the scaleMeter. You could also use a CCTintTo action here.

        scaleMeter.color = ccRED;

      }

      scaleMeter.scaleX = percent;

// scaleX value to the percent once again

      scaleMeter.position = ccp((-1 * scaleMeter.contentSize.width / 2) + (percent *
                           (scaleMeter.contentSize.width / 2)) ,
                           scaleMeter.position.y);

// use the same position equation in the init method

    }

}

Include your usual **dealloc** method, and that's it for the HealthMeter class.

Back to the GameEngine class, in the header file be sure to write: #import "HealthMeter.h" and while you are there declare a few more variables:

HealthMeter *meter;

float currentHealthUnits;

float maxHealthUnits;

First, we declare a HealthMeter named meter to which we will add to the scene in the **init** statement in just a moment. We also declare two float type variables called currentHealthUnits and maxHealthUnits. When injured, the player will lose currentHealthUnits, whereas, the maxHealthUnits will stay the same over time. We figure out the percentage of the meter by dividing the currentHealthUnits by the maxHealthUnits. Be sure these are float values, otherwise we'll have issues passing the value into our class method for the HealthMeter.

Now in the **init** statement of the GameEngine add these lines:

maxHealthUnits = 500;

currentHealthUnits = maxHealthUnits;

meter = [HealthMeter **createWithPercentage**: (currentHealthUnits / maxHealthUnits)];

[self **addChild**:meter **z**: kInterfaceElements];

meter.position = ccp(200, screenHeight − 30);

If you want to set the currentHealthUnits and maxHealthUnits values on a per-level basis using the ***GameData.plist*** file, no one is going to stop you. It's an excellent idea, but to keep things simple in this section, I'll just set them to 500. If you plan on always keeping these the same amount for each level, there's nothing wrong with that.

Next, our meter is created passing in the value of currentHealthUnits / maxHealthUnits, which of course will equal one on first run, so the meter will be 100 percent full. Then we add the child to the scene. I'm placing the meter at a **z** depth of kInterfaceElements, or fifty because that's what I have defined in my ***Constants.h*** file. Then I'm positioning the meter at 200 on the x and 30 minus the screenHeight, just in case the screenHeight of the iPad ever changes, this should still keep the bar right up on top of the screen.

Now we can add the code to decrease health on impact with an Enemy. Find your **checkEnemyCollisions** method, and within the existing if statement below add a new method called **enemyCollisionOccurred**. We'll do anything related to an impact in this method.

if (**CGRectContainsPoint**(enemyRect, player.position)) {

    [self **enemyCollisionOccurred**];

    // [player **showBruisedState**];

}

Notice I'm commenting out the code that was previously in that if statement. We'll keep it, but let's move it to the new method which we'll begin writing on the next page. Just don't forget to copy in the line we're removing to this new method.

-(void) **enemyCollisionOccurred** {

    [player **showBruisedState**];

    // this line is moved to here

    currentHealthUnits = currentHealthUnits − 1;

```
[meter adjustPercentage: (currentHealthUnits / maxHealthUnits) ];
if (currentHealthUnits <= 0 ){
        [self reloadLevel];
    }
}
```

I'm only subtracting one from currentHealthUnits because with our current setup this method can get called multiple times when the player collides with an Enemy. Unlike our ScoreObject instances, which disappear on impact, the enemies stay on screen. So most likely your player will trigger this code five to ten times per impact, making small decrements in the health meter each cycle, which I think looks better than decreasing a larger chunk at a time. Micro injuries basically. If you wanted to trigger a bigger decrease in health and then temporarily give the player a reprieve from any health reduction, you could do that with a bool variable similar to the one used in the Player class called isBruised. If you remember, we toggle between the normal state and bruised state of the player in that class, and you can't bruise the player if he's already been hurt using a simple bool variable. So refer to that code if you want something different.

As you can see, we call the adjustPercentage method in the HealthMeter class and pass in the division of currentHealthUnits by maxHealthUnits, the same way we did in creating the meter. We can now include an if statement to see if the currentHealthUnits is at or below zero, in which case we can call reloadLevel. This is a somewhat abrupt restart to the level, since we don't flash any sort of message to the player telling them they've failed, but we can finesse this method later. For now though, we've got a functional reset, and you can remove the previous method call that automatically reloaded the level for testing purposes.

Finally, *if you wanted to*, you could easily add back health units when the player collides with ScoreObjects by simply writing:

```
currentHealthUnits = currentHealthUnits + 10;
```

```
[meter adjustPercentage: (currentHealthUnits / maxHealthUnits) ];
```

Keep in mind, you've only got one chance to run this code because every ScoreObject disappears on first contact, so you might want to add back a larger value like 10 units.

Player Lives

No one lives forever, Mr Bond … Uh, whoops, in our game you pretty much do. So let's make use of the currentLivesLeft in our AppData class that is mostly set up already. If you need a refresher here's what we have so far in the implementation file:

```
-(int) returnLives {
        return currentLivesLeft;
}
```

```
-(void) subtractLife {
     currentLivesLeft = currentLivesLeft -1;
     if (currentLivesLeft == 0) {
          [self resetGame];

     }
}
```

The currentLivesLeft variable is initially set from the **GameData.plist**.

In our GameEngine implementation file the init statement already calls the **returnLives** method in AppData giving value to a lives variable. Again, here's a refresher:

lives = [[AppData **sharedData**] **returnLives**];

So now all we need is a visual representation of that lives value on screen, and to find a place to decrease the lives. The latter task is easy because in our **enemyCollisionOccurred**, we just added an if statement to check if currentHealthUnits is less than zero. So let's add more to that:

```
     if (currentHealthUnits <= 0 ){
          [self unschedule:@selector(mainLoop:)];
          [[AppData sharedData] subtractLife];
          [self reloadLevel];

     }
```

First off, I'm unscheduling the **mainLoop** because it becomes a bit more important now that we don't accidentally call this same if statement twice. If we did, it would call **subtractLife** more than once. Now that our **mainLoop** isn't firing repeatedly this entire engine is essentially shut off. We won't even be keeping the player within the screen bounds, which we could use to our advantage if you wanted the player to just drop off screen when a life has ended. Let's save that for later though.

For now let's just focus on showing the user that the stockpile of lives has decreased by one. You could do this with another label in the scene, but since we've already done that with the scores, let's get a bit fancier and use an icon for the number of lives left.

Your Resources folder will need an icon of course. Add your own, or steal mine from the finished project files at **www.focalpress.com/cw/Dike**. Mine are named **player_icon.png** and **player_icon-ipadhd.png**.

Go to the **init** statement of your GameEngine class and add everything after this first line you already have in place:

lives = [[AppData **sharedData**] **returnLives**];

CGPoint iconPos = ccp(400, screenHeight − 30);

for (int i=1; i <= lives; i++) {

    CCSprite* icon = [CCSprite **spriteWithFile**:@"player_icon.png"];

    [self **addChild**: icon **z**:kInterfaceElements **tag**:i];

    icon.position = ccp(iconPos.x + (i * icon.contentSize.width), iconPos.y);

}

First, I'm creating a CGPoint called iconPos, which will be used as a starting location for the row of icons. The icons will all be staggered off of this location by their width.

The for statement iterates through the number lives, each time creating a new CCSprite icon. I'm adding them to the scene with a z depth defined in my **Constants.h** file called kInterfaceElements but you could use any number out of range of your other objects. Then I'm tagging each icon with a value that is the same as the variable named i in my for loop.

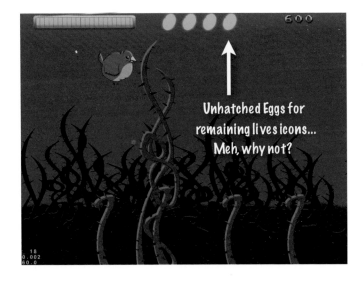

Unhatched Eggs for remaining lives icons... Meh, why not?

So the first icon is tagged 1, the second 2, and so on. I'll use this **tag** later to identify the icon to remove when a life is lost. Since no other objects have been tagged in this project, it's safe to use tags 1 through whatever the value of lives is at the time, but if you wanted to **tag** them with a larger, more specific number you could always add something like 1000, so your tags would then be 1001, 1002, 1003, and so on. Finally, I'm positioning each with a simple addition equation based on the value of i multiplied by the icon.contentSize.width plus the iconPos.x value.

Now I want to remove the furthest icon to the right when a player loses a life, so let's return once again to the **enemyCollisionOccurred** method and add/modify the highlighted lines on page 376.

```
-(void) enemyCollisionOccurred {
    [player showBruisedState];
    currentHealthUnits = currentHealthUnits - 2;
    [meter adjustPercentage: (currentHealthUnits / maxHealthUnits) ];

    if (currentHealthUnits <= 0){
        [self unschedule:@selector(mainLoop:)];
        [[AppData sharedData] subtractLife];

        CCFadeOut *fade = [CCFadeOut actionWithDuration:1.0f];
        CCBlink *blink = [CCBlink actionWithDuration:1.0 blinks:5];
        CCSpawn *spawn = [CCSpawn actions:fade, blink, nil];
        [[self getChildByTag:lives] runAction:spawn];
        [self scheduleOnce:@selector(reloadLevel) delay:1.0f]; // delay reloadLevel
        [self reloadLevel]; // remove this, instead we will call reloadLevel using the line above

    }
}
```

The first four lines create a CCSpawn action which fades out the icon while simultaneously blinking it five times. We use [self getChildByTag:lives] as the object to run the action on, which will always be the icon to the far right. So that we actually see the action before the level reloads, I'm delaying the **reloadLevel** call instead of firing it immediately like we were before.

Advancing to the Next Level

I've left this aspect of the project a bit vague until now because there's so many ways to level up. Meditate for a moment. Comb your vast library of video game knowledge and think about the most common ways. "Mmmm, Happy thoughts … River Raid, Missile Command, Joust." Ah, Memory Lane. So here's what my years of growing up with an Atari and Nintendo got me:

- **Survival Time**—you've played long enough without dying. In our project, we could simply test if the ticker variable has got to a certain value, for example 30000. This value could be set in the *GameData.plist* file on a per level basis. Or you could **schedule** a new method that runs once per second, and test the actual time that way.

- **Point/Object Accumulation**—you've got enough points to pass the level, or collected enough magical widgets. In our project, this is essentially the same thing because our ScoreObjects are an item to collect and they give us points. So we could either test to see if the score is high enough, or create a int variable like objectsCollected that starts at zero each level and increments up for the amount of ScoreObjects collided with. Testing for a level-up this way also lends itself to failing the level if enough points haven't accumulated by a certain point. So you might need to use the ticker here as well, to test when the user hasn't accomplished this goal.

- **Enemies Bested**—you've crushed enough of your foes, Conan-style. In our project, this doesn't make much sense since we aren't destroying the enemies on collision, we're just trying to avoid them. So there isn't a great way to count the enemies we crushed.

- **Finish Line**—you've reached a challenging position on the board, or simply made it to the flagpole in front of the castle at the end of the board. In our project we could include a CGPoint item in the **GameData.plist** that marks an end spot, or at least an end x location to exceed. Since the player automatically moves forward without stopping, our ticker variable is tracking both the x amount moved and survival time, depending on how you want to look at it. Either way, you're testing the ticker value essentially.

- **Marker Contact**—you've collided with a special class, perhaps an object that only shows up at random. The Golden Snitch basically. We could easily add this to our project, we would just need to create a special class and go through the same steps used to add or test contact with either the Enemy or ScoreObject classes.

- **End Boss/Swarm**—this is a combination of getting to the end of the board and then having to deal with a final enemy or onslaught of many enemies. Again, this doesn't make much sense in our project since we aren't killing enemies on contact.

No matter what you decide to go with, we can have a common method that's triggered when the player has accomplished board victory. Let's call it **levelPassed**, and make a few things happen:

1. Stop the **mainLoop**.
2. Tell the AppData class to advance a level (this method is already set up from before).
3. Slide the player off the screen.
4. Show the user that they've passed the level with a message like, "Level 1 Passed".
5. Then we can call the same **reloadLevel** method used in failing the board, because all it really does is transition the GameEngine scene out and the same GameEngine scene back in again (this time though with a new level value from the AppData class).

Let's get to it:

```
-(void) levelPassed {
    [self unschedule:@selector(mainLoop:)];
    [ [AppData sharedData] advanceLevel ];
```

```
CCMoveBy *move = [CCMoveBy actionWithDuration:2.0 position:ccp( screenWidth, 0) ];
[player runAction: move];
// move the player off screen

NSString* message = [NSString stringWithFormat:@"Level %i Passed", level];
[self showMessage:message];
// we'll create a new method called showMessage on the next page

[self scheduleOnce:@selector(reloadLevel) delay:3.0f];
}
```

The first and last lines we've already seen in our **enemyCollisionOccurred** method, the only difference is that I'm adding more of a delay.

We're then calling **advanceLevel** in the AppData class, which adds to the currentLevel variable and saves an NSUserDefaults int for the level we just passed. Something to remember now is that while testing your application, you'll be restarting the app at the most recent level passed *if* the **init** statement in AppData includes: currentLevel = levelsPassed + 1;

Until we get a menu in the game to forcibly reset the game back to level 1, this might trip you up (like it did me). After testing the game and advancing levels a few times, I forgot that the game was sending me to the most recent level passed. An easy mistake since right now *all* my level info in the **GameData.plist** is identical. So visually, level 1 looks like level 2 and level 3, and so on. I finally ran out of level data in the **.plist** and crashed when restarting a level that tried to pull in data that wasn't there. Which is something we'll make sure doesn't happen later.

So moving on, literally, we have a CCMoveBy action, which will send our player the distance of the screenWidth forward off screen.

Next, I'm creating an NSString variable called message, which is initialized using **stringWithFormat**, where I'm combining "Level" plus the string text from the current level variable and the word "Passed". So this will read "Level 1 Passed" after the first level. The message variable gets passed into the new method below, called **showMessage**, which receives an NSString variable as a parameter.

```
-(void) showMessage:(NSString*) theMessage {
    CCLabelTTF *message = [CCLabelTTF labelWithString:theMessage fontName:@"Marker
    Felt" fontSize:40];
    [self addChild:message z: kInterfaceElements ];
    message.position = ccp(0, screenHeight / 2);
```

```
CCMoveTo *move = [CCMoveTo actionWithDuration:0.5 position:ccp( screenWidth / 2 ,
screenHeight / 2)];

CCDelayTime *delay = [CCDelayTime actionWithDuration:2.0];

CCMoveTo *move2 = [CCMoveTo actionWithDuration:0.5 position:ccp( screenWidth +
200, screenHeight / 2)];

CCCallFuncN *callFunc = [CCCallFuncN actionWithTarget:self selector:@selector(
finishSeq:)];

CCSequence* sequence = [CCSequence actions: move, delay, move2, callFunc, nil];

[message runAction:sequence];
}
```

Before you test that code, be sure to write the **finishSeq** method that gets called from the CCCallFuncN action.

```
-(void )finishSeq:(id) sender {
    CCLOG(@"removing message");
    [self removeChild:sender cleanup:NO];
}
```

The **showMessage** method on the previous page can now be used for creating and temporarily showing any text we want in the scene. All we have to do is call it with an NSString parameter to display. The message will be displayed mid-screen after moving in from the left, it will stay there for 2 seconds, then move off to the right. The CCCallFuncN will trigger the method above, which receives the CCLabelTTF as a sender parameter that gets removed.

So let's use this same method to display text when the level begins. In the **init** statement, include:

```
NSString* message = [NSString stringWithFormat:@"Level %i", level];
[self showMessage:message];
```

Just be sure you write those lines anywhere after you've already established the value for level.

Then in the **enemyCollisionOccurred** method, within the if (currentHealthUnits <= 0) statement, include:

```
NSString* message = [NSString stringWithFormat:@"Level %i Failed", level];
[self showMessage:message];
```

Easy right? That adds a lot to make the game feel like you are keeping the player informed.

▼ Levels		Array	(5 items)
▼ Item 0		Dictionary	(8 items)
LevelPassedAt	⊕ ⊖	Number	▲▼ 2,500
▶ ScoreObjects		Array	(2 items)

Now all you have to decide is when you'll call the **levelPassed** method. I'm just going to make this easy on myself and let the ticker value decide when the board is done. First, I should set up a new **Number** Item in each of my items in the **Levels** Array. I'll call that **LevelPassedAt** and for now, I'll just set it at something low like 2500 for testing purposes.

Then in the header file for the GameEngine I'll declare an int variable called levelPassedAt:

int levelPassedAt;

Next, in the **init** statement in the implementation file, I'll make that equal to the **LevelPassedAt** item:

levelPassedAt = [[levelDict **objectForKey**:@"LevelPassedAt"] **integerValue**];

Just be sure to write that at some point after you've already established a value for levelDict. Finally, in my **mainLoop**, I'll test the value of the ticker to see if it equals levelPassedAt:

```
-(void) mainLoop: (ccTime) delta {
    ticker ++;
    if ( ticker == levelPassedAt ){
        [self levelPassed];
}
// etc., leave in everything else you had before ...
```

Once it does, the **levelPassed** method gets called and you've got one level in the "win" column!

Let's add a quick fix to the problem of running out of level data in the *plist* file. All we need to do is find out the number of **Level** items and if our **advanceLevel** method in the AppData class makes currentLevel greater than that value, we'll call **resetGame**. So in the header file for AppData declare:

int totalLevelsInGame;

Then jump over to the implementation file of AppData and add the following lines to the end of your **init** statement:

NSMutableArray* levelArray = [NSMutableArray **arrayWithArray**:[plistData **objectForKey**:@"Levels"]];

totalLevelsInGame = [levelArray **count**];

CCLOG(@"total levels in game is %i", totalLevelsInGame);

// might as well check this value with a log statement

So now totalLevelsInGame is equal to [levelArray **count**], which is simply the number of items in that array.

Now you can add the highlighted if statement to your existing **advanceLevel** method in AppData:

-(void) **advanceLevel** {

    levelsPassed = currentLevel;

    [defaults **setInteger**:levelsPassed **forKey**:@"levelsPassed"];

    currentLevel ++;

    [defaults **synchronize**];

```
if (currentLevel > totalLevelsInGame){
     [self resetGame];
}
```

}

Of course you might want to make a bigger deal out of passing every level, because I'll admit sending players back to level 1 isn't exactly enthralling. If so, you'll want the GameEngine to also know the value of totalLevelsInGame, and your **levelPassed** method can check if level equals totalLevelsInGame. If so, then you can add some fireworks and play some epic music. I'll let you carry the torch from here, I think you've earned the chance to fly solo. If you want the project files so far, they are in the *GameStructure_Interface* folder at www.focalpress.com/cw/Dike.

Game Menu with Unlocked Level Buttons

Like the last section, we'll keep building on our previous project but again, what you learn here can apply to an endless number of other games. The title of this section underplays what's ahead, because we've got a lot of odds and ends to patch up to really complete this game. The good news is that the end result should start to "feel" like an actual game instead of a prototype. Our main tasks are:

- Set up a bool variable in the existing *plist* to begin the game with either an opening **Game Menu** or go directly into Level 1.

- Use the same **Game Menu** as a pause screen during the game.

- Create a sub-menu of **Locked or Unlocked Level Buttons** (once unlocked, players can jump to boards they have passed).

- Create a **Reset Game** button, **Sound Enabled** button and **Return to Level** button (that last one just resumes the current level).

- Modify the current code to send players to the **Game Menu** when they lose all their lives.

The first thing I can do to make this feel more "real" is stop using the *IntroLayer.png* file I've included in every project so far. If you've been working with my source files, you've seen it. I'm going to put ten minutes on the clock and make a proper logo screen ... starting ... NOW!

This looks like the title card of a Beavis and Butthead episode, but that's not a bad thing. Since I'm just replacing

my current **IntroLayer.png** and **IntroLayer-ipadhd.png** files, I don't need to make any changes to the code in the IntroLayer, but since we are on the topic of this class, let's make some quick additions to it. In the **IntroLayer.h** file, declare one variable: bool startGameWithMenu; Then switch over to **IntroLayer.m**.

This class doesn't have an **init** statement (it is kind of odd that I just noticed that), instead it runs with the **onEnter** method. Take a look at what I'm adding.

You can copy the first three lines from any of our past code where we pulled data from our *GameData.plist* file. You will need to add a **GameOpensWithMenu** Item to the Root of your *plist* file.

Key	Type	Value
▼ Root	Dictionary	(4 items)
GameOpensWithMenu	Boolean	YES
LivesAtGameStart	Number	3
▼ Levels	Array	(5 items)
▶ Item 0	Dictionary	(8 items)
▶ Item 1	Dictionary	(8 items)
▶ Item 2	Dictionary	(8 items)
▶ Item 3	Dictionary	(8 items)

After we give startGameWithMenu a value, we use it to determine which scene to run.

```
-(void) onEnter {

    [super onEnter];

    CGSize size = [[CCDirector sharedDirector] winSize];

    CCSprite *background = [CCSprite spriteWithFile:@"IntroLayer.png"];

    background.position = ccp(size.width / 2, size.height / 2);

    [self addChild: background];

    [self scheduleOnce:@selector(makeTransition:) delay:2];

    NSString *path = [[NSBundle mainBundle] bundlePath];

    NSString *finalPath = [path stringByAppendingPathComponent:@"GameData.plist"];

    NSDictionary *plistData = [NSDictionary dictionaryWithContentsOfFile: finalPath]

    startGameWithMenu = [[plistData objectForKey:@"GameOpensWithMenu"] boolValue];

}

-(void) makeTransition:(ccTime) dt {

    if (startGameWithMenu == YES) {

        [[CCDirector sharedDirector] replaceScene:[CCTransitionFade
        transitionWithDuration:2 scene:[GameMenu scene] withColor:ccWHITE]];

    } else {

        [[CCDirector sharedDirector] replaceScene:[CCTransitionFade
        transitionWithDuration:2 scene:[GameEngine scene] withColor:ccWHITE]];

    }

}
```

You're probably thinking, "Yar! I see a new class on the horizon." Yes, pirates, the GameMenu class is sailing straight at us.

Go to **File > New > File**, find the usual Cocos2d row of templates and select CCLayer for the subclass, then name this **GameMenu.m.**

Now go back to your **IntroLayer.h** or **IntroLayer.m** file and be sure to import in this new class: #import "GameMenu.h"

Congrats. The IntroLayer is done. You now have a quick way to switch between opening with the menu or a level. Your end user won't appreciate this, but for you as a developer, it can be nice to have a fast way of going back and forth. Just don't try to test this yet, since our GameMenu doesn't have a **scene** method written yet.

Defining Game States

Precious few times have I heard a grown man talk to his food, but after waiting an hour for a burrito to arrive at a crowded Mexican restaurant, my cousin George, straight-faced, leaned over his plate and said, "You got some 'splaining to do."

I've got some 'splaining to do too. Of course, when don't I as the author of a programming book? I just wanted to tell that story.

By the end of this section, a lot of things will harmoniously be working together, and hopefully you'll have some appreciation for the AppData, our almighty singleton. The AppData class is going to manage some "game states" that will need defining in our **Constants.h** file. It's not many, so go ahead and paste these in now:

Game Structure

```
#define kGameNotInProgress 0
#define kGameEnginePaused 1
#define kGameEngineRunning 2
```

In plain speak, the three states are:

- **No Game in Progress**—this would occur when the game first runs OR a game has ended after all the player's lives have been lost. This is our kGameNotInProgress state.
- **Game In Progress but Paused**—in this case, a game was previously started, but the game engine isn't running its schedules because we've opened the GameMenu class on top of the GameEngine. Cocos2d completely manages pausing this class, but I need to define the kGameEnginePaused for other reasons.
- **Game in Progress, the Engine is Running**—in this case, you're playing an actual level of the game. This state is defined as kGameEngineRunning.

Go ahead and import in your ***Constants.h*** file to all our classes. AppData, GameMenu, GameEngine, let's just get that over with.

```
#import "Constants.h"
```

The main reason I need these three states is because we are using the same GameMenu class to both open/restart the game *or* pause it. In the first case, I can just use **replaceScene,** exchanging the GameMenu with the GameEngine. In the latter case, I need to call **popScene** to dump the GameMenu which in turn, will resume the GameEngine.

As I mentioned before, our wonderful AppData class will be the one managing these states. "Managing" sounds fancy—all this means is the variables will be stored there, and the GameMenu class will query the AppData class as to how it should proceed in certain cases. Notice in the screenshot of my GameMenu class (on the page opposite), I have seven buttons that could potentially go to different levels: the row of five icons, the "Return To Level" button, and the "Reset Game" button. All of those will end up calling the same method named **jumpToThisLevel**, which takes in an int parameter to specify which level to go to. Using the game state we just have a simple if statement that acts as a gateway to handle almost all the functionality of the GameMenu (aside from the sound preferences). That's good news, people! We are getting a lot of bang for our buck, especially since this class doubles as the opening and pause menu.

The AppData Class

Let's go ahead make the necessary changes to AppData because it isn't much, and by the time we've written all the code in the GameMenu, you'll be chomping at the bit to test something out.

Head over to your **AppData.h** file, and declare this variable:

int gameStatus;

This will only ever equal the value of either kGameNotInProgress, kGameEnginePaused, or kGameEngineRunning. Like all int variables, by default it will equal zero, which by no accident is also what kGameNotInProgress equals. Next, declare these methods in the header:

-(void) **setGameStatus**:(int)status;

-(int) **returnGameStatus**;

-(bool) **canYouGoToThisLevel**:(int) desiredLevel;

-(void) **changeLevelTo**:(int) desiredLevel;

The first two are pretty obvious—they will set and return the gameStatus. The **canYouGoToThisLevel** method will be used to test whether you can go to a specific level, and the **changeLevelTo** method will change the AppData class to a new level. So in **AppData.m**, add the following:

-(void) **setGameStatus**:(int)status {
    gameStatus = status;
}

-(int) **returnGameStatus** {
    return gameStatus;
}

- No surprises here, just setting and returning gameStatus. Looking at how little is occurring here now, setting up gameStatus as a property would have made sense. Either way works though.

-(bool) **canYouGoToThisLevel**:(int) desiredLevel {
    if ((levelsPassed +1) >= desiredLevel) {
        return YES;
    } else {
        return NO;
    }
}

- The **canYouGoToThisLevel** method takes in one parameter, the desiredLevel to unlock. The unlocking aspect occurs in the GameMenu class. Here, the method just needs to return YES or NO. The condition would be NO if the desiredLevel is greater than the existing variable, levelsPassed plus 1.

-(void) **changeLevelTo**:(int)desiredLevel {
    currentLevel = desiredLevel;
}

- Finally, this method does nothing more than set the currentLevel to the desiredLevel.

That does it for the AppData class (for now). Although, you could go to your **init** statement and add: gameStatus = kGameNotInProgress; The only reason you might want to do that, is if you accidentally made the value of kGameNotInProgress something other than zero.

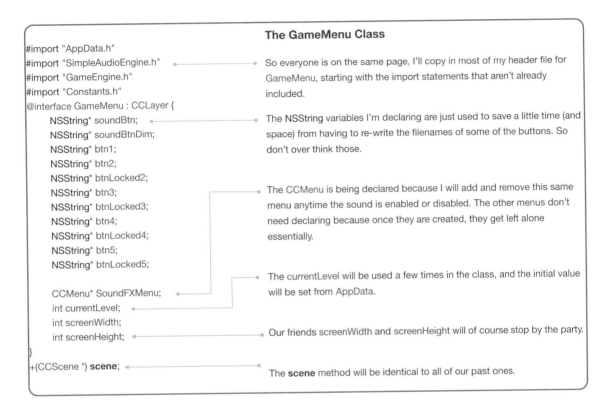

The GameMenu Class

```
#import "AppData.h"
#import "SimpleAudioEngine.h"
#import "GameEngine.h"
#import "Constants.h"
@interface GameMenu : CCLayer {
    NSString* soundBtn;
    NSString* soundBtnDim;
    NSString* btn1;
    NSString* btn2;
    NSString* btnLocked2;
    NSString* btn3;
    NSString* btnLocked3;
    NSString* btn4;
    NSString* btnLocked4;
    NSString* btn5;
    NSString* btnLocked5;

    CCMenu* SoundFXMenu;
    int currentLevel;
    int screenWidth;
    int screenHeight;
}
+(CCScene *) scene;
```

So everyone is on the same page, I'll copy in most of my header file for GameMenu, starting with the import statements that aren't already included.

The NSString variables I'm declaring are just used to save a little time (and space) from having to re-write the filenames of some of the buttons. So don't over think those.

The CCMenu is being declared because I will add and remove this same menu anytime the sound is enabled or disabled. The other menus don't need declaring because once they are created, they get left alone essentially.

The currentLevel will be used a few times in the class, and the initial value will be set from AppData.

Our friends screenWidth and screenHeight will of course stop by the party.

The **scene** method will be identical to all of our past ones.

Let's jump over to the GameMenu implementation file. The scene method will look like it usually does:

```
+(CCScene *) scene{
    CCScene *scene = [CCScene node];
    GameMenu *layer = [GameMenu node];
    [scene addChild: layer];
    return scene;
}
```

Then add the following to the **init** statement:

```
-(id) init {
    if( (self=[super init])) {
        CGSize size = [[CCDirector sharedDirector] winSize];
        screenWidth = size.width;
        screenHeight = size.height;
        btn1 = @"levelButton1.png";
        btn2 = @"levelButton2.png";
        btnLocked2 = @"levelButton2_locked.png";
        btn3 = @"levelButton3.png";
        btnLocked3 = @"levelButton3_locked.png";
        btn4 = @"levelButton4.png";
        btnLocked4 = @"levelButton4_locked.png";
        btn5 = @"levelButton5.png";
        btnLocked5 = @"levelButton5_locked.png";
        soundBtn = @"soundButtonOn.png";
        soundBtnDim = @"soundButtonOff.png";

        CCSprite* theBackground = [CCSprite spriteWithFile:@"menu_background.png" ];
        theBackground.position = ccp (screenWidth / 2 , screenHeight / 2);
        [self addChild:theBackground z:0];

        currentLevel = [[AppData sharedData] returnLevel];

        [self createLevelMenu];
        // creates the unlocked or locked buttons
        [self createSoundMenuOn];
        // creates the sound menu in "on" state
        [self createResetMenu];
        // creates the reset game menu
        [self createReturnMenu];
        // creates the return to current level menu
    }
    return self;
}
```

Most of this is self-explanatory. The NSString variables are just getting the name of the file for their particular button. As usual, you can pull out those images from the source files at **www.focalpress.com/cw/Dike.**

The CCSprite named theBackground uses a file called ***menu_background.png***, which is shown above. All of our buttons will be created on top of this backdrop. Other than being a visual, it does nothing.

The currentLevel variable is getting it's value from the **returnLevel** method in AppData.

Then I'm calling four methods, **createLevelMenu**, **createSoundMenuOn**, **createResetMenu**, and **createReturnMenu**. These are their own methods mostly for organization, but the **createSoundMenuOn** method also has a counter method named **createSoundMenuOff**, so it was practical to separate the sound menu creation code from the init statement. This will be a similar setup to what we did back in Section 2 of Chapter 8, when we emphasized the last icon selected, but on a smaller scale because we only have two states, either "On" or "Off". The ***soundButtonOff.png*** is simply a dimmer version of the ***soundButtonOn.png***.

On the next page, we'll begin writing the **createLevelMenu**, but so you can avoid warnings, go ahead and write blank methods for **createSoundMenuOn**, **createResetMenu**, and **createReturnMenu**.

Create the Level Locked or Unlocked Buttons

Let's get right into the code, and then I'll explain.

```
-(void) createLevelMenu {
     CCMenuItem *button1;
     CCMenuItem *button2;
     CCMenuItem *button3;
     CCMenuItem *button4;
     CCMenuItem *button5;
     button1 = [CCMenuItemImage itemWithNormalImage:btn1 selectedImage:btn1
     block:^(id sender) {[self jumpToThisLevel:1 ];}];
     // button 2 ...
     if ( [[AppData sharedData] canYouGoToThisLevel:2] == NO ) {
          button2 = [CCMenuItemImage itemWithNormalImage:btnLocked2 selectedImage:
          btnLocked2 target:self selector:@selector(bloop)];
     } else {
```

Locked level.

```objc
    button2 = [CCMenuItemImage itemWithNormalImage:
    btn2 selectedImage:btn2 block:^(id sender) {[self
    jumpToThisLevel:2 ];}];
}
// button 3 ...
if ( [[AppData sharedData] canYouGoToThisLevel:3] == NO )
{
    button3 = [CCMenuItemImage itemWithNormalImage:
    btnLocked3 selectedImage:btnLocked3 target:self
    selector:@selector(bloop)];
} else {
    button3 = [CCMenuItemImage itemWithNormalImage:btn3 selectedImage:
    btn3 block:^(id sender) {[self jumpToThisLevel:3 ];}];
}
// button 4 ...
if ( [[AppData sharedData] canYouGoToThisLevel:4] == NO ) {
    button4 = [CCMenuItemImage itemWithNormalImage:btnLocked4 selectedImage:
    btnLocked4 target:self selector:@selector(bloop)];
} else {
    button4 = [CCMenuItemImage itemWithNormalImage:btn4 selectedImage:
    btn4 block:^(id sender) {[self jumpToThisLevel:4 ];}];
}
// button 5 ...
if ( [[AppData sharedData] canYouGoToThisLevel:5] == NO ) {
    button5 = [CCMenuItemImage itemWithNormalImage:btnLocked5 selectedImage:
    btnLocked5 target:self selector:@selector(bloop)];
} else {
    button5 = [CCMenuItemImage itemWithNormalImage:btn5 selectedImage:
    btn5 block:^(id sender) {[self jumpToThisLevel:5 ];}];
}
CCMenu *menu = [CCMenu menuWithItems:button1, button2, button3, button4,
button5, nil];
menu.position = ccp( screenWidth/ 2, screenHeight / 2 );
[menu alignItemsHorizontallyWithPadding:10 ];
[self addChild: menu z:1];
}
```

Unlocked level.

Obviously each one of the buttons gets a different **itemWithNormalImage / selectedImage** and @selector depending on the return value of **canYouGoToThisLevel**. If AppData returned NO, then the @selector set is **bloop**, which we can write in a moment. All it does is play a sound called **bloop.mp3.** Otherwise, if AppData returned YES, then we use the unlocked images, and introduce this new **block** parameter. Block programming is interesting to say the least. It hasn't completely "clicked" with me, some of the examples I've read make me squint my eyes, but this example is pretty easy to understand.

Take this snippet: ^(id sender) {[self **jumpToThisLevel**:1];} ... and break it into three lines instead.

```
^(id sender) {
    [self jumpToThisLevel:1 ];
}
```

A bit more normal now.

Don't worry about the ^(id sender) part, because we don't need to use the sender anyway. The rest of the block is just a method call like we've seen before. The nice thing is that I can pass in the int parameter to **jumpToThisLevel** with a different value for each button.

The rest of the **createLevelMenu** method, just takes all five buttons and adds them to a CCMenu, aligned in a row with ten points between each. If one day, you want more than five levels, repeat the same pattern, and to accommodate more buttons, you might want more than one CCMenu.

Finally, if it's not obvious, our lock and unlock menu is finished. So basically, if you can see a button that doesn't say "LOCKED" across it, you can tap that button to jump to that level. Speaking of, let's actually write the **jumpToThisLevel** method:

```
-(void) jumpToThisLevel:(int) theLevel {
    if ( [[AppData sharedData] returnGameStatus] == kGameNotInProgress) {
        CCLOG(@"GAME NOT IN PROGRESS, NEW LEVEL STARTING");
        [[AppData sharedData] changeLevelTo:theLevel];
        [[CCDirector sharedDirector] replaceScene:[CCTransitionFade
        transitionWithDuration:1.0 scene:[GameEngine scene] withColor:ccBLACK]];
    } else if ( currentLevel == theLevel ) {
        CCLOG(@"RETURNING TO THE SAME LEVEL");
        [[AppData sharedData] setGameStatus:kGameEngineRunning];
        [[CCDirector sharedDirector] popScene];
    } else if (currentLevel != theLevel) {
        CCLOG(@"CHANGING LEVELS");
```

```
    [[CCDirector sharedDirector] popScene];

    [[AppData sharedData] resetGame];

    [[AppData sharedData] changeLevelTo:theLevel];

    [[CCDirector sharedDirector] replaceScene:[CCTransitionFade
    transitionWithDuration:1.0 scene:[GameEngine scene] withColor:ccBLACK]];

    }

}
```

That method is broken down into three conditions. The first if condition tests if the gameStatus (in AppData) is equal to kGameNotInProgress. If that's true, we simply tell AppData to **changeLevelTo** the parameter we passed in, which is theLevel (the level we want to go to). Then we call **replaceScene**, and bring in the GameEngine. Easy, right?

The first else if condition doesn't even need to test the game state because if we're seeing this menu at all and the first condition failed, the game must be paused. So all I want to test now is if currentLevel is equal to theLevel, which means the user paused the game but is going to return to the same level. In which case, we **setGameStatus** back to kGameEngineRunning, and call **popScene**, which removes the GameMenu class and returns to the GameEngine.

The last else if condition is similar, but now we are testing if the currentLevel does not equal theLevel we want to go to. In which case, we still need to call **popScene**, then we tell the AppData class to **resetGame** and **changeLevelTo** the value of theLevel. Finally we call **replaceScene** and transition in the GameEngine. We don't need to call **setGameStatus** back to kGameEngineRunning, because in the init statement of the GameEngine we will call it from there anyway. By using **replaceScene**, the GameEngine is being reinitialized, so the **init** will run again.

Finally, we still need to write the **bloop** method:

```
-(void) bloop {
    // play a sound indicating this level isn't available
    [[SimpleAudioEngine sharedEngine]
        playEffect:@"bloop.mp3"];
}
```

Now the **bloop.mp3** file will play if the user tries to tap a level button that hasn't been unlocked.

Opening the Menu from the GameEngine

Most of you are probably going crazy wanting to test this, so let's quickly go over to the **GameEngine.m** file and add a button to open the GameMenu. At the end of your **init** statement, add:

```
CCMenuItem *button1 = [CCMenuItemImage
    itemWithNormalImage:@"gameMenu.png"
    selectedImage:@"gameMenu.png"
    target:self selector:@selector(showMenu )];
CCMenu *menu = [CCMenu menuWithItems:button1, nil];
menu.position = ccp( screenWidth −150, 60 );
[self addChild:menu z: kInterfaceElements];
```

The CCMenuItem and CCMenu shouldn't need any explaining. Then somewhere in the init statement, add the line below, so that any time the instance is initialized we set the game status to "running": [[AppData **sharedData**] **setGameStatus**:kGameEngineRunning];

Finally, just add the **showMenu** method, which gets called when tapping the button we just created:

```
-(void) showMenu {
    [[AppData sharedData] setGameStatus:kGameEnginePaused];
    [[CCDirector sharedDirector] pushScene:[GameMenu scene]];
}
```

Be sure you've written #import "GameMenu.h" in either the GameEngine's header or implementation.

So there it is! We're ready for a quick test before moving onwards (don't forget to include all the image files that correspond to the code we wrote). After building, you should be seeing the GameMenu first, and the first level button should start the game. Also any previous levels you've passed from earlier builds should be unlocked. You can delete the app to clear out previous NSUserDefaults data if you choose. When you land on Level 1, you should be able to tap the "Game Menu" button and get back to the menu. *To fact-check myself, I retraced my steps with the project as it was at the end of last section, just to be sure I didn't miss mentioning anything. So far, so good. Which means, we're ready to continue on.*

The Reset Game Menu

Head back over to your *GameMenu.m* file and let's fill in the **createResetMenu** method.

```
-(void) createResetMenu {
CCMenuItem *button1 = [CCMenuItemImage itemWithNormalImage:@"resetButton.png"
                          selectedImage:@"resetButton.png" target:self
                          selector:@selector(resetGame)];
    //calls the method below
    CCMenu *menu = [CCMenu menuWithItems:button1, nil];
    menu.position = ccp( screenWidth/2 - 200, 200);
    [self addChild:menu z:10];
}
```

That's pretty straight forward, once tapped it will call the **resetGame** method below.

```
-(void) resetGame{
    [[AppData sharedData] resetGame];
    [self jumpToThisLevel:1];
}
```

Test that code, and you might notice there's one big problem here. If I'm just resetting the game after playing a lousy outing on Level 1, I'll be returned to Level 1 with the same health and lives because even though I call **resetGame** on AppData, the GameEngine isn't being replaced. As is, the **jumpToThisLevel** method will see that the currentLevel equals theLevel I pass in, and just resume the game by popping out the GameMenu. One way to fix this is to go to your *Constants.h* file and define the following:

#define kGameNeedsHardReset 123456

Now change the method to:

-(void) **resetGame**{

    [self **jumpToThisLevel**: kGameNeedsHardReset];

}

Notice, I'm not changing the gameStatus in the AppData class, I'm just passing in a *very* specific value (kGameNeedsHardReset, or 123456) to the **jumpToThisLevel** method. As you can probably guess (sigh), we need to modify that method.

We are going to add one more condition before our existing ones. This means the existing if statement will become an else if statement and it will end up being the second condition tested instead of the first. The new condition will test if theLevel passed in equals kGameNeedsHardReset and within an interior if statement test the gameStatus in AppData. Again, we have to determine if the GameMenu is the primary scene or popped scene.

-(void) **jumpToThisLevel**:(int)theLevel {

  if (theLevel == kGameNeedsHardReset){

      if ([[AppData **sharedData**] **returnGameStatus**] == kGameNotInProgress) {

        CCLOG(@"GAME NOT IN PROGRESS, FULL RESET");

        // not really necessary, but I'd like to check this anyway

      } else if ([[AppData **sharedData**] **returnGameStatus**] == kGameEnginePaused) {

        CCLOG(@"GAME PAUSED, FULL RESET");

        // not really necessary, but I'd like to check this anyway

        [[CCDirector **sharedDirector**] **popScene**];

        // first pop the scene if the GameEngine was paused

      }

    [[AppData **sharedData**] **resetGame**];

    [[AppData **sharedData**] **changeLevelTo**:1];

    // hard code in 1, instead of using theLevel

    [[CCDirector **sharedDirector**] **replaceScene**:[CCTransitionFade
    transitionWithDuration:1.0 **scene**:[GameEngine **scene**] **withColor**:ccBLACK]];

  } else if (

  // continue with the original if statement from before ...

The Return to Level Button

Alright, this is an easy one, I swear. Nothing out of left field this time. In fact, our CCMenuItem can call the **jumpToThisLevel** method directly using the **block** parameter, which our other level buttons have in place. So without further ado:

```
-(void) createReturnMenu {
    CCMenuItem *button1 = [CCMenuItemImage itemWithNormalImage:@"returnButton.png"
                              selectedImage:@"returnButton.png" block:^(id sender)
                              {[self jumpToThisLevel:currentLevel ];}];
    CCMenu *menu = [CCMenu menuWithItems:button1, nil];
    menu.position = ccp( screenWidth/ 2 + 200, 200);
    [self addChild:menu z:10];
}
```

The parameter we pass into **jumpToThisLevel** is simply the currentLevel.

The Sound Button (Kinda)

I'm going to leave out the code that actually mutes the audio from this sub-section, for a proper dedicated section where we create a singleton class to handle the audio. Until then, you can just set up the "on" and "off" states of the button:

```
-(void) createSoundMenuOn {
    [self removeChild:SoundFXMenu cleanup:NO];
    // harmless if the button doesn't already exist, which would be the case on first run
    CCMenuItem *button1 = [CCMenuItemImage itemWithNormalImage:soundBtn
    selectedImage:soundBtn target:self selector:@selector(createSoundMenuOff)];
    // calls the method on the next page
    SoundFXMenu = [CCMenu menuWithItems:button1, nil];
    SoundFXMenu.position = ccp( screenWidth/ 2, 200);
    [self addChild:SoundFXMenu z:10];
}
```

When the "Sound Enabled" button is tapped, it will call the method below, which destroys the menu and recreates it with the alternate artwork. Likewise, this button will now call the method on the previous page. So this is just a simple toggle switch basically.

```
-(void) createSoundMenuOff {
    [self removeChild:SoundFXMenu cleanup:NO];
    CCMenuItem *button1 = [CCMenuItemImage itemWithNormalImage: soundBtnDim
                    selectedImage:soundBtnDim target:self selector:
                    @selector(createSoundMenuOn)];
    // calls the method on the previous page
    SoundFXMenu = [CCMenu menuWithItems:button1, nil];
    SoundFXMenu.position = ccp( screenWidth/ 2, 195);
    // you could lower the button slightly for the off state
    [self addChild:SoundFXMenu z:10];
}
```

Sending Players Back to the Menu After a Game Loss

As is, the game automatically restarts when the player has lost all their lives. Instead, we should send them to GameMenu. To do this, let's first visit the **AppData.m** file and modify the **subtractLife** method. All we need it to do is this now:

```
-(void) subtractLife {
    currentLivesLeft = currentLivesLeft - 1;
    // remove the existing code from before
}
```

Also, if you didn't already do this, be sure the totalScore is being set back to zero in the **resetGame** method. I can't think of a good reason not to do this, but it wasn't in the previous project.

```
totalScore = 0;
```

Now jump over to your ***GameEngine.m*** file and locate the existing **enemyCollision Occurred** method. Find this line:

[self **scheduleOnce**:@selector(**reloadLevel**) **delay**:1.0f];

That will still run, but only as the else condition of the if statement below that we will crowbar in. First, we will test to see if the currentLivesLeft variable in the AppData class is at zero. If so, we change the game status, reset the game, and replace the GameEngine with the GameMenu scene. Otherwise, we just run the line from before, which simply reloads the same level.

```
if ( [[AppData sharedData] returnLives] == 0 ) {

    [[AppData sharedData] setGameStatus: kGameNotInProgress];

    [[AppData sharedData] resetGame];

    [[CCDirector sharedDirector] replaceScene:[CCTransitionFade transition
    WithDuration:3.0 scene:[GameMenu scene] withColor:ccBLACK]];

} else {

    [self scheduleOnce:@selector(reloadLevel) delay:1.0f];

}
```

That should be all it takes to send the GameEngine back to the GameMenu. Before you give it a test fire, let's head back to the ***GameMenu.m*** file and add a **dealloc** method. Since this class gets dumped from memory quite often, we should be double-checking that actually ***is*** what's happening. So I'll include a log statement within the method.

```
- (void) dealloc {

    CCLOG(@"MENU HAS BEEN REMOVED");

    // I tend to shout a lot for these important logs

    [super dealloc];

}
```

That's all for now! You can check out the project, as is, at **www.focalpress.com/cw/Dike** in the folder called ***GameStructure_StartMenu***.

Singleton Class for Sound

In the last section we created a toggle button to enable or disable sound in the game, except we didn't actually do anything sound related. I saved that for this section, where we will create another singleton class, this one called GameSounds, and use it to manage any code related to audio.

Since this is a brand new class, go to **File > New > File**, select the Cocos2d starting template, and subclass it from CCNode. Name it **GameSounds.m** then go ahead and #import it to any other class you'll play sound from, which for this project is at least the GameEngine and GameMenu.

Now in the GameSounds header file, add in everything below (of course leave in the existing #import statements in the class).

#import "SimpleAudioEngine.h"

> *// can't play sound without importing this*

@interface GameSounds : CCNode {

    bool isAudioMuted;

}

@property (readwrite, nonatomic) bool isAudioMuted;

> *// make it a property*

+(GameSounds*) **sharedSounds**;

-(void) **playSoundFX**:(NSString*)fileToPlay;

-(void) **playBackgroundMusic**:(NSString*)fileToPlay;

@end

As you can see, there isn't much to this class, at least for this example project. I've created GameSounds singletons in other projects and they've been quite a bit more involved, but to demonstrate the usefulness of this class, I don't need much more.

We will set the isAudioMuted property any time someone toggles the "Sound Enabled" button in the GameMenu class. So that the GameMenu class can change the value directly, I'm declaring isAudioMuted as a readwrite property.

Jump over to the GameSounds implementation file and @synthesize the isAudioMuted property under the @implementation line:

@implementation GameSounds

@synthesize isAudioMuted;

Next, we will make this into a singleton by writing our **sharedSounds** class method. If you need a refresher on the hows and whys of doing this, jump back to Section 2 in this chapter, where I introduced how to create a singleton. The code set-up below is identical to the AppData singleton, aside from the obvious name changes. You can go ahead and write the init method now too. All we need to do here is set sharedSounds = self;

static GameSounds *sharedSounds = nil;

+(GameSounds*) **sharedSounds** {
        if (sharedSounds == nil) {
                sharedSounds = [[GameSounds **alloc**] **init**];
        }
        return sharedSounds;
}

-(id) **init** {
if ((self = [super **init**])) {
                sharedSounds = self;
        }
        return self;
}

These next two methods are fairly obvious. In both we just test the value of isAudioMuted and if it is NO, then we play the sound through the SimpleAudioEngine. That sound is determined by the NSString variable that was passed into this method (the audio file name).

-(void) **playSoundFX**:(NSString*)fileToPlay {
        if (isAudioMuted == NO) {
                [[SimpleAudioEngine **sharedEngine**] **playEffect**: fileToPlay];
        }
}

-(void) **playBackgroundMusic**:(NSString*)fileToPlay {
        if (isAudioMuted == NO) {
                [[SimpleAudioEngine **sharedEngine**] **playBackgroundMusic**: fileToPlay];
        }
}

So essentially, the GameSounds class is just a gateway to either play audio or not. In our project, we don't have too many possible classes to play audio from, but the more you have, the better it is to manage the audio with one single class. Plus, our project has only one option, which is to mute everything, but you could give users multiple sound options. For example, "mute only voice FX," "mute only background music," or "mute only sound FX."

When I introduced the SimpleAudioEngine, I mentioned you might want to create a method that randomly plays a certain type of sound. Suppose your game involves moving farm animals around, and every time you drag a pig into the barn, you want to play a squeal sound. The same sound will get annoying after a while (especially for a parent listening to their kid play that game), but if your GameSounds class plays a random selection of pig squeals every time, then partner, you got yourself a humdinger of a good game.

Also keep in mind, not **all** your calls to handle audio have to come through this class now. For example, you could stop the background music by using the SimpleAudioEngine directly.

Using GameSounds with the GameMenu Class

Alright, I'll stop selling you on the GameSounds singleton, and actually use it now. Be sure to import it to the header file of the GameMenu class. Reason being, we are going to declare a GameSounds variable called sharedSounds. For example:

#import "GameSounds.h"

@interface GameMenu : CCLayer {

GameSounds* sharedSounds;

// leave in everything else from before.

That's interesting, right? Why do this? Well, check out this next line I'm going to write in the init statement of the **GameMenu.m** file:

sharedSounds = [GameSounds **sharedSounds**];

Now any time I write sharedSounds in the implementation file, I'm essentially writing [GameSounds sharedSounds]. So this is just a bit of shorthand for referring to the singleton. The two examples below are exactly the same:

[[GameSounds **sharedSounds**] **playSoundFX**:@"bloop.mp3"];

[sharedSounds **playSoundFX**:@"bloop.mp3"];

Cool, right? Come to think of it, let's change the **bloop** method to include that line instead of what we currently have:

-(void) **bloop** {

    [sharedSounds **playSoundFX**:@"bloop.mp3"];

    // comment out or delete the line below …

    // [[SimpleAudioEngine sharedEngine] playEffect:@"bloop.mp3"];

}

Now go back to your **init** statement, and find this line:

[self **createSoundMenuOn**];

… and replace it with an if … else statement, which tests the value of isAudioMuted in the GameSounds class to determine whether the "Sound Enabled" button should initially appear on or off.

    if (sharedSounds.isAudioMuted == NO) {

        [self **createSoundMenuOn**];

    } else {

        [self **createSoundMenuOff**];

    }

Ah, how nice. We can simply write sharedSounds.isAudioMuted when we need to test that property.

Now in the **createSoundMenuOn** method, include this line:

sharedSounds.isAudioMuted = NO;

Then in the **createSoundMenuOff** method, include this line:

sharedSounds.isAudioMuted = YES;

That's it! You should be able to test this out and press the locked level icons to trigger the *bloop.mp3* sound, depending on whether or not the GameSounds class has audio muted.

If you wanted to take this a bit further, you *could* save the isAudioMuted preference to the NSUserDefaults, but I think you can flip a coin as to whether that's necessary. If someone force quits their app, they might intentionally be trying to return audio because somehow they missed that big mute button they accidentally pressed. In which case, you want the audio to return for them.

As usual, you can find the newly modified project, now titled ***GameStructure_GameSounds*** in the zip file at **www.focalpress.com/cw/Dike**.

The Empty Starter Kit

The Ark?

I started this chapter thinking, "Wouldn't it be great to leave readers with an Empty Starter Kit?" Honestly, I didn't imagine back then what we would end up with was going to be as good as it turned out to be. The reason I say that, is because I actually started modifying this chapter's project recently to see how easily it could be changed, and it went pretty darn smoothly. The core code of the GameEngine class didn't need much changing at all, but I was able to combine our project from way back in Chapter 5 on Platform Collisions. So I've added the Platform class to "The Kit" and included the code to do collision detections with it. Like everything else, the Platform locations can be set up in the **GameData.*plist***.

I also added a bit to the *plist* file so now each level can disable using the accelerometer and if enabled, you can choose between the tilt variable affecting the player vertically or horizontally.

In the Fat Bird project, tilting moved the bird up or down, now in the Kit, the farmer character will slide left or right instead. The two bool variables in the *plist* are called **UseAccelerometer** and **TiltUpDown**.

I didn't feel like making an entirely new sprite sheet and running animation for the character, so as is, the Kit just uses static images for his default state and injured state. The **PlayerProperties** Dictionary in the *plist* file now includes a **UseSpritesheet** bool so I had to make some minor adjustments to the Player class for this.

The last player change was that I unscheduled the method in the Player class, which moves the position down based on the gravity variable in the *plist*. Instead that has been moved to the GameEngine class. I did this so it was easier to disable gravity when the player collided with a Platform instance.

The Kit actually has two "engines" now. The regular GameEngine class and one called EmptyEngine. As is, the Kit builds with the EmptyEngine now, which looks like the screenshot on this page. I wanted to strip out as much code as possible because, even though I've titled this section "The Empty Starter Kit", there's still plenty of code in place. So the EmptyEngine doesn't create any Enemy or ScoreObject instances. At any time though, you can switch the code in the GameMenu to run the full GameEngine instead (just do a Find and Replace). Also, if you set the *plist* file to open directly into the game, the IntroLayer is still set to open with the GameEngine. The ScoreObjects are little green bushes now (which don't move), and the Enemy instances are snakes on clouds, which still move from right to left.

Regardless of whether you're running the GameEngine or EmptyEngine, if you go to Level 5 the Fat Bird artwork is back, which hopefully demonstrates that the same engine can run two potentially different games, both in looks and gameplay.

Are you ready to download **The Empty Starter Kit**? Have a look at it, at **www.focalpress.com/ cw/Dike**.

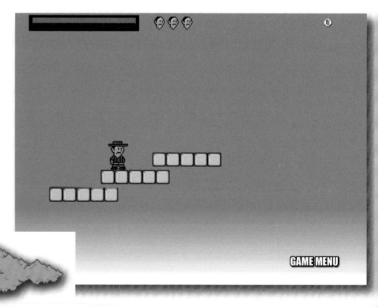

Chapter 10

Extending Cocos2d

In this chapter, I'll give you some code to extend Cocos2d to the Outer Reaches of the Universe ... Meaning, things like Twitter, Facebook, In-App purchases, streaming video, and more.

It's easy to bask in the little walled garden of Cocos2d because there's A LOT of code there to explore, but these iOS devices can do quite a lot. So in this chapter we will bridge the gap between Cocos2d and the true power of your shiny iPhone or iPad!

Don't worry, it's not THAT much more code.

Connecting to Twitter or Facebook (iOS 6 or Higher)

When iOS 6 was released, connecting your app to Facebook or Twitter became incredibly easy. Using nearly the same code we can post to both social networks, so we can kill two birds with one stone in this section.

The first thing we'll do is add a new Framework to the project. Frameworks add extra functionality to your app, and in this case, we want the aptly named **Social.framework**. Make your way to the **Build Phases** tab of your project (see the circled portion of the image below for a hint). Then unfurl the section called **Link Binary with Libraries**. Click the + sign in the lower left, and you'll see a new window to choose the framework you'd like to add. In the search bar you can type in "Social," and easily find it that way. Select **Social.framework** and click the Add button. We're done with the Build Phases tab, so you can go back to whatever class you want to add this code to. For this example, I'll just use the steadfast HelloWorldLayer class. So in the header or implementation file, add:

#import <Social/Social.h>

Next add the **tweetSomething** method written on the following page:

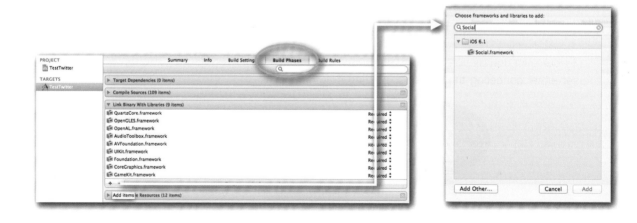

```
-(void) tweetSomething {
    if ( [SLComposeViewController isAvailableForServiceType:SLServiceTypeTwitter] ) {
        // check if Twitter is accessible and one account is set up
        AppController *app = (AppController*) [[UIApplication sharedApplication] delegate];
        SLComposeViewController *controller = [SLComposeViewController compose
        ViewControllerForServiceType:SLServiceTypeTwitter];
        [[app navController] presentViewController:controller animated:YES completion:nil ];
        // present the view
    }
}
```

This is about as simple as it gets. Calling [self **tweetSomething**]; would bring up a nice-looking Tweet window and keyboard, where the user can enter whatever they want. Actually, it could be simpler. We could remove the if statement above, but calling **isAvailableForServiceType** and specifying SLServiceTypeTwitter checks to see if the Twitter network is accessible and if the device has the account credentials already in place for Twitter. Otherwise, what's the point of opening a Tweet window at all?

The next three lines just handle presenting the **SLComposeViewController**, which has an instance name of controller and a type of SLServiceTypeTwitter. The last line presents the view controller with your choice of **animated** being YES or NO, and a **completion** parameter set to nil. In the example that follows, we'll modify this method and add our own completion handler to respond to the user either canceling the Tweet or posting it.

When dealing with a UIView and Cocos2d you'll spot this line often...
AppController *app = (AppController*) [[UIApplication sharedApplication] delegate];

That app variable is used to present the UIView over our Cocos2d. Like so...
[[app navController] presentViewController:controller animated:YES completion:nil];

Now let's create a similar method, which sets some initial text in the window, adds a URL and image to the potential Tweet.

```
-(void) tweetWithInitialText:(NSString*) text {
    if ( [SLComposeViewController isAvailableForServiceType:SLServiceTypeTwitter] ) {
    // check if Twitter is accessible and one account is set up
    AppController *app = (AppController*) [[UIApplication sharedApplication] delegate];
    SLComposeViewController *controller = [SLComposeViewController
    composeViewControllerForServiceType:SLServiceTypeTwitter];
    [controller setInitialText:text];
    // set the initial text of the message (this is the NSString we passed into the method)
    [controller addImage:[UIImage imageNamed:@"Icon-72.png"]];
    // the name of an image in your app's resources to be attached to the tweet
    [controller addURL:[NSURL URLWithString:@"www.cartoonsmart.com"]];
    // add a URL to the tweet
    [[app navController] presentViewController:controller animated:YES completion:nil ];
    // present the view
        [controller setCompletionHandler:^(SLComposeViewControllerResult result){
        // do something based on the completion handler's result
            [[app navController] dismissViewControllerAnimated:YES completion:nil];
            NSString *output = [[NSString alloc] init];
            switch (result) {
                case SLComposeViewControllerResultCancelled:
                output = @"Post Cancelled";
                // The user cancelled composing a tweet
                break;
                case SLComposeViewControllerResultDone:
                output = @"Post Done";
                // The user finished composing a tweet
                default:
                break;
            }
            UIAlertView *alert = [[UIAlertView alloc] initWithTitle:@"Twitter" message:output
            delegate:nil cancelButtonTitle:@"Ok" otherButtonTitles:nil ];
            // create an alert window regarding the completion
```

```
        [alert show];
    }];
  }
}
```

To call that method, we could write:

[self **tweetWithInitialText:**@"Check out CartoonSmart …"];

In that example, the text we passed into the method was "Check out CartoonSmart …".
It is added to the Tweet window as initial text, which is what this line in the method does:

[controller **setInitialText**: text];

The user could still delete that text from their tweet before sending it. Sorry, you can't force your users to Tweet something set in stone by suggesting their initial text. Doing so would interfere with that whole Free Will thing.

We're also adding a URL to the Tweet using:

[controller **addURL:**[NSURL **URLWithString:**@"www.cartoonsmart.com"]];

This URL won't be visible in the Tweet composition window, but if I were to actually send the Tweet, we'd see it tacked onto the end of the message.

Then to really ice the cake, we can add an image to the Tweet using:

[controller **addImage**: [UIImage **imageNamed:**@"Icon-72.png"]];

In that example, it is attaching the file ***Icon-72.png***, which is included in with every Cocos2d template. This could be any image file you've added as a Resource to your app.

You can also include the **setCompletionHandler** block to do something when the user is done composing the tweet or has cancelled it. In our example, you'll just read either "Post Cancelled" or "Post Done" in an alert window following either outcome. Tapping the "Ok" button closes the alert.

Ready for some great news? You could copy that last method, and simply replace "Twitter" with "Facebook" to create this one:

```
-(void) facebookWithInitialText:(NSString*) text {
if ( [SLComposeViewController isAvailableForServiceType:SLServiceTypeFacebook] ) {
// check if FB is accessible and one account is set up
AppController *app = (AppController*) [[UIApplication sharedApplication] delegate];
SLComposeViewController *controller = [SLComposeViewController
composeViewControllerForServiceType:SLServiceTypeFacebook];
[controller setInitialText:text];
// set the initial text of the message *(this is the NSString we passed into the method)
[controller addImage:[UIImage imageNamed:@"Icon-72.png"]];
// the name of an image in your app's resources to be attached to the tweet
[controller addURL:[NSURL URLWithString:@"www.cartoonsmart.com"]];
// add a URL to the tweet
[[app navController] presentViewController:controller animated:YES completion:nil ];
// present the view
    [controller setCompletionHandler:^(SLComposeViewControllerResult result){
    // do something based on the completion handler's result
        [[app navController] dismissViewControllerAnimated:YES completion:nil];
        NSString *output = [[NSString alloc] init];
        switch (result) {
            case SLComposeViewControllerResultCancelled:
            output = @"Post Cancelled";
            // The user cancelled composing a tweet
            break;
            case SLComposeViewControllerResultDone:
            output = @"Post Done";
            // The user finished composing a tweet
            default:
            break;
        }
        UIAlertView *alert = [[UIAlertView alloc] initWithTitle:@"Facebook" message:output
        delegate:nil cancelButtonTitle:@"Ok" otherButtonTitles:nil];
        // create an alert window regarding the completion
```

```
        [alert show];
      }];
    }
}
```

To call that method, we could write:

[self **facebookWithInitialText:**@"Hey friends and family I found this great app …"];

How's that for some easy in-app marketing? Again, like the Tweet window, users can delete any initial text you've populated the Facebook composition window with. And once again, you can add either a URL or image to the message.

If you would like to download the project files, go to **www.focalpress.com/cw/Dike**.

Connecting to Twitter (iOS 5)

When iOS 5 was released, Apple baked in an easy way to integrate Twitter (the code is almost identical to what we saw in the last section), but Facebook was excluded from the fun. So if you're looking for an easy solution to post to both services, the **Social.framework** for iOS 6.x apps is the way to go. Just keep in mind, the iPad 1 isn't upgradeable to iOS 6, it's capped at 5.1, so if all you're looking for is a Tweet window that's fine for iOS 5, here's your solution.

First thing we'll do is add some Frameworks to the project. One is optional, one is required, but let's add both for fun. Make your way to the **Build Phases** tab of your project (see the circled portion of the image below for a hint). Then unfurl the section called **Link Binary with Libraries**. Click the + sign in the lower left, and you'll see a new window to choose the framework you'd like to add. In the search bar you can type in "Twitter," and easily find it that way. Select **Twitter.framework** and click the **Add** button.

Do the exact same thing for the **Accounts.framework** and you are done with the **Build Phases** tab.

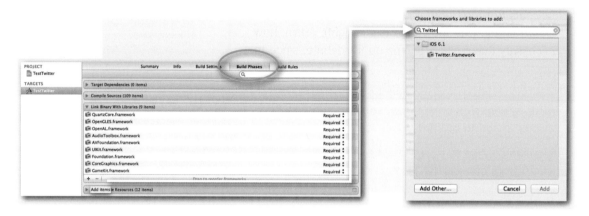

Now you'll need to add the following import statements to the top of either the header or implementation file of the class you want to add Tweet functionality to (in testing this I added them to my *HelloWorldLayer.m* file).

#import <Twitter/TWTweetComposeViewController.h>

#import <Accounts/Accounts.h>

Gaining account access to Twitter seems to be optional, but I have a feeling some of you will appreciate this code down the road anyway. From what I can tell though, whether you ask the user beforehand if your app can be used to Tweet doesn't have much affect on the method we'll use to launch a Tweet window.

-(void) **requestTweetAuthorization** {

    ACAccountStore *accountStore = [[ACAccountStore **alloc**] **init**];

    ACAccountType *accountType = [accountStore **accountTypeWithAccountTypeIdentifier**:ACAccountTypeIdentifierTwitter];

    [accountStore **requestAccessToAccountsWithType**:accountType **withCompletionHandler**:^(BOOL granted, NSError* error) {

        ACAccount *account = [[ACAccount **alloc**] **initWithAccountType**:accountType];

    }];

}

And to call this method, you just need to write:

[self **requestTweetAuthorization**];

At which point, it displays a dialog to the user confirming whether the application can have access to their Twitter account credentials. If access is granted, then asking again won't be necessary and in the **Twitter** section of the device's **Settings** app, you'll see your app's name next to an **On** switch (like the image to the right). Again, how necessary this really is seems up for debate, since the next block of code apparently works the same whether or not the **requestTweetAuthorization** method is called.

Now go ahead and write the **tweetWithInitialText** method below and we'll talk more about this on the next page:

-(void) **tweetWithInitialText**:(**NSString***) text {
// pass in text to initially add to the Tweet window
    if ([TWTweetComposeViewController **canSendTweet**]) {
    // YES if Twitter is accessible and at least one account is set up; otherwise NO
        CCLOG(@"Can send Tweet");
        AppController *app = (AppController*) [[UIApplication **sharedApplication**] **delegate**];
        TWTweetComposeViewController *controller = [[TWTweetComposeViewController **alloc**] **init**];
        // initialize the Tweet window
        [controller **addImage**: [UIImage **imageNamed**:@"Icon-72.png"]];
        // the name of an image in your app's resources
        [controller **addURL**:[NSURL **URLWithString**:@"www.cartoonsmart.com"]];
        // NOTE: the URL won't show in the Tweet window
        [controller **setInitialText**: text];
        // set the initial text to the NSString we passed into the method
            controller.completionHandler = ^(TWTweetComposeViewControllerResult result) {
                [[app navController] **dismissModalViewControllerAnimated**:YES];
                switch (result) {
                // do something based on the completion handler's result
                    case TWTweetComposeViewControllerResultCancelled:

```
        CCLOG( @"Cancelled" );
            // The user cancelled composing a tweet
            break;
        case TWTweetComposeViewControllerResultDone:
            CCLOG( @"Sent" );
            // The user finished composing a tweet
            break;
        default:
            break;
        }
    };
    [ [app navController] presentModalViewController: controller animated:YES];
} else {
    CCLOG( @"Twitter was not accessible or more likely, at least one account has not
    been set up.");
    }
}
```

To call that method, we could write:

`[self tweetWithInitialText:@"Check out CartoonSmart …"];`

In that example, the text we passed into the method was "Check out CartoonSmart …" It is added to the Tweet window as initial text, which is what this line in the method does:

`[controller setInitialText: text];`

I could still delete that text from the potential tweet before sending it. We're also adding a URL to the Tweet using:

`[controller addURL:[NSURL URLWithString:@"www.cartoonsmart.com"]];`

This URL won't be visible in the Tweet composition window, but if I were to actually send the Tweet, we'd see it tacked onto the end of the message. Then to really ice the cake, we can add an image using:

`[controller addImage: [UIImage imageNamed:@"Icon-72.png"]];`

In that example, it is attaching the file *Icon-72.png*, which is included in with every Cocos2d template. This could be any image file you've added as a Resource to your app.

Optionally, you can use the **canSendTweet** class method to check if Twitter is set up and reachable before presenting this view to the user. This will also check to see if at least one Twitter account has been set up on the device. The final else statement in the method could be used to tell the user that they won't be tweeting today (maybe add the sound of a bird flying into a plate glass window).

You can also set a handler using the completionHandler property to do something when the user is done composing the tweet or has cancelled it. In our example, you'll just read either "Cancelled" or "Sent" in the Output Window, but you could add more code here to do something fancier.

Finally, you might be most intrigued that we've popped up this little Tweet window to begin with. That magic happens with just a few lines. You could remove everything but these three lines from that entire method and still have a functional Tweet window:

AppController *app = (AppController*) [[UIApplication **sharedApplication**] **delegate**];

TWTweetComposeViewController *controller = [[TWTweetComposeViewController **alloc**] **init**];

[[app navController] **presentModalViewController**: controller **animated**:YES];

What you won't get is obviously the initial text, URL, image or handlers for completing or canceling the Tweet.

Saving the Screen to the Camera Roll

Saving the entire screen to the camera roll is quite easy. Keyword being "entire" because I've trimmed out the functionality to start at a specific node. So the code below is the "what you see is what you get" version of saving the screen (which I think is what most people want anyway).

I hope this camera has film in it.

```
-(void) screenshot {
    [CCDirector sharedDirector].nextDeltaTimeZero = YES;
    // CCDirector will ignore a big leap in time (to account for saving the photo)
```

```
    CGSize size = [CCDirector sharedDirector].winSize;

    CCRenderTexture* rtx = [CCRenderTexture renderTextureWithWidth: size.width
    height: size.height];

    // draws a node and all of it's children into a CCRenderTexture ...

    [rtx begin];

    [self visit];

    [rtx end];

    UIImage *img = [rtx getUIImage];

    // create a UIImage from the render texture

    UIImageWriteToSavedPhotosAlbum( img, nil, nil, nil );

    // save the UIImage to the users Camera Roll or Photo Library if there's no camera
}
```

Then just call:

```
[self screenshot];
```

If you would like to download the project files, go to **www.focalpress.com/cw/Dike**.

Section 4

Adding Video

Hopefully by now you've got the hang of
adding new Frameworks to your project,
because we've got another one that needs
including. Once again, from your **Build
Phases** tab, under **Link Binary with
Libraries**, click the + icon and locate the
MediaPlayer.framework. This will give us the
ability to use the **MPMoviePlayerController**
class which—you guessed it—plays movies.
It'll also add AirPlay functionality by default
too. Cool, huh?

So let's get started. In whatever class you want to play a movie from you'll need to add an import statement to either the header or implementation file:

#import <MediaPlayer/MediaPlayer.h>

First let's play a movie from a URL, this way you can test without adding a video to your project (I'll show you the code for that too though). Somewhere in the implementation file of the class you're adding video to, add these lines:

MPMoviePlayerController *player = [[MPMoviePlayerController **alloc**] **initWithContentURL**: [NSURL **URLWithString**:@"www.cartoonsmart.com/ocean.mp4"]];

    // will play ocean.mp4 file from my site

[player **prepareToPlay**];

    // apparently this gets called anyway before playing, but its recommended we call it first

[player.view **setFrame**: [[CCDirector **sharedDirector**] view].**bounds**];

    // player's frame must match parent's

[[[CCDirector **sharedDirector**] view] **addSubview**: player.view];

    // add the player's view to our view

[[NSNotificationCenter **defaultCenter**] **addObserver**:self **selector**:@selector (**videoPlayBackDidFinish**:) **name**: MPMoviePlayerPlaybackDidFinishNotification **object**:nil];

    // this will notify us when playing is done

[player **play**];

    // start playing the movie

We aren't done yet, we still need to write a separate method called **videoPlayBack DidFinish**, which will basically just close the movie when it's done playing, but first let's pick apart the code so far.

We are initializing the player with content from a URL, which is the *ocean.mp4* file on my website.

Then we are calling **prepareToPlay**, which Apple says this about: "If a movie player is not already prepared to play when you call the play method, that method automatically calls this method. However, to minimize playback delay, call this method before you call play." Sounds good to me.

Next we are calling **setFrame** on the player.view and making this equal to the **bounds** of [[CCDirector **sharedDirector**] view].

Then we are calling **addSubview** on [[CCDirector **sharedDirector**] view], and the subview we are adding is of course the player.view.

Then before playing, we are adding an observer to the default NSNotificationCenter to "listen out" for a particular notification (once "heard," it will call the method **videoPlayBackDidFinish)**. We haven't talked yet about notifications in this book, but they are pretty useful to say the least. In this case we need to do something when the movie finishes playing. Fortunately the movie will automatically post a notification called MPMoviePlayerPlaybackDidFinishNotification when it has finished or if it was cancelled. That notification goes to the **defaultCenter,** which is where we are listening for it. Later in this chapter, we will look at notifications again.

Finally, it's time for the real playas to play. Call **play** on the movie player.

Now let's write the **videoPlayBackDidFinish** method:

```
-(void) videoPlayBackDidFinish:(NSNotification*)notification {
    [[NSNotificationCenter defaultCenter] removeObserver:self
    name:MPMoviePlayerPlaybackDidFinishNotification object:nil];
    MPMoviePlayerController *player = notification.object;
    [player stop];
    [player.view removeFromSuperview];
    [player autorelease];
}
```

Let's go through that method now. First, we are removing the MPMoviePlayerPlaybackDid FinishNotification observer from the **defaultCenter**. Since the movie is finished, we no longer need to listen for it finishing again.

Then we are casting MPMoviePlayerController *player as the notification.object. So whatever object initiated this notification is going to be referred to as player throughout the rest of this code block. Which, as we know, is the movie player from before. So we're basically just giving it the same name as before (and we aren't creating a new movie player here, we're just casting the existing one).

Next we tell the player to stop, which stops playback of the movie and resets the playhead to the start.

Then we call **removeFromSuperview** on player.view, which to put it simply, just removes the view.

And finally, player is set to **autorelease**.

Playing a Movie from the App's Resources

If your movie is relatively small in file size it's perfectly okay to add it as a Resource so the user could watch it even if they weren't connected to the Internet. To try this out, add a movie file to your app, then remove (or comment out) this line:

MPMoviePlayerController *player = [[MPMoviePlayerController **alloc**] **initWithContentURL**: [NSURL **URLWithString**:@"www.cartoonsmart.com/ocean.mp4"]];

Then replace it with these two lines:

NSString *path=[[NSBundle **mainBundle**] **pathForResource**:@"ocean" **ofType**:@"mp4"];

MPMoviePlayerController* player =[[MPMoviePlayerController **alloc**] **initWithContentURL**: [NSURL **fileURLWithPath**:path]];

The path variable is created in the first line to specify that ocean.mp4 is in the **mainBundle** of the app. Then, in the next line, the player is initialized using that path as the NSURL. That's it. The rest of your code can remain the same.

Fine Tuning MPMoviePlayerController

One property you might want to explore would be setting:

player.shouldAutoplay = NO;

… which will obviously stop the movie from automatically playing. Instead you'll just see the first frame of it. If you do this, you'll need to remove:

[player **play**];

You can also set the style of the playback controls with the controlStyle property. For example:

player.controlStyle = MPMovieControlStyleFullscreen;

This would give you controls for full-screen playback, which includes a start/pause button, a scrubber bar, forward and reverse seeking buttons, a button for toggling between full screen and embedded display modes, a button for toggling the aspect fill mode, and a Done button. In our example, tapping the Done button would call **videoPlayBackDidFinish**.

Other options would be:

```
player.controlStyle = MPMovieControlStyleNone;
```
        // No controls, you're flying solo

```
player.controlStyle = MPMovieControlStyleDefault;
```
        // The default controls are displayed (the Done button only appears after toggling to full screen)

```
player.controlStyle = MPMovieControlStyleEmbedded;
```
        // Controls include start/pause button, scrubber bar and the full screen toggle

That's it for a short introduction to the MPMoviePlayerController class. You should be able to follow along with the official documentation for any other tweaking you need. You can access that from Xcode by going to the Help menu, then selecting Documentation and API Reference.

If you would like to download the project files go to **www.focalpress.com/cw/Dike**.

Quick Start Guide to In-App Purchasing

In this section we'll look at what is probably the most popular form of **In-App Purchasing** which is the **Non-Consumable** type. Non-Consumable in-app purchases are those that don't need to be bought twice and can be shared across multiple devices—as opposed to Consumable purchases, which can get used up over time. For example, in-game money would be a Consumable purchase, whereas unlocking all the chapters of a book app would be a Non-Consumable purchase.

It probably goes without saying to anyone that owns an iOS device, but in-app purchases are a huge part of the App Store. Chances are you've downloaded a free app and paid to unlock extra features to either enhance the app or simply play more levels. With what you already know about programming, the code to either allow or disallow gameplay past a certain level is very simple. An if ... else statement and bool variable could handle it like so:

```
if ( isAppUnlocked == YES) {

    [ self loadNextLevel ];

    // keep playing

} else {

    [ self showUpsellPage ];

    // keep paying

}
```

If the app hasn't been unlocked, you can show the user an "upsell" page where you prompt them to purchase the upgrade. It's your chance to don your salesmen cap, and bestow your wiles. Or just show an awesome image of the next level. Speaking of images, don't underestimate your most devoted player's willingness to buy upgrades, which could simply be a picture. For example, one of my free pinball games regularly gets upgrade purchases to unlock a zombie version of the table, which wasn't more work than adding a few more images. That same zombified table can also be unlocked by getting a high score, but heck, $0.99 is a pretty fair price for what's essentially a cool cheat code.

Have dollar signs replaced your normal pupils yet? Cool, let's get started. This is a decent amount of code to rewrite, so while I don't usually recommend this, I have no problem with you just copying the classes into your example project. So if you want to grab those now from **www.focalpress.com/cw/Dike** and speed through the set-up, I won't be offended. The project is titled **NonConsumablePurchase**.

The classes you'll want to copy into your project are InAppManager and InAppObserver. Grab the **.h** and **.m** files for each, and drag them into any project you want to add purchasing too. Be sure all the checkmarks you see in the image below are checked on.

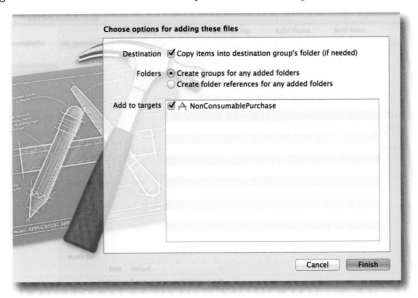

If you don't want to copy in my files then pat yourself on the back for being a purist and just wait a bit because I'll guide you through creating these files from scratch. To speed along those of you copying the files, we'll talk about the nitty gritty details of those classes last, and first discuss setting up In-App purchases in iTunes Connect and how to make test purchase calls using the usual HelloWorldLayer class (or any other class on your end).

One nice thing about the InAppManager and InAppObserver classes (aside from them making money rain) is that once they've been written there's nothing really to change other than the IDs, which we will set up in a moment in iTunes Connect.

Import the StoreKit Framework

Like we've done a few times already this chapter, head over to the **Build Phases** window of Xcode and add the **StoreKit.framework** to your project.

If you copied in those two classes, any errors should now be gone. Both headers included:

#import <StoreKit/StoreKit.h>

... so without the **Storekit.framework** in your project, you would be pretty doomed. Speaking of doom, I'll give you a quick review of what needs to happen in the **Provisioning Portal** before we get started programming because your In-App products need a properly signed app to work.

Provisioning Portal and Xcode's Organizer

The Provisioning Portal and Organizer Window in Xcode play a big part in making your app submittable to Apple and your in-app purchase functional. As we talked about in Chapter 1, you eventually need to sign up for the **iOS Developer Program**. That day has come. Once you've signed up, log into the iOS Dev Center, then head to the Provisioning Portal. Most of what you need to do in the portal you can also do from **Xcode** by going to the **Window** menu, then opening the **Organizer**. I'll sum up what you need to do using either the Portal or Organizer.

- **Certificates**—You need to install two certificates in your Keychain app (every Mac already has this application even if you've never opened it). The **Development** and **Distribution** certificate play a part in code-signing your application. These can be set up from the portal or from the Organizer, where you should be prompted if your certificates need installing. At which point you'll need to provide the Organizer with your iOS Developer log-in credentials.

- **Devices**—You can add a test device from the Provisioning Portal by following the instructions on the site. Or you can open the Organizer, connect your iOS Device (it should show up in the left column), select it, then click the **Add to Portal** button.

- **App IDs**—Unless the Organizer has snuck in this feature, I think you still need to create **New App IDs** from the Provisioning Portal. You'll be asked to enter a **Description** (for your own benefit), which could simply be your app's title. Your **Bundle Seed ID** can be set to **Use Team ID** (as seen in the screenshot to the right). Most important is your **Bundle Identifier** which is a unique ID for your app. It is recommended to use the reverse of your domain name (if you own a domain) then the title of your app. For example, my identifier might be *com.cartoonsmart.somecoolapp.* The Bundle Identifier you enter into Xcode must match this same ID (for reference see the screenshot on the right).

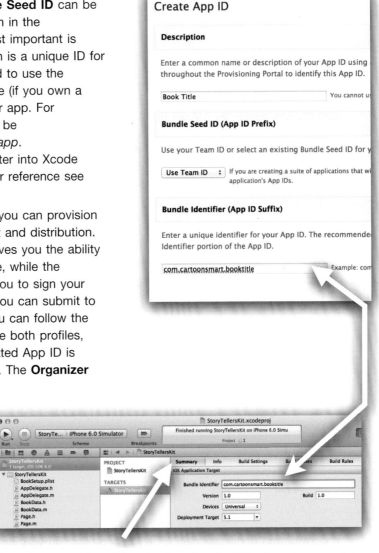

- **Provisioning**—In the portal you can provision your device for development and distribution. The **development profile** gives you the ability to test on your actual device, while the **distribution profile** allows you to sign your finished application, which you can submit to Apple for the App Store. You can follow the prompts on the site to create both profiles, just be sure your newly created App ID is associated with each profile. The **Organizer** can also be used to create profiles (go to Library > Provisioning Profiles > New). Again, be sure the App ID is associated with each profile.

If you have trouble editing the **Bundle Identifier from here, switch from the Summary to Info tab, and edit it from there.**

The tough part is hopefully over now, and you are set up to properly code sign your application. By default Xcode should automatically sign your app with the **Development Provisioning Profile** if you are testing on your own device. Keyword being "should." Sometimes restarting Xcode is needed if the wrong profile is associated with your app (it happens to me all the time).

Troubleshooting: If you get a code signing error, first double check that your Bundle Identifier matches the one you created in the Provisioning Portal. Second, go to the Build Settings panel in Xcode (seen in the screenshot below) and type in "Code Signing" in the search bar. This will bring up your **Code Signing Identity** options. In Xcode, pull down in the same areas where I've placed arrows on the screenshot. Make sure the profiles selected match that of your Bundle Identifier. You should see them along with your profile names.

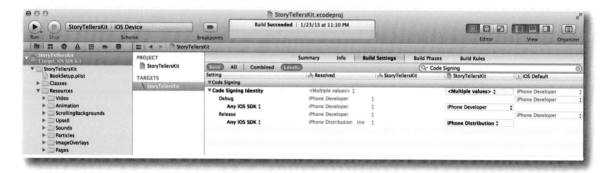

Setting Up the In-App Purchase

Yup, there's more to set up. This time you'll need to head over to iTunes Connect. Once you sign in with your developer credentials, go to **Manage Your Applications**, then click on **New App**. You'll see the same window below:

The **App Name** will be the title displayed in the store. The **SKU Number** is up to you. The **Bundle ID** is a pull-down selection showing all active bundle identifiers. Choose the one you created for this app.

At this point you'll need to provide, at the very least, some basic meta data (keywords, description), a **512** by **512** icon, and at least one screenshot (you can add more screenshots later).

After providing this information, you can then click the "Manage In-App Purchases" button (see the screenshot below).

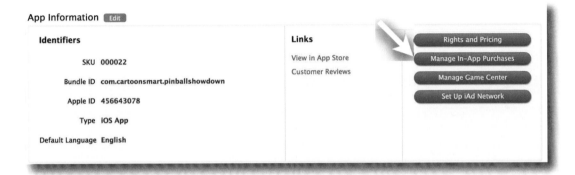

From here, click **Create New**, then select **Non-Consumable**. On the next page, you've got a few more options and we're done!

The **Reference Name** is for your internal reference of the In-App purchase (reports and such). The most important part is the **Product ID**. This value can be whatever you want, but you need to make a note of it, because we'll enter it into our InAppManager class later.

From here, you just need to fill in the rest of the info for the In-App Purchase.

> **Cleared for Sale**—Yes.
>
> **Price Tier**—Tier 1 is $0.99, Tier 2 is $1.99 and so on.
>
> **In-App Purchase Details**—Click Add Language, then fill in the prompts.
>
> **Hosting Content with Apple**—No
>
> **Review Notes**—You probably don't need to enter anything here.
>
> **Screenshot for Review**—This will only be seen by your app reviewer.

You are almost ready to test your In-App Purchase.

Create a Test User

Back at the main menu of iTunes Connect, click on **Manage Users**, then select **Test User**. Click on **Add New User**. The email and password you enter here can be used to test unlocking the book. The email can be completely made up by the way.

Important: When testing the in-app purchase on your device, be sure to first sign out of the iTunes store (in the Settings app). When you try to make a purchase, you'll get prompted to use either an Existing Account or Create a New Account. Choose Existing Account and enter in your Test User credentials.

Add the Product ID to the InAppManager Class

Before we begin writing the code to buy and unlock a product, let's take that In-App **Product ID** we just created and add it to the InAppManager class (if you decided to just copy in the class files from the sample project).

At the very top of the ***InAppManager.m*** file, you'll find:

```
static NSString *productID1 = @"SOME_ID1";
```

Remove SOME_ID1 and enter in exactly the same text as your Product ID for the In-App Purchase.

Keep in mind, this is **NOT** your bundle identifier. It is only your In-App Purchase Product ID.

Once you enter this in the InAppManager class, you can forget about it. From here on out, we'll refer to this as "Product 1." If you created another In-App Product, do the same thing on the next line:

```
static NSString *productID2 = @"SOME_OTHER_ID";
```

From here on out, consider that to be "Product 2." Do the same thing for more products. The sample project has code for up to five different in-app purchases.

Buying and Unlocking a Product

Now the fun begins. If you had trouble code-signing your app, then implementing this code will seem like a breeze. In whatever class you'll be working with (I'm using HelloWorldLayer), add the following import statement:

```
#import "InAppManager h"
```

The next eleven lines of code will be written in the init statement of ***HelloWorldLayer.m*** but you can add them to any method. These will create a menu with three buttons labeled Product 1, Product 2, and Restore Purchases. Apps with in-app purchases are now required to have a button that allows the user to restore purchases. If someone did try to buy the same Non-Consumable product twice they wouldn't get charged but they would step through the buying process again unnecessarily, so a Restore Purchases button adds a lot more peace of mind for the user and saves time.

This first line below will initialize the InAppManager singleton and trigger some messages to the Output window about what products are are found in iTunes Connect and purchasable. You'll see the description, price and ID for each product.

[InAppManager **sharedManager**];

Next we'll create the CCMenu:

CGSize size = [[CCDirector **sharedDirector**] winSize];

CCMenuItem *product1 = [CCMenuItemFont **itemWithString**:@"Product 1" **target**:self **selector**:@selector(**buyProduct1**)];

CCMenuItem *product2 = [CCMenuItemFont **itemWithString**:@"Product 2" **target**:self **selector**:@selector(**buyProduct2**)];

CCMenuItem *restore = [CCMenuItemFont **itemWithString**:@"Restore Purchases" **target**:self **selector**:@selector(**restoreProducts**)];

CCMenu *menu = [CCMenu **menuWithItems**: product1, product2, restore, nil];

[menu **alignItemsVerticallyWithPadding**:10];

[menu **setPosition**:ccp(size.width / 2 , size.height / 2)];

[self **addChild**:menu];

Finally, before we leave the **init** statement (or whatever method you're writing in), we need to add a couple notifications to the **NSNotificationCenter**. The notification center provides an easy way to communicate between classes. Basically we add an observer (which is what the two lines below are doing) to listen out for another class to post a notification with a matching name. In our examples, those **name** values are @"feature1Purchased" and @"feature2Purchased." If either of those notifications are observed than this class will call the methods **unlockProduct1** or **unlockProduct2**.

[[NSNotificationCenter **defaultCenter**] **addObserver**:self **selector**:@selector (**unlockProduct1**) **name**:@"feature1Purchased" **object**:nil];

[[NSNotificationCenter **defaultCenter**] **addObserver**:self **selector**:@selector (**unlockProduct2**) **name**:@"feature2Purchased" **object**:nil];

Next, type outside of wherever you added the previous lines and include the two methods for unlocking Product 1 and Product 2:

-(void) **unlockProduct1** {

    CCLOG(@"Do whatever needs doing to unlock product 1");

}

```
-(void) unlockProduct2 {

        CCLOG(@"Do whatever needs doing to unlock product 2");

}
```

These will get called after a successful purchase of either product, or they will get called if the user restores a past purchase. If they previously had purchased both products, then both methods would run above. You don't necessarily need to use these methods to alert the user that their purchase was a success or restored, because the InAppManager already has code to do that via a UIAlertView window. So what you do to unlock your products in these methods varies depending on what your product is. It could be as simple as increasing a variable for something like maxNumberOfPlayableLevels. Or you could do nothing at all here!

Why's that? Well, if you aren't at a place in your app where you need to unlock anything, it's fine not to. The InAppManager and NSUserDefaults will both be holding onto bool variables noting that a particular product was unlocked. So at anytime you could write something like: if ([InAppManager **sharedManager**] **isFeature1PurchasedAlready**] == YES … to find out the unlock status.

Finally, we need to include our methods to initiate buying or restoring products. These are the methods called from each CCMenuItem:

```
-(void) buyProduct1{

        CCLOG(@"Will attempt to buy Product 1");

        [[InAppManager sharedManager] buyFeature1];

}

-(void) buyProduct2{

        CCLOG(@"Will attempt to buy Product 2");

        [[InAppManager sharedManager] buyFeature2];

}

-(void) restoreProducts {

        CCLOG(@"Will attempt to restore products");

        [[InAppManager sharedManager] restoreCompletedTransactions ];

}
```

That's all you need to do. A **UIView** will step the user through the buying process. As I've said before in this book, "ignorance is bliss," but if you want to really explore the InAppManager and InAppObserver classes, you can get your hands dirty in the next section.

The In-App Purchasing Classes

If you'd like to create the InAppManager and InAppObserver classes from scratch and get a better understanding of what's happening behind the scenes of the In-App purchasing process, I'll step you through everything I know. I created these classes using code from Apple's official documentation and some inspiration from an early version of Mugunth Kumar's MKStoreKit, which has now progressed to support a lot more than Non-Consumable purchases (his store-kit classes can handle things like hosted content and more). So feel free to check out his classes as well. Mine are relatively simple since they are just for Non-Consumable upgrades and I tried to make the code similar to past examples we've already seen in this book.

To follow along, be sure you've already gone through the same steps in the previous section. You should have:

- A properly code-signed app (added your Bundle ID and provisioning profiles).

- Created an In-App product in iTunes Connect.

- Added the StoreKit framework to your project.

Once these classes are written we'll add the same code from last section to buy and unlock the In-App products. If you've already written that code in your project, simply comment it out for now.

Let's begin. In Xcode, go to **File > New > File** … and you can choose the usual **CCNode class** option. Name the file **InAppManager.m**, then do the same thing again for **InAppObserver.m**. The code we'll be writing really has nothing to do with Cocos2d. So where you see CCNode in the header files, that could also be NSObject (switching it at any time is fine). The class headers don't need the #import "cocos2d.h" line, but it won't hurt us either and it gives you the option to write CCLOG instead of NSLog to send a message to the Output window.

Readers of this book might have CCLOG engrained in their brains by now.

The InAppManager Class

At the top of the *InAppManager.h* file, add these lines:

#import <StoreKit/StoreKit.h>

#import "InAppObserver.h"

Remember what C-3PO was programmed for, mostly etiquette and protocol? Actually, to fully jog our geek memory, let's check the Star Wars Wiki entry … "A protocol droid was a type of droid designed to assist sentients in their relations with one another." Well that's not too far off from the type of protocol programming we get to do. Our InAppManager needs the SKProductsRequestDelegate protocol to receive a list of products from the Store. So you could think of this like we need a few lines of protocol code to act as an interpreter. To do this, we must mark the class as implementing the protocol in the class extension, like so:

@interface InAppManager : CCNode <SKProductsRequestDelegate> {

}

> *// Keep in mind, CCNode or NSObject can be interchanged in that line above*

The only addition to the existing code is this: <SKProductsRequestDelegate> … which on it's own, will give you the warning below.

> Incomplete implementation,
> Method 'productsRequest:didReceiveResponse:' in protocol not implemented

I'll be your protocol droid and interpret that. We aren't done implementing the protocol because it needs the **productRequest** method to be complete. So let's jump over to the *InAppManager.m* file and add that in:

- (void) **productsRequest**:(SKProductsRequest *)request **didReceiveResponse**:(SKProductsResponse *)response {

> *// add more here later*

}

All is right again in the world. Eventually this method will actually do something (like help us organize possible products we can buy from the store), but for now the compiler will leave us alone regarding the warning above. Once the class was marked as implementing the <SKProductsRequestDelegate> protocol, we essentially agreed to including that method above (regardless of how we used it).

Next, let's go back to our InAppManager header file, and declare some variables and methods we'll use in the class.

@interface InAppManager : CCNode <SKProductsRequestDelegate> {

    NSMutableArray *purchasableProducts;

    // an array of the possible products to purchase

    NSUserDefaults *defaults;

    // we'll store a bool variable marking products that have already been unlocked

    bool product1WasPurchased;

    // YES or NO (noting whether product 1 was purchased)

    bool product2WasPurchased;

    // YES or NO (noting whether product 2 was purchased)

}

@property (nonatomic, retain) NSMutableArray *purchasableProducts;

    // retain the array so we don't lose it

+ (InAppManager*)**sharedManager**;

    // the InAppManager will be a singleton class accessed through the sharedManager

- (void) **requestProductData**;

    // In my example project, no other class calls this, so it's questionable if this is worth declaring. It's harmless if we do though

We'll return to the header later to add more, but for now this is plenty. Jump over to the **InAppManager.m** file and let's just start at the top of the file and work our way down. Anything I can't explain with comments, I'll break from the code and discuss further

@implementation InAppManager

@synthesize purchasableProducts;

    // synthesize the array, no different than what we usually do for properties

static NSString *productID1 = @"MOREVEHICLES";

    // the string value will be the exact product ID you added in iTunes Connect

static NSString *productID2 = @"MOREVEHICLES2";

    // the string value will be the exact product ID you added in iTunes Connect

If you don't have a second In-App product to sell, that's okay. Just enter any string value in here. Worst case the product isn't found (nothing bad will happen). You won't initiate any code to try to sell that product anyway. These lines might look curious because we don't often create static variables anyway, and we definitely haven't created static NSString's in this book. Just remember, a static variable belongs to the class as a whole, and is shared by all objects of the class. Granted, we're writing this in a singleton class anyway, and singletons themselves are shared, so we're kind of just doubling-down on making these product IDs set at those values throughout the lifespan of this app. Speaking of singletons, let's continue with that:

```
static InAppManager *sharedManager = nil;

+(InAppManager*) sharedManager {
        if (sharedManager == nil) {
                sharedManager = [[InAppManager alloc] init] ;
        }
        return sharedManager;
}
```

If you forgot how the secret sauce to these work, just refer back to our recent section on singletons. Just remember, there's **only ever one instance** of this class. So once we initialize it, it's there for good (and we don't have a reason to deallocate it). Calling the **sharedManager** class method will initialize the InAppManager (if it wasn't already) by calling the **init** method below:

```
-(id) init {
   if( (self=[super init])) {
        sharedManager = self;
        defaults = [NSUserDefaults standardUserDefaults];
        // the defaults variable just refers to the standard user defaults
        product1WasPurchased = [defaults boolForKey:productID1];
        // check the defaults to see if the key already has a bool value
        product2WasPurchased = [defaults boolForKey:productID2];
        // check the defaults to see if the key already has a bool value
        purchasableProducts = [[NSMutableArray alloc] init];
        // allocate and initialize our array for products
        [self requestProductData];
        // as soon as we initialize the class, we want to get product info from the store
   }
   return self;
}
```

The **init** method will set the variables for product1WasPurchased and product2Was Purchased to whatever the defaults last stored bool values for keys that match productID1 and productID2. (Those keys are the same string values as your In-App product IDs in iTunes Connect). If this is the first time the app has been run, then obviously there aren't previously stored values for the defaults. What happens then? Nothing really. The variables for product1WasPurchased and product2WasPurchased are still NO, which is what bool variables are by default anyway.

The last line in the **init** statement calls **requestProductData**, which is our next method to write:

- (void) **requestProductData**{

    SKProductsRequest *request= [[SKProductsRequest **alloc**] **initWithProductIdentifiers**:
                                  [NSSet **setWithObjects**: productID1, productID2, nil]];

    // add more products here if you had them

    request.delegate = self;

    // the request's delegate is this same class

    [request **start**];

    // start the request

}

These three lines create the SKProductsRequest variable called request, which is initialized with a set of our product identifiers (again we are making use of our static NSString variables, which are the values of our In-App product ID's from iTunes Connect). We set the request.delegate to self, which goes back to why we marked this class as implementing the SKProductsRequestDelegate protocol. After we **start** the request, we'll get back the response in the method we've already written some of below. For now just add a couple more lines inside that method:

- (void) **productsRequest**:(SKProductsRequest *)request **didReceiveResponse**: (SKProductsResponse *)response {

    NSArray * skProducts = response.products;

    // create (and log) a quick array from the products we got back

    NSLog (@"This is kind of a vague response ... %@ ...but at least it's a response ", skProducts);

}

Let's give this a quick test. Before hitting the almighty Run button on the project, add this line to your HelloWorldLayer class (or any class you want to add purchasing to):

[InAppManager **sharedManager**];

> *// be sure the #import "InAppManager.h" statement for InAppManager.h is also included*

If you had your Bundle Identifier in place and some products in iTunes Connect to test, you should get a response. It's not the world's greatest response though. You should see a line in the Output window for each product in the store, but it will look like this:

"<SKProduct: 0x437f40>"

Whoa. That feels like an ominously short text message from a girlfriend. You might be thinking, "Oh no, what'd I do wrong this time?" but fortunately everything is okay. We just need to pry some details from that response. Here's the complete block of code, which I'll explain in a moment:

```
- (void) productsRequest:(SKProductsRequest *)request didReceiveResponse:
(SKProductsResponse *)response {
    NSArray * skProducts = response.products;
    if ( [skProducts count] != 0 && [purchasableProducts count] == 0) {
    for (int i=0; i<[skProducts count]; i++) {
        [purchasableProducts addObject:[skProducts objectAtIndex:i ]];
        SKProduct *product = [purchasableProducts objectAtIndex:i ];
        // I'm only creating this product to log info below
        NSLog(@"Feature: %@, Cost: %f, ID: %@",[product localizedTitle], [[product price]
        doubleValue], [product productIdentifier]);
    }
    }
    // after the for statement is run, let's make sure the purchasableProducts array has the
    right number of products in it
    NSLog (@"We found %i In-App Purchases in iTunes Connect", [purchasableProducts
    count]) ;
    [request autorelease];
}
```

The if statement checks two things. First if the number of objects in the skProducts array *does not* equal zero. If it did, that would mean zero In-App purchases were found in the Store. Then if our purchasableProducts array *does* equal zero. If so, then we need to populate it with our products found in the store. This double condition just protects against the **productsRequest** being run twice and unnecessarily adding duplicate products to the purchasableProducts array. To be honest, even if that happened, it's really not a big deal.

So once we proceed within the if statement, we have a for statement, which will iterate for as many products were counted in the response back from the Store. The only line that really matters here is:

[purchasableProducts **addObject**:[skProducts **objectAtIndex**:i]];

… the other two lines are just used to send messages to the Output window. That line above is what actually adds an object from the skProducts array to our purchasableProducts array. Keep in mind the "object" itself is an SKProduct, or Store Kit Product, which provides information about the product you previously registered in iTunes Connect (like price, title, ID).

Some of you might wonder, why use the skProducts array at all here? Why not just make purchasableProducts array immediately equal the response.products? And if you did notice that, then hey, good observation. That is possible of course. One thing this code leaves the door open for is syphoning out which products have already been purchased before adding them to the purchasableProducts array. You might want to do this if you were presenting a fancy menu of **only** products the user hadn't yet bought. Food for thought.

Moving on, there's one last log statement that just tells you the [purchasableProducts **count**], which is the number of products you have in the store to purchase. Then finally the request is set to autorelease.

Now when you build and run the app, you should see something far less vague like this:

> **Feature:** Unlock More Vehicles—Set 1, **Cost:** 0.990000, **ID:** MOREVEHICLES
>
> **Feature:** Unlock More Vehicles—Set 2 , **Cost:** 0.990000, **ID:** MOREVEHICLES2
>
> **We found 2 In-App Purchases in iTunes Connect**

Congrats. We aren't done with the InAppManager, but it's time to side-step over to the InAppObserver for a bit.

The InAppObserver Class

While I'd rather just barrel roll through the rest of the InAppManager class, we've got to a point where we can't do much else without getting the InAppObserver involved. As far as this book goes, this class is a bit of a rarity since it doesn't even have an **init** statement. As the class name implies, it is kind of an etheric observer. A pair of eyes and binoculars, watching what happens with any product we send to the SKPaymentQueue (basically the checkout line at the grocery store). So this class will be notified if the purchase was completed, a past purchase was restored, or if the payment failed. It could fail if the buyer cancelled it or their account wasn't authorized for purchases.

Open the **InAppObserver.h** file and add the following to what's already there:

#import <StoreKit/StoreKit.h>

*// NOTE: do **not** import "InAppManager.h" here, we'll do that in the implementation file*

@interface InAppObserver : CCNode <SKPaymentTransactionObserver> {

// again CCNode could be interchangeable with NSObject here

}

- (void) **paymentQueue**:(SKPaymentQueue *)queue **updatedTransactions**:(NSArray *) transactions;

- (void) **failedTransaction**: (SKPaymentTransaction *)transaction;

- (void) **completeTransaction**: (SKPaymentTransaction *)transaction;

- (void) **restoreTransaction**: (SKPaymentTransaction *)transaction;

The <SKPaymentTransactionObserver> protocol will require us to add the **paymentQueue** method you see declared above. The other three methods simply deal with whatever result we get back from the **paymentQueue** method.

Now jump over to your **InAppObserver.m** file and add the import statement for the InAppManager class:

#import "InAppManager.h"

// this import statement MUST be added to the implementation instead of the header file or we get errors

Now let's write the **paymentQueue** method:

@implementation InAppObserver

- (void) **paymentQueue**:(SKPaymentQueue *)queue **updatedTransactions**:(NSArray *) transactions {

    for (SKPaymentTransaction *transaction in transactions) {

        switch (transaction.transactionState) {

            case SKPaymentTransactionStatePurchased:

                [self **completeTransaction**:transaction];

                break;

            case SKPaymentTransactionStateFailed:

                [self **failedTransaction**:transaction];

                break;

            case SKPaymentTransactionStateRestored:

```
        [self restoreTransaction:transaction];
        break;
      default:
        break;
    }
  }
}
```

Again, this will get called on it's own when a transaction in the queue is observed doing something. The for statement just iterates through the transactions array that got passed into the method. When buying a Non-Consumable product there should be just one transaction to observe, but if the app was restoring multiple products, the transactions array could have more than one object.

Each one of those case values (SKPaymentTransactionStatePurchased, SKPaymentTransactionStateFailed or SKPaymentTransactionStateRestored), has a corresponding method in this class that receives the SKPaymentTransaction (named transaction) as a parameter. Those corresponding methods follow:

```
- (void) failedTransaction: (SKPaymentTransaction *)transaction{
  NSLog(@"Transaction Failed ...");
  if (transaction.error.code != SKErrorPaymentCancelled) {
  // if the error was anything other than the user canceling it
    [[InAppManager sharedManager] failedTransaction:transaction];
    // we imported the InAppManager so we could make calls like this to it
  }
  [[SKPaymentQueue defaultQueue] finishTransaction: transaction];
  // finished with this transaction
}
```

The **failedTransaction** method checks the transaction.error.code and as long as that doesn't equal SKErrorPaymentCancelled, meaning the buyer cancelled the payment on their own, then we pass the transaction back to the [InAppManager **sharedManager**] and call **failedTransaction** with it as a parameter. We've yet to write that method though, so until we do, you'll get a warning in Xcode.

Then like the other two methods below, our last line simply tells the default SKPaymentQueue that we've finished observing this transaction.

```
- (void) completeTransaction: (SKPaymentTransaction *)transaction {

    NSLog(@"Purchases was complete, will notify the InAppManager …");

    [[InAppManager sharedManager] provideContent: transaction.payment.productIdentifier];

    [[SKPaymentQueue defaultQueue] finishTransaction: transaction];

}

- (void) restoreTransaction: (SKPaymentTransaction *)transaction {

    NSLog(@"Found purchase, will notify the InAppManager …");

    [[InAppManager sharedManager] provideContent:
    transaction.originalTransaction.payment.productIdentifier];

    [[SKPaymentQueue defaultQueue] finishTransaction: transaction];

}
```

The last two methods in the class are very similar. Both pass the transaction's productIdentifier (an NSString of the Product ID of what was bought) to the **provideContent** method in the [InAppManager **sharedManager**]. Again, we haven't written that yet, but since that's a wrap for the InAppObserver class, we won't have to deal with that pesky warning for long.

There and Back Again (to the InAppManager)

Let's go to the header file of InAppManager one more time, and finish it for good. I'll paste in most of the header, and note the additions:

```
@interface InAppManager : CCNode <SKProductsRequestDelegate> {

    NSMutableArray *purchasableProducts;

    NSUserDefaults *defaults;

    InAppObserver *theObserver;

    // an instance of the InAppObserver we just spent a few pages discussing

    bool product1WasPurchased;

    bool product2WasPurchased;

}

@property (nonatomic, retain) NSMutableArray *purchasableProducts;

@property (nonatomic, retain) InAppObserver *theObserver;

    // retain it

+ (InAppManager*) sharedManager;

- (void) requestProductData;
```

- (void) **buyFeature1**;

// declared so any class can call it to initiate a purchase of Product 1

- (void) **buyFeature2**;

// declared so any class can call it to initiate a purchase of Product 2

-(bool) **isFeature1PurchasedAlready**;

// declared so any class can check if Product 1 was purchased before doing something

-(bool) **isFeature2PurchasedAlready**;

// declared so any class can check if Product 2 was purchased before doing something

- (void) **provideContent**: (NSString*) productIdentifier;

// declared so the InAppObserver can call it

- (void) **failedTransaction**: (SKPaymentTransaction*) transaction;

// declared so the InAppObserver can call it

- (void) **restoreCompletedTransactions**;

// declared so any class can call this to attempt to restore purchases

@end

Now, go over to your **InAppManager.m** file and let's quickly take care of everything related to the InAppObserver variable we just declared in the header. To synthesize it, we can just add it after the purchasableProducts on the same line:

@synthesize purchasableProducts, theObserver;

Then in our **init** statement, we just need these two lines:

theObserver = [[InAppObserver **alloc**] **init**];

[[SKPaymentQueue **defaultQueue**] **addTransactionObserver**:theObserver];

The **defaultQueue** now has theObserver instance monitoring the results of whatever we send through there. We will send a product through the **defaultQueue** in just a moment but as far as theObserver goes we are finished with it. Now let's work on actually buying something. Type in these next two methods to the class:

```
- (void) buyFeature1 {
    [self buyFeature:productID1];
}
- (void) buyFeature2 {
    [self buyFeature:productID2];
}
```

Both of these methods just call the **buyFeature** method (which we'll write next), the only difference is the parameter we pass to it. If you remember, productID1 and productID2 are the static NSString variables that are equal to our In-App product IDs in iTunes Connect.

You might be wondering, why hard-code those variables into their own method when we could just call **buyFeature** directly with the product ID like @"UNLOCKSTUFF." Well, you could. The only harm in doing that is having to write the product ID in more than one place (or class). Ideally once we enter that ID, we don't *want* to write it again. We've already used productID1 and productID2 in multiple places in this class and that cuts down on possible errors or typos from rewriting the actual product ID. Plus if we copy these class files for re-use in another project, it's much easier to implement a different product ID if it's only written once, and in one class.

Next let's write the **buyFeature** method. This will either proceed with the purchase if the user passes the **canMakePayments** check or it will show a UIAlertView telling the buyer they are not authorized to purchase. If they can pay, we create an SKProduct variable called selectedProduct, make that equal to the product stored in the purchasableProducts array using the for loop, then attach the selectedProduct to an SKPayment variable aptly called payment. Finally, we send the payment to the SKPaymentQueue. If any of that isn't clear, see the comments following each line below:

```
- (void) buyFeature:(NSString*) featureID {
    if ([SKPaymentQueue canMakePayments]) {
        NSLog(@"Can make payments");
        // worth logging to make sure you get this far in the purchase
        SKProduct *selectedProduct;
        // create the product we will use with the SKPayment variable below
        // search the purchasableProducts array and find one with a productIdentifier
        equal to that of the featureID
        for (int i=0; i < [purchasableProducts count]; i ++ ) {
        // iterate through the purchasableProducts array
            selectedProduct = [purchasableProducts objectAtIndex:i ];
            // make the selectedProduct equal to the current object in the array
            if ( [[selectedProduct productIdentifier] isEqualToString: featureID] ) {
            // if selectedProduct's identifier equals the featureID
                SKPayment *payment = [SKPayment paymentWithProduct:selectedProduct];
                // create the payment variable with product
                [[SKPaymentQueue defaultQueue] addPayment:payment];
                // send the payment to the default payment queue
```

```
        break;
    }
  }
} else {
    UIAlertView *alert = [[UIAlertView alloc] initWithTitle:@"Oh no" message:@"You can't
    purchase from the App Store"
    delegate:self cancelButtonTitle:@"OK" otherButtonTitles: nil];
    [alert show];
    //show the alert above
    [alert release];
  }
}
```

Once the payment goes to the SKPaymentQueue, we just wait for the InAppObserver to do its thing, which if you remember, results in methods to complete the transaction, restore past transactions or tell us it failed. The first two of those possible outcomes both call the **provideContent** method below. This method takes in the productIdentifier as a parameter and depending on that value sets different variables or calls different methods (see the notes below). At the end it shows a UIAlertView to tell users the purchase was a success.

```
-(void) provideContent: (NSString*) productIdentifier {
    NSNotificationCenter *notification = [NSNotificationCenter defaultCenter];
    // used below to post notifications to the defaultCenter
    NSString* theMessageForAlert = nil;
    // we'll use this string later in the UIAlertView, but create it now to set a different
    message per product
    if ([productIdentifier isEqualToString:productID1]) {
    // if productIdentifier is equal to productID ...
        NSLog(@"Item 1 was purchased- the ID was %@", productIdentifier );
        // log it
        theMessageForAlert = @"Your App Now Has Product 1's Content Available";
        // message for the UIAlertView
        product1WasPurchased = YES;
        // set to YES now
        [defaults setBool:YES forKey:productID1];
        // set to YES for the defaults as well
```

```
[notification postNotificationName:@"feature1Purchased" object:nil];
// post a notification with name@"feature1Purchased"
} else if ([productIdentifier isEqualToString:productID2]) {
// if productIdentifier is equal to productID ...
    NSLog(@"Item 2 was purchased- the ID was %@", productIdentifier );
    // log it
    theMessageForAlert = @"Your App Now Has Product 2's Content Available";
    // message for the UIAlertView
    product2WasPurchased = YES;
    // set to YES now
    [defaults setBool:YES forKey:productID2];
    // set to YES for the defaults as well
    [notification postNotificationName:@"feature2Purchased" object:nil];
    // post a notification with name @"feature1Purchased"
}
UIAlertView *alert = [[UIAlertView alloc] initWithTitle:@"Thank You!" message:
theMessageForAlert delegate:self cancelButtonTitle:@"OK" otherButtonTitles: nil];
[alert show];
// show the alert with a different message depending on the value of theMessageForAlert
[alert release];
}
```

The **provideContent** method above is really the first in a possible chain of methods to provide "actual content." You might have noticed we didn't actually do anything significant in the way of displaying more images or adding new levels, but as far as the InAppManager goes, what is set in that method is really all that needs to happen in this class. Think about what we did:

- The product1WasPurchased variable or product2WasPurchased variable was set to YES.
- The defaults for the app also stored a YES value for the particular product that was bought.
- A notification was posted for other classes to be made aware that the purchase was made.

The notification *could* be what results in showing something unique following the purchase (aside from the UIAlertView that is). In the last section, I showed you the code to add an observer (or notification listener). To jog your memory, here's an example:

[[NSNotificationCenter **defaultCenter**] **addObserver**:self **selector**:@selector
(**unlockProduct1**) **name**:@"feature1Purchased" **object**:nil];

Once a notification is posted with a matching name of @"feature1Purchased", the method
unlockProduct1 would be called. In my example project, **unlockProduct1** and
unlockProduct2 both output log messages to show that the purchase result trickled all the
way back to that class.

Continuing with the *InAppManager.m* file (we're almost done), other classes need to be
able to call the **restoreCompletedTransactions** method written below. And when I say
"need," I really mean it. You must implement some way for users to restore past purchases
or else your app will be rejected at review time. Fortunately this method is short and sweet:

- (void) **restoreCompletedTransactions** {

    [[SKPaymentQueue **defaultQueue**] **restoreCompletedTransactions**];

}

That's all there is to it. If past purchases are found, each one will call the **provideContent**
method written on the previous page, so in turn, each product will call it's corresponding
notification and a UIAlertView will pop up for each product. Don't worry, they don't pile up
on top of each other. One alert will follow another after tapping OK to dismiss the one
showing.

Failure will not be tolerated in this class! … er, actually it will be a little tolerated. The
failedTransaction method below gets called from the InAppObserver if something
prevented the order from succeeding (other than the user canceling it themselves).
A clever thing Apple has done is given us code to not only tell the potential buyer the
reason it failed, but also suggest a solution. So the first line in the method creates an
NSString called failMessage, which combines the **localizedFailureReason** and
localizedRecoverySuggestion into a **message** for the alert window we will **show**.

- (void) **failedTransaction**: (SKPaymentTransaction *)transaction {

    NSString *failMessage = [NSString **stringWithFormat**:@"Reason: %@, You can try: %@",
                [transaction.error **localizedFailureReason**], [transaction.error
                localizedRecoverySuggestion]];

    UIAlertView *alert = [[UIAlertView **alloc**] **initWithTitle**:@"Unable to complete your
                purchase" **message**: failMessage **delegate**:self
                cancelButtonTitle:@"OK" **otherButtonTitles**: nil];

    [alert **show**];

    [alert **release**];

}

Finally, let's write two very simple methods, which do nothing more than return a bool value (to see if a particular product was purchased).

```
- (bool) isFeature1PurchasedAlready {

    return product1WasPurchased;

}
- (bool) isFeature2PurchasedAlready {

    return product2WasPurchased;

}
```

Even if you didn't use the NSNotificationCenter to provide purchased content right away, at anytime (soon after the purchase *or* far later in the lifespan of the app) you could check with these methods to see if content should be shown/unlocked. Keep in mind, our InAppManager is a singleton that just kind of "hangs around." It's not going anywhere as long as this app is running so we can query it any time. Think of it like the bullies in front of the Springfield Kwik-E-Mart—as long as there's a chance to get someone to buy them beer, they'll be there.

So for example, your **HelloWorldLayer.m** file could call:

```
if ( [[InAppManager sharedManager] isFeature1PurchasedAlready] == YES ) {

    // do something because it was purchased

}
```

The code to create some actual Buy and Restore buttons was already taught last section. So there you have it. If you get into any trouble, you can pick up my example project at **www.focalpress.com/cw/Dike**.

NSURL and UIAlertView

Throughout this entire book, we somehow skipped over how to **go to a webpage** from our app, so let's get right to it:

[[UIApplication **sharedApplication**] **openURL**:[NSURL **URLWithString**: @"www.cartoonsmart.com"]];

If you had multiple URLs in your app, consider creating a method that takes in an **NSString** as a parameter for theURL, like so:

-(void) **useURL**:(NSString*)theURL {

    [[UIApplication **sharedApplication**] **openURL**:[NSURL **URLWithString**:theURL]];

}

To call this method you would simply write:

[self **useURL**:@"www.cartoonsmart.com"];

You could also use the same shortened method to **go to the Mail app** with a pre-populated email like so:

[self **useURL**:@"**mailto**:cartoonsmart@mac.com**?subject**=Hi%20Justin**&body**= My%20question%20is …"];

    // body and subject are optional

I've made the **mailto:**, **?subject=** and **&body=** bold so it's a little easier to pick apart the sections making up the string. The greyed out %20 portions in the string represent spaces in the text. So the subject would read "Hi Justin" and the body would read "My question is."

Last but not least, you could even **initiate a phone call** like so:

[self **useURL**:@"tel:555–555–5555"];

// The dashes are optional by the way, and feel free to test that number. No one picks up

UIAlertViews

We saw plenty of **UIAlertView** examples in
the sections dealing with In-App purchasing,
but if you're bouncing around this book
I can't expect you to read thirty pages of
unrelated code for a measly UIAlertView.
Plus we didn't get a chance in those
examples to add more than one button to
respond to the alert. Previously, we just tapped "OK" and dismissed the alert with no
follow-up code. Go ahead and write the following code into your example project:

```
UIAlertView * alertView = [[UIAlertView alloc] initWithTitle:@"Dial the number now?"
                          message:@"Are you sure?" delegate:self cancelButtonTitle:
                          @"Cancel" otherButtonTitles:@"Dial", nil];
alertView.tag = 101;
    // add a tag to identify the alert when we respond to the button tap
[alertView show];
[alertView release];
```

Most the code to create the alert is pretty self-explanatory (especially if you compare it to
the example image above). Unlike past UIAlertView examples in this book, instead of only
writing nil after **otherButtonTitles** we'll add in another string value that will create a second
button titled "Dial." Now obviously, we need to respond to which button is tapped. We'll do
that with this separate method:

```
- (void) alertView:(UIAlertView *)alertView clickedButtonAtIndex:(NSInteger)buttonIndex {
    if (alertView.tag == 101) {
    // the tag we set earlier, so we know which alert we're responding to
        if (buttonIndex == 0) {
        // the first button has an index value of 0
            NSLog(@"Canceled Alert");
        } else {
        // since we only have two buttons, our else statement must have caught us tapping
        the Dial button
            NSLog(@"Okay let's dial");
            [[UIApplication sharedApplication] openURL:[NSURL URLWithString:
            @"tel:555-555-5555" ]];
        }
    }
}
```

Now usually when we have methods that magically know to respond to events in the app, we need to implement a protocol so the class (or some class) knows they are in charge of that response. Oddly enough, in testing the **alertView: clickedButtonAtIndex** method it worked the same with or without adding the <UIAlertViewDelegate> protocol.

Better safe than sorry though, so I'll go ahead and mark the class as implementing it.

@interface HelloWorldLayer : CCLayer <UIAlertViewDelegate> {

}

In case it wasn't obvious from my notes, if you had multiple UIAlertViews in the same class, they could all be responded to with the same **alertView: clickedButtonAtIndex** method by using if statements to check the tag on each alertView. So you might have:

if (alertView.tag == 101) {

    // test which buttonIndex was tapped for the alert tagged as 101

} else if (alertView.tag == 102) {

    // test which buttonIndex was tapped for the alert tagged as 102

}

Phew, I think that's it. And not a moment too soon, as we're in danger of this becoming a Cocoa book instead of Cocos2d book.

The Back

I suppose it's time to wrap things up. We can talk a little about the app review process, what to expect after approval to the App Store, and, most important, how to measure success. At least, what I consider to be success.

I've mentioned plenty of great resources throughout the book, and I've left too many unmentioned. I can correct that this chapter and leave you with some great places to continue your epic journey.

Of course, I'll leave you with some parting words of wisdom. You've made it this far, what's a few more rambling paragraphs to read?

Submission and Review

Way back in Chapter 1 we talked about the most difficult aspect of delivering your finished app for review, which in my opinion, is properly code-signing it. Review that section if you've already forgotten how to sign your app with your **Distribution Profile**. Usually, once my code-signing is ready, I simply go to Xcode's **Product** menu, and select **Archive**. If the **Archiving** option is greyed out, you are probably set to build for the iOS Simulator instead of your device. Switch your scheme off the Simulator, and you should be ready now.

Hopefully, your app builds fine without any code-signing issues. If you run into a problem at this stage, you are *not* alone. Most developers have done something wrong here, and turned a few more hairs grey as a result. Copy and paste any errors you received into Google and you'll probably find a solution within a couple minutes. Your most likely culprit is the Provisioning Profile, so again, refer back to Chapter 1.

In that section, we also talked about where your actual apps are located once they are built. Both the **Debug app** (signed with Developer Profile) and **Release** app (signed with the Distribution Profile) are actual files on your computer. To find them, I think it's easiest to Right-Click on the app in the Products folder in Xcode, which will take you to the Debug app, and from there, you can go up one folder to find the Release folder, which contains the Distribution-signed app. If you want to locate the Products folder by digging deep into your hard drive, you can probably follow the same path in the screenshot shown on the right.

Once you find the app, right-click on it, and select **Compress**, to create a zip file of it. You can ignore the *.dYSM* file in the folder.

This zip file is what gets delivered to Apple through Application Loader (search for the program on your computer, you'll find it got installed with Xcode). This is a very simple application that is primarily used for delivering the compressed app, or binary, as it is also called. First, you'll need to sign in with your developer credentials, then afterwards, just click the **Deliver Your App** button, and you'll be guided through the rest.

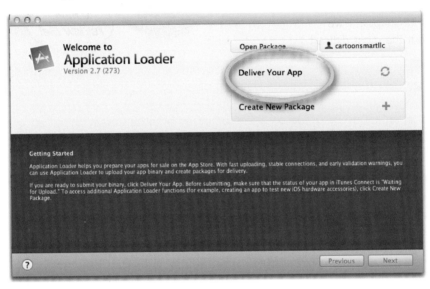

Prior to doing anything in Application Loader, be sure the status of your app in iTunes Connect is "Waiting for Upload." Otherwise, the program will tell you "No Eligible Applications Found," when you try to deliver the app.

The Review

When it comes to your app's review, I want you to remember this going into it: *I haven't taught a student yet that didn't get their app included in the App Store*. That doesn't mean they didn't get rejected initially. It means, they all got their apps in eventually. Issues you can't possibly foresee prior to submission can cause a rejection. One student told me his app got rejected because of a trademark issue with the title of the app (mind you, nothing to do with the actual content). The trademark holder was in Germany, so the easiest solution was to re-submit his app and exclude it from the German App Store.

Another app got rejected because it included a cartoon version of President Obama as a zombie. No disrespect was intended, but even the President can succumb to a zombie apocalypse. Regardless, someone could have seen that as inflammatory. The solution was to just not call that character "The President." No artwork needed changing, just a label.

So don't fret if your first review comes back negative. Most likely, a minor tweak is all that's needed. I would suggest every developer get familiar with the App Store Review Guidelines (at https://developer.apple.com/appstore/guidelines.html). Unfortunately, it is for registered developers only, because it is a terrific document. Apple casually outlines what they expect from their apps (so casually it feels a bit like my writing). Since it's obviously being kept somewhat confidential for a reason, I won't quote anything directly from it, but they make a good point about creating something ***useful***, ***entertaining*** or ***unique***.

Try to keep those words in mind when you are developing your app. Actually I would combine those expectations and go one step further now that the store has almost one million apps. Strive for either: ***uniquely entertaining*** or ***uniquely useful***.

I think to satisfy those qualities, you'll need to submit something that took a while to build. Take the time to do it right. A week's worth of development probably isn't enough time to "wow," anyone. Commit a hundred hours and then see what you can come up with. Don't slap together an app to get a feel for the submission process to test if you can get something approved. The Secret Order of App Developers won't mail you a Member's Only Cloak for doing such a thing (I'm kidding, there's no Secret Order … yet).

Fortunately, I haven't heard that any of my students got rejected for the simple reason that their work "just wasn't good enough." I would like to think that is because my students consistently do excellent work, although the more likely reason is that no one confessed to getting that rejection letter.

Finally, this should go without saying, but a good attitude goes a long way in this world, and if your app gets rejected initially, you'll probably find out exactly why. If not, be polite and inquire. The keywords in that sentence are "be" and "polite."

Section 2

Approval

Now that your app is in the store, and you've been treated to multiple celebration dinners by your wife or husband, girlfriend or boyfriend, parents, brothers, sisters, and best friends, you'll become an iTunes Connect statistics addict overnight

(it'll take longer for all those meals to digest). You'll know the exact time of day Apple posts new download numbers in iTunes Connect. You'll check those paid or free download stats religiously every day. If you aren't seeing the numbers you expected, it can be a little disenchanting. Worse, eventually you'll have to start telling all those people that bought you dinner, the mini-yacht you promised to buy them might not be in the water by next summer. Fortunately, I have some advice for everyone that has to drydock their dreams another year.

You have a product now. Starbucks has coffee drinks. Gillette has razors. Tropicana has juice (I'm just thinking of companies I've used today), oh, and Apple has computers. When those companies need to sell another one of those "things," they have to do more work again. Some laborer has to labor again. Some manufacturer has to manufacture again. Some barista has to … (hmm, there's no verb for barista) … keep being a barista.

Those old rules don't apply to you. **You have an intangible product**. It is simply copied when someone wants to buy it. There's an endless supply, and it doesn't even collect dust on a shelf when demand goes down. There's never too many or too few. Oh, and the store that sells your product is **always open**, and their location is **anywhere**! People are walking around in cargo shorts with the ability to buy what you sell in a few touches. If a super villain created the perfect thing to sell, it would be an app. This is coming from someone who already sells intangible products! Apps are even more perfect. They require almost no customer service and most of them are just considered entertainment by the user. There's no ten-year warranty or guarantee of satisfaction. They give you a dollar or two, and you give them something to keep their eyes and fingers busy for a little while.

Now that you are the creator of the **perfect type of product**, you have to do two things:

1. **Make the product itself perfect.** Listen to what people say about your first version. The comments you get in the App Store from users might not be pretty, but they will be honest. These aren't your friends, they are your customers. They'll tell you when something is messed up. Even if you don't like what those people have to say, they are saying something worth listening to. If you get a couple of comments like, "the physics seem off," then it's time consider that maybe they are. This is why you can submit unlimited revisions of your app. Apple reviews those revisions in a timeframe close to the initial approval (probably a week), which I think is smart because it will make you appreciate spending significant time on your next version. Otherwise, if it was an automatic un-approved update, developers would be sending in nightly, or twice-daily updates to their apps. That would lead to sloppy repairs and users would constantly see that your app has another update.

2. **Study the business.** You absolutely need to read articles and books on marketing apps. I've heard back from students that assumed their app's approval was like crossing the finish line when playing The Game of Life. Mansions awaited. The reality is, every product sells more with more publicity. Apple isn't your company's PR Department though. No one in Cupertino is organizing a pub crawl sponsored by your new app. They will list

your product in the App Store and they will make it so someone can search for it with certain keywords, but they have around 699,999 other apps on their shelves. Special attention to yours is rare. You might see a nice initial spike of downloads because your app is newly listed but sooner than later, *you* have to help get your work seen. Moving your app up the ranks in the store is completely possible even with long-established favorites for certain search terms like, "ninja" or "zombie."

Marketing can be a rewarding adventure on it's own. When I released my first pinball game, I got in touch with strangers. You're not supposed to do that as a kid, but as an adult, it's called networking. I found some small pinball user groups online, even pinball machine repair websites, and told them about the app. I got some great responses, and good suggestions to make it more realistic. You might stumble into someone that runs a message board or newsletter list that has 20,000 people, and if you make a friend, that person can help your app move up significantly in the ranks. App marketing can be done in your spare time too. Don't tell me you can't search the Internet while *also* watching TV at night. You are an iron tiger of multi-tasking, I know you can.

In the upcoming section on Resources, I'll give you some websites to explore that should help before and after publishing your app. That is a section bound to grow, so if you ever notice this book has been updated, look specifically in that section for a new link or two.

Section 3

Success

I'll have to paraphrase this quote because I can't find the exact source right now, so here goes, "If you suddenly find yourself rich, be in a dark place when you jump for joy." Hmmm. Interesting. Kinda dark too. I like it. I read that on a wall at Disney's

Animal Kingdom Resort. No, it wasn't some profound graffiti followed by a sweet tag. Disney printed tribal quotes like that all over the place.

Take what you will from the quote, that was just a misleading segue to talk about Disney vacations. Well, vacations in general. You probably won't get filthy rich selling apps. I don't know anyone personally that has, but I do know a lot of people that can treat themselves to a vacation every year from app sales. I think that's a *very* realistic goal for many of you, and one that certainly means your app was a success. Ten paid downloads a day is really all it takes for a great vacation. Assuming those are 99 cent apps, that's about $10 multiplied by 365 days a year, so $3,650 dollars, of which a generous 70 percent is yours, bringing you to an extra $2,555 a year. That might just be from one app too. You can judge your success by how many vacations you can you fund through app sales, or hey, "think different" and don't make money a determining factor at all. Create something that's personal, even free, and simply be proud of what you've given away to like-minded people that can appreciate it. That too is a successful use of your talents.

When I had a modicum of more free time many, many years ago, I created a free app called Werewolf: Curse of Pandora. My extended family loves playing the card version of this game, which has gone by many names over the years. Some people know it as Mafia, and probably before it had any name, I've read that soldiers stuck in bunkers would play this game to pass the time. The basic premise in every version is that there's a killer in the group, who points out the next victim to a moderator during a "blind" phase of the game where everyone closes their eyes. Then the group accuses each other, and votes to kill off someone they decide is the killer. Problem is, someone is always stuck being the moderator. So I wanted to make a version where my Aunt Peaches didn't have to graciously volunteer for this role over and over again.

That was my main motivation for the game. Make something for people that already loved the "And-then-there-was-one" genre of games, and **try** to make something better, or at least based on that premise. How unsuccessful could I have been making a free game for a niche group? ***One free download a day, is a pleasure to see***.

In fact, looking back on the art for that game now, I would love to remake that in Cocos2d, take an entirely new pass at it, and give everyone a fabulous free update. That would be completely satisfying to me, even though I would probably spend fifty hours on it and my financial return would be next to nothing (the current version has an in-app purchase but for the most part, the game is entirely free).

Discover what makes you satisfied in this world of app development. Are you in it for the love of the game, or just hoping to find a pot of gold out there? Like me, you'll probably be motivated by different reasons for different games. You might even laugh at yourself one day, when you look back at the time you spent on a project and have a Napoleon Dynamite moment counting up your pay day, "That's like a dollar an hour!"

In future versions of this book, I might have to include a Memorial Wall for all the developers who had that thought and didn't laugh at themselves. Those are sad souls that made one app and quit forever. Those of you that can do this for the sheer love of development will be happy with whatever gains come your way. You'll also have a great attitude going into the creation of your next app.

Section 4

Resources

Behind every good developer is an even better browser cache of websites, and most of this list is pulled from my Safari History over the past few months. This section will probably be updated with every new version of the book, so check back often for new links to even more great resources.

Cocos2d Related

Official Cocos2d Site—www.cocos2d-iphone.org

Steffen Itterheim's Learn Cocos2d / Kobold Site—www.learn-cocos2d.com

A Bit Of Code—http://abitofcode.com

Ray Wenderlich's Tutorials—www.raywenderlich.com

Indie Dev Stories—http://indiedevstories.com

Stack Overflow—Tagged for Cocos2d—http://stackoverflow.com/questions/tagged/cocos2d

Ricardo Quesada on Twitter—The Main Author of Cocos2d—https://twitter.com/RicardoQuesada

Search "Cocos2d" on Twitter—Read the Latest Mentions—https://twitter.com/
search?q=cocos2d&src=typd

CartoonSmart's 20-Plus Hour Cocos2d Course—
www.cartoonsmartcode.com/ios_app_programming.php5

Programming Tools

Particle Designer—www.71squared.com

Fuel Collective—www.fuelcollective.com

Level Helper—www.gamedevhelper.com

Zwoptex - Sprite Sheet Generator—www.zwopple.com/zwoptex/

Fonts / Font Software

Blambot—Comic Fonts and Lettering—www.blambot.com

Fonts For Flash—www.fontsforflash.com

Graphic River Fonts—http://graphicriver.net/category/fonts

bmGlyph—Bitmap Font Generator—www.bmglyph.com

Art Tools / Design Resources

Arsenal Vector Packs—http://arsenal.gomedia.us

iStockPhoto—Stock Graphics—www.istockphoto.com

Royalty-Free Cartoon Templates—www.cartoonsmartart.com

GraphicRiver—Stock Graphics—http://graphicriver.net

Sound

Audio Micro—www.audiomicro.com

Audio Sparx—www.audiosparx.com

Sound Cloud—https://soundcloud.com

Artists for Hire

Justin Cook's—Seen Creative—www.seencreative.co.uk

Sin Ars Studios—www.sinars-studios.com

Andy Gertler's FlashBooty.com (Flash Site)—www.flashbooty.com

Code Templates/Starter Kits

CodeCanyon—Sorted by Mobile Category—http://codecanyon.net/category/mobile

iPhone Game Kits—http://iphonegamekit.com

Steffen Itterheim's Line Drawing Game Kit—www.learn-cocos2d.com/store/line-drawing-game-starterkit/

More App Starter Kits—www.cartoonsmartkits.com

Marketing Your App

Games Brief—The Business of Games (Blog and Book)—www.gamesbrief.com

Free App Report—Submit Your Free App—http://freeappreport.com

Crazy Mike's App Reviews—www.crazymikesapps.com

The Author's Website

CartoonSmart—www.cartoonsmart.com

Parting Words

By now, you've probably figured out I've been creating video tutorials for a long time. My website, CartoonSmart.com, has an amazingly loyal fan base that follows my own educational adventures with new software or coding languages. Too often, I teach as I learn. You've probably heard teachers confess that they just stay a chapter ahead of the students, well, I'm definitely one of those teachers. I tend to get excited about what I'm currently learning, every new thing is the "next, best, greatest thing ever," but enthusiasm is contagious in a good way. Seven or eight months ago when I began this book, I wrote that I wanted to teach people that were on the fence about Cocos2d, because I'll gladly take the credit for pulling someone into this new world. Learning Cocos2d is a small part of a larger universe though, which is simply application development (including devices beyond the iOS).

Hopefully I can take a wee bit of credit for introducing you to this new medium. I know there's some try-before-you-buy readers out there, and maybe something you read lit a fire to get you started. Which is good. I don't like to see anyone miss out on a fantastic opportunity. I've heard a lot of success stories, and I don't necessarily mean financial success. I think every developer can add a giant checkmark in their own personal Win Column following their app's inclusion in the App Store. In essence, you've got a gallery piece and it's time to invite people to the showing. Celebrate. Your friends, family, co-workers, new employers (if you're looking for a job) should all see what you've accomplished. Those times when you create or do something you can truly be proud of, come along far fewer than they should. In life, how often do you earn a PhD, or single-handedly build a deck, or receive a military medal of honor, or save someone's life?

Heck, most of us don't even have notable graduations to celebrate that often. Publishing an app is a relatively small moment to be proud of, but still, you've earned the pride you will feel. If it's your first app, then "Welcome to the Clubhouse."

As of late 2013, there are nearly one million apps in the store but there probably aren't 700,000 developers. I'm guessing solo developers like myself average at least three or four apps in the store. So for every big production app, that was worked on by a team developers, there's far more indie developers like you and I. Think about that. You're part of a relatively small group once you are a published developer. Regardless of sales, you are one of us now ... (queue chanting), "One of us, one of us, one of us!"

As I said, oh so many months ago (for me at least), this book will end with you needing to fly solo. Or did I edit that part out? Maybe I did. Well, I'm saying it now. The father bird is leaving the nest. I've regurgitated enough juicy worms into your baby beaks. You have to leave the nest. New eggs are on their way and they need your spots. So fly my hatchlings. Fly ...

Okay, I see someone just dropped straight to the ground. Perhaps it was too early to completely let you go. I'm available to email whenever. I get a ton of mail already, but I don't mind Twitter-length messages. So feel free to ask anything. You can reach me anytime through my website, CartoonSmart.com.

Seriously though, it has been a pleasure writing this book. Every one that emailed me during the making of it was incredibly encouraging about the early previews I uploaded. My sincerest thanks to all of you that started reading this book back in those unedited early days, **and** to any of you that just started
reading it and made it this far!

Thank you!

Justin Dike

Glossary-Index

Absolute value 170, 184

Converts a negative number to a positive. The absolute value of −40 is 40.

Accelerometer 187, 188–192, 340, 401

That cool piece of equipment in iOS devices that detects the tilt of the device. You can get tilt readings on the **x, y** and **z** axis.

Adding children 59

Add a child to a parent. For example:

CCSprite* player = [CCSprite **spriteWithFile**:@"player.png"];

[self **addChild**: player];

You can also extend the statement above to add a z depth and tag.

[self **addChild**: player **z**:1 **tag**: 12345];

If you move a parent object, the children would follow. If you removed a parent, the children would also be removed.

Anchor point 60

Every class derived from CCNode will have an anchorPoint property. When rotating an object, it will rotate around it's anchorPoint, as if a pin were placed at that point. The default anchor point of a CCSprite is 0.5, 0.5 . Or center. You can change the anchorPoint like so:

CCSprite* player = [CCSprite **spriteWithFile**:@"player.png"];

[self **addChild**: player];

player.**anchorPoint** = **ccp**(1, 1);

The anchorPoint is a relative value (not pixel value). So 1, 1 is 100 percent on the x and 100 percent on the y, making the anchor in the top right corner. So rotating the object now would rotate it around the top right.

The anchor point can also be set to outside of the object. For example:

player.**anchorPoint** = **ccp**(2, 2);

The anchor would now be set in a location at double the width and height of the object.

Append zeros 230

Adding zeros to the front of a number. You might have to do this if your file numbering in an animation sequence includes zeros in front (and you didn't rename the images without them).

Fortunately the **%i** integer replacement syntax has some variations that will automatically append zeros. So for example, using **%04i** will always make the integer be four places long. Keep in mind, it isn't adding four zeros. If frame was equal to 131, the integer inserted in the string would be **0131**. Or if frame was equal to 2345, then a zero wouldn't be added at all.

Syntax	Example number...
%04i	file**0001**.png
%03i	file**001**.png
%02i	file**01**.png
%i	file**1**.png

Arc4random 43

Used for generating a random number. For example:

int diceRoll = **arc4random**( ) % 20;

… in this case, diceRoll would equal a whole integer from 0 to 19.

Asterisk pointer 36

When declaring a variable you include it after a class name for object types, and you don't need to include it for number data (like float and int types) or data structs.

Autoreleased 101, 247

Automatically released from memory.

Block 15, 44, 50

A block is a section of code which is grouped together.

Bool 30, 34, 36–37, 39, 45, 47, 125, 163, 298, 315, 351, 371, 380, 431

A Boolean value, this variable type only holds two values. NO or YES. The NO essentially equals 0 and the YES equals 1. Don't believe me? Test this:

bool someBool = YES;

CCLOG(@"someBool actually equals %i" , someBool);

Your output will come back as:

> *someBool actually equals 1*

I like my bool variable names to read like questions, and since booleans equal NO by default, then the question by default should be NO. For example:

isThrowInProgress = NO;

Bounding boxes 132, 134, 139

Your CCSprites can be enabled to show bounding boxes (the actual size of the image, not just the visible area) with a simple number change in your ***ccConfig.h file***. To do this. Unfold your **Libs** folder, then **Cocos2d,** locate ***ccConfig.h,*** and find #define CC_SPRITE_DEBUG_DRAW 0 and change it to 1 instead. Your next build should show white rectangles around each sprite. Of course, you'll want to switch back this variable when you're done testing.

boundingBox 125, 131–132, 134, 145

Property that returns a CGRect for the x, y, width and height of a CCNode. Most commonly used with CCSprites as an easy property to test in a collision detection method.

Break 52–54

Writing: break; in a for or while statement will stop the current loop and continue to an outer loop (if there is one), or break outside of the for or while loop completely. For example:

while (bullets < 100) {

    bullets ++ ;

    if (bullets == 50) {

        break;

    }

}

Breakpoints 10, 16–17

A breakpoint will pause the app and wait at the breakpoint marker you created (whatever line of code that is in a particular class). You might add multiple breakpoints to isolate a problem. If your app never makes it to that first breakpoint, then you know the error is before that point. If you resume the app (by pressing the Continue Program Execution button), and it crashes before the second breakpoint, you know the error is somewhere between the first two breakpoints.

Bundle Identifier 10, 26, 28, 421–422

Your app's Bundle Identifier, or App ID Suffix, will need to match the same App ID given to Apple in the Provisioning Portal. Typically this will be a combination of your domain name (in reverse) followed by a period, then the title of your app. For example:

com.cartoonsmart.pinballkingpin

In Xcode you can set your project's Bundle Identifier from the Summary panel (to get there click the project name in the top left). If you have trouble editing the Bundle Identifier, switch to the Info tab (next to Summary) and edit it from here.

Casting 80, 204

To cast one variable for another. This doesn't create two variables, it gives you access to the same variable through another instance name. So I could write:

CCSprite *enemy = [CCSprite **spriteWithFile**:@"enemy.png"];

[self **addChild**:enemy];

Then later:

CCSprite* tintedEnemy = enemy;

tintedEnemy.color = ccRED;

This would simply tint the original enemy, it wouldn't create a second enemy.

CCActionManager 200

A singleton class which deals with CCActions. For example, the line below:

[[CCActionManager **sharedManager**] **pauseTarget**: ninja] ;

… would pause all actions running on the ninja variable.

CCActions 192–201, 253

CCActions are classes, but you can think of them more like *orders* given to an object (any CCNode really) to do something. Using CCActions is a great shortcut to handling many common tasks such as making an object move, scale, jump, etc.

CCAnimate 247, 251

Used with a CCAnimation action to run an animation sequence.

CCAnimation 247, 251

A CCAnimation action will use an array of sprite frames, and set the time delay between each frame. Typically used with CCAnimate to play an animation sequence.

CCBezierBy 195, 196

Bézier curves are smooth paths. Using a CCBezierBy action will move an object along this path to an end position.

CCBezierTo 195

Bézier curves are smooth paths. Using a CCBezierTo action will move an object along this path to an end position.

CCBlink 198

An action used to make an object blink, going from visible to invisible.

CCCallFunc 203–204, 212, 259, 377

A CCAction to call a function (method). Typically used in a CCSequence to make something happen while other actions are occurring.

CCCallFuncN 203–204, 212

Similar to a CCCallFunc action, used to call a function (method), but this variation will use the object as a parameter in the method called.

CCCallFuncND 204

Similar to a CCCallFuncN action, used to call a function (method) and use the object as a parameter in the method called. This variation can also send data along with the sender as a parameter.

CCDelayTime 206

A CCAction used for delaying time between actions in a sequence.

CCFadeIn 199

An action that fades in an object from zero transparency.

CCFadeOut 199

An action that fades out an object to zero transparency.

CCFadeTo 199

An action to fade an object to a specific transparency.

CCMoveTo 192, 194
An action used for moving an object to a specific x and y location.

CCNode 69, 79, 119–120, 162–163, 192, 231, 240, 277, 321
CCNode is the base class for anything that gets drawn or contains things that get drawn. So your CCScene, CCLayer, CCSprites, CCMenu classes are all subclasses for CCNode.

CCParticleExplosion 265
A particle system that creates an explosion effect.

CCParticleFire 265
A particle system that creates a fire effect.

CCParticleFireworks 265, 267
A particle system that creates a fireworks effect.

CCParticleFlower 265
A particle system that creates a flowering effect.

CCParticleGalaxy 265–266
A particle system that creates a galaxy effect.

CCParticleMeteor 266–267
A particle system that creates a meteor effect.

CCParticleSmoke 268
A particle system that creates a smoke effect.

CCParticleSpiral 267
A particle system that creates a spiral effect.

CCParticleSun 265
A particle system that creates a sun object.

CCParticleSystem 264
Used in creating a particle effect of varying kind. For example:

```
CCParticleSystem* system = [CCParticleSnow node];
[self addChild: system ];
```

or

```
CCParticleSystem* system = [CCParticleSun node];
[self addChild: system ];
```

The only difference is specifying CCParticleSnow or CCParticleSun.

CCPlace 197

An action used to place an object. Typically used in a sequence to start an object somewhere or return an object to a starting position, perhaps for a looping effect.

CCRepeat 205

An action to repeat a sequence a set number of times.

CCRepeatForever 206, 215, 247

An action to repeat a sequence forever.

CCRipple3D 217

An action that applies a ripple effect on an object.

CCRotateBy 197

An action used to rotate an object *by* a certain amount.

CCRotateTo 197

An action used to rotate an object *to* a certain amount.

CCScaleBy 197

An action used to scale an object *by* a certain amount.

CCScaleTo 197

An action used to scale an object *to* a certain amount.

CCScene 59

The parent of your CCLayers. You have one CCScene running at a time, but you can pause a scene and display another. Also one CCScene can transition out another CCScene. When that occurs the original scene is autoreleased.

CCSequence 202, 205, 212, 254

An action defined by a list of actions that will be executed one after another in order.

CCShaky3D 215

An action that applies a shaky effect on an object.

CCShow 198

An action used to immediately show an object. This affects the .visible property, not the opacity.

CCSpawn 205, 212, 254, 374

An action defined by a list of actions that will be executed all at once. The duration of a CCSpawn is the longest action in the list.

CCSprite 46, 58–60, 68–69, 72, 78–80, 84–85, 96, 119, 125, 247

A class used mostly for displaying images, although you can make a CCSprite a parent of other objects, so it could be used like a container. Move the parent sprite and you move the children.

See the following example code to create a CCSprite, and add it to the layer with **z** depth and **tag**.

```
CCSprite* skeleton = [ CCSprite spriteWithFile:@"skeleton_in_chains.png"];
[self addChild: skeleton z:1 tag:12345 ];
```

You can change a CCSprite's texture with this line:

```
[enemy setTexture:[ [CCSprite spriteWithFile:@"skeleton_talking.png"] texture] ];
```

CCSpriteFrame 250, 259

Instead of making a CCSprite display a file directly by calling **spriteWithFile** , you can call **spriteWithSpriteFrame**, in which case you'll need to pass in a CCSpriteFrame instance.

CCSpriteFrame uses an image from the [CCSpriteFrameCache **sharedSpriteFrameCache**] in the example code below:

```
[[CCSpriteFrameCache sharedSpriteFrameCache]
addSpriteFramesWithFile:@"hanksheet_poses.plist"];

CCSpriteFrame *defaultPose = [[CCSpriteFrameCache sharedSpriteFrameCache]
spriteFrameByName:@"hank_fighting_default.png"];

zombie = [CCSprite spriteWithSpriteFrame: defaultPose ];
```

CCTextureCache 226, 239

A singleton class for managing stored textures in memory. You could preload an image to the cache with the following line:

```
[[CCTextureCache sharedTextureCache] addImage:@"logo.png"];
```

You could clean out the CCTextureCache with this line:

[[CCTextureCache **sharedTextureCache**] **removeUnusedTextures**];

CCTintBy 199

An action to tint an object *by* an amount.

CCTintTo 199

An action to tint an object *to* a specific amount.

CCToggleVisibility 198

An immediate action used to reverse whether the object is hidden or visible.

CCTouchDispatcher 166

The CCTouchDispatcher is a singleton class that handles all touch events. You don't really need to do much with it unless you are setting touch priorities for your objects.

ccTouchesBegan 149, 151, 157, 163, 168

The method selector name for detecting the beginning of a touch event. For example:

```
-(void) ccTouchesBegan:(NSSet *)touches withEvent:(UIEvent *)event
{
    UITouch *touch = [touches anyObject];
    CGPoint location = [touch locationInView:[touch view]];
    location = [[CCDirector sharedDirector]convertToGL: location];
    //do something with the location values
}
```

ccTouchesCancelled 149, 157, 163

The method selector name for detecting the cancellation of a touch event. For example:

```
-(void) ccTouchesCancelled:(NSSet *)touches withEvent:(UIEvent *)event
{
    UITouch *touch = [touches anyObject];
    CGPoint location = [touch locationInView:[touch view]];
    location = [[CCDirector sharedDirector]convertToGL: location];
    //do something with the location values
}
```

ccTouchesEnded 149, 151, 163, 168

The method selector name for detecting the end of a touch event. For example:

```
-(void) ccTouchesEnded:(NSSet *)touches withEvent:(UIEvent *)event
{
    UITouch *touch = [touches anyObject];
    CGPoint location = [touch locationInView:[touch view]];
    location = [[CCDirector sharedDirector]convertToGL: location];
    //do something with the location values
}
```

ccTouchesMoved 149, 151, 163

The method selector name for detecting the movement of a touch event.

```
-(void) ccTouchesMoved:(NSSet *)touches withEvent:(UIEvent *)event
{
    UITouch *touch = [touches anyObject];
    CGPoint location = [touch locationInView:[touch view]];
    location = [[CCDirector sharedDirector]convertToGL: location];
    //do something with the location values
}
```

CCTurnOffTiles 220

An action which makes the tiles disappear from a CCAction that transformed the object in a tiled fashion.

CCTwirl 218

An action that applies a twisting, twirl effect on an object.

CCWaves 216–217

An action that applies a wave effect on an object.

CCWaves3D 216–217

An action that applies a 3D wave effect on an object.

CGPoint 62–64, 131

A data structure that holds two values: x and y. For example, if I created this CGPoint below:

```
CGPoint myPoint = CGPointMake( 50, 100 );
```

I would then be able to access these two properties:

myPoint.x

//which is currently 50

myPoint.y

//which is currently 100

I could also change those values, like so:

myPoint.x = 200;

myPoint.y = 10;

Using Cocos2d, instead of CGPointMake, I could write the shorter ccp:

CGPoint myPoint = ccp(50, 100);

I could also make an object's position equal that of a CGPoint. For example:

CCSprite* player = [CCSprite **spriteWithFile**:@"player.png"];

[self **addChild**: player];

player.position = myPoint ;

CGRect 131–132, 145

A data structure containing values for the x location, y location, width and height of a rectangle.

CGRect enemyRect;

enemyRect = **CGRectMake**(0, 10, 200, 50);

The enemyRect is defined now at an x location of 0, y is 10, the width is 200 and the height is 50.

CGRectContainsPoint 136

Tests whether a CGRect contains a CGPoint. For example:

if (CGRectContainsPoint (joyStickBall.boundingBox, location)){

// collision was true

}

CGRectIntersectsRect 131, 145–146

Tests the intersection of two rectangles. For example, where bullet and wolf are both CCSprites:

```
if ( CGRectIntersectsRect ( bullet.boundingBox , wolf.boundingBox ) ) {
        //collision occurred , CGRectIntersectsRect returned YES
}
```

CGSize 63

A structure that holds a width and height value. For example, if I created this CGSize variable below:

CGSize mySize = **CGRectMake**(300, 200);

I would then be able to access these two properties:

mySize.width

> //which is currently 300

mySize.height

> //which is currently 200

Class 36–37, 39, 44, 47, 58–59, 95–126

In Objective-C, classes are defined in two parts:

- An interface that declares the methods and properties of the class and names it's superclass (usually this is the header file or .h file).

- An implementation that contains the code that implements it's methods (usually this is a separate implementation or .m).

Class method 99–100, 103, 109, 234, 321–324

Instance methods operate on an object, while a class method operates on a class as a whole. Class methods are usually used to create instances of that class. When declaring a class method in your header file, remember to write the plus sign (not minus) in front:

+ (id) createWithLocation ;

Cleaning 15

The Xcode equivalent of giving C3PO an oil bath. Sometimes useful when strange warnings appear. In Xcode the Product > Clean menu option cleans up the build directory for all targets by deleting the app and dSYM files along with the precompiled headers. You can also hold down the option key and the Clean button will change to Clean Build Folder. Use this option if you really need to clean things up. The only time I've had to scrub a project this clean was when I deleted a project I made some serious mistakes in, and replaced it with a back-up of the same name. For whatever reason, Xcode kept building with errors from the deleted project. Clean Build Folder solved that issue.

Comment out code 15

Commenting out code, can be done in two ways. By writing **//** in front of a single line of code. For example:

> *// code here won't run*

As you can see, I've got a special format in this book for text that is being commented out. In general, comments aren't for code, but rather they are notes to yourself. So in this book, I'll often leave you notes after a line of code to explain it further. You can also comment out larger blocks of code by writing an opening mark like this **/*** and then a closing mark like this ***/.**

For example:

> */* Game of Thrones was great this season I should really read the books*
> *Pick up milk later from the grocery store */*

That's an even worse example of a worthy note to yourself, but it's been commented out, so as far as your final app is concerned, it doesn't exist.

Comparison operators 41, 42

The syntax that compares one thing to another. In the example below the **>=** is the comparison operator:

if (myVar **>=** 20) {

> *//do something*

}

Other common comparison operators:

Operator Name	Syntax
Equal to	someNum == otherNum
Not equal to	someNum != otherNum
Greater than	someNum > otherNum
Less than	someNum < otherNum
Greater than or equal to	someNum >= otherNum
Less than or equal to	someNum <= otherNum

Composition actions 202

Actions used for composing other actions, such as in sequence (possibly repeating) or spawning multiple actions to perform at once.

Constant variable 34

A variable whose value does *not* change over time. These are often defined in a shared header file called **Constants.h** like so:

#define MAX_ENEMIES 20

Constants created in this way are typically written in all caps, but if that looks too loud to you, it's fine to write:

#define maxEnemies 20

Defining constants is one of the rare times when the line of code doesn't have a semicolon after it.

We will use constants often in programming games, so readers coming to this definition early need not worry much about it now.

CONTROL + ⌘ Up 65, 141

This hot key is too essential to *not* add to the book's index. Pressing these keys will switch your document between the header and implementation file, or vice versa.

Convenience method 124, 130, 136

A method you write or that has been included in your code framework library that shortens or aids in writing a much longer chunk of code. Like the term implies, it's just downright convenient! Don't be afraid to write your own.

Convert an int to an NSNumber 76

Occassionally you need to convert a basic number type like int to an object like NSNumber. For example:

int myInt = 3;

NSNumber* myNumObj = [NSNumber **numberWithInt**: myInt];

Other NSNumber methods are **numberWithFloat** or **numberWithBool** (and quite a few more).

convertToWorldSpace 336

Converts the location of an object inside of another object to the world space, as if the interior object were a child of the main scene.

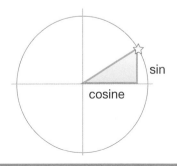

Cosine 175

Cosine is the horizontal coordinate of the arc endpoint.

Dealloc 106, 141, 247, 248, 249, 275

As in deallocating something from memory. With Cocos2d we typically don't have much to release from memory in the **dealloc** method, but it should be written in most of your classes like so:

-(void) **dealloc** {

    // release anything else that needs it

    [super **dealloc**];

}

Deallocate 106, 159, 248

Delete from memory. See the related term "dealloc" for more details.

Declare 64, 65, 67, 121–125, 247, 264, 365, 437

You declare variables so you can access them throughout your entire class.

Define a constant 81

Make a constant variable, or one that doesn't change. As a good practice, done in a file called **Constants.h.** For example:

#define kEnemyTag 12345

Notice you don't need to add a semicolon after the line.

Delegate class 163

Delegation is where an object, instead of performing one of it's stated tasks, delegates that task to an associated helper object.

Deprecated code 14

Code that's on it's way out. You might see a warning about deprecated code. This shouldn't cause your app to crash or get rejected when reviewed, but just be aware that some time in the future that code could be more of a problem if you're using it.

Design pattern 313–404

An "ideal" game design pattern is a large part of what Chapter 9 goes into, which focuses on a GameEngine class and AppData class. "Ideal" is in quotes, because like many things in this book, it's ideal *to me*. Your design pattern is simply how *you* choose to design your game. I'll give you some tips of my own. Take 'em or leave 'em. If in the end, your first game builds and plays fine, the design is a success because no matter how sloppy your code, you still made an app. Nobody playing it will peak under the hood. Your app reviewer will test your game enough to see that it doesn't crash repeatedly but they won't take a magnifying glass to your actual code. When you mature as a programmer, you'll begin adopting better practices and strategies for managing your own code. Most likely, *your* code will stay *yours*. You'll be the only one that ever has to deal with any poor practices. So when you get tired of rereading your own hard-to-understand code or rewriting large chunks of code to create new levels, you'll begin to explore ways to save yourself time.

Development Profile 25, 26, 421, 448

A provisioning profile you'll download as a registered developer from Apple. You'll use this profile to test your app on your device (instead of testing on the Simulator).

Distribution Profile 25, 421, 448

A provisioning profile you'll download as a registered developer from Apple. You'll use this profile to sign your finished application before sending it to Apple. This profile does not get used for testing the app on your device.

Dot notation 61

The short definition here is to just call dot notation the dot (or period on the keyboard) between a variable and one of it's properties. For example, CCNode variables all have a position property. To set values for that property, we could write:

player.position = ccp(0, 0);

Notice the dot between player and position. This can simplify setting or getting values for the position versus accessing them through longer written methods.

Draw calls 359

The top number in your Cocos2d app's display stats. Objects being drawn to the screen are tallied here. An object removed from the scene shouldn't add to this number.

Float 34, 38, 47, 315

Short for floating point number. Float variables can be positive or negative decimal values. Money would be represent by a float variable, like:

float cashMoneyInDaBank = 200.52 ;

For Statements 53–54, 118–119, 143, 250–251

The for statement is very similar to a while loop in usage, in that they iterate through code until a condition is untrue. In the example below, that would be until bullets is equal to or greater than 100 instead of less than 100:

```
for ( int bullets = 0 ; bullets < 100 ; bullets ++ ) {

    //the code in here repeats until the condition above is no longer true

}
```

Inside of the parenthesis we have three parts of code separated by semicolons. The first part sets up a variable, the second part is our conditional expression, and the last part is the increment for the loop. The bullets ++ is just a shorter way of writing:

    bullets = bullets + 1;

or

    bullets += 1 ;

We could have written those statements as well though.

Game data   47, 298, 318

Some programmers like to put their game's data into a separate class. When planning out your game consider doing this as a good practice. Some examples of game data might be:

- int variables for the current level or score;
- NSString* variables for image file names;
- bool variables for preferences like whether the sound is muted;
- float variables for how much money your game character has.

A wave-attack-style game is a good example of how a game engine and separate game data class work together. The game engine (which handles the bulk of the game play) can get info from the game data and spawn a certain number of enemies to increase the difficulty every time the game engine reloads (or every level essentially). The code in the game engine doesn't really need to change at all every time it reloads.

This scheme doesn't work for all games, but for some it's a great design pattern.

Game engine   47, 61, 125, 140, 319, 320, 330–364, 383

A vague term for the main code that really drives your game. If it was a space game, your game engine would probably be considered the code that handles moving the ship, events that occur because of collisions or accomplishments, adding enemies to the screen, and so on. As a good practice, your game engine might access a separate class for data that persists through various levels (or reloads of the game engine), like the score or current level.

A wave-attack-style game is a good example of how a game engine and separate game data class work together. The game engine can get info from the game data and spawn a certain number of enemies to increase the difficulty every time the game engine reloads (or every level essentially). The code in the game engine doesn't really need to change at all every time it reloads.

This scheme doesn't work for all games, but for some it's a great design pattern.

Gesture recognition states 177

The following are conditions of a gesture recognizer:

UIGestureRecognizerStateBegan

UIGestureRecognizerStateCancelled

UIGestureRecognizerStateChanged

UIGestureRecognizerStateFailed

UIGestureRecognizerStatePossible

UIGestureRecognizerStateRecognized

UIGestureRecognizerStateEnded

You can use these definitions in an if statement when handling your gesture, for example:

```
-(void) handleRotation:(UIRotationGestureRecognizer *)recognizer {

if ( recognizer.state == UIGestureRecognizerStateBegan ) {

CCLOG(@"the gesture just began");

    }

}
```

Gesture recognizers 172–174, 178–185

Apple's code for handling some of the most common touch events such as: finger rotations, finger pinches, taps, long presses, swipes and panning. Many of these will allow you to set how many fingers must be touching for the gesture to be recognized, and you can differentiate between states of the gesture, like when it began or ended.

Go to a webpage 443

If you want to go to a webpage from your app, simply call:

[[UIApplication **sharedApplication**] **openURL**:[NSURL **URLWithString**: @"http://www.CartoonSmart.com"]];

Go to the Mail app 443

To open a pre-populated email from your app, you can call:

[[UIApplication **sharedApplication**] **openURL**:[NSURL **URLWithString**: @"mailto:address@mac.com"]]

You can also add a subject and body message.

Hard-coded 62

Giving something a specific value, as opposed to a variable.

Headers and Implementation files 35

In Objective-C, classes are defined in two parts:

- An interface that declares the methods and properties of the class and names it's superclass (usually this is the header file or .h file).

- An implementation that contains the code that implements it's methods (usually this is a separate implementation or .m).

If statements 40–43

If statements will test if a condition is true and run code if so. For example:

```
int myVar = 40;
if ( myVar == 40 ) {
        // if the condition above is true, the code here runs
}
```

If ... else if ... else statement 41, 160, 284, 302

If ... else if ... else statements will test if multiple conditions are true, or run an else statement if nothing was true. The final else statement is optional.

```
int myVar = 40;
if ( myVar == 41 ) {
        // the code here wouldn't run because the condition above isn't true
} else if ( myVar == 42 ) {
        // the code here wouldn't run because the condition above isn't true
} else {
        // the code in here runs because no statement above is true
}
```

If ... else statement 41, 45, 170, 418

If ...else statements will test if a condition is true and run code accordingly, or else perform the negative conditional code. For example:

```
int myVar = 40;
if ( myVar == 41 ) {
        // the code here wouldn't run because the condition above isn't true
} else {
        // the code in here would run instead
}
```

In-App Purchasing 418–442

Products you can sell within the app. Typically for free apps, the "product" is simply to unlock the full version of the game.

Initiate a phone call 443

To open the phone app and dial a number you could call:

[[UIApplication **sharedApplication**] **openURL**:[NSURL **URLWithString**:@"tel: 555–555–5555"]];

Instance 58

An instance is a variable of a class. In the example below, player is the instance:

CCSprite* player ;

In a game, you might have many instances in the scene of the same class. For example, 100 instances of an Enemy class could be trying to attack the player.

Instance methods 100, 103, 108–109, 322–326

Instance methods are called on an object of a class. After you've created (instantiated) the object to operate on you could call methods like the last three lines below:

Enemy* theEnemy = [Enemy **create**];

[self **addChild**: theEnemy **z**:0 **tag**:123];

[theEnemy **walkAround**];

[theEnemy **setSpeedToLow**];

[theEnemy **tintRedToShowFuriousAnger**];

Notice we wrote the instance name of theEnemy instead of the class name Enemy when calling the instance methods.

Instant actions 198

Actions that do not have a duration, they are performed immediately.

Instantiated 102, 105

Create an instance of a class.

Int 30, 34–39, 47–50, 76–77

Short for integer. Here's an example of an int variable:

int myNum = 10;

Int variables are whole numbers and can be either positive or negative.

Leading zeros 230

Refers to sequential file names that have zeros in front. For example:

CartoonSmart1.jpg

> // no leading zeros

CartoonSmart0001.jpg

> // leading zeros

Local variable 66

A variable that exists only within the block of code it has been written, as opposed to a variable that has been declared outside of the scope of that block.

-(void) **someMethod** {

> int myVar = 5;
>
> // this is a local variable, it is defined in this method and won't exist outside of it

}

Other methods would have no idea what myVar referred to.

Log statement 38, 132, 189, 203, 268, 275, 315, 350, 433

CCLOG ( ) and NSLog ( ) are both log statements that can send messages to the output window at runtime (when the app is running on the device or simulator). Here's an example:

CCLOG(@"I am a message");

Here's an example of how you can add a variable into a log statement:

int myVar = 200;
CCLOG(@"My variable equals %i" , myVar);

Notice the %i . That syntax will get replaced by myVar in the output message. That message would read:

My variable equals 200

Logical AND 42

In a conditional statement the **&&** is called a Logical AND operator. We are testing if both statements are true in the example below:

if (mySpeakers == 10 **&&** myGuitarIsLoudEnough == NO) {

> // both statements are true, do something

}

Logical NOT operator 46

You can add an exclamation point in front of a condition and test if the value returns NO.

bool myBoolVar = NO;

if (**!** myBoolVar) {

// if the method returns NO, then this code is run

}

That exclamation point is called a Logical NOT operator.

Logical Operator 42

Logical operators are used in conditional statements. Common ones are:

&& for **Logical AND,** one condition AND another condition are both true

|| for **Logical OR.** one condition OR another condition is true

! for **Logical NOT** one condition is not true

See the related glossary terms for examples.

Logical OR 42

In a conditional statement the double pipe symbol syntax **||** is called a Logical OR operator.

We are testing if at least one statement is true

if (mySpeakers == 10 **||** myGuitarIsLoudEnough == NO) {

// if at least one statement is true, do something

}

MediaPlayer.framework 414

Importing this framework gives you the ability to playback various media types, either streaming or locally.

Messages with arguments 48

The more Objective-C way of saying, *methods with parameters* or *functions with properties*. It's all semantics, really. Here's an example:

-(void) **checkForNewHighScore**: (int) theScore {

//now we can use theScore somewhere in this method

CCLOG (@"the variable passed in equals **%i**", theScore);

}

This part: (int) theScore, is the parameter we've tacked on. Inside the squiggly brackets we can use theScore in some way. It will equal the value of whatever we set it to when we called the method.

To call a method with a parameter we would write:

[self **checkForNewHighScore**: 10500];

Method selector 44, 47, 59, 70, 100, 163

In this example method:

-(void) **dropNinja** {

}

... **dropNinja** is the method selector. In this next example method with parameters:

-(void) **dropNinjaWithLocation**:(CGPoint) theLocation **andWeapon**:(int)weapon{

}

... the method selector is **dropNinjaWithLocation.** The term "selector" shows up a lot in our code, for example:

[self performSelector:@selector(**dropNinja**)];

Methods 30, 44–50

When defining this term, I feel like I should be standing up and giving a toast. "What can be said that hasn't been said before about methods? Helluva guy." I'll try to keep this short and simple:

- Methods are blocks of code that help to organize things (*functions* or *messages* are other common terms for *methods*).

- Methods can perform simple calculations in a couple of lines of code or be hundreds of lines long, and even call other methods.

- Methods are a great way to keep from writing the same code in multiple places.

- Methods can optionally return a value *and* be used as the value to a variable or be used in a conditional statement.

- Methods can optionally have parameters passed in (*argument* or *property* are other common terms for *parameter*).

Methods with parameters 47, 49

Methods can be called with data passed into them. Here's an example:

-(void) **checkForNewHighScore**: (int) theScore {

    // now we can use theScore somewhere in this method

CCLOG (@"the variable passed in equals %i", theScore);

}

This part: (int) theScore, is the parameter we've tacked on. Inside of the squiggly brackets we can use theScore in some way. It will equal the value of whatever we set it to when we called the method. To call a method with a parameter we would write:

[self **checkForNewHighScore**: 10500];

MPMoviePlayerController 414–418

A movie player (of type MPMoviePlayerController) manages the playback of a movie from a file or a network stream. Playback occurs in a view owned by the movie player and takes place either full screen or inline. You can incorporate a movie player's view into a view hierarchy owned by your app, or use an MPMoviePlayerViewController object to manage the presentation for you.

Nested loops 53–54

A for statement within another for statement would be an example of a nested loop. For example:

for (int bullets = 0 ; bullets < 100 ; bullets ++) {

    // do code to add a bullet to the scene

for (int grenades = 0 ; grenades < 10 ; grenades ++) {

    //do code to add a grenade to the scene

  }

}

Non-Consumable 418, 423, 435

Non-Consumable in-app purchases are those that don't need to be bought twice and can be shared across multiple devices. As opposed to Consumable purchases, which can get used up over time. For example, in-game money would be a Consumable purchase, whereas unlocking all the chapters of a book app would be a Non-Consumable purchase.

NSArray 159–160

An object that contains an ordered list of other objects. The first object has an index number of 0, the second object is 1, and so on. For example:

CCSprite * enemy1;

CCSprite * enemy2;

NSArray *spriteArray = [NSArray **arrayWithObjects**: enemy1, enemy2, nil];

CCLOG(@"spriteArray has this many items %i", [spriteArray **count**]);

    // logs 2

CCLOG(@"The second object is %@", [spriteArray **objectAtIndex**:1]);

    // cast another sprite as enemy2

CCSprite* castSprite = (CCSprite*)[spriteArray **objectAtIndex**:1];

NSMutableArray 250, 256–258, 316, 337–338

Like an NSArray (see also that term) but an NSMutableArray can be changed. Objects can be added or dropped from it.

NSNotificationCenter 415–416, 425, 442

The notification center provides a way of broadcasting information within a program. This is a great way to communicate between classes.

NSObject 315

NSObject is the root class of most Objective-C class hierarchies. All objects inherit from NSObject. Akin to what CCNode is in Cocos2d.

NSString 30, 34, 36, 46–47, 50, 159, 316, 376, 430, 443

An NSString* variable is a string of characters. For example:

NSString* myString = @"CartoonSmart is a great site";

Just be sure to include the @ symbol in front of whatever is in quotes. NSString variables are used frequently throughout this book, and are Objective-C (not Cocos2d).

NSURL 406–417

An NSURL object lets you manipulate Uniform Resource Locators (URLs). These could be used for streaming video, sending emails, going to webpages, initiating phone calls, etc.

NSUserDefaults 298–301, 327–329, 426

An easy place to store basic user preferences or data you want to persist in the app, even if it were to close completely.

Object Oriented Programming 96–97

Describes a style of programming where classes are objects, with their own properties and methods. For example, your game might create twenty instances (copies) of an Asteroid class. Ideally, each instance could know how to interact within the *"universe"* without always being told by a parent class what to do. Suppose the asteroid went out of bounds of the screen, it might reappear on the other side of the screen or bounce off of the screen because it has it's own logic regarding how it moves and interacts with things.

A parent class could call methods on the asteroid to examine it's properties or tell it what to do a certain times. If the asteroid collided with a ship, a method could be called on the instance to make it explode.

onEnter 162, 164–166, 381

An optional method you can include in your class that will fire when the object instance has been added as a child. So your initialization would already have occurred when the onEnter statement runs:

- (void) **onEnter** {

    //Gets called when the object is added to the scene

    [super **onEnter**];

    //be sure to include this

}

onExit 162, 164–166

An optional method you can include in your class that will fire when the object instance has been removed from the scene or layer. This would get called before anything in the deallocation method.

- (void) **onExit** {

    //Gets called when the object is removed from the scene

[super **onExit**];

    //be sure to include this

}

Plist 241–250, 312–319

Short for Property List, or the *.plist* file format. Property lists are XML files used to organize data read in by your app. You can define entire levels in your game by editing a property list and parsing that data at runtime.

Powers of 2 227

Cocos2d works with powers of 2 when it comes to textures in memory. Powers of 2 go like this: 2, 4, 8, 16, 32, 64, 128, 256, 512, 1024. So if possible, try to work with those numbers when creating your images. Reason being, a 120 by 250 pixel image gets loaded into memory as if it were 128 by 256. Yet a slightly bigger image at 130 by 260 will take up the same amount of memory as the next powers up, which is 256 by 512. So *if* you can work with your images at those dimensions, you should. If you forget, and use an image that's 33 pixels by 66, you'll be no different than all us other developers that do the same thing from time to time.

Procedural 96

Procedural programming follows a pattern of executing code from the top to the bottom of the file. One thing does something, that triggers the next, and so on in a linear fashion though a program. Conversely object oriented programming follows a different pattern.

Property List 241–250, 312–319

Property lists are XML files used to organize data read in by your app. You can define entire levels in your game by editing a property list and parsing that data at runtime.

Release 26, 448, *see also* dealloc

In reference to releasing an object from memory. See the related dealloc term for more.

Retain 247, 254

When declaring objects you can retain them, meaning they won't automatically be released from memory. You can become responsible for releasing them.

Return 45–50

A method can return a value. For example:

```
-( bool ) doWeNeedToAddMoreNinjas {
    if ( numberOfNinjasInGame > 10 ) {
        return NO ;
    } else {
        return YES ;
    }
}
```

Notice where we wrote bool above. A method that returned nothing would have void there. By writing bool we are committing to returning a bool value in the method (and you *must* return something or you will get an error). So the method above could now be used as the value of a variable. For example:

```
bool someBool = [self doWeNeedToAddMoreNinjas ];
    // will equal YES or NO
```

or in a conditional statement like:

```
if ( [ self doWeNeedToAddMoreNinjas] == YES ) {
    //perform code here if the method returns YES
}
```

Reverse 206, 217

An action that reverses another action.

Runtime 38

Testing a variable at runtime would mean we tested it while the app was running. For those of you that like defining terms, then design time would be the antonym for this term. Design time would be when you are actually coding your app.

Scene transitions 272–275

Replacing one scene with another. This can be done over a set duration with a variety of transition effects.

Scheduled method 70–72

A scheduled method is one that performs at a certain interval. The example below is a method call with a scheduled interval of 1/60th of a second:

[self **schedule**:@selector(**updateMyNode**:) **interval**:1.0f/60.0f];

The method would look like this:

-(void) **updateMyNode**: (ccTime) delta {

    // do stuff 60 times per second

}

Scope 65–66

Basically where a variable can be "seen" from. A variable could be created within a block of code that makes it hidden to other blocks of code. We declare variables so we don't have scope issues, or problems accessing the variable.

Set the text of a label 213

You can set the text of a label, with the following line:

[points **setString**:@"hi!"];

In this example, points is a CCLabelTTF.

setDisplayFrame 259

Sets the display frame of a CCSprite, requires a CCSpriteFrame variable to set to. For example:

[zombie **setDisplayFrame**: defaultPose];

Above, defaultPose is a CCSpriteFrame variable.

Sin 175

Sin is the vertical coordinate of the arc endpoint.

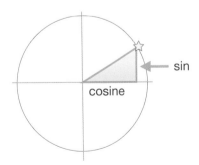

Singleton 320–330, 397–399

A class typically made for sharing data to other classes. Singletons are unique in that there's *only ever one instance* of this class. So when our app first runs, it initializes this class, and that class stays initialized for the life of the app.

Static variable 273, 275

A static variable defined inside a class body. This variable belongs to the class as a whole, and is shared by all objects of the class.

StoreKit.framework 420

Adds the Store Kit functionality to your project for In-App purchasing.

Swallowing touch 162

Captures a touch and doesn't allow any other object detect that touch.

Swap the depth of two objects 83

If you wanted to swap the depth of two objects, in this case, player and enemy, you could write:

[self **reorderChild**: enemy **z:** [player **zOrder**]];

Switch statements 43

Switch statements are another way to compare a lot of values without having to write a ton of *else if* statements. Suppose you wanted to test the value of an int called diceRoll .

```
switch ( diceRoll ) {
    case 0:
        //do something if the value is 0
        break;
    case 1:
        //do something if the value is 1
        break;
    case 2:
        //do something if the value is 2
        break;
    case 3:
        //do something if the value is 3
        break;
    case 4:
        //do something if the value is 4
        break;
```

default:

   //do something if none of the cases above were true
   break;
}

The comments above could be replaced by multiple lines of code, or calls to methods.

Tag 77–83, 193

A numerical ID you can give the children you add. For example:

CCSprite* player = [CCSprite **spriteWithFile:** @"player.png"];

[self **addChild:**player **z:**100 **tag:**12345] ;

It is common practice to define a constant for your tags. For example:

#define playerTag 12345

You could then change the line above to be:

[self **addChild:** player **z:**100 **tag:** playerTag] ;

Texture atlases 241–246

Sprite sheets, or texture atlases as they are also called, are textures that contain more than one image.

Touch priority 162–167

How touchy an object is. The lower the priority number, the more priority it has. So if your object set it's priority at zero, for example:

[[[CCDirector sharedDirector] **touchDispatcher**] **addTargetedDelegate:** self **priority:**0 **swallowsTouches:** YES];

Then it would capture the touch versus an object with 100:

[[[CCDirector sharedDirector] **touchDispatcher**]**addTargetedDelegate:** self **priority:**100 **swallowsTouches:** YES];

UIAlertView 443–445

Use the UIAlertView class to display an alert message to the user.

UIGestureRecognizerStateEnded 177–477

The end state condition of a gesture recognizer. You can use this definition in an if statement when handling your gesture, for example:

-(void) **handleRotation**:(UIRotationGestureRecognizer *)recognizer {

if (recognizer.state **==** UIGestureRecognizerStateEnded) {

    CCLOG(@"the gesture ended");

}

}

UILongPressGestureRecognizer 183

Gesture for detecting a press down on the screen of a minimum length.

UIPanGestureRecognizer 184

Gesture for detecting a panning motion. You can set minimum and max numbers that should be touching to detect this gesture.

UIPinchGestureRecognizer 180

Gesture for detecting a pinch. You can detect whether the pinch is inwards or outwards using the scale property of the recognizer.

UIRotationGestureRecognizer 172–176

Gesture for detecting finger rotation. For example:

UIRotationGestureRecognizer * rotationGR = **[[** UIRotationGestureRecognizer **alloc]**

initWithTarget: self **action**:@selector(**handleRotation**:) **]**;

[[[CCDirector **sharedDirector**] **view**] **addGestureRecognizer**: rotationGR **]**;

[rotationGR **release**];

-(void) **handleRotation**:(UIRotationGestureRecognizer *)recognizer {

    CCLOG(@"rotation in radians is **%f**", recognizer.rotation);

    // log the value of the rotation in radians

}

UISwipeGestureRecognizer 180–182

Gesture recognizer for detecting UP, DOWN, LEFT or RIGHT swipes. Separate handlers are created for each direction.

UITapGestureRecognizer 182–183

Gesture for detecting a number of quick taps to the screen. You can set the number of taps to detect and number of fingers that must be touching to detect this gesture.

UITouch 159–161

A UITouch object represents the presence or movement of a finger on the screen for a particular event. You can access the location of the touch with the UITouch object.

Universal app 20

An app that runs on the iPhone, iPod touch and iPad.

unscheduleAllSelectors 75

A method which stops all scheduled selectors on a node.

[self **unscheduleAllSelectors**];

Variables 34–37, 65–69

Variables can change their value over time. They can equal something at one point in a program, and then another value later. Creating a variable then assigning a value to it can be done as a one- or two-step process. You can do this:

int myNumber = 10 ;

Or you can do this:

int myNumber ;

Take a nap, and come back later and give it a value:

myNumber = 10 ;

While you were taking a nap, that variable named myNumber existed because you created it, but it just had a default value of zero for that variable type.

You can create **constant variables** which don't change their value over time. See the related term for more info there.

Velocity 184

How fast something is moving.

Void 44

Methods that return nothing, use void like so:

```
-( void ) dropNinja {
    // code goes here
}
```

Our method doesn't return anything. It just runs the code in the squiggly brackets.

Warning 14

I hope you didn't look this term up expecting a solution to whatever strange Warning you're currently facing. You can get Warnings for as many ways as you can write typos in code.

The silver lining is that Warnings are not full-blown Errors. You can get Warnings for simple things like **unused variables**. The app won't crash, it won't get rejected on review for the App Store, but you probably don't want to see a bunch of easily-fixable warnings every time you build the app.

While Loop 51–54

While statements are very similar to for statements in usage, in that they iterate through code until a condition is untrue. With while loops you just want to make sure you don't create an infinite loop, which is a dangerous possibility.

```
int myVar = 0;
while (myVar <= 100) {
    // this code runs over and over again until myVar is greater than 100
myVar = myVar + 1;
    // add 1 to myVar so eventually the condition isn't true
}
```

In the example above if I had forgotten to add 1 to myVar in the loop, then the condition would never become false, and the app would get stuck running this infinitely. While loops are useful for many things, one of which would be to do something based on all the children in a scene. In which case, you could write something like:

```
while (myVar < self.children)
```

Or you could use the children of a specific object:

```
while (myVar < enemy.children)
```

Z depth 83

A positive or negative integer specifying the visual depth of an object. The higher the number, the higher on the stack of objects it will be. An object with a z depth of 100 will visually appear above an object with a z depth of −100.

zOrder 83

If you were curious about a child's **z** depth, you could query it with a log statement like so:

```
CCLOG( @"the depth is %i " , [player zOrder] );
```